ANCILLA TO CLASSICAL READING

ANCILLA

TO

CLASSICAL

READING

MOSES HADAS

COLUMBIA UNIVERSITY PRESS

MORNINGSIDE HEIGHTS · NEW YORK

Columbia Bicentennial Editions and Studies

THE ENERGETICS OF DEVELOPMENT
By Lester G. Barth *and* Lucena J. Barth

NEW LETTERS OF BERLIOZ, 1830–1868
Text with Translation, edited by Jacques Barzun

ON THE DETERMINATION OF MOLECULAR WEIGHTS
BY SEDIMENTATION AND DIFFUSION
By Charles O. Beckman *and Others*

Luigi Pirandello
RIGHT YOU ARE
Translated and edited by Eric Bentley

THE SCULPTURE OF THE HELLENISTIC AGE
By Margarete Bieber

THE ALGEBRAIC THEORY OF SPINORS
By Claude C. Chevalley

Henry Carter Adams
THE RELATION OF THE STATE TO INDUSTRIAL ACTION
and ECONOMICS AND JURISPRUDENCE
Edited by Joseph Dorfman

Ernst Cassirer
THE QUESTION OF JEAN-JACQUES ROUSSEAU
Translated and edited by Peter Gay

THE LANGUAGE OF TAXONOMY
By John R. Gregg

ANCILLA TO CLASSICAL READING
By Moses Hadas

James Joyce
CHAMBER MUSIC
Edited by William Y. Tindall

APOKRIMATA: DECISIONS OF SEPTIMUS SEVERUS
ON LEGAL MATTERS
Edited by William L. Westermann *and* A. Arthur Schiller

General Editor's Preface

THE MODERN UNIVERSITY HAS BECOME A great engine of public service. Its faculty of Science is expected to work for our health, comfort, and defense. Its faculty of Arts is supposed to delight us with plays and exhibits and to provide us with critical opinions, if not to lead in community singing. And its faculty of Political Science is called on to advise government and laity on the pressing problems of the hour. It is unquestionably right that the twentieth-century university should play this practical role.

But this conspicuous discharge of social duties has the effect of obscuring from the public—and sometimes from itself—the university's primary task, the fundamental work upon which all the other services depend. That primary task, that fundamental work, is Scholarship. In the laboratory this is called pure science; in the study and the classroom, it is research and teaching. For teaching no less than research demands original thought, and addressing students is equally a form of publication. Whatever the form or the medium, the university's power to serve the public presupposes the continuity of scholarship; and this in turn implies its encouragement. By its policy, a university may favor or hinder the birth of new truth. This is the whole meaning of the age-old struggle for academic freedom, not to mention the age-old myth of academic retreat from the noisy world.

Since these conditions of freedom constitute the main theme of Columbia University's Bicentennial celebration, and since the university has long been engaged in enterprises of public moment, it was doubly fitting that recognition be given to the activity that enlarges the world's "access to knowledge." Accordingly, the Trustees of the University and the Directors of its Press decided to signalize the 200th year of Columbia's existence by publishing some samples of current scholarship. A full representation was impossible: limitations of time and space exercised an arbitrary choice. Yet the Bi-centennial Editions and Studies, of which the titles are listed on a neighboring page, disclose the variety of products that come into being on the campus of a large university within a chosen year. From papyrology to the determination of molecular weights, and from the state's industrial relations to the study of an artist's or poet's work in its progress toward perfection, scholarship exemplifies the meaning of free activity, and seeks no other justification than the value of its fruits.

JACQUES BARZUN

Preface

A WHIMSICAL TITLE IS PROBABLY OMINOUS for a book innocent of whimsy. What this book attempts to do is set forth in the Introduction, and a glance at the Contents will make its scope apparent. "Companion" might be a proper description, but as a book title that word has come to designate a reference work that is alphabetically arranged and reasonably complete. This is neither. Much of it is the by-product of my short histories of Greek and Latin literature, but I have not written it merely to salvage what had to be left in the inkwell and what could be swept up from unemptied filing drawers. Long preoccupation with a subject begets curiosity about matters essentially peripheral or even irrelevant to its main issues, and I have thought that others interested in ancient books might enjoy such partial satisfaction of similar curiosity as I am able to offer.

Though there is no single work that deals with all the subject matter of this book—perhaps for all too good a reason!—there are many good books that deal with sections of it. Those I have found most useful, and to which readers who desire further information may turn, are listed in the Bibliographical Notes at the end of the volume. I myself have always believed that text is more useful than commentary, and so have cited ancient authors freely. Most of the versions I have used are from the Loeb Classical Library, published by the Harvard University Press, many are older versions of merit, and some I have translated myself; in many that I have borrowed I have made changes. The sources of the translations are listed in the Bibliographical Notes at the appropriate pages. In order not to overload the body of the book I have expanded the Index into a brief prosopography, supplying dates and identifications wherever appropriate.

The suggestion that I write this book came from my colleague Jacques Barzun, who also read and criticized part of my first draft.

I wish to express my gratitude to him, to Professor Joseph Mazzeo, who read the entire MS and made useful suggestions, to Mrs. Margaret Davidson for generous and meticulous secretarial assistance, and to Henry Wiggins and William Bridgwater of the Columbia University Press for their unfailing helpfulness and courtesy.

MOSES HADAS

Columbia University in the City of New York
November 8, 1953

Contents

Part II: Literary Gossip

CONTENTS

Part I

PRODUCTION, RECEPTION
AND PRESERVATION

1 : *The Leaf and the Fruit*

THE SIMPLEST EXPLANATION FOR THE SURVI-
val of the classics is that ordinary readers have found them
worth preserving. Their vogue has naturally fluctuated with vicissitudes of history and vagaries of taste, but periodic renascences
have returned to them with renewed zeal and fresh advocacy. At
one time the classics have provided ideal paradigms for all phases
of intellectual life; at another they have been exploited for purely
antiquarian interests. But justifications for concern with classics
are afterthoughts of guilty Puritans, and those who feel constrained
to advance them are always one-sided and often wrong. Our grandfathers justified the study of Homer, for example, on the grounds
that he marked the beginning of profane history as Abraham did of
sacred history. We now know that both Homer and the Old Testament had literary antecedents, and in the cuneiform writings of
the ancient Near East we actually possess documents a millennium
older than either which palpably influenced the writers of the Old
Testament and which throw incidental light on the poetry of
Homer.

But in an essential sense our grandfathers were right. Coming to
Homer from the antecedent literatures of the Near East is like
coming to the Greek gallery from its predecessors in a museum of
antiquities. The products of the older civilizations are curiosities,
remote and alien. With the Greeks we feel an immediate kinship,
and in their works we recognize the cultural stream in which we
ourselves move and live. Greek literature is European in a sense
in which its Near Eastern predecessors are not. To acclimatize ourselves to the preoccupations of the latter requires an effort of the
imagination, and even if the personalities of their authors were more
clearly limned for us we should still require either a microscope or
a telescope to examine their nature. But a Greek author can be
apprehended with the naked eye; he offers no greater obstacles to

understanding than does a modern French or Russian author. We understand his motives and objectives; his loves and hates and ambitions evoke familiar responses. Upon the personality and the working habits of the Greek author, then, we may properly bestow such interest as we commonly bestow upon literary figures in the later history of Europe, and we may expect that the Greeks will prove as rewarding of our efforts.

The proper basis for judging any author is of course his book. Ancient authors have customarily been judged exclusively by their books, because little outside their books is known of them and because their books tend to possess an elemental and universal character which makes the personality of the author as impertinent as the personality of the man for whom a mountain is named. But because classic authors are serious men who are likely to question the assumptions of their society or advocate a program of reform, knowledge of the intellectual and political and social backgrounds against which they worked can enlarge our understanding of their books. Here numerous expositors and interpreters offer guidance. Easily available also is such information as is appropriate to a history of literature—biographies, literary genealogies, inventories, and evaluations. But none of these things quickens the rigid library busts into life, replaces their blank eyes with expressions that show human emotions in the ordinary encounters of life or, more important, strips the formal drapery away and reveals the craftsman in his tunic fashioning his products and marketing them. The intimate and sometimes banausic details concerning the daily preoccupations of the craftsmen who wrote and preserved our classics, such information as might be gleaned from a house-organ of a writer's guild rather than a formal history of literature, may be profitable as well as entertaining.

A curious reader of an ancient work might well wonder how his text was first committed to writing, how it was preserved and transmitted, and how faithful his fresh edition is likely to be to its author's autograph, and he might well profit from the answers. What, to begin with, were the physical resources of the writer—paper, alphabets, handwritings? How did he publish, and how make his living? How large was his public and what were his relations to it? Did he enjoy a special prestige, and was he charged with special responsibilities? How was his work cared for, kept intelligible, transmitted through the ages? What have been the functions of professional criticism and scholarship in antiquity and subsequently? Aside from professional and traditional judgments, can vulgar opinion and gossip throw light upon our authors and help bring them to life?

Insofar as knowledge permits, the pages which follow will attempt to suggest answers to such questions as these. The first part of this work will deal with the general theme of the ancient writer as craftsman and as citizen, and with the history of the preservation and study of his work. The second part will retail such items of literary gossip concerning the major writers of antiquity (in roughly chronological order) as may enable the modern reader to see them as their contemporaries, or at least men in their own uninterrupted tradition, saw them. To repeat slanderous reports that Simonides was avaricious, Sophocles a pederast, Demosthenes venal, may be frowned upon as a surrender to Philistinism and a needless reinforcement of the complacency of the vulgar; but surely the realization that these authors shared the character of their age (and were subjected to reproach for their failings) must enhance rather than diminish the worth as well as the understanding of their works.

Boswell's preface to his Johnson explains his inclusion of apparent trivialities by reference to David Kimhi's exegesis of Psalm 1: "And he shall be like a tree planted by the rivers of water, that bringeth forth his fruit in his season; his leaf also shall not wither." This signifies, Kimhi had said, that not only the serious discourse of the sages (which is their fruit), but their lighter utterances and commonplace activities (which is merely their leaf) must be attended to. There can be no fruit without leaves, and it is to leaves rather than fruit that we shall now turn our attention.

2: *The Outward Manifestations*

I. THE ALPHABET

GENERATIONS OF GREEKS WHO HAD NEVER looked into a text of Homer must have been intimately familiar with *Iliad* and *Odyssey*, just as moderns to whom a printed score is meaningless may yet be intimately familiar with a Beethoven symphony. But it is no longer necessary to believe, as all scholars a generation or two ago and many today still believe, that either the poems were composed without the art of writing or, alternatively, that the date of their composition must be brought down to the 6th century. In Mesopotamia, Egypt, Asia Minor, Crete, writing was used in the third millennium B.C., and though we cannot premise a *reading* public in Greece much before the classical age, there is every probability that Homer, however high we date him, could use writing for the composition of his poems, and that the rhapsodes who recited them possessed manuscript copies to study.

The Greeks themselves attributed the introduction of their alphabet to Cadmus, whom they imagined to have lived long before the Trojan War, and whose name consists of the Semitic radicals for "east." The oldest and best statement on the subject is that of Herodotus (5.58):

Now the Phoenicians who came with Cadmus . . . introduced into Greece upon their arrival a great variety of arts, among the rest that of writing, whereof the Greeks till then had, as I think, been ignorant. And originally they shaped their letters exactly like all the other Phoenicians, but afterwards, in course of time, they changed by degrees their language, and together with it the form likewise of their characters. Now the Greeks who dwelt about those parts at that time were chiefly the Ionians. The Phoenician letters were accordingly adopted by them, but with some variation in the shape of a few, and so they arrived at the present use, still calling the letters Phoenician, as justice required, after the name of those *who were the first to introduce them into Greece. Paper rolls (bybloi) were called from of old "parchments" (diphtherai) by the Ionians, the skins of sheep and goats—on which material many of the barbarians are even now wont to write.*

The names and early forms of the Greek letters make it plain that they were indeed taken from Phoenician models. The principal innovation of the Greeks was the adaptation of the letters A E I O Y, which in Semitic have consonantal values not required in Greek, to serve as vowels. Of several early varieties of writing the East Ionic became predominant. Since Ionic had lost the *h* sound, *H* came to be used for long *e*; and when the Ionic alphabet was accepted in Athens the aspirate was expressed by a mark (ʻ) which signifies "rough breathing."

II. PAPYRUS ROLLS

As far as memory went in Herodotus' day, as the close of the passage cited shows, papyrus was the material normally used for writing. Papyrus made into rolls continued to be the regular material for books until the introduction, mainly by Christians for the convenience of having the Gospels in a single volume, of the codex form and hence of vellum which is more suitable to that form. Of the various other materials which might on occasion be used to receive writing, some form of leather was the only practicable alternative to papyrus. Today the only books regularly written on parchment rolls are the scrolls of the Pentateuch intended for ritual use in the Synagogue, which suggests that, as Herodotus says, parchment was at one time the regular writing material among "barbarians." That parchment was used among Greeks only in times of stress we learn both from the Herodotus passage and from Varro's story (cited by Pliny, below) to the effect that parchment was invented in the reign of Eumenes II of Pergamum (197–159 B.C.). Parchment must surely have been invented much earlier, but its Greek name *pergamene* does suggest some significant connection with Pergamum. Perhaps parchment did come into more general use for literature under Eumenes, for the reason Varro states, but even so its use must have been local and temporary. Throughout classical antiquity papyrus remained the regular material for books.

For the manufacture and marketing of papyrus, and for other details germane to the subject, the fullest information is to be found in Pliny, N.H. 13.21.68 ff.:

Before we leave Egypt we shall also describe the nature of papyrus, since our civilization or at all events our records depend very largely on the employment of paper. According to Marcus Varro we owe even the discovery of paper to the victory of Alexander the Great, when he founded Alexandria in Egypt, before which time paper was not used. [This is not true.] First of all people used to write on palm leaves and then on the bark of certain trees, and afterwards folding sheets of lead began to be employed for official muniments, and then also sheets of linen or tablets of wax for private documents; for we find in Homer [Iliad 6.168] that the use of writing tablets existed even before the Trojan period. . . . Subsequently also, according to Varro, when owing to the rivalry between King Ptolemy and King Eumenes about their libraries Ptolemy suppressed the export of paper, parchment was invented at Pergamum; and afterwards the employment of the material on which the immortality of human beings depends spread indiscriminately.

Papyrus, then, grows in the swamps of Egypt or else in the sluggish waters of the Nile where they have overflowed and lie stagnant in pools not more than about three feet in depth; it has a sloping root as thick as a man's arm, and tapers gracefully up with triangular sides to a length of not more than about 15 feet, ending in a head like a thyrsus; it has no seed [wrong] and is of no use except that the flowers are made into wreaths for statues of the gods. The roots are employed by the natives for timber, and not only to serve as firewood but also for making various utensils and vessels; indeed the papyrus itself is plaited to make boats, and the inner bark is woven into sail-cloth and matting as well as blankets and ropes. It is also used as chewing-gum, both in the raw state and when boiled, though only the juice is swallowed. Papyrus also grows in Syria . . .

nevertheless up to the present the Parthians prefer to embroider letters upon cloths.

The process of making paper from papyrus is to split it with a needle into very thin strips made as broad as possible, the best quality being in the center of the plant, and so on in the order of splitting up. [There follows an inventory of the classes of manufactured papyrus.]

Paper of all kinds is "woven" on a board moistened with water from the Nile, muddy liquid supplying the effect of glue. First an upright layer is smeared on to the table, using the full length of papyrus available after the trimmings have been cut off at both ends, and afterwards cross strips complete the lattice-work. The next step is to press it in presses, and the sheets are dried in the sun and then joined together, the next strip used always diminishing in quality down to the very worst of all. There are never more than twenty sheets to a roll [i.e., as a marketing unit; for a book several such rolls might be joined].

There is a great difference in the breadth of the various kinds of papers: the best is 13 inches wide, the hieratic two inches less, the Fannian measures ten inches and the amphitheater paper one less, while the Saitic is still fewer inches across and is not as wide as the mallet used in making it, and the emporitic kind is so narrow that it does not exceed six inches. . . .

Roughness is smoothed out with a piece of ivory or shell, but this makes the lettering apt to fade, as owing to the polish so given the paper does not take the ink so well, but has a shinier surface. . . . The common kind of paste for paper is made of fine flour of the best quality mixed with boiling water, with a very small sprinkle of vinegar; for carpenter's paste and gum make too brittle a compound. But a more careful process is to strain the crumb of leavened bread in boiling water; this method requires the smallest amount of paste at the seams, and produces a paper softer even than linen. But all the paste used ought to be exactly a day old—not more nor yet less. Afterwards the paper is beaten thin with a mallet and run over with a layer of paste, and then again has its creases removed by pressure and is flattened out with the mallet. This process may *enable records to last a long time; at the house of the poet and most distinguished citizen Pomponius Secundus I have seen documents in the hand of Tiberius and Gaius Gracchus written nearly 200 years ago; while as for autographs of Cicero, of his late Majesty Augustus, and of Vergil, we see them constantly.*

Pliny's account is generally corroborated by papyrus finds in Egypt. Single papyrus sheets were normally 5 or 6 inches wide and 8 or 9 inches tall. Such sheets were glued together to make a roll, which might extend to 30 feet or more. Upon this roll the writing was arranged in columns, usually 2 or 3 inches wide for prose and somewhat wider for poetry. Lines ran to 20 or 25 letters, and there were normally 30 to 40 lines in a column. Margins between columns were small, but somewhat larger at top and bottom, where forgotten words might be written in. Hands naturally varied in legibility, but reading was in any case more difficult than today because words were not separated and punctuation was uncertain and arbitrary. In cases of ambiguity a rough breathing might be employed, cola might be set off with a single point, and a horizontal stroke (*paragraphos*) indicated a sharp break or a change of speaker in dramatic pieces. Titles were placed at the end of writings; a label attached to a scroll identified its contents.

In addition to this information, based on actual remains from Egypt, we have in the Latin poets a number of helpful allusions to the appearance of books, though no ancient Roman books have survived, except for badly charred scrolls from Herculaneum. Catullus, Propertius, Ovid, and especially Martial all speak of books; a single passage in Catullus (22.3.8) supplies a number of details:

Suffenus makes many more verses than anyone else. I suppose that he has got some 10,000 or even more written out in full, and not, as is often done, put down on old scraps; imperial paper (chartae regiae), new rolls, new bosses (umbilici), red ties, parchment wrappers, all ruled with lead and smoothed with pumice.

The bosses referred to were decorative knobs for the ends of the rollers, with which books of the better class were furnished. When not in use the roll was kept in a parchment sheath, which might be colored and fitted with colored strings. To improve its durability and appearance a papyrus book might be tinted with cedar oil. A number of rolls would be kept together in boxes or buckets (*capsa*, *scrinium*), or laid in shelves or in pigeonholes (*nidi*). Several passages speak of booksellers' stalls at Rome, and of announcements of their wares posted in front of them.

III. TABLETS, CODICES, VELLUM

For school work, temporary memoranda, or correspondence tablets of wood or occasionally of ivory were used. A depression in the surface of the tablet was nearly filled with wax, so as to leave a raised rim about the edges, like the frame of an old-fashioned slate. Letters were incised on the wax with a metal or ivory stilus, pointed at one end for writing and flat at the other for erasing. Sets of two or more tablets were often fastened together at one edge by wire hinges, and these so-called *codicilli* became the pattern for the form of book called the codex.

The codex, which is in effect the modern book, consisting of leaves arranged in quires, is obviously more compact than a roll and makes more complete use of the writing space. In a codex a group of Gospels or Epistles could be reduced to the convenient size of a pocket edition, and that advantage is usually taken to explain the general adoption of the codex form by Christians in the 4th century. There are indeed traces of 2nd century A.D. papyrus codices of pagan writings; but through the 3rd century the great majority of pagan remains are in rolls, while the great majority of Christian works are in codex form. The usual size of the codex was about 10 × 7 inches. The quires were formed of 10 or 12 leaves, and each page usually carried a single column of writing.

For the codex vellum or parchment is a much more satisfactory material than papyrus, and it is during the 4th century also that we note the general change from papyrus to vellum. Constantine the Great ordered 50 copies of the Scriptures written on vellum for the churches of Constantinople, and Jerome records that the worn papyrus MSS in the library at Caesarea were replaced by copies on vellum. The finest books that have come down from antiquity are the great codices of the Greek Bible, the Vaticanus and Sinaiticus, which were made about this period. To the 4th or early 5th century also are dated our earliest Latin codices—Vergil, Cicero, Terence, and Livy.

IV. PENS AND INK

The tools for writing, as we learn from ancient representations and descriptions, were not very different from ours. They are listed in this epigram by Paul the Silentiary (A.P. 6.64), composed for a superannuated scribe who was dedicating his now useless equipment to Hermes:

Philodemus, now that his wrinkled brows owing to old age come to hang over his eyes, dedicates to Hermes the round lead that draws dark lines, the pumice, rough whet-stone of hard pens, the knife, flat sharpener of the split-reed pens, the ruler that takes charge of the straightness of lines, the ink long kept in hollow caverns, and the notched pens blackened at the point.

The "notched pens" were of reed, pointed and cleft at the end as quills used to be. The "hollowed caverns" doubtless refer to the two compartments generally seen in ancient pictures of ink-wells; the second was for red ink, which was much used for headings (hence "rubrics"), ornaments, and the like. There are good remarks on ink in Persius' lines on the sluggish student (3.12 ff.):

Now he takes the book in his hand, and the parchment, which has had the hair taken off and shows two colors, and the paper, and the jointed reed. Next we begin to complain that the ink is thick and clots on the pen; and then, when water is poured in, that the liquor (or "its blackness") is ruined and that the implement makes two washy drops instead of one.

The parchment mentioned in this passage refers either to the sheath of the papyrus book-roll, or to the use of parchment as a sort of scratch-pad. For the manufacture of ink our best passage is in the Elder Pliny (N.H. 35.41–43):

Ink can be made in a variety of ways from the soot produced by burning resin or pitch, owing to which factories have actually been built with no exit for the smoke produced by this process. The most esteemed black paint is obtained in the same way from the wood of the pitch-pine. It is adulterated by mixing it with the soot of furnaces and baths, which is used as a material for writing. Some people calcine dried wine-lees, and declare that if the lees from a good wine are used this ink has the appearance of Indian ink. The very celebrated painters Polygnotus and Micon at Athens made black paint from the skins of grapes, and called it grape-lees ink. Apelles invented the method of making black from burnt ivory; the Greek name for this is elephantinon. There is also an Indian black, imported from India, the composition of which I have not yet discovered. A black is also produced with dyes from the black florescence which adheres to bronze pans. One is also made by burning logs of pitch-pine and pounding the charcoal in a mortar. The cuttle-fish has a remarkable property in forming a black secretion, but no color is made from this. The preparation of all black is completed by exposure to the sun, black for writing ink receiving an admixture of gum and black for painting walls an admixture of glue. Black pigment that has been dissolved in vinegar is difficult to wash out.

V. CHAPTERS AND VERSES

Divisions of large works into separate "books" originated in Alexandria, but authors naturally conceived of their work in well-defined parts. Each part of the Anabasis closes with a kind of summary; the book-division of the *Republic* may well be Plato's own. By the time of Pliny division into books was so well established that he can make of his first book a table of contents for the rest. Publication was frequently by groups of five or ten books; that is why the losses in such large histories as those of Livy or Polybius are in batches of five or ten books.

Chapter divisions are modern, and date only from the Renaissance, but the ancients did count lines, at first of poetry, and then of prose. A statement of the number of lines in the author's autograph would protect the purchaser of a copy against large omissions. At the conclusion of his *Antiquities* Josephus gives the size of his work as 60,000 lines. Sometimes, for the purpose of protecting the integrity of an important text, words and even letters might be counted. The Masoretic text of the Bible marks such detailed divisions.

Titles for books are also a later development. Homer himself did not call his poems *Iliad* and *Odyssey*, and both Herodotus and Thucydides describe their books, but give them no title, in their opening sentences. Frequently a book was cited by its opening words. Titles were given to Alexandrian books by their authors. Apollonius called his epic *Argonautica*, just as Vergil called his *Aeneid*.

VI. HANDWRITINGS

Boys learned to write as they learned to read. Plato makes Socrates explain (*Republic* 2.368b) that discussing justice in the state rather than in the individual is like writing large for easier legibility, and the Elder Cato wrote a history of Rome for his young son in "large letters" (Plutarch, *Cato* 19.5). That the method of teaching writing has not much altered we see from a schoolboy's tablet found in Egypt; on the top is the master's fair copy, and underneath the scrawling and incorrect imitation. Latin schoolboy hands can be seen in the remains of schools in the Forum of Caesar and on the declivity of the Palatine. Quintilian (1.1.27–29) recommends a method for teaching writing and insists on the usefulness of a legible hand:

As soon as the child has begun to know the shapes of the various letters, it will be no bad thing to have them cut as accurately as possible upon a board, so that the pen may be guided along the grooves. Thus mistakes such as occur with wax tablets will be rendered impossible; for the pen will be confined between the edges of the letters and will be prevented from going astray. Further by increasing the frequency and speed with which they follow these fixed outlines we shall give steadiness to the fingers, and there will be no need to guide the child's hand with our own. The art of writing well and quickly is not unimportant for our purpose, though it is generally disregarded by persons of quality. Writing is of the utmost importance in the study which we have under consideration and by its means alone can true and deeply rooted proficiency be obtained. But a sluggish pen delays our thoughts, while an unformed and illiterate hand cannot be deciphered, a circumstance which necessitates another wearisome task, namely the dictation of what we have written to a copyist. We shall therefore at all times and in all places, and above all when we are writing private letters to our friends, find gratification in the thought that we have not neglected even this accomplishment.

As we should expect and as the papyri from Egypt show, there is a marked difference between the writing of an individual intended for his own or his friends' eyes and that of a professional scribe. Formal documents as well as books were written by professionals, and busy men normally dictated to trained scribes. Cicero sometimes dictated to Tiro, and sometimes, as he notes, wrote with his own hand. Caesar dictated in his carriage, as we read in Plutarch (Caesar 17.3):

Most of his sleep he got in cars or litters, making his rest conduce to action, and in the daytime he would have himself conveyed to garrisons, cities, or camps, one slave who was accustomed to write from dictation sitting at his side, and one soldier standing behind him with a sword.

The indefatigable Elder Pliny dictated all the time, even in the bath, except when submerged (as his nephew tells us in 3.5), and even when traveling:

A shorthand writer, with book and tablets, constantly attended him in his carriage, who, in the winter, wore a particular sort of warm gloves, that the sharpness of the weather might not occasion any interruption to his studies; and for the same reason my uncle always used a sedan chair in Rome.

The shorthand here referred to was introduced into Rome by Cicero, who once made political capital of the device (Plutarch, Younger Cato 23):

The preservation of Cato's only extant speech was due to Cicero the consul, who had previously given to those clerks who excelled in rapid writing instruction in the use of signs, which, in small and short figures, comprised the force of many letters; these clerks he had then distributed in various parts of the Senate-house. For up to that time the Romans did not employ or even possess what are called shorthand writers, but then for the first time, we are told, the first steps towards the practice were taken.

Later shorthand is called notae Tironianae from Cicero's freedman-secretary. Cicero himself refers to shorthand by a Greek word (Atticus 13.32) and its invention was surely Greek. Diogenes Laertius (2.48) says that Xenophon first used "signs" to note down the conversation of Socrates, and actual shorthand manuals, with a complete system, have been found in Egypt. Perhaps the most interesting note on shorthand is that in which Eusebius (Ecclesiastical History 6.23) describes the prodigious output of Origen:

Such was the inception of Origen's commentaries on the sacred Scriptures. Ambrose [not, of course, the Latin Father] urged him with a thousand encouragements, and not only with persuasive words but by most generous provision of the necessary appliances. Stenographers, more than seven in number, attended him as he dictated, and they worked in fixed shifts, spelling one another. There were an equal number of book-scribes, and also young women trained in calligraphy. The necessary expense for all this assistance Ambrose provided with ungrudging hand.

Ciphers as well as stenography were used. Suetonius (*Julius* 56.6) has this:

There are also letters of Caesar's to Cicero as well as to his intimates on private affairs, and in the latter, if he had anything confidential to say, he wrote it in cipher, that is, by so changing the order of the letters of the alphabet, that not a word could be made out. If anyone wishes to decipher these and get at their meaning, he must substitute the fourth letter of the alphabet, namely D, for A, and so with the others.

Of Augustus Suetonius tells us (*Augustus* 88):

Whenever he wrote in cipher he wrote B for A, C for B, and the rest of the letters on the same principle, using AA for X.

When style was a consideration even people who had amanuenses wrote by hand. So Suetonius (*Nero* 52) tells us of the emperor who said "I wish I had never learned to write" when he was asked to sign a death warrant:

I have had in my possession note-books and papers with some well-known verses of his, written in his own hand and in such wise that it was perfectly evident that they were not copied or taken down from dictation, but worked out exactly as one writes when thinking *and creating; so many instances were there of words erased or struck through and written above the lines.*

The difference between bookhands and everyday cursive is something like the difference between printing and writing. The former were like letters carved on stone, and always tended to be conservative, but they were constantly influenced by cursive forms. Palaeography, or the study of ancient handwritings, is an important tool for the philologer. Of the scholars who used this tool to protect the integrity of our texts we shall speak in a succeeding chapter; here a word may be said of the handwritings in which the texts were handed down. Greek uncials are merely rounded forms of letters used in inscriptions and changed little until the use of parchment encouraged thick vertical strokes. About A.D. 800 scholars in Constantinople deliberately designed a new minuscule book hand based on cursive, which remained in use until the introduction of printing. Printed books at first retained and then abolished the capricious forms and arabesque ligatures which had developed in this hand; to the uninitiate early Greek printing is as puzzling to read as a manuscript.

The Latin uncial, which was the regular book hand from the 4th to the 8th century, was similarly the product of the earlier capitals ("square" or "rustic") with an admixture of cursive forms. By A.D. 800 cursive itself, as developed on wax and papyrus, came to be used for books, and developed into "national" hands—Lombardic, Visigothic, and Merovingian. Book production was then systematized at Tours under Charlemagne. Capitals, square or rustic, were used for headings, initials, and the like, and the text was in a minuscule based on cursive but without its ligatures. The best MSS of the bulk of our extant literature are in this Carolingian hand, which persisted with little change until the 12th century, when the Gothic or blackletter was developed in several national styles. In the 15th century humanist scholars revived the Carolingian, on the false assumption that it was the hand of the ancient Romans, and their writing was the model for early printing, which developed into the forms current today. The decipherment of MSS, as of early printed books, is made difficult not only by ligatures but by abbreviations and signs indicating certain omitted letters which probably go back to ancient shorthand. Only gradually do words become divided and punctuation helpful. Occasionally a MS carries a colophon at its end, giving the place and date of writing and the copyist's name, and more rarely a subscription by a reader who has corrected the copy.

VII. THE USE OF BOOKS

Although, as far as we can tell, there was no organized book trade or public collections in classical Greece, copies of the poets very likely existed in sufficient numbers to assure their preservation until such time as libraries were instituted; undoubtedly scientific writers like the Hippocratics and meticulous historians like Thucydides had the work of their predecessors in writing. Aristophanes could not have acquired his verbal knowledge of the plays of Aeschylus and Euripides merely from stage presentations; in the *Frogs*, for example, the chorus assures these poets that the audience can follow their lines, "for each has his book and knows what's right" (1114). In *Phaedo* (97b, 98b) Socrates refers to a book of Anaxagoras which he heard read and subsequently procured, and in *Apology* (26d) he says that anyone can buy an Anaxagoras for a drachma. At *Phaedrus* 274d ff. Socrates shows his contempt of dependence upon books in an apologue. When Theuth boasted of the advantages his invention of writing would bring to the Egyptians, Thamus replied:

O most ingenious Theuth, he who has the gift of invention is not always the best judge of the utility or inutility of his own inventions to the users of them. And in this instance a paternal love of your own child has led you to say what is not the fact; for this invention of yours will create forgetfulness in the learners' souls, because they will not use their memories; they will trust to the external written characters and not remember of themselves. You have found a specific, not for memory but for reminiscence, and you give your disciples only the pretense of wisdom; they will be hearers of many

*things and will have learned nothing; they will appear to be omnis-
cient and will generally know nothing; they will be tiresome, having the reputation of knowledge without the reality.*

In Xenophon's *Memorabilia* 4.2 Socrates' scorn for mere book-
learning is made plainer—and incidentally proves that there were
people, like his interlocutor Euthydemus, who relied upon books.
In the course of a conversation Socrates asks (4.2.8):

*"Tell me, Euthydemus, am I rightly informed that you have a large
collection of books written by the wise men of the past, as they
are called?"*

*"By Zeus, yes, Socrates," answered he, "and I am still adding
to it, to make it as complete as possible."*

Socrates' adroit dialectic quickly persuades Euthydemus of the futility of his book learning. On the other hand, also in the *Memorabilia* (1.6.14), Socrates says:

*The treasures that the wise men of old have left us in their writings
I unroll and explore with my friends. If we come on any good thing
we extract it, and we set much store on being useful to one another.*

From Xenophon too (*Anabasis* 7.5.14) we learn that in the cargoes
of ships wrecked near Salmydessus on the north coast of Asia Minor
many books were included.

On the other hand, an author's copy of his own work, of which
copies had not been multiplied, naturally possessed a special
value; so gossip such as Aulus Gellius (3.17) reports might gain
currency:

*The story goes that the philosopher Plato was a man of very slender
means, but that nevertheless he bought three books of Philolaus
the Pythagorean for 10,000 denarii. That sum, according to some
writers, was given him by his friend Dion of Syracuse. Aristotle too,
according to report, bought a very few books of the philosopher
Speusippus, after the latter's death, for three Attic talents. The*

bitter satirist *Timon* wrote a highly abusive work which he entitled Silloi. In that book he addresses the philosopher Plato in opprobrious terms, alleging that he had bought a treatise on the Pythagorean philosophy at an extravagant figure, and that from it he had compiled that celebrated dialogue the Timaeus.

From the Younger Pliny (3.5.17) we know that his uncle was offered 400,000 sesterces for his 160 rolls of notes, written on both sides of the papyrus.

VIII. LIBRARIES PUBLIC AND PRIVATE

Platonic teaching depended on direct contact between pupil and master, but for the systematic and painstaking research instituted by Aristotle and prosecuted by the Peripatetic school it is obvious that libraries were essential. With Aristotle the use of books changed to something like their function in our own day, and the fact was noted in antiquity. Aristotle himself speaks (*Rhetoric* 1413*b*) of books of even belles-lettres that were intended for reading rather than recitation. The story of Aristotle's own library and its vicissitudes, as told in Strabo 13.1.54, is famous:

Aristotle bequeathed his own library to Theophrastus, to whom he also left his school; and he is the first man, so far as I know, to have collected books and to have taught the kings in Egypt how to arrange a library. Theophrastus bequeathed it to Neleus; and Neleus took it to Scepsis and bequeathed it to his heirs, ordinary people, who kept the books locked up and not even carefully stored. But when they heard how zealously the Attalid kings to whom the city was subject were searching for books to build up the library in Pergamum, they hid their books underground in a kind of trench. But much later, when the books had been damaged by moisture and moths, their descendants sold them to Apellicon of Teos for a large sum of money, both the books of Aristotle and those of Theophrastus. But Apellicon was a bibliophile rather than a philosopher; and therefore, seeking a restoration of the parts that had been eaten through, he made new copies of the text, filling up the gaps incorrectly, and published the books full of errors. The result was that the earlier school of Peripatetics who came after Theophrastus had no books at all, with the exception of only a few, mostly exoteric works [i.e., meant for larger audiences, in contrast to "esoteric" works, which were limited to the inner circle], and were therefore able to philosophize about nothing in a practical way, but only to talk bombast about commonplace propositions, whereas the later school, from the time the books in question appeared, though better able to philosophize and Aristotelize, were forced to call most of their statements probabilities, because of the large number of errors. Rome also contributed much to this; for, immediately after the death of Apellicon, Sulla, who had captured Athens, carried off Apellicon's library to Rome, where Tyrannion the grammarian, who was fond of Aristotle, got it in his hands by paying court to the librarian, as did also certain booksellers who used bad copyists and would not collate the texts—a thing that also takes place in the case of the other books that are copied for selling, both here and in Alexandria. However, this is enough about these men.

Later ages believed that Pisistratus himself founded a public library, as can be seen from a passage in Aulus Gellius (7.17):

The tyrant Pisistratus is said to have been the first to establish at Athens a public library of books relating to the liberal arts. Then the Athenians themselves added to this collection with considerable diligence and care; but later Xerxes, when he got possession of Athens and burned the entire city except the citadel, removed that whole collection of books and carried them off to Persia. Finally, a long time afterwards, King Seleucus who was surnamed Nicanor had all those books taken back to Athens.

But Pisistratus is a dim figure, and in what appears to be intended as a full list of well known collectors Athenaeus (1.3ab) can name none except Euripides between him and Aristotle, whom he too makes indirectly responsible for the establishment of the Alexandrian library. The greatest epoch in the history of literary scholarship is marked by the establishment of the library at Alexandria. It was founded by Ptolemy I, at the suggestion of the Aristotelian Demetrius of Phalerum, and much enlarged by Ptolemy II Philadelphus. The oldest of our notices of it is in *Aristeas to Philocrates* 9–11, which tells the story of the translation of the Septuagint:

When Demetrius of Phalerum was put in charge of the king's library he was assigned large sums of money with a view to collecting, if possible, all the books in the world; and by arranging purchases and transcriptions he carried the king's design to completion as far as he was able. When he was asked, in my presence, about how many thousands of books were already collected, he replied, "Above two hundred thousand, Your Majesty; and in a short while I shall exert every effort for the remainder, to round out the number of half a million. I am informed that the laws of the Jews also are worthy of transcription and of being included in your library."

"What is to prevent you from doing so?" the king replied; "all the necessary means are at your disposal."

But Demetrius said, "Translation is required; in the country of the Jews they use a peculiar script, just as the Egyptians employ their arrangement of letters, and they have their own language. They are supposed to use Syrian, but that is not the case, for theirs is another dialect."

When the king learned these particulars he gave word that a letter should be addressed to the High Priest of the Jews, in order that the design above mentioned might be carried to completion.

Other notices give the size of the library at from 100,000 to 700,000 volumes. A series of distinguished scholars—Zenodotus, Eratosthenes, Aristophanes of Byzantium, Aristarchus—served as its directors. Apollonius of Rhodes and Callimachus worked in it; the latter's catalogues of its contents (*Pinakes*) were in effect literary histories. Part of a catalogue of a library at Rhodes has turned up in a papyrus of the 2nd century B.C. There was at Alexandria a second, smaller, library in the Serapeum, and there were others in other Hellenistic cities. The second largest appears to have been established at Pergamum by Eumenes; Plutarch (*Antony* 58) says that it contained 200,000 volumes when Antony presented it to Cleopatra. Plutarch also tells us (*Aemilius* 28) that Perseus of Macedon had a library. According to Plutarch (*Caesar* 49), the great library at Alexandria was burned when Caesar was besieged there. Other writers speak of the total destruction of both libraries and their contents.

At Rome we hear of no libraries before the 1st century B.C., when we have mention of several private collections and the beginnings of public ones. Lucullus (Plutarch, *Lucullus* 42) made his large collection accessible, especially to Greeks. Atticus and Cicero possessed many books. Varro, the greatest scholar of his age, was commissioned by Julius Caesar (Suetonius, *Julius* 44) "to procure and classify the greatest possible libraries of Greek and Latin books and open them to the public," but this was one of the projects prevented by Caesar's death. Asinius Pollio founded a public library in Rome (Pliny, *N.H.* 7.30, 35.2), but the Roman libraries were the two established by Augustus. Each was connected with a temple, had Greek and Latin sections, and a reading room where conversation was possible (Aulus Gellius 13.19). Succeeding emperors followed Augustus' example, until there were 28 libraries in Rome alone; the finest appears to have been that built by Trajan. Even Domitian, who had little sympathy for literature, was concerned for the libraries (Suetonius, *Domitian* 20):

At the beginning of his rule he neglected liberal studies, although he provided for having the libraries, which were destroyed by fire, renewed at very great expense, seeking everywhere for copies of the lost works, and sending scribes to Alexandria to transcribe and correct them.

Benefactors might provide a library for a provincial town as they would a school or a bath; the Younger Pliny, he himself tells us (1.8.2), gave one to his native Como.

In Nero's day private libraries had become as common as baths in the houses of the rich, as we learn from an always relevant passage of Seneca (*On Tranquillity* 9). Livy had spoken of libraries as "the most distinguished achievement of the good taste and solicitude of kings." But Seneca demurs:

There was no "good taste" or "solicitude" about it, but only learned luxury—nay, not even "learned," since they had collected the books not for the sake of learning but to make a show, just as many who lack even a child's knowledge of letters use books, not as the tools of learning, but as decorations for the dining-room. Therefore let just as many books be acquired as are enough, but none for mere show. "It is more respectable," you say, "to squander money on these than on Corinthian bronzes and on pictures." But excess in anything becomes a fault. What excuse have you to offer for a man who seeks to have bookcases of citrus-wood and ivory, who collects the works of unknown or discredited authors and sits yawning in the midst of so many thousand books, who gets most of his pleasure from the outsides of volumes and their titles? Consequently it is in the houses of the laziest men that you will see a full collection of orations and history with the boxes piled right up to the ceiling; for by now among cold baths and hot baths a library also is equipped as a necessary ornament of a great house. I would readily pardon these men if they were led astray by their excessive zeal for learning. But as it is, these collections of the works of sacred genius with all the portraits that adorn them are bought for show and a decoration of their walls.

Such a private library as Seneca speaks of has been uncovered at Herculaneum. This was a room about 12 feet square, lined with bookcases ornamented with inlaid woods, and furnished with a table for readers. The rolls lay on shelves or pigeonholes in cupboards or stood in boxes, and a tag (*titulus*) projecting from each roll gave its title and author. Over the cases were portraits of authors, in the form of busts or medallions fixed to the walls. These libraries, public or private, may not have given the impetus to such intense scholarly industry as centered in the library at Alexandria, but they are evidence for the large-scale multiplication of books. That a gentleman was expected to be well read we infer from another satirical passage in Seneca (*Letters* 27.5 f.):

Calvisius Sabinus had a memory so faulty that he would sometimes forget the name of Ulysses or Achilles or Priam—names which we know as well as we know those of our own attendants. . . . But none the less did he desire to appear learned, so he devised this short cut to learning: he paid fabulous prices for slaves—one to know Homer by heart and another to know Hesiod; he also delegated a special slave to each of the nine lyric poets. You need not wonder that he paid high prices for these slaves; he did not find them ready to hand, but had them made to order. After collecting this retinue he began to make life miserable for his guests; he would keep these fellows at the foot of his couch, and ask them from time to time for verses which he might repeat, and then frequently break down in the middle of a word. Sutillius Quadratus . . . suggested to Sabinus that he should have philologists to gather up the bits.

In the later Empire librarians were regularly attached to the court. The duties of a librarian may be learned from a letter of Theonas, bishop of Alexandria (282–300) to Lucianus, a chamberlain of Diocletian at his great palace in Nicomedia (*Ante-Nicene Fathers* 6.158–61):

The chief chamberlain ought, therefore, to know all the books which the emperor possesses; he should often turn them over and arrange them neatly in their proper order by catalogue; if, however, he shall have to get new books, or to have old ones transcribed, he should be careful to obtain the most accurate copyists; and if that cannot be done he should appoint learned men for the work of correction, and recompense them justly for their labors. He should also cause all manuscripts to be restored according to their need, and should embellish them, not so much with mere super-

stitious extravagance as with useful adornment; and, therefore, he should not aim at having all the manuscripts written on purple skins and in letters of gold unless the emperor has specially commanded that. With the utmost submission, however, he should do everything that is agreeable to Caesar. As he is able, he should, with all modesty, suggest to the emperor that he should read, or hear read, those books which suit his rank and honor, and minister to good use rather than pleasure. He should himself be thoroughly familiar with those books, and he should often commend them in presence of the emperor, and set forth in an appropriate fashion the testimony and the weight of those who approve them, in order that he may not seem to lean upon his own understanding only.

IX. LOSSES AND SURVIVALS

Of the books known to antiquity not a tithe has survived. Papyrus is perishable, and unless popular demand or princely patronage encouraged the periodic copying of books they crumbled into oblivion. Great and irreparable losses were caused by such catastrophes as the burning of the Alexandrian library or the more devastating destruction of libraries at Constantinople by the Crusaders in 1204. Of lost authors or works we have modern collections of "fragments" culled from such indefatigable quoters as Plutarch or Athenaeus or Aulus Gellius or from examples cited by grammarians. But in more recent times numerous fragments in the physical sense have been recovered from the sands of Egypt, for only there does the climate permit the survival of papyrus. From 1788 onwards, and in a steady flow since 1891, papyri from the 3rd century B.C. onwards have come to our knowledge, and some 20,000 pieces, varying widely in extent and significance, have been published. Far the greater number are private or official papers of all descriptions, of interest chiefly to the social and economic historian. Only some 2,000 contain literary texts, but among these are a number of important works not previously known—the mimes of Herondas, Aristotle's *Constitution of Athens*, considerable fragments of Menander and of Sophocles' *Ichneutae*, orations of Hyperides, and odes of Bacchylides, as well as fragments of the lyric and tragic poets. For works known through ordinary channels the papyri are an important aid to textual criticism, since some are a full millennium older than texts handed down in the usual manuscript tradition.

The distribution of the fragments from Egypt, chronologically and by authors, throws considerable light on the literary tastes and educational practices of later antiquity. In an inventory of literary papyri (excluding Christian works) published by Professor Roger Pack in 1952 no fewer than 554 items are Homeric—382 containing portions of the *Iliad*, 112 of the *Odyssey*, and the remainder being commentaries, lexica, and the like. This great preponderance shows the importance of Homer in education. Next in order are Demosthenes, 75; Euripides, 57; Callimachus, 38; Plato, 36; Menander, 23; Herodotus, 22; Thucydides, 21; Sophocles and Pindar, 19 each; Apollonius of Rhodes, 14; Theocritus and Sappho, 11 each; Aeschines, 10; Hippocrates, 7. Pieces dating from the last three centuries B.C. are relatively few. There are twice as many from the first century A.D. as from any previous century, and twice as many in the second or third century, when the dissemination of books was widest, as in the first. From the fourth century onwards the numbers drop sharply, due to the rise of Christianity and the decline of Roman civilization. The Arab conquest in the 7th century brought both pagan and Christian literature to an end. It is likely that these observations based on Egypt would apply to other areas of the eastern Mediterranean also.

Not only in Alexandria but throughout the Mediterranean world the decline in Roman civilization and the initial hostility of Christianity made the survival of the pagan legacy precarious. Even before the Alexandrian scholars had done their work of organizing and preserving the existing body of Greek literature much had been lost, and much that the Alexandrians knew perished later. Though many of the losses (as well as the survivals) are largely accidental, in general it is pleasant to assume that the law of the survival of the fittest operated. Homer, as Theocritus said, criticizing the niggardliness of patrons, was "sufficient for epic," and the poets of the Cycle met the doom they doubtless deserved. Herodotus overshadowed his Ionian rivals Charon, Xanthias, and Hecataeus, who apparently never even entered the Athenian tradition. Authors whose language was difficult or contents obscure, an Aeschylus or an Aristotle, could only survive through the patronage of a Ptolemy or other Maecenas, or else by being made into a textbook. Portions of a poet's work which were included in an anthology or chrestomathy had an excellent chance of survival, but for that very reason the remainder of his work was doomed. The plays of Aeschylus and Sophocles which we possess are doubtless a schoolmaster's selection from the whole corpus for purposes of teaching; we can only trust that the schoolmaster's judgment was sound. A handful of books possess such vitality and continuing appeal that they survive without benefit of princely patronage and despite the anthologizer; thus of Homer and Plato we possess all that antiquity knew, and their works have apparently never been in danger of perishing.

Works no longer extant we know by title and frequently by quotation from later writers. Plutarch gives us hundreds of lines from lost tragedies, and Athenaeus is a mine for Middle and New Comedy. Scissors-and-paste authors like Diogenes Laertius or Diodorus Siculus present large excerpts from their sources. Cicero quotes a substantial quantity of the poetry of his favorite Ennius. Our principal poem of Tyrtaeus is quoted by the orator Lycurgus to enforce a lesson in patriotism; our two considerable poems of Sappho are cited by Dionysius of Halicarnassus and "Longinus" to illustrate comments on style. Numerous tantalizing fragments, no more than a word or two, are cited by grammarians to illustrate unusual forms or meanings. Of the hundreds of Greek authors mentioned by Athenaeus or listed by Photius only a small number are extant. "It is as though of all the works quoted in Burton's *Anatomy of Melancholy*," writes F. G. Kenyon, "only those survived which are included in the World's Classics or Everyman's Library."

After its conquest of Egypt, Rome succeeded to primacy in scholarship; Antioch rose to prominence as a center for rhetoric; Athens retained something of its venerable prestige as a seat of learning. But Constantinople, from its foundation in 330 to its fall in 1453, was the hearth and bulwark of Greek learning, and successfully resisted hostile waves of Persians and Arabs, Bulgarians and Slavs, and for a long while, under the significantly named Palaeologi, the Turks themselves. In however tenuous a form Byzantium assured the continuity of the ancient tradition, and so was able, when the time came, to impart that tradition to the West.

For the survival of Latin literature the critical period was the 4th century, when Roman Christianity acquired the power to make its antagonism to the pagan tradition effective. A figure of first-class importance for the preservation of ancient literature is the aristocratic Symmachus (ca. 345–405), whose position can be understood from the role he played in the significant episode of the statue of Victory. The statue, in fact little more than a symbol of empire, had always stood in the senate-house. It was removed as a pagan image by Constantius in 357, restored by Julian called the Apostate, and again removed by Gratian in 382. Symmachus headed a group of pagan senators who petitioned for the restoration of the statue, and pleaded eloquently on behalf of ancient tradition. He is indifferent to the religious associations of the statue but insists that its abolition would entail the loss of the accumulated legacy of ancient civilization. Only the energetic intervention of the powerful St. Ambrose prevented a pagan victory. Subscriptions on extant MSS of Livy show that Symmachus was particularly concerned with preserving and circulating that author. The choice is significant: no other communicates so high a sense of the dignity of Rome and of the responsibility of Romans to their tradition. It cannot be accident, moreover, that a gentle visionary like Vergil, who was justly regarded as an *anima naturaliter Christiana*, was frequently copied and continuously read, whereas a Catullus who could speak of *pietas* due to Love, or a hard-bitten pagan like Tacitus who was especially intolerant of alien superstitions, survive imperfectly and accidentally in isolated MSS, like brands saved from the burning.

But the chief credit for the physical preservation of the classics by continuous copying through the Middle Ages belongs to a Cassiodorus Senator (ca. 487–583) who, because he was connected by blood and loyalty to what had been the highest aristocracy of pagan Rome and was himself the founder of a Christian monastery, represents in his own person the symbiosis of what had been mutually hostile traditions. Cassiodorus was concerned for the propagation of ancient texts, and drew up a work on orthography and spelling for the use of the monks of Vivarium. His provision that in the intervals of copying sacred texts the monks should copy secular works was of great importance, for the practice of Vivarium set an example for similar foundations elsewhere. Using the text "Of the making of books there is no end" in Ecclesiastes, Richard de Bury (b. 1287) writes in his *Philobiblon:*

For as the bodies of books, made of a mixture of their contraries, must experience a continuous wasting of their elements, so by the wisdom of clerks there ought to be found a remedy by which a sacred book, after paying the debt of nature, may obtain a substitute by inheritance, and thus a like seed be raised up to the dead brother.

Why books should need to be replaced is made clear in a passage of timeless validity which must strike a sympathetic chord in the heart of every lover of books:

You shall chance to see some stiff-necked youth sluggishly seating himself for study, and while the winter frost is sharp his nose, all watery with the biting cold, begins to drip. Nor does he deign to wipe it with his cloth until he has wet the books spread out before him with the vile dew. Would that such a one were given instead of a book a cobbler's apron! He has a nail almost as black as jet and reeking with foul filth, and with this he marks the place of any matter that pleaseth him. He sorts out innumerable straws which he sets in divers places, evidently that the mark may bring back to him what the memory cannot hold. These straws, because the stomach of the book does not digest them and no one takes them out, at first distend it beyond its wonted place of closing and at length, being quite overlooked, begin to rot. He halts not at eating fruits and cheese over the open page, and, in a slovenly way, shifts his cup hither and thither. And because he has not his alms bag at hand, he casts the residue of the fragments into the book. With endless chattering he ceases not to rail against his companions and . . . wets the book spread out in his lap with the sputtering of his spittle. Soon, doubling his elbows, he reclines upon the book and by his short study invites a long sleep and, by spreading out the wrinkles, bends the margins of the leaves. . . . [In the summer] he will stuff his book with the violet, the primrose and the rose and even with clover. Then he will apply his watery hands, all damp with sweat, to turning over the volumes. . . . At the nip of a biting flea the book is flung aside, and scarcely being shut within a month's time, becomes so swollen with the dust that has fallen in it that it cannot obey the effort of one who would close it. . . . when opportunity offers they scribble uncouthly on the best volumes, and where they see a large margin about the text they display their monstrous letters; and if any other triviality whatsoever occurs to their imagination, their unchastened pen hastens at once to draw it out.

3: *The Poet and His Work*

I. THE ESSENTIAL COMMODITY

MORE SIGNIFICANT THAN OUR TANGIBLE borrowings from the ancients, which can be examined in isolation, are certain cultural attitudes, which are so pervasive as not to be recognized. The view of society which we call democratic and the restless intellectual questioning which characterizes Western society are almost as obviously derived from the Greek legacy as columns in architecture or unified construction in drama. Less tangible but more important is a product of the combination of democracy and intellectual curiosity which makes of literature not an indulgence for leisure or a preserve for clerks but an essential ingredient of civilized life. It is so among ourselves because it was so in Greece. For no Western people, surely, does literature seem to be a more natural and necessary commodity than to the Greeks.

For us, of course, the value of the Greek legacy lies in the things the Greeks thought and in the books in which they recorded their thoughts. But the Greeks themselves were no less clearly aware of the basis of their distinction. Isocrates, who was their most articulate educator, wrote (3.5):

In the other powers which we possess we are in no respect superior to other living creatures; nay, we are inferior to many in swiftness and in strength and in other resources; but because there has been implanted in us the power to persuade each other and to make clear to each other whatever we desire, not only have we escaped the life of wild beasts, but we have come together and founded cities and made laws and invented arts; and, generally speaking, there is no institution devised by man which the power of speech has not helped us establish.

Just as human preeminence rests on ability to use words, so does Athenian preeminence (15.293):

You, Athenians, are preeminent and superior to the rest of the world, not in your application to the business of war, nor because you govern yourselves more excellently or preserve the laws handed down to you by your ancestors more faithfully than others, but in those qualities by which the nature of man rises above the other animals, and the race of Hellenes above barbarians, namely, in the fact that you have been educated as have been no other people in wisdom and in speech.

It is its character as an essential and nearly universal commodity that sets Greek literature apart from its predecessors and many of its successors. The Greek writer was not the spokesman for an organized religion, as most of his Near Eastern predecessors had been, nor a self-conscious artist insulated from the community, as many of his successors have been. He was a craftsman like other craftsmen, supplying a recognized communal need.

II. THE POET'S MISSION

But this is not to imply that special perceptions and a special responsibility as well as superior craftsmanship were not demanded of the writer. As compared with antecedent and contemporary literatures of the Near and Middle East, Greek literature is to a peculiar degree anthropocentric in substance and secular in outlook. It is the palpable humanism of Greek literature, indeed, which makes it more sympathetic than its predecessors to modern readers—and tempts them to apply to it the same critical canons as are appropriate to other European literatures. Hence it becomes important to notice that even the Greek writer, as soon as his personality was clearly asserted, regarded himself and was regarded by his audience as an instrument of inspiration and as such responsible to the requirements of something approaching a sacerdotal office. Dedicated poets like Pindar are deeply convinced of their mission and speak of it explicitly, but even in Homer the minstrel holds a commission from supernatural powers. Of Demodocus, for example, it is said (Odyssey 8.63) that "the Muse had greatly loved him and had given him good and ill: she took away his eyesight but gave him delightful song." The bard's productions are regularly characterized as "charming" or "enchanting," and we must remember that such expressions were not yet reduced to mere metaphor but in all likelihood reflected a belief that an actual magical power had been communicated by a divine patron. When Hesiod received his call he was given a rod as a manifest symbol of this magical power; the Muses, he says (*Theogony* 29–35)

> A branch of laurel gave, which they had plucked,
> To be my sceptre; and they breathed a song
> In music on my soul, and bade me set
> Things past and things to be to that high strain.
> Also they bade me sing the race of gods,
> Themselves, at first and last, ever remembering.

Hesiod cannot be dismissed as a primitive, for his ethical formulations retained great authority throughout the classical period.

Pindar, who lived in the bright light of the fifth century and who is in many ways the most Greek of poets, is as deeply convinced of the poet's supernatural endowment and of his own election to the high office of poet. Repeatedly he emphasizes the antitheses between natural genius (*phya*) and craftsmanship (*techne*), between the man who knows by nature and the man who learns (*Olympian* 2.94, 9.100; *Nemean* 3.40). "To me," he says with simple assurance (*Paean* 7b), "the Muses have handed on this immortal task." It is by virtue of his office that Pindar can confer immortality on the subjects of his epinician odes—such as Homer had conferred on Ajax (*Isthmian* 4.37). Yet Pindar also has sufficient assurance to criticize Homer for giving Odysseus undeserved fame by his fictions (*pseudesi: Nemean* 7.20 f.), and he righteously rejects poetic tales discreditable to the gods (*Olympian* 1.28 ff.)

Nor is the theory of inspiration peculiar to dedicated poets like Hesiod or Pindar; it persisted throughout the classical period and is repeatedly set forth by Plato. "The poet," he wrote (*Ion* 534b), "is a light and holy and winged thing, and there is no invention in him until he is inspired and out of his senses, and the mind is no longer in him." "Whoever knocks at the door of poetry without the Muses' frenzy, persuaded that by art alone he will be a sufficient poet, fails of perfection, and the work of the sober is forthwith eclipsed by that of the frenzied" (*Phaedrus* 245a). In the *Apology* Socrates discovers that poets do not themselves well understand the things they write, though he looks forward to meeting Hesiod and Homer as well as Orpheus and Musaeus after death.

But Plato's view, it may be, was somewhat old-fashioned. His emphasis is everywhere spiritual and his bias aristocratic, and we may question the propriety of accepting his views as evidence for a period which was dominantly democratic and rationalist. Suspicion of special gifts or of priestly pretensions was a natural concomitant of the democratic and rationalist currents of the late fifth century, and the poet's claim to special spiritual endowment may actually have contributed to the eclipse of poetry at the end of that century. The substitution of *poietes* ("maker") for *aidoios* ("bard"), which we first encounter in Herodotus and Aristophanes, is an index of the change. It was in an age of enlightenment in Italy that *vates* was similarly supplanted by *poeta*.

But even if the doctrine of inspiration had lost its full force it continued to survive as a formula. The process of weakening can be illustrated from Aristotle. In the *Rhetoric* (1408b), Aristotle repeats and apparently accepts the doctrine, but in the *Poetics* (1455a) it is qualified: "Poetry implies either a happy gift of nature (*euphuia*) or ecstasy (*manike*)"—and the whole of the *Poetics*, as of most subsequent criticism, really rests on the former alternative. It is hard to assess the effectiveness of traditional formulae in sophisticated periods, but it is surely worth noticing that the organization of the Museum and Library at Alexandria, as of the schools of philosophy, took the form of a cult of the Muses, with the chief librarian as high priest. Contemporaries may have been perfectly aware that this was the only device for validating the legal fiction of a corporation, and it is hard to believe that a Callimachus could feel that his inspiration was as direct as Hesiod had felt his to be; and yet the connection cannot have been entirely meaningless. The rhapsodes who recited Homer believed that they possessed an extension of Homer's original inspiration, and even in a rationalist age the incumbent of a sacred office may feel that he somehow reincarnates the special powers of the founder.

In the case of the Romans, as perhaps of the Alexandrians, it is hard to determine how much more is to be deduced from a claim to inspiration or an appeal for the Muses' assistance than that a given poet's classical models contained such claims or appeals. The primitive *vates* surely had a sacerdotal character: to what degree was his sophisticated successor believed to share in it? Or, proceeding from a different approach, the great poems of Lucretius and Vergil are more specifically religious in aim than any analogous works in Greek: to what degree were the poets regarded, by themselves and their audience, as possessed of spiritual authority? This much may be said: where Roman poetry is not frivolous it is consciously and austerely devoted to the service of the Roman ideal, and its tone, in the *Aeneid* or in the patriotic odes of Horace, is one of lofty patriotism perhaps more truly religious than the formal cults. Where disciplined orthodoxy is the ideal, prophecy is suspect, and the temper of the Roman state was more hospitable to the priest than to the prophet. Hence in Rome the spokesman for the state may have carried the kind of authority which was elsewhere associated with a more literal concept of inspiration.

III. THE LICENSE TO TEACH

Whether as an active belief, then, or merely as a suggestive literary formula, it was held in antiquity that the poet worked under external inspiration. A companion belief, equally persistent, maintained with greater conviction, and more effective in determining the course of poetry, held that the poet's prime function was to teach. Among ourselves even advocates of pure poetry would doubtless grant the poet the *privilege* of teaching and the possibility that even pure poetry might be instructive; what is striking in the ancient concept is the *obligation* of the poet to teach and the consequent

assumption that the principal consideration in judging a poem is
its doctrinal value. In a familiar line of the *Frogs* (1055) Aristophanes gives it as a truism that "Boys have a master for their schooling;
men have the poets," and at the end of that play Aeschylus receives
a *poetic* award for *political* advice.

Doubtless it was from the concept that poetry was inspired and
the use made of poetry in education that this view of the poet's function arose. Poetry was in fact the staple of all education. After children have learned their letters, writes Plato (*Protagoras* 325e)

*they are furnished with works of good poets to read as they sit in
class, and are made to learn them off by heart: here they meet with
many admonitions, many descriptions and praises and eulogies of
good men in times past, that the boys in envy may imitate them
and yearn to become even as they.*

Even the Spartans used poets like Tyrtaeus to indoctrinate their
embryo warriors. Not only the gnomic and lyric poets but the dramatists also were continually quarried for wholesome tags, and then
not merely for tags but for wise counsel in all the concerns of life.

An age which accepted the exclusively didactic treatises of Aratus
and Nicander on astronomy and antidotes as poetry demanded that
Homer too should be a teacher of specific subjects of the curriculum,
such as medicine or cookery, and in particular, of course, of morality.
It was to a poet that Agamemnon had intrusted the care of Clytem-
nestra when he went off to the Trojan War, and Aegisthus had to
kill him before he could corrupt the lady (*Odyssey* 3.267 ff.). Stoic
exegesis (represented by Strabo 1.2.3 and Athenaeus 1.14b)
naturally took this passage to imply that the poet must be a moral
instructor. If claim to inspiration was one factor in the eclipse of
poetry during the age of the orators, the view of the poet as teacher
was surely another, for such rhetoricians as Isocrates could now insist that their own artistic productions had taken over the didactic
functions of poetry.

In what appears to have been a recognized opposition between
a Hesiodic and a Homeric view of the function of poetry, then, the

Hesiodic prevailed. To Hesiod the Muses had said (*Theogony* 27–28), "We know how to speak many false things as though they were true; but we know, when we will, to utter true things." This is doubtless a rebuke to the Homeric type of poetry, and an affirmation of the moral obligation of the poet. The difference between the Homeric and Hesiodic type of poetry is of course manifest, and was pointed up by the Spartan king who observed that Homer was the poet of Spartiates and Hesiod of helots (Plutarch, *Sayings of the Lacedaemonians* 223a). The rivalry of the two schools may be the issue in the Contest at Chalcis where Hesiod boasts he won a tripod (*Works and Days* 654), and may be reflected in the *Contest of Homer and Hesiod*, which is of Hadrianic date but embodies earlier matter. In any case it is worth noticing that presentation of poetry at a public contest is a very old practice. The institution is suggested in the *Homeric Hymn to Apollo* (157 ff.), in Thamyris' competition with the Muses (*Iliad* 2.595), Apollo's with Marsyas, and even in the singing matches in Theocritus. The influence of the *agon* was not wholly salutary. The umpire (*krites*) became the "critic," and tended to formulate his judgment on irrelevant grounds, as we have seen in the award at the close of the *Frogs*, or in the exclusion of good poets from Plato's *Republic* on political grounds.

The earliest condemnation of poetry, made in the spirit of Hesiod's concept of the poet's function and employing such criteria as Plato was to use, made Hesiod himself a culprit. In the 6th century Xenophanes complained that "Homer and Hesiod assigned to the gods all that is disgraceful and blameworthy among men— stealing and adultery and mutual deceit" (11b, Diels). When Pythagoras visited Hades he saw Homer and Hesiod enduring Dantesque punishments for what they had said about the gods (Diogenes Laertius 8.21), and Heraclitus used to say that "Homer deserved to be chased out of the lists and beaten with rods, and Archilochus likewise" (*ibid.* 9.1). The same sixth century which saw these attacks saw a defense, based on the same mistaken grounds. This was the allegorical method of interpretation, which is said to have been introduced by Theagenes of Rhegium. Both parties accepted the principle that the poet is a teacher, but whereas the literalists found the teaching morally inadequate, the allegorists discovered hidden meanings which must have been the poet's true intention and which were ethically edifying. Whenever an ancient and revered text falls short of the ethical requirements of a more refined age it is natural that recourse be had to allegorical interpretation; Philo's treatment of Scripture is a perfect analogy. Nor is the method as absurd as it might at first glance appear, for in many instances interpreters only made explicit what must actually have been part of the author's intention. Homer must surely have been aware of the sermons implicit in such texts as that describing Circe's transformation of Odysseus' men into swine.

Literalists and allegorists alike, then, proceeded on the assumption that the poet's account must be instructive and, by implication, ultimately true. Part of the difficulty was an accident of language: the only word available for "fiction" was *pseudos*, and in ordinary parlance pseudos meant "falsehood." In the succeeding chapter we shall see how long it took the ancients to formulate the distinction between artistic creation and ordinary deception so as to surmount the difficulty. But before the distinction was clarified and without the benefit of allegorical acrobatics, it is easy to see that the demand for moral instruction in poetry would subject the poet to criticism for passages which might be offensive on moral grounds, even when such passages were uttered "in character" and clearly did not represent the poet's own moral views. Aristophanes presents some first-class criticism of Euripides and Aeschylus on proper aesthetic grounds in the *Frogs*, but the real basis for his unremitting campaign against Euripides is that the poet is giving countenance to moral turpitude: Euripides is a chatterer and a skeptic, his heroes are lame and tattered, his heroines love sick or incestuous, he degrades heroism to the level of the commonplace. The unfairness as well as the irrelevance of such criticism becomes obvious when Hippolytus' unfortunate "My tongue has sworn, my mind is unsworn," spoken in character, is twice cited for excoriation, and the persistence of this view is demonstrated by the fact that Plato and Aristotle both use the same line for the same purpose.

The comic poet held a general brief for criticizing society in all

its aspects and a general license which permitted comic exaggera-
tion, as in the travesty of Socrates in the *Clouds*. It is more startling
to find so earnest and thoughtful a philosopher as Plato, who amply
proves his appreciative perception of poetry, applying the same exclusively moral and hence essentially irrelevant gauge. Indeed, the
better a work is as poetry the more liable it is to Plato's condemnation. In the last analysis Plato's criticism is political; it is because
poetry is a corrupting influence that he would banish it from his
society. In *Hippias Minor* (369b), to take an example, *Iliad* is declared a better poem than *Odyssey* on the ground that Achilles is
morally superior to Odysseus. In the *Republic*, *Iliad* too is rejected,
because Achilles' unrestrained display of emotion sets the reader a
bad example. Not only, then, are poems to be judged on the basis
of their morality, but the poet is responsible for the conduct of his
characters even when their conduct is perfectly true to their nature.

Our own protests against such criteria would likely invoke the
principle of artistic integrity, and Plato's successors saw clearly
enough that a distinction must be drawn between poetic and actual
truth. But the very intensity of Plato's onslaught shows that besides
inspiration and instruction poetry was regarded as an instrument
of pleasure. Affording the pleasure which is poetry's province was
so self-evident a part of the poet's function as to be assumed in the
definition of poet. This aspect of poetic activity is implied in the
epithets "delightful" or "sweet" which Homer regularly applies to
minstrelsy; perhaps the victory of the Hesiodic school over the
Homeric implies that this aspect of poetry is no longer emphasized.
But though the element of pleasure giving appears not to have been
discussed in isolation, it is clearly premised not only in Plato's treatment of poetry and in such scattered critical remarks as that of
Simonides, to the effect that poetry is vocal painting and painting
silent poetry (Plutarch, *On the Glory of the Athenians* 347), or in
Corinna's advice to Pindar to sow with the hand and not with the
full sack (*ibid.* 348), but, indeed, in Aristotle's *Poetics* and the
entire body of subsequent criticism. The Why and the What
seemed to concern later critics little; their chief business was with
the How.

IV. TRUTH AND IMAGINATION

Where God is both omnipotent and benevolent it is a corollary that inspired utterances must be true. But in the Greek view there was no necessary connection between inspiration and truth, as such writers as Hesiod and Plato, each singularly devout in his way, well realized. What then are the poet's obligations in regard to truth? The validity of poetic truth, which may be the creation of the poet and independent of actual happenings, was first maintained by Aristotle, who taught that poetry is "a more philosophical and higher thing than history, for poetry tends to express the universal, history the particular." So far, then, from adhering to actual happenings the poet should even prefer probable impossibilities to improbable possibilities in creating a truthful work of art.

But it was long before Greek criticism acknowledged the poet's right to independent creativeness, possibly because it mistook the poet's prerogative to teach for an obligation, and then, as we have seen, proceeded to judge his effectiveness on irrelevant grounds. The older view is illustrated by a story told, aptly if not truly, of Solon. When Solon, now retired but as always mentally alert, had gone to see Thespis perform, he was scandalized and he scolded the actor for having uttered so many lies before so many people (Plutarch, Solon 29).

Thespis replying that it was no harm to say or do so in a play, Solon vehemently struck his staff against the ground: "Ah," said he, "if we honor and commend such play as this, we shall find it some day in our business."

Solon himself had used poetry as a means of persuasion, and it was natural for him to be dismayed when he found the instrument of persuasion could be applied to fictions. Because they recognized the potentialities of persuasion in the art of the word (logos), practical sophists who discredited the Pindaric afflatus turned to grammatical and rhetorical investigations. Protagoras and Prodicus are among the more prominent of the sophists who wrote on words

and their use. Gorgias of Leontini, a disciple of Empedocles, who
introduced the rage for rhetoric when he came to Athens in 428,
frankly looked on tragedy as an art of persuasion and, as became
a sophist, was not shocked at its "lies." "Tragedy," he said (Plutarch,
On the Glory of the Athenians 348), "deceives by myths and en-
ticements, and the tragic poet who deceives is more just than one
who does not deceive." The sophist's art first invaded poetry, as
we can perceive most plainly in Euripides, and then, as we shall
see, supplanted it.

If poetry is a means of persuasion like oratory, we can legitimately
demand that it observe the canons of truthfulness appropriate to
oratory. When, as notably in the *Phaedrus*, Plato imposes upon the
orator strict requirements of knowledge and truth as well as art,
modern feeling can only applaud. But when he insists that the same
gauge be applied to poetry Plato denies the validity of poetic truth,
and the poet's creations are reduced to mere "lies." As we should
expect from such premises, the greatest leniency is shown to hymns
and eulogies of the dead (and even there under strict surveillance:
Laws 801b), and the greatest severity, all through Plato's writings,
to tragedy. If the tragic poet is in fact another kind of rhetorician
he might indeed be suspected of endeavoring to please the mob by
flattery and to avoid giving offense by wholesome doctrine which
they might not like. To us the subjection of frankly creative works
of the imagination to such a gauge seems not only intolerable Puri-
tanism but irrelevant—as if one were asked the dimensions of a
reservoir and reported that the water it held was insufficiently
chlorinated.

The emancipation of the poet as a legitimate creator was the
work of Aristotle, who clarified the province of criticism for all time
by pointing out (in the *Poetics*) that each art must be judged in
accordance with its efficacy in producing the *pleasure appropriate
to it*. Aristotle recognizes the independence of poetic creativity in
his differentiation between the historian and the poet. The distinction, he tells us, is not that the one writes prose and the other
verse, but that one tells what did happen and the other what might
happen. Aristotle's dictum appears to have been the point of de-

parture for opposing attitudes toward the relationship between history and tragedy or between fact and fiction in all subsequent criticism.

But it was criticism, not necessarily new composition, which Aristotle's formulation affected. His analysis of tragedy was not intended as legislation for future tragedians but rather, like his analysis of biological specimens, as a basis of criticism for existing examples. And, as in his analysis of political institutions in the *Politics*, Aristotle was oblivious to developments in his own day. He believed that the traditional city-state could survive as an independent power, not realizing that the day of empires and great kingdoms had arrived, and he apparently believed, similarly, that tragedies like those of Sophocles could still be written. But the same conditions which put a period to the city-state also made tragedy of the old type impossible. Actually Aristotle's discussion of tragedy envisages Sophocles as the norm; even Euripides diverges essentially from this norm. Large questions of man and fate recede before concern with contemporary problems, and the influence of rhetoric becomes prominent. Just as the *dramatis personae* of the heroic age are retained while the characters are in actuality contemporaries, so in the tragedies as a whole it is the form rather than the spirit which survives. The result was inevitably an artificial "literary" production in which preoccupation with form and erudition concerning heroic legends took the place of interpretation. In such works as Lycophron's *Alexandra* and in lost tragedies of the Alexandrian "Pleiad," questions of poetic truth are irrelevant.

But if poetry is eliminated there is a more immediate concern with truth in more pedestrian works. Hellenistic philosophers could have no doubt of their special truths and were notoriously unconcerned with form, and so cannot be properly considered in this connection. For the historians, however, and for "orators" who dealt with historical subjects, their canon of veracity is of high importance, and we shall see how Aristotle's formula concerning poetic truth was applied to expository prose.

In the writing of history the competing claims of art and science have never been adjudicated to the complete satisfaction of all parties. As we should expect, the question was mooted in antiquity as soon as criticism became conscious. The influence of epic in the early historians, of rhetoric in the later, and of the desire to enthrall the reader at all times, naturally tended to embellish historical writing with elements of the marvelous and the pathetic. But from Isocrates and in the succession of historians—Ephorus, Theopompus, Timaeus, and others—influenced by him, we may discern something like a school which favored such embellishment. From the criticism of historians of this school by others—chiefly Polybius —who apparently followed the Peripatetic tradition, we find another which eschewed adventitious adornment and adhered to fact. Naturally there were cross-currents between the two schools, and scholars are not at one in assessing the influence of each, but the essential distinction between the realms of historical and poetic truth was never again lost sight of, though opinions differed on the proper proportion of each to be included in a given type of composition.

A favorite form of historical composition, in later antiquity, which admitted of both fact and fiction in recognized proportions is the prose narration (*diegesis, narratio*), which is defined as "a discourse expository of things which happened or might have happened." The fact that this definition is given in virtually identical terms by Cicero, Auctor ad Herrenium, Quintilian, and Theon, shows how rigid and potent was the doctrine of the schools. An insight into the canon of the narratio is afforded by Cicero's invitation to Lucceius (*Ad familiares* 5.12) to write a treatise on his life and to make it as attractive as possible. Cicero's letter is carefully written and is an important document in the history of criticism. Whereas history serves *veritas* and *utilitas*, says Cicero, a *narratio* may supply *delectatio* also. But how much may be yielded to *delectatio* without impairing *veritas*? In other words, What is literary truth?

As to this we have a highly significant canon, set down in a clear statement by the grammarian Asclepiades of Myrlea (in Sextus Empiricus, *Adversus Grammaticos* 252). Three categories of truth are distinguished: *alethes historia* or "true history," for what is literally true; *pseudes historia* or "false history" for what is wholly imaginary; and *plasmata, hos genomena* or "fiction," "as might happen," for imaginative writing. In the first two categories no reader could be in doubt as to the quality of belief expected; the first is to be accepted as a purely factual account, like a historical chronicle; the second as a complete fantasy, like Lucian's *True History*. But in the third category the quality of truth depends upon the art and conscience of the writer and its correct apprehension depends upon the literary experience of the reader. The *plasma* must have a core of actual history; the treatment of this history might be imaginative, but it must preserve historical verisimilitude and convey edification. A conscious literary artist might, like the tragic poets, enhance historical legends and characters by whatever means might serve a higher poetical truth, and his audience would understand that the treatment might be imaginative but that the moral or ethical burden of the piece was to be accepted seriously.

Gorgias' paradox of the honest deceiver and his shrewdly willing victim had now become a commonplace in the theory of fiction. But there have at all times been critics like Solon, who would countenance no liberties with truth and insist that a given writing must belong to one or the other of the first two categories: if it was not completely true it must be wholly false and hence utterly rejected. In later antiquity this attitude was characteristic of the Latin Fathers of the Church, as in the 19th century it was that of certain critics who denied all historical value to an ancient document if it contained demonstrable errors of fact.

For the secular literature of their own day the attitude of the Fathers was not without justification. By the time the theorists had formulated their canon of truth for *plasmata* the problem itself had become academic, for life and letters alike seem to have confined themselves to the first two categories. The period of the so-called Second Sophistic, which begins with Hadrian, seems utterly sterile in products of the imagination, and hence unconcerned with poetic truth. Only Christian teachers and certain philosophic sectaries hardly less grimly devout had any convictions of truth, and to them truth was absolute. In the fabricators of belles-lettres associated with the Second Sophistic indifference to substance was equally purposeful and absolute. It is hard to conceive how generations of writers who made a fetish of the style of 5th- and 4th-century masters could be so completely indifferent to and untouched by what those masters had to say. And where substance is a matter of indifference truth is irrelevant. Men blind to the essential falseness in the "oratory" of the Second Sophistic are surely bound to remain blind to the essential truth in Homer or tragedy.

Antiquity's latest species of imaginative literature was the novel, which took the form of historical narrative and embodied plots and intrigue like those of drama and a narrative scheme like that of epic. In origin the novel may well have been a serious device for aggrandizing and perpetuating national traditions of defeated peoples; for its own audience, in any case, the Greek novel provided entertainment combined with edification, somewhat as drama had done in the 5th century or the novel among ourselves. The chronological order of development constitutes an interesting commentary on the canons of truth as set forth by Aristotle for poetry and Asclepiades for prose. In the earlier examples of which we know, as long as edification was an important consideration, the author starts with a historical personage (or one accepted as such in legend) and milieu, upon which he lavishes imaginative treatment to effect his twofold aim. He may still be said to follow Aristotle's conception of poetic truth, though his execution may be faulty, or else he follows Asclepiades' conception of the *plasma*. In the later specimens, probability in incident and character is so far disregarded that the production can no longer be regarded as *plasma*, but must be classified as "false history." But apparently "false history" was usually indicated to be such—Lucian starts his *True History* by saying that the only true statement in his book is that it is all untrue—whereas the novels are represented as true. The novels, then, represent a final abdication of truth in creative literature. That is in fact the great weakness of these novels, and of other imaginative productions of later antiquity.

Solon's apprehensions, and Plato's, would appear to be realized, despite the reassurances of Thespis and of Gorgias. Apparently the web of deceit must inevitably grow so tangled as to lose value altogether. In adherence to truth we have, incidentally, a gauge of value which yields critical results remarkably congruous with those yielded by other criteria. The poetry of Homer, for example, is strikingly free of exaggerated hyperbole. Even the most stalwart heroes in their most dangerous crises lifted stones which two men of the present day could scarcely lift—not six, as in Apollonius or twelve as in Vergil.

V. APPLIED POETRY

Readers who attribute to the Greeks a pure cult of beauty are disconcerted to find that most poetry of the classical age was written on commission. Like the sculptor, the poet supplied a requirement of religion or patriotism or family loyalty or pride for pay, and without compromising his personal dignity or artistic integrity. Simonides, Pindar, and Bacchylides received commissions to compose their elaborate epinician odes to celebrate the victories of reigning princes at the national athletic festivals. Their fees were generous, for only rich men could afford to stage the majestic odes with their requisite choruses, and there was rivalry for commissions among the poets. Simonides and others also received commissions for epigrams from the Athenian state and from individuals for inscriptions upon tombs or votive offerings.

Commissions for such epigrams continued to be given throughout antiquity. Dramatic poets cannot properly be said to have been commissioned, though they worked for the state, for their plays had to be approved before they were accepted. The authors of the *Homeric Hymns* sometimes concluded a piece with a personal advertisement for future employment. Solon and other elegiac poets composed for political or patriotic reasons, and it is conceivable that Solon might have engaged a professional if he were himself incapable of poetry, just as professionals were later engaged to compose political speeches.

The only poets of whom we cannot say definitely that they composed for a specific market are the authors of epic and of solo (as contrasted with choral) lyric. In the case of Homer and Hesiod, though their prime motive may have been to teach nobility and morality, it is reasonably clear that they expected to live by their work. Only writers of personal lyric like Alcaeus or Sappho could have been as disinterested as nightingales, but even lyricists, if we take Hipponax or Anacreon as examples, wrote their songs for gain. Romantics who thrill to Homer's description of the chivalrous exchange of weapons by Glaucus and Diomedes in the sixth *Iliad* tend to condemn as a vulgar interpolation Homer's remark that some god had bereft Glaucus of his wits, in that he changed gold armor for bronze, the value of a hundred oxen for the value of nine. A saner view can perceive that the appended price-tag enhances the worth of the gesture. To practical men who know how to add chivalry is more than a gesture: nor need a price-tag diminish the permanent worth of other lofty reaches of the human spirit.

4: *Distribution and the Consumer*

I. THE SUBSTANCE OF SOUND

TODAY THE PURCHASER OF A NEW BOOK PAYS for more than printed and bound sheets of paper. He can be charged more because copyright laws assure the producer owner-ship of nonphysical elements of his book, and because the invest-ment involved in printing makes it impractical for him to copy a borrowed copy of the book he desires. Without the safeguard of copyright laws and the deterrent of printing costs, nothing could prevent the owner or borrower of a book from making copies of it and disposing of them for his own account. The concept of litera-ture as something to be listened to in public rather than scanned silently in private in itself makes the notion of literary property more difficult to grasp. We ourselves are more conscious of an author's contribution when we read his book than we are of a com-poser's when we hear his work performed. Among the Greeks the regular method of publication was by public recitation, at first, significantly, by the author himself, and then by professional read-ers or actors, and public recitation continued to be the regular method of publication even after books and the art of reading had become common. How this affected the poet's livelihood we shall see in another connection; here we may pause to notice the effect of oral presentation on the character of the literature.

All classic literature, it may be said, is conceived of as a conversa-tion with, or an address to, an audience. Ancient drama is signif-icantly different from modern because plays acted in bright sun-light before 40,000 spectators cannot be like plays acted before 400 in a darkened room. Similarly, a piece intended for declamation at a festival cannot be like a piece intended for the perusal of a cloistered student. Poetry in particular shows that all its varieties were in-tended for oral presentation. Even epigrams represent a vocal ad-dress to the passer-by ("Go, stranger," or the like) and sometimes, as in some of the epigrams of Callimachus and of his imitators, the stone is thought of as carrying on a brief dialogue with the passer-by. Homeric epic was of course designed for public reading, and long after private reading became common, rhapsodes made a profession of reciting epic. Pisistratus, who had something (we do not know how much) to do with regularizing the text of Homer, also instituted the public reading of his poems at the Panathenaic festival. From Diogenes Laertius (1.2.57) we learn that

Solon provided that the public recitations of Homer shall follow a fixed order: thus the second reciter must begin from the place where the first left off.

Prose no less than poetry was presented orally, as we know from reports concerning Herodotus and others, and the practice of oral presentation affected the nature of prose as it did of poetry. The elaborate attention to sound which characterizes Gorgias' pioneer productions would have been meaningless unless his pieces were intended for recitation. It was the artfulness which Gorgias gave it that enabled Isocrates to maintain that prose was the legitimate successor of poetry and must replace it. Later critics like Dionysius of Halicarnassus judge historians by the same gauge as oratory and make comparisons between their works with no allowances for what we should consider necessary differences in genera.

Throughout antiquity and long thereafter even private readers regularly pronounced the words of their text aloud, in prose as well as poetry. Silent reading was such an anomaly that St. Augustine (Confessions 5.3) finds Ambrose's habit a very remarkable thing: "But when he was reading his eye glided over the pages and his heart searched out the sense, but his voice and tongue were at rest." Visitors came to watch this prodigy, and Augustine conjectures explanations:

Perchance he dreaded lest if the author he read should deliver anything obscurely, some attentive or perplexed hearer should desire him to expound it, or to discuss some of the harder questions; so that his time being thus spent, he could not turn over so many volumes as he desired; although the preserving of his voice (which a very little speaking would weaken) might be the truer reason for his reading to himself. But with what intent soever he did it, certainly in such a man it was good.

II. RHAPSODES

The artists who presented public recitations of heroic poetry were called rhapsodes, and their profession carried high dignity. On the profession of rhapsode we get most light from Plato's Ion. Here are some sentences, somewhat tongue-in-cheek, from that dialogue:

I often envy the profession of a rhapsode, Ion; for you have always to wear fine clothes, and to look as beautiful as you can is a part of your art. Then, again, you are obliged to be continually in the company of many good poets. . . . When you produce the greatest effect upon the spectators in the recitation of some striking passage, such as the apparition of Odysseus leaping forth on the floor, recognized by the suitors and casting his arrows at his feet, or the description of Achilles rushing at Hector, or the sorrows of Andromache, Hecuba or Priam, are you in your right mind? Are you not carried out of yourself, and does not your soul in an ecstasy seem to be among the persons or places of which she is speaking? . . . What are we to say of a man who at a sacrifice or festival, when he is dressed in holiday attire, and has gold crowns upon his head, of which nobody has robbed him, appears weeping or panic stricken in the presence of more than twenty thousand friendly faces when there is no one spoiling or wronging him; is he in his right mind or is he not?

What Plato is trying to show is that the inspiration of the poet works like a magnet through the rhapsode and upon his auditors. Despite his exclusion of poets from his ideal state Plato himself appears to have listened to their readings. According to a story in Cicero (Brutus 191),

Once upon a time Antimachus was reading to a select company that lengthy poem of his [the Thebais] with which you are acquainted, and before he had finished everybody left except Plato. "I shall proceed nevertheless," he said; "to me Plato is worth a hundred thousand."

III. LYRIC PERFORMANCE

According to Aelian (7.15) rhapsodes recited lyric as well as heroic poetry:

From the mouths of traveling bards the people learned the new heroic poems. Rhapsodes not only recited the poems of Homer and Hesiod, but also the iambic poetry of Archilochus and Semonides of Amorgos. The numerous poems and songs went from mouth to mouth, from city to city. Gradually the knowledge of reading and writing became more general.

Not much confidence can be placed in Aelian, for he cannot have known much more of the matter than we do. But it is clear that elegiac poetry was presented orally by the author. Solon, for example, obviously delivered his own verses, and Plutarch (*Solon* 8.2) has an interesting anecdote on the subject:

Solon secretly composed a poem in elegiac verse. Then, after he had committed it to memory, he rushed out suddenly into the market place, with a small cap on his head, and when a great crowd had gathered he mounted the herald's rostrum and chanted the poem which begins, "As my own herald have I come from beloved Salamis, to sing you a poem I have fashioned in lieu of a speech."

Iambics like Archilochus', though less solemn than Solon's elegiacs or even Theognis', still presuppose oral delivery by the author. The *agentia verba Lycamben* (Horace, *Epistles* 1.19.25) would not have driven Neobule's unfortunate father to suicide if they had been merely written. In solo lyric like Sappho's it is of the essence that it be sung; and the intricacies of elaborate choral lyric like Pindar's are meaningless without vocal, instrumental, and choreographic performance.

Beginning with the Alexandrian age poets composed their works as we do, to be read, and not as the classics did, to be recited. It is hard to see how the enigmatic allusiveness of a Lycophron, or frequently even that of an Apollonius, could be deciphered without a text in hand. Poets now addressed one another rather than the entire community, and the recitation like the composition of poetry had about it the hothouse air which seems inevitable when public support is replaced by princely patronage. Vitruvius (7, preface 4–7) has preserved a fine story of a reading at Alexandria:

The Attalid kings, impelled by their delight in literature, established for general perusal a fine library at Pergamum. Then Ptolemy, moved by unbounded jealousy and avaricious desire, strove with no less industry to establish a library at Alexandria after the same fashion. When he had completed it with great diligence, he did not think it enough unless he should provide for its increase by sowing and planting. So he consecrated games in honor of the Muses and Apollo, and established prizes and honors for the successful writers of the day, in the same way as for successful athletes.

When the arrangements were completed and the games were at hand, learned judges had to be chosen to examine the competitors. When the king had chosen six persons from the city and could not quickly find a seventh person suitable, he consulted the governors of the library whether they knew anyone prepared for such a duty. They gave the name of Aristophanes who read each book in the library systematically day by day with comprehensive ardor and diligence. Therefore at the assemblage for the games special seats were allotted to the judges, and Aristophanes, being summoned with the rest, took his seat in the place allotted to him. The competition for poets was first on the list; and when their poems were recited, the whole multitude by its utterances warned the judges what to approve. When, therefore, the judges were asked one by one, the six agreed and gave the first prize to the poet who, they observed, most pleased the audience; the second prize to the person who came next in their approval. Aristophanes, however, when his opinion was asked, voted that the first place should be given to the candidate who was least liked by the audience. When the king and all the company showed great indignation, he rose and obtained permission to speak. Amid a general silence he informed them that only one of the competitors was a true poet; the others recited borrowed work; whereas the judge had to deal with original compositions, not plagiaries. The assembly were surprised and the king was doubtful. Aristophanes relying upon his memory produced a large number of papyrus rolls from certain bookcases, and comparing these with what had been recited he compelled the authors to confess they were thieves. The king then ordered them to be brought to trial for theft. They were condemned and dismissed in disgrace, while Aristophanes was raised to high office and became librarian.

The circumstances of this reading show clearly enough that it was a special case. Poets must always have read their works to one another and upon occasion to larger gatherings, but probably in Alexandria, as surely in Rome, ordinary publication was through the book trade, of which a few words will be said in a later section.

IV. DRAMATIC PRESENTATION

The one form for which oral presentation is to this day a condition of its being is the drama. In antiquity as today a piece might be written in dramatic form without being intended for performance on the stage; so Cynics and Stoics are said to have written doctrinaire plays to promote their propaganda, and some scholars hold that even the *Prometheus* is not the work of Aeschylus but of a 4th century sophist, and not intended for actual presentation. Nor is it likely that the plays of Seneca were acted out; they were more probably declaimed by a cast of readers. But true drama is by definition impersonation of speaking characters.

In Athens dramatic performances were a function of the state and constituted a part of religious worship. Their importance in the life of the community can be paralleled in no other society. The place of drama in Greek life is documented not only in literature but also by the numerous remains of Greek theaters with their capacious auditoria; the best preserved, at Epidaurus, could accommodate 40,000 spectators. Even so brief a summary of Athenian history as that inscribed on the Parian Marble, which dates from the 3rd century B.C., finds room to record victors in Dionysiac contests. Only on these festival occasions could the Greeks attend the theater. Dramatic performances were supervised by the state, acting through an archon. To this official, playwrights submitted their work and he selected, for the dramatic contest at each festival, three poets, to whom he was said to "grant a chorus." To each poet was assigned a choregus, who bore the special costs of mounting a play as a liturgy, or income tax in the form of a public service; another liturgy was to equip a battleship. The choregus was as eager for distinction as the poet, and would mount the play as lavishly as he could afford. Of the wealthy Nicias we are told (Plutarch, *Nicias* 3) that every tetralogy that he mounted obtained the prize. To each poet the archon also assigned a chief actor (*protagonist*), who provided his own subordinates. In his day, Aristotle tells us (*Rhetoric* 3.1), the actors were more important than the poets, and to obviate unfairness to the poets it was arranged that each protagonist should perform in one tragedy only of each poet. For determining the winner an ingenious combination of expertness and the democracy of the lot was contrived. Names of persons competent to judge were selected from each of the ten tribes and placed in urns some days before the contest. At the opening of the festival the archon drew one name from each urn, and the ten persons so chosen were sworn in as judges and given special seats. At the conclusion each deposited his ballot, and of the ten ballots five drawn at random settled the award. One famous exception to this method of selecting judges is recounted by Plutarch in his *Life of Cimon* (7):

Sophocles, still a young man, had just brought forward his first plays; opinions were much divided, and the spectators had taken sides with some heat. So, to determine the case, Apsephion, who was at that time archon, would not cast lots who should be judges; but when Cimon and his brother commanders with him came into the theater, after they had performed the usual rites to the god of the festival, he would not allow them to retire, but came forward and made them swear (being ten in all, one from each tribe) the usual oath; and so being sworn judges, he made them sit down to give sentence.

Despite such safeguards we hear of instances of skulduggery. In Lysias 4.3–4 a prosecutor openly avows that he had been nominated as judge in the Dionysia on the understanding that he would vote for a particular contestant.

In Greece acting was a respected profession. "Artists of Dionysus" enjoyed important privileges and immunities, and they took their art seriously. Heavily draped as they were, and wearing buskins and a mask, they could represent fine gradations of feeling only by the skillful use of the voice and by statuesque postures, but they appear to have been adequate to the most exacting demands of the poet and of the audience. The generally high level is indicated by the fact that a single slip could be so famous as to survive in a scholiast. When Hegelochus was playing the title role in Euripides' *Orestes* he turned "After the billows once more I see calm" into "Once more do I see a cat coming out of the billows" by giving a single syllable the wrong pitch. Perhaps the best known actor's story of all is that (told by Gellius 6.4) of Polus, who, playing the title role in Sophocles' *Electra*, carried the ashes of his own recently deceased son in the urn to make his expression of grief authentic. The audience showed its appreciation by sitting through entire tetralogies, from dawn to late afternoon. They cried encore when a speech was well delivered, and whistled and stamped when they were displeased. Demosthenes makes it a charge against his rival Aeschines, whom he admits to have possessed a fine voice and bearing, that when he was an actor audiences pelted him with fruit and stones. Aristotle (*Ethics* 10, 1175b) provides a homely note: "People who eat sweetmeats in the theater do so with most abandon when the performers are bad."

The infinitely lower status of the actors at Rome, who were mostly slaves—rated on a level with thieves, panders, and gladiators, and flogged to encourage better performances—is in itself a sufficient index of the lower status of the drama at Rome. The two outstanding exceptions were the comedian Roscius, whom Sulla made a knight and Cicero befriended, and the tragedian Clodius Asopus, who was his near contemporary. Both these men amassed fortunes and trained pupils. In the empire an outstanding actor might enjoy imperial favor, but the profession as a whole was regarded as infamous, and it may well be that the Roman attitude was partly responsible for the lasting prejudice against actors in modern times.

Stage entertainment of a less pretentious kind was afforded by mimes, who functioned from the 5th century B.C. onwards and survived antiquity to become the jongleurs of the Middle Ages; the Empress Theodora was herself a mime. Plato is said to have learned the art of the dialogue from the mimes of the Sicilian Epicharmus, and we have the titles of literary mimes by the Sicilian Sophron. The poems of Theocritus are in effect mimes; it is doubtful whether they were performed, but such a piece as his *Women at the Festival of Adonis* is admirably suited to the talents of a Ruth Draper or of a Cornelia Otis Skinner. The realistic and often bawdy mimes of Herondas probably were performed. In Rome the mime leaves the domain of literature, for gesticulation and lascivious posturing seem to have usurped the place of words; certainly Theodora's art required no verbalization.

Somewhat akin to the mime is the moralizing prose discourse interspersed with bits of verse which Menippus apparently learned in Semitic Gadara, and which is called Menippean satire. Here, as in the clearly cognate Arabic *maqama*, the performer dealt humorously with some moral theme (the Greeks said *spoudogeloion*, "serious-laughable"; the Romans spoke of *ridendo dicere verum*, "to speak truth with a smile") and brightened his remarks with snatches of verse. None of Menippus' own work is extant, though we do have many titles and some snatches of Varro's imitation of Menippean satires. Seneca's satire on the deification of Claudius called *Apocolocyntosis,* Boethius' *Consolation of Philosophy,* Martianus Capella's *Marriage of Philology and Mercury,* and the romance of *Aucassin and Nicolette* are all adaptations of the Menippean satire.

V. ORATORY AND HISTORY

Another literary form of which oral presentation is a condition *sine qua non* is oratory. Indeed virtuosity was relatively more important in oratory than in drama, as is shown by the success of such empty speeches as those of Gorgias or of those of Phaedrus, Pausanias, and Agathon reported in Plato's *Symposium.* In Plato's dialogue named for him Phaedrus is represented as memorizing a show piece of Lysias which Socrates thinks not only empty but immoral. Even when a speech had substance it was largely admired for form. Aeschines, the Younger Pliny tells us (4.5.1), recited Demosthenes' as well as his own speech to the Rhodians, and was roundly applauded for both alike. The adulation which later ages heaped upon the artists of the Second Sophistic who attracted enormous crowds to their displays of elegant emptiness is astonishing. But oratory included other things than speeches. Isocrates' "orations," which have many serious things to say about education and politics, were never delivered by Isocrates, but from the first circulated as pamphlets. Speeches which were in fact delivered, like those of Demosthenes, were also circulated as books; we know that Cicero published speeches whose delivery had been rendered unnecessary, like those *Against Verres,* or which had been badly delivered, like the *Defense of Milo.*

What is most striking, from the point of view of modern practice, is the publication of even history by oral recitation. That Herodotus recited from his work is indicated by the disparaging remark of Thucydides and by a number of later writers, as for example Lucian, in the opening of his *Herodotus:*

From the use Herodotus made of his writings and the speed with which he attained the respect of all Greece you or I or anyone else might take a hint. As soon as he had sailed from his Carian home for Greece, he concentrated his thoughts on the quickest and easiest method of winning a brilliant reputation for himself and his works. He might have gone the round, and read them successively at Athens, Corinth, Argos, and Sparta; but that would be a long toilsome business, he thought, with no end to it; so he would not do it in detail, collecting his recognition by degrees and scraping it together little by little; his idea was, if possible, to catch all Greece together. The great Olympic Games were at hand, and Herodotus bethought him that here was the very occasion on which his heart was set. He seized the moment when the gathering was at its fullest, and every city had sent the flower of its citizens; then he appeared in the temple hall, bent not on sightseeing but on bidding for an Olympic victory of his own; he recited his Histories and bewitched his hearers.

Herodotus cannot have been alone in this practice, though histories like those of Thucydides seem intended for readers rather than hearers. Herodotus calls his work *historie*, which means "inquiries," and hence may be more suitable for oral narration; Thucydides calls his *syngraphe*, or "written composition," which would seem to imply reading rather than hearing. Hellenistic histories of the "pathetic" school, like some of those Polybius excoriates, may possibly have been intended for oral presentation. But in general it seems safe to say that from Aristotle onwards prose works other than those intended for oratorical display were published in writing.

VI. ROMAN RECITATIONES

A new era for publication by recitations, with effects patent in the literature thus published, is inaugurated by the Roman *recitationes*. The practice, which aroused the just indignation of later satirists, was introduced by Asinius Pollio, who, as the Elder Seneca (*Controv. 4, praef. 2*) tells us, was the first to read his works before an audience. But the practice goes back to the beginnings of Roman interest in literature. Suetonius (*On Grammarians* 2) tells us that Crates of Mallos introduced the practice of public readings to the Romans, who then imitated him:

Their imitation, however, was confined to careful criticism of poems which had as yet but little circulation, whether those of deceased friends or others that met with their approval, and to making them known to the public by reading and commenting on them.

Asinius Pollio's innovation soon hardened into a regular practice. When politics no longer offered an avenue to ambition and the world's talent was congregated at Rome, it was natural that men of letters, who constantly met at the houses of the same patrons, should form coteries, with strong partisanship on such questions as ancients versus moderns. Poets and poetasters attended each other's readings scrupulously, as a means of assuring an audience for themselves when their turn should come. Vergil himself read his own works, and his delivery, as Donatus and Servius report, was much admired. When he read the lines on the recently deceased Marcellus (*Aeneid* 6.860) the Empress Livia swooned. Vergil was also read in the theater, as we learn from Tacitus (*Dialogue on Orators* 13):

We have the testimony of the letters of Augustus, the testimony too of the people themselves, who, on hearing in the theater some of Vergil's verses, rose in a body and did homage to the poet, who happened to be present as a spectator, just as to Augustus himself.

Horace (*Satires* 1.4.73–74) declares that he himself "recites to no one except friends, and then under constraint; not just anywhere or in the presence of just anyone." Ovid refers to his own recitations repeatedly. From his exile at Tomis on the Black Sea he complains (*Letters from Pontus* 3.14.39–40) that he can there find no audience to appreciate his recitations; at 4.13.18 ff. he says that he recited at Tomis a poem in praise of Augustus in the Getic language.

"Lucan so admired the writings of Persius," says Suetonius (*Persius*), "that when the author recited them in the usual way he could hardly wait until he finished before saying that they were true poems, and his own mere child's play." Lucan's own poetry aroused the jealousy of Nero, who deliberately "walked out when he was giving a reading, with no other motive than to throw cold water on the performance" (Suetonius, *Lucan*). Martial (2.88) implies that no one could be regarded a poet unless he did recite: "You recite nothing Mamercus, and yet would pass for a poet."

The great promoter of recitations is Pliny, whose *Letters* have many comments on the subject. He speaks of his own and his friends' readings, encourages aspirants to perform, and in the following selection (5.3.8–11) justifies the practice:

My reasons for reciting are these; firstly the reciter himself becomes a keener critic of his work, under the diffidence inspired by an audience; secondly, he can settle any points on which he feels doubtful by the advice of assessors, so to speak. He has, moreover, the advantage of receiving many hints from different persons; and, failing this, he can discover his hearers' sentiments from the air of a countenance, the turn of a head or eye, the motion of a hand, a murmur of applause, or even silence itself; signs which will plainly enough distinguish their real judgment from the language of civility. And indeed, if anyone of my audience should have the curiosity to peruse the same material which he had heard me read, he may find several things altered or omitted, and perhaps too upon his judgment, though he did not say a single word to me.

Pliny regarded recitations as much more than an opportunity for display, yet he took great satisfaction in the applause they brought him, and rejoiced that his wife shared his pleasure (4.19.3): "Whenever I recite my works she sits close at hand, concealed behind a curtain, and greedily overhears my praises."

Pliny wrote some verses—and was criticized for their levity—but it is to be noted that his chief productions were in prose. Of

an unfortunate reading of a prose work by the Emperor Claudius
we have an entertaining account in Suetonius (*Claudius* 41):

*Claudius began to write a history in his youth with the encourage-
ment of Livy and the direct help of Sulpicius Flavus. But when he
gave his first reading to a large audience, he had difficulty in finish-
ing, since he more than once threw cold water on his own performance. For at the beginning of the reading the breaking down of
several benches by a fat man raised a laugh, and even after the dis-
turbance was quieted, Claudius could not keep from recalling the
incident and renewing his guffaws. Even while he was emperor he
wrote a good deal and gave constant recitals through a professional
reader.*

We should expect that Nero recited, and Suetonius (*Nero* 10)
confirms that he did:

*He read his poems too, not only at home but in the theater as well,
so greatly to the delight of all that a thanksgiving was voted because
of his recital while part of his poems was inscribed in letters of gold
and dedicated to Jupiter of the Capitol.*

We read that several other of the emperors, including Augustus
himself, gave public readings.

Attendance at a reading was by invitation, and as many as a thousand might be present. They expressed their appreciation by rising
to their feet, crying bravos and encores and blowing kisses. That
such enthusiasms were not always genuine we see from the satirists,
who tell us that auditors often loitered in the corridor until they
heard the scroll was nearing its end and then came in to give their
applause. We hear too of hired claques. Not only satirists but
philosophers complained of the essential frivolity of the applause.
Here is what Musonius (as quoted in Aulus Gellius 5.1) says:

*When a philosopher is uttering words of encouragement, of warn-
ing, or persuasion, or of rebuke, or is discussing any other philosophical theme, then if his hearers utter trite and commonplace*

*expressions of praise without reflection or restraint, if they shout
too, if they gesticulate, if they are stirred and swayed and impas-
sioned by the charm of his utterance, by the rhythm of his words
. . . then you may know that speaker and hearers are wasting their
time, and that they are not hearing a philosopher's lecture, but a
flute-player's recital. . . . Great applause is not inconsistent with
admiration, but the greatest admiration gives rise, not to words, but
to silence.*

The practice of *recitationes* continued in full flower until Hadrian's day, and survived thereafter. Its effect on literary expression
is very perceptible in what is called the Pointed Style. Because the
reciter's success was measured by the rounds of applause he received, he strained to prick the auditor's attention by conceits of
sense and sound and strove to coin epigrammatic utterance. That
is why Silver prose and poetry alike are apt to be brilliant in quotation but cloying in extended passages.

VII. THE BOOK TRADE

We have seen that even very early authors used written books, and
there must have been some common way of procuring them.
Though a book might first be published through recitation, copies
of it were apparently soon available to readers. There must have
been booksellers in 5th century Athens, as is indicated by Socrates'
remark in the *Apology* (26d) that anyone could buy an Anaxagoras
for a drachma, and other similar references. The accumulations in
the Alexandrian and other Hellenistic libraries suggest that the
manufacture and sale of books was fairly well organized. Polybius,
comparing his own universal history with the partial histories of
others, says (3.32) that it is easier to buy his 40 books, which are
a single lot. Elsewhere (16.14) Polybius speaks of certain Greeks
who wrote "with no view to gain," which implies that others did
write with a view to gain. But aside from deductions of this character, we have no evidence for the systematic publication of books
until the time of Cicero.

From several of Cicero's letters to Atticus and from Nepos' *Life* of him we know that Atticus possessed slaves and other resources for multiplying and distributing books. Though it is likely that he engaged in this business at least in part for profit, there is no certain evidence that he did so, and still less evidence that the author of a book shared in the profits that might accrue from its sale. Nor do we find unequivocal statements on how a writer might profit from the sale of his books. (Patronage is another matter, and will be glanced at presently.) How far the Romans were from recognizing the concept of literary property may be seen from the following application of the doctrine of acquisition by *accessio* as applied to literature (*Digest* 41.1.9.1):

Writing, even if in letters of gold, follows the papyrus or parchment, just as things built on land, or things planted in it, go with the soil. Thus, if I write a poem or history or oration on your papyrus or parchment, it is to be understood that you are the owner, not I. But, if you want back your material and are unwilling to pay the expenses of writing, I can defend myself on a plea of fraud if I have come into the possession of the material in good faith. On the other hand, painting reverses this arrangement, and the material follows the ownership of the painting.

But if literature could not be bought and sold, the books upon which it was written could be and were. For trade purposes a single reader would very likely read a text to a number of scribes who worked simultaneously; Pliny (*Epistles* 4.7) says that Regulus had the life of his son transcribed in a thousand copies, which would imply some such procedure. Rapid copying increased the possibility of error, and so Martial (2.8) explains:

If, reader, some places in these pages seem obscure or not good Latin, the mistake is not mine but the copyists', who hurried overmuch to give you the verses you awaited.

Careful authors corrected copies of their works, as Cicero claims to do in *To Atticus* 16.6, and as Martial (7.11) refuses to do:

You require me, Pudens, to correct my poems with my own hand and pen. This is to esteem and love me too much, to want my trifles in autograph!

Booksellers appear to have been fairly numerous. Cicero mentions dealing with them several times, and in the *Second Philippic* (9) he says that Clodius took refuge on the staircase of a bookshop when he was pursued. Martial has several allusions to booksellers:

Whenever you meet me, Lupercus, you say at once: "May I send a boy to you for your book of epigrams? I will return it promptly when I have read it." There is no need, Lupercus, to bother your boy. He has a long way to come to the Pear-tree, and I live three flights—long ones—up. You can seek nearer for what you want, for you are accustomed to frequent the Argiletum. Opposite Caesar's Forum, there is a shop with doors covered over with titles, so that you can read the list of poets in a moment. Look for me there. Ask Atrectus (that is the name of the shopkeeper). From the first or second shelf, he will offer you Martial, smoothed with pumice and ornamented with purple, for five denarii. "You are not worth it!" you say. You are wise, Lupercus (1.117).

You urge me, Quintus, to give you my books. I have none, but Tryphon the bookseller has (4.72.1–2).

Would you prefer, my little book, to live in the bookshops at the Argiletum? . . . Go, fly then, but you would be happier here at home (1.3).

All the Xenia in this little book you can buy for four sesterces. Is four too much? You might get it for two, and Tryphon the bookseller would still make a profit (13.3).

An anecdote in Aulus Gellius (5.4) tells us something of the book trade in his day:

*I chanced to be sitting in a bookshop in the Sigillaria with the poet
Julius Paulus, the most learned man within my memory: and there
on sale were the Annals of Fabius (Pictor) in a copy of good and
undoubted age, which the dealer maintained was without errors.
But one of the better known grammarians, who had been called in
by a purchaser to inspect the book, said that he had found in it one
error.*

VIII. PATRONAGE

In the absence of the legal concept of literary property, how could
an author make a living? In special cases, as we have noted in the
alleged purchases of Plato and Aristotle and the offer for Pliny's
books, an author might sell his work to an individual, but here
the purchaser's object is private enjoyment, plagiarism, or a collection of rarities. What of books meant for general circulation? In
the absence of a regulated book trade with established safeguards
against "piracy" which enables the entrepreneur to pay the author
an honorarium, the writer's only recourse, unless he is a prophet
or inordinately eager for publicity, has always been patronage. "Let
there be Maecenases," says Martial (8.56.5), "and there will be no
lack of Vergils." In the early classical age the tyrants of various
Greek cities, particularly those of Sicily and the Pisistratids in
Athens, surrounded themselves with men of letters, and we know
that such poets as Arion, Alcman, Pindar, Bacchylides, and Simonides received princely commissions and support. Pausanias, possibly
judging from conditions in his own day, assumes that patronage
always existed. Speaking of the cenotaph of Euripides in Athens,
he writes (1.2.2):

*He himself went to King Archelaus and lies buried in Macedonia;
as to the manner of his death (many have described it), let it be
as they say. So even in his time poets lived at the courts of kings,
as earlier still Anacreon consorted with Polycrates, despot of Samos,
and Aeschylus and Simonides journeyed to Hiero at Syracuse. Dionysius, afterwards despot in Sicily, had Philoxenus at his court, and*

Antigonus, ruler of Macedonia, had Antagoras of Rhodes and Aratus of Soli. But Hesiod and Homer either failed to win the society
of kings or else purposely despised it, Hesiod through boorishness
and reluctance to travel, while Homer, having gone very far abroad,
depreciated the help offered by despots in the acquisition of wealth
in comparison with his reputation among ordinary men. And yet
Homer too in his poem makes Demodocus live at the court of
Alcinous, and Agamemnon leave a poet with his wife.

In the burgeoning democracy official and public competitions
tended to take the place of private patronage. Dramatic poets who
"received choruses" must also have received subsidies, though we
do not know the details; even so both Aeschylus and Euripides
died as pensioners of foreign princes. Epigrams, whether for tombs
or votive offerings, and other occasional compositions were paid
for. It is more difficult to know how prose writers were paid. Political speeches were a necessary contribution to a political career.
Speeches in private law-suits were commissioned and well paid for.
Treatises like those of a Protagoras or an Isocrates were a by-product
of the teaching career of these men, which might not have been
so remunerative if their reputation had not been confirmed by published work. Isocrates and Plato were moved by a genuine impulse
to enlighten their public, and since they were men of means and
their regular incomes were derived from their work towards public
enlightenment, it was natural for them to supplement their oral
teaching by publication. So today a professor of only ordinary vanity
will publish an unremunerative book in his field. Herodotus received public patronage; Thucydides was a rich man and was motivated by a zeal to educate.

In the Alexandrian age patronage is of paramount importance.
The literary protégés of the Ptolemies lived and worked, as Timon
said, "in the bird-cage of the Muses." In early Rome the traditional
patron-client relationship made it easy for literary men, who were
usually of a humble social position, to be attached to noble patrons.
Livius Andronicus, Ennius, Terence, each had his patron. Playwrights whose work was performed at the public games were paid

by the aediles; otherwise the only work we know to have been commissioned by the state was a translation of the Carthaginian Mago's Greek treatise on agriculture. The beginning of the Empire was the great age of Roman patronage. The amiable Maecenas, who was in effect Augustus' minister of propaganda, was patron to both Vergil and Horace, and in their works both poets express generous but dignified gratitude. The tradition of imperial patronage was maintained during the first century, and other wealthy men followed the custom. In Silius Italicus we have a wealthy man who was himself a poet and helped humbler poets. The Younger Pliny helped Martial, among others, and Martial himself acknowledges help from patrons, though he, like Juvenal, occasionally complains of the stinginess of some patrons. Whether, aside from subsidies he might receive from a patron, an author received income from the sale of his books is a difficult question. Without copyright laws and without the expense of producing a printed edition to deter anyone who wished to make a copy of the book, it is hard to see how a bookseller could pay an author more than the price of a single copy; and yet the Martial passages cited above do suggest that some little profit accrued when a bookseller sold his work.

IX. PLAGIARISM

Whether or not a literary property had monetary value, pride of authorship would naturally in itself make ownership important, and ancient writers often speak of plagiarism. Aristophanes (*Clouds* 553 ff.) charges that Maricas only distorted his *Knights* and that others pilfered his similes. Isocrates (12.16) accuses his rivals of living on his writings. Diogenes reports that Anaxagoras, Plato, and Epicurus plagiarized. Alexandrian scholars devoted special attention to the subject of plagiarism. Aristophanes of Byzantium wrote a treatise entitled *Menandrian Parallels and Selections Whence He Purloined*, and Eusebius preserves Porphyry's first century list of treatises *On [Literary] Theft*. But it must be remarked that the limits of permissible use of the work of others was wider in antiquity than in modern times, though contemporary poets seem to have

reverted to the ancient practice. Every teacher of literature urged
emulation of great authors upon his students, and from emulation
to imitation is but a short step, as "Longinus" (13–14) shows. At
all periods, but perhaps especially in the 2nd century A.D., writers
deliberately aped the mannerisms of some classic. How successful
aping could be is shown by the story of a man who imitated for
malice rather than profit (Pausanias 6.18.5):

Anaximenes [a late 4th century historian] is known to have retaliated on a personal enemy in a very clever but ill-natured way. He
had a natural aptitude for rhetoric and for mimicking the style of
the rhetoricians. Having a quarrel with Theopompus [a better known
historian] he wrote a treatise abusing Athenians, Lacedaemonians,
and Thebans alike. He imitated the style of Theopompus with perfect accuracy, inscribed Theopompus' name upon the book, and
sent it round to the cities. Though Anaximenes was author of the
treatise, hatred of Theopompus grew throughout the length of
Greece.

Xenophon, as we shall see, was praised, because when he might have
published Thucydides' work as his own he refrained from doing so.
    Writers of history or of works of scholarship in particular re-
garded the work of their predecessors as in the public domain, and
usually mention them only to criticize or disagree with them. So
Herodotus must have used Hecataeus in many more than the four
passages where he disagrees with him. And when a later writer lists
the differing opinions of four or five predecessors, it is a safe guess
that he himself consulted only the last in the series.
    In Rome literary borrowing was regarded even as a virtue if the
original work was Greek. When Terence is accused of plagiarizing
Naevius and Plautus he righteously insists that he borrowed directly
from Menander. The Romans did not set a high value upon complete originality; for them it was a sufficient boast to claim primacy
in introducing one or another Greek literary genre into Latin. The
Romans also felt free to borrow from one another. By modern
standards Horace's debt to Lucilius and Vergil's to Ennius (as

pointed out in the ancient commentators) exceed the limits of propriety. Again we must remember the inordinate prestige enjoyed by accepted classics and the insistence upon imitation of the best models as the only road to acceptable authorship. In other literatures movements initiated by a master spirit have had numerous recognizable progeny, but it is hard to cite an analogy for the dominance of Vergil, for example, over subsequent Latin epic. Even Shakespeare's influence upon verse drama is not so palpable.

The Humanists, eagerly emulous of each other, were much exercised over the problem of plagiarism and originality. The climate of their cock-pit (as Ascham calls their world) is reflected in *Democritus to His Reader*, which opens Burton's *Anatomy of Melancholy* (words not italicized are translations of Latin in the text):

If that severe doom of Synesius be true, "It is a greater offense to steal dead men's labour than their clothes," *what shall become of most writers? I hold up my hand at the bar among others, and am guilty of felony in this kind,* the defendant pleads guilty, *I am content to be pressed with the rest.* 'Tis most true an incurable malaise of writing seizes many, and "there is no end of writing of books," *as the wise man found of old, in this scribbling age especially,* "wherein the number of books is without number" (as a worthy man saith), "presses be oppressed," *and out of an itching humour that every man hath to show himself, desirous of fame and honour,* we all write, learned and ignorant alike, *he will write no matter what, and scrape together it boots not whence.* "Bewitched with this desire of fame, even in the midst of illness," *to the disparagement of their health, and scarce able to hold a pen, they must say something,* "and get themselves a name," *saith Scaliger,* "though it be to the downfall and ruin of many others." *To be counted writers, to be addressed as authors, to be thought and held polymaths and polyhistors,* among the ignorant crowd, to get a name for a worthless talent; with no hope of gain but great hope of fame, in this precipitate, ambitious age *('tis Scaliger's censure).* . . . *As apothecaries we make new mixtures every day, pour out of one vessel into another; and as those old Romans robbed all the cities* of the world to set out their bad-sited Rome, we skim off the cream of other men's wits, pick the choice flowers of their tilled gardens to set out our own sterile plots.

X. CENSORSHIP

In the classical Greek period we know of only one attempt at official censorship of literature, and that is the law of Morychides which attempted to restrain the license of Comedy in 440–39 and the year following, when the war between Athens and Samos was in progress, and was then withdrawn. Other alleged curbs rest on misunderstandings of texts or chronological confusion on the part of writers of late antiquity. This is true of perhaps the most familiar passage of all, Horace, Ars Poetica, 282–85:

Liberty degenerated into license and violence that deserved legal restraint; a law was adopted, and the chorus, deprived of its right to wound, fell into ignominious silence.

On the other hand, our extant plays prove that the dramatic poets enjoyed the fullest freedom of expression. At performances under state sponsorship, Aristophanes could utter, in his Knights, the most virulent invective against the leader of the government in the presence of the leader himself and a huge audience, and Euripides in his Trojan Women could hint openly that the Syracusan expedition was doomed when preparations for it were at their height.

For religious offenses we hear of divine, but not human, retribution. So Stesichorus was said to have been blinded for maligning the character of Helen—and to have recovered his vision because of his Palinode. The condemnation of Socrates (and reports of similar perils to other unorthodox teachers) may be regarded as political, but Socrates' career is rather a proof of the absence of censorship than of its presence. Demosthenes was hounded to death for having spoken and written against Macedonian imperialism, but that persecution was due to the force majeure of a conquerer. Under the suzerainty of Macedonia and the other successor king-

doms freedom of speech was plainly dangerous and we know of
no recalcitrants unless we wish to include the Maccabeans under
Antiochus Epiphanes. The "dangerous thoughts" of the Alexandrians were limited to questions of philology.

In the Roman republic Naevius (noted below) suffered imprison-
ment because he had offended the powerful Metelli, but his case
is unique. Republican writers with senatorial affiliations were in
thorough sympathy with their government, and those of humbler
station exercised self-discipline. Catullus, as we shall see, incurred
Caesar's displeasure by lampooning one of his creatures, but Caesar
invited him to dinner as soon as he apologized. Epicureanism became politically suspect, so that Cicero, towards the end of his life,
pretended he had not read Lucretius; but *On the Nature of Things*
was not prohibited reading. Antony's persecution of Cicero after
the assassination of Caesar is like Antipater's persecution of Demosthenes. It is with the empire that official censorship begins, as
Tacitus (*Annals* 1.72) tells us:

It was Augustus who first, under color of "majesty of Rome" ap-
plied legal inquiry to libelous writings, provoked, as he had been,
by the licentious freedom with which Cassius Severus had defamed
men and women of distinction in his insulting satires. Soon after-
wards, Tiberius, when consulted by Pompeius Macer, the praetor,
as to whether prosecutions for treason should be revived, replied
that the laws must be enforced. He too had been exasperated by the
publication of verses of uncertain authorship, pointed at his cruelty,
his arrogance, and his dissensions with his mother.

At *Agricola* 3 Tacitus speaks of the reign of Domitian as "those
many years which brought the young in dumb silence to old age,"
and at *Histories* 1.1 he speaks of the reigns of Nerva and Trajan
as "that period of rare happiness when we may think what we please
and express what we think."

The best known case of prosecution for subversive writings is
that of Cremutius Cordus, who was condemned under Tiberius.
Because the case served as a precedent, and because Cremutius'

defense is a classic protest against censorship, Tacitus' account (Annals 4.34–35) may be quoted rather fully:

In the year of the consulship of Cossus and Agrippa, Cremutius Cordus was arraigned on a new charge, now for the first time heard. He had published a history in which he had praised Marcus Brutus and called Caius Cassius the last of the Romans. His accusers were Satrius Secundus and Pinarius Natta, creatures of Sejanus. This was enough to ruin the accused; and then too the emperor listened with an angry frown to his defense, which Cremutius, resolved to give up his life, began thus:

"It is my words, Senators, which are condemned, so innocent am I of any guilty act; yet these do not touch the emperor or the emperor's mother, who are alone comprehended under the law of treason. I am said to have praised Brutus and Cassius, whose careers many have described and no one mentioned without eulogy. Titus Livius, preeminently famous for eloquence and truthfulness, extolled Cneius Pompeius in such a panegyric that Augustus called him a Pompeian, and yet this was no obstacle to their friendship. Scipio, Afranius, this very Cassius, this same Brutus, he nowhere describes as brigands and traitors, terms now applied to them, but repeatedly as illustrious men. Asinius Pollio's writings too hand down a glorious memory of them, and Messala Corvinus used to speak with pride of Cassius as his general. Yet both these men prospered to the end with wealth and preferment. Again, that book of Marcus Cicero, in which he lauded Cato to the skies, how else was it answered by Caesar the dictator, than by a written oration in reply, as if he was pleading in court? The letters of Antonius, the harangues of Brutus contain reproaches against Augustus, false indeed, but urged with powerful sarcasm; the poems which we read of Bibaculus and Catullus are crammed with invectives on the Caesars. Yet the Divine Julius, the Divine Augustus themselves bore all this and let it pass, whether in forbearance or in wisdom I cannot easily say. Assuredly what is despised is soon forgotten; when you resent a thing, you seem to recognize it.

Of the Greeks I say nothing; with them not only liberty, but even license went unpunished, or if a person aimed at chastising, he retaliated on satire by satire. It has, however, always been perfectly open to us without any one to censure, to speak freely of those whom death has withdrawn alike from the partialities of hatred or esteem. . . . To every man posterity gives his due honor, and, if a fatal sentence hangs over me, there will be those who will remember me as well as Cassius and Brutus."

He then left the Senate and ended his life by starvation. His books, so the Senators decreed, were to be burned by the aediles; but some copies were left which were concealed and afterwards published. And so one is all the more inclined to laugh at the stupidity of men who suppose that the despotism of the present can actually efface the remembrances of the next generation. On the contrary, the persecution of genius fosters its influence; foreign tyrants, and all who have imitated their oppression, have merely procured infamy for themselves and glory for their victims.

Suetonius (Tiberius 61.3) gives us another instance of Tiberius' repression:

A poet was charged with having slandered Agamemnon in a tragedy, and a writer of history of having called Brutus and Cassius the last of the Romans. The writers were at once put to death and their works destroyed, although they had been read with approval in public some years before in the presence of Augustus himself.

Prosecution for disrespectful treatment of an Agamemnon suggests that mythological themes might indeed have been used for covert criticism of the Emperor. We hear of cases where theater audiences roundly applauded lines in ancient plays which seemed applicable to current abuses. We know from Suetonius that the fabulist Phaedrus was severely punished by Sejanus because he suspected that Phaedrus used some of his animal pieces to mask criticism of himself. Martial, who can speak well even of Domitian, refers (3.20.5) to "the jokes of wicked Phaedrus," but the fables we have show no trace of wickedness in the ordinary sense. An Italian

scholar exiled by Mussolini maintained (but without much probability) that Vergil ordered the *Aeneid* burned because the draft
he left contained covert criticisms of Augustus which might involve
his friends in trouble, that Varius and Tucca expurgated the more
dangerous passages, and that the otherwise inexplicable half-lines
are relics of this expurgation.

Repression under Nero is alluded to in the Younger Pliny's account of his uncle's writings (3.5.3):

*He wrote in the later years of Nero's reign, when tyranny made it
dangerous to engage in studies of a more free and upstanding spirit.*

As examples of Domitian's repression Suetonius (*Domitian* 10.3)
cites the following:

*He put Mettius Pompusianus to death because it was commonly
reported that he had an imperial nativity and carried about a map
of the world on parchment and speeches of the kings and generals
from Livy, besides giving two of his slaves the names of Mago and
Hannibal.*

Sufficient evidence of the weight of the repression is afforded by
the innocuous character of post-Augustan literature, which tends
to be pretty rather than profound. When indignation drives a
Juvenal to utterance, he too must complain (1.152), "Where find
that freedom of our forefathers to write whatever the burning soul
desired?"

A new era of external control of literature enters when Christianity attains secular power. Plato's provisions for the strict censorship of literature in his ideal state (which of course were never
put into practice) show that any system which undertakes to direct
the intellectual life of its adherents must exercise similar control.
The Christian Fathers were educated in the classics, as their writings amply prove, but they were fearful of the impulses to heresy
the classics contained. St. Augustine (*On Christian Doctrine* 3.11)
suggests as a proper procedure that the pagans be "spoiled," as the

Israelites spoiled the Egyptians in their exodus from Egypt. In the 4th and 5th centuries Christian teachers sought to check the reading of pagan books by ridiculing their folly and inveighing against their immorality, and authors in the pagan tradition, even when they were, like Ausonius or Claudianus, Christians, avoided allusions to Christianity except in set pieces where the Christian note was called for. The informal censorship thus established on both parts was hardened into law, on the Christian side, by the provisions of Theodosian Code, the 16th book of which begins with the curt command "Superstition shall cease" (*cesset superstitio*). To be sure, the 25 decrees which follow have to do mainly with cult observances, but (though we have no specific cases) it is easy to see that the determination to uproot all "superstition" must inevitably result in the suppression of such books as were not assimilable to Church approval. The cases of architecture and the plastic arts are parallel. In Rome only such above-ground pagan edifices were preserved as were early transformed to Church use. Pagan statuary, like literature, preserved a kind of underground existence and, like manuscripts, was unearthed from hiding places, often in quite a literal sense, during the enthusiastic revival of interest in such matters in the Renaissance. It cannot be accident that such unredeemably pagan authors as Catullus, Lucretius, or Tacitus have survived in an extremely tenuous manuscript tradition, whereas an *anima naturaliter Christiana* like Vergil never went out of circulation.

5: *Criticism*

I. THE VULNERABILITY OF THE SECULAR

AS COMPARED WITH THE AUTHORITARIAN ages which preceded and followed, the most striking aspect of the temper of the classical age in Greece is its restless questioning of all tradition. Because Greek literature, unlike its predecessors in the Near East, was anthropocentric and intended from the first to provide pleasure as well as edification, it was from the first subject to criticism. Its audience freely brought to bear upon it such judgments as they might apply to other products fashioned for their use and pleasure. Grand figures of antiquity were venerated for their wisdom and their art, but no amount of veneration could shield either their content or their form from the probing wit of their critics; so Aristophanes reveres Aeschylus in the *Frogs*, and Plato Simonides in the *Protagoras*, but Aristophanes is outspoken on Aeschylus' shortcomings and Plato on Simonides'. Not until the Roman Empire do we hear of actual or tacit censorship of works which might subvert popular attitudes to traditional institutions.

From the 5th century B.C. onwards we have professional criticism by experts, but critical attitudes to predecessors or rivals are implied from the time of Homer. Homer, we now realize, undoubtedly followed a long tradition of heroic poetry. His own innovations, in matter or form and especially in ethical refinement, were then tantamount to criticism of his predecessors. So Homer's own art and ethics are tacitly criticized in later works, which are themselves in turn subjected to similar criticism.

II. POETS ON POETRY

When authors' personalities become distinct criticism becomes outspoken. When Hesiod in his account of his own mission says that "the Muses know many falsehoods also" he is surely thinking of Homer. The "pair of crows" of whom Pindar says (*Olympian* 2.86 ff.) that "they have only learnt the art of song" are almost certainly Simonides and Bacchylides. It is in the nature of dramatic poetry that the author may not speak in his own person, but the work of even the tragic poets contain palpable hits at their rivals. The plainest and most familiar instance is the parody of the recognition scene of Aeschylus' *Choephoroe* in Euripides' *Electra*. Euripides not only ridicules Aeschylus' tokens—lock of hair, footprint, scrap of cloth—but shows how the thing should be done properly —by a scar. And when, at *Phoenicians* 751, Eteocles is made to say "To tell each chieftain o'er were costly waste of time," the criticism of the procedure in *Seven against Thebes* is plain. Again, the simplest explanation for certain peculiarities in Sophocles' *Trachinian Women*, *Electra*, and *Philoctetes* is that they were intended as "corrections" of similar things in plays by Euripides which had preceded them. Poets sometimes allude to their own work. It is hardly an accident that Sophocles' valedictory *Oedipus at Colonus* brings upon the stage the persons and events of his highly successful *Antigone* and *Oedipus Rex*. In a different category is Euripides' inexplicable but indubitable parody of his own *Iphigenia among the Taurians* in the *Helen*, which was written the same year.

In the tragedians, criticism could only be incidental and by indirection, but for the comic poet who took all aspects of contemporary life as his province, so important an educational force as poetry was conceived to be a legitimate object of examination. All of Aristophanes' comedies do in fact contain allusions to or parodies of the tragedians, and the first parabasis of the *Knights* supplies most of what we know of Aristophanes' predecessors in the art. Euripides is the main object of Aristophanes' criticism, and two of his comedies, the *Thesmophoriazusae* and the *Frogs*, are largely taken up with criticism of Euripides. Most of the strictures proceed, as we have seen, from moral grounds, like Plato's; but Aristophanes also scrutinizes certain fundamental poetic techniques from an aesthetic point of view, and so deserves the title of pioneer in technical criticism.

The sum of Aristophanes' criticism is that Euripides had robbed tragedy of its dignity, not only by his vulgar themes and personages but also by a certain monotony in rhythm and syntax, and above all by his commonplace diction. It must be remarked that Aeschylus' opposite vices of bombast and misplaced grandiloquence are also shrewdly noted. Acute and accurate as Aristophanes' objections are, they are nonetheless unjust for, as even later antiquity realized, the style of each is appropriate to his theme. Whereas Aeschylus' plays are heroic and remote and grand, Euripides designed his to conform to contemporary characters and problems. We must assume that Aristophanes was as aware of Euripides' design as are we, and hence that even his aesthetic criticism had a moral basis. For us the significant implication is that to the Greeks of the 5th century even technical literary criticism must proceed from a moral basis. To them the doctrine of art for art's sake would have been unintelligible and perhaps monstrous.

When literature lost contact with reality and became erudite or precious, questions of technique assumed central importance and themselves became the substance of even imaginative literature. For the present we shall leave the prose theorists in Aristophanes' and succeeding generations and continue with works of the imagination which involve critical judgments. Of New Comedy, which was the major fictional form after Euripides and Old Comedy, we know too little to hazard meaningful conclusions in this connection. In the Latin adaptations of New Comedy we do have critical notices of rival poets, specifically in the prologues of Terence, but these refer not to the originals, which were accepted as canonical, but to rival Latin adapters. It is in the Alexandrian age that pure literature, written by professional litterateurs, makes its appearance.

To the Alexandrian men of letters literary doctrines were of great importance, and became issues in resounding literary feuds. The most considerable single work of the age, Apollonius of Rhodes' Argonautica, was apparently written to disprove Callimachus' assertion that epic could no longer be written. "A big book," Callimachus had maintained, "is a big evil," and the whole tendency of the Alexandrian school was towards the art of the miniature—

small works carefully elaborated and highly polished. Doubtless in some of Callimachus' own compositions the chief intention was to illustrate a literary doctrine. Emphasis on form is illustrated by the stricter rules of prosody: by Callimachus' rules the opening lines of the *Iliad* contains three faults. The most deeply felt poem of Callimachus, except possibly for some of his epigrams, was apparently the (lost) *Ibis*, which was an attack upon Apollonius.

Modern taste finds Theocritus the most genuine poet of the Alexandrian age, yet for all his unquestioned originality and charm, Theocritus is always a conscious professional. Literary allusions and parody have been detected in almost all his poems, and are clearly the heart of the much imitated *Thalysia* (No. 7). Here Lycidas, Tityrus, Simichidas, Sicelidas, and Aratus all represent actual poets, and the reader is expected to understand the criticisms of their several manners. Among the epigrams of the *Greek Anthology* there are many on literary figures, and often these will not only praise a writer but also characterize him in a single felicitous phrase. Nothing could be more apt or more concise than the floral symbols of Meleager's "Garland"—myrtle for Callimachus, honeysuckle for Anacreon, thorn for Archilochus, and red rose for Sappho.

The Roman poets modeled themselves on the Alexandrians. Catullus' longer pieces and Vergil's *Eclogues* are adaptations of Alexandrian work, and even when Vergil looks to Homer and Hesiod or when Horace adapts Archilochus or Alcaeus their procedure is Alexandrian. As with the Alexandrians, their productions often designedly illustrate doctrines of literary technique.

III. PHILOSOPHERS ON POETRY

Greek poetry preceded prose by a half a millennium, and it was late in the history of poetry that its practitioners became preoccupied with technical doctrine; artistic prose was recognized as a novelty from its very inception, and at once became the object of professional study. Such Sophists as Protagoras, Prodicus, and Hippias prosecuted studies in prose style, and Gorgias raised persuasion to an art. Plato took a different view, and insisted that rhetoric was rather a knack acquired by practice (*Gorgias* 463b). He rejected the spurious arguments based on probability rather than on knowledge and truth (*Gorgias* 453 ff.), and condemned the arbitrary divisions which the Sophists substituted for organic unity (*Phaedrus* 264 ff.). Plato's own prescriptions were native endowment (*physis*), knowledge (*episteme*), practice (*melete*), and due regard for psychological verisimilitude (*Phaedrus* 269 f.). Plato's paramount regard for substance made him suspicious of a mechanical system which professed ability to make the worse appear the better cause.

But the doctrine of the Sophists was not so immoral as this program might suggest. If for "worse" and "better" we substitute "weaker" and "stronger," then in a given case it might serve the cause of truth to make the apparently weaker appear stronger. In practical questions of politics and citizenship the "culture" which the Sophists professed to teach might well be more useful than philosophy. It was Isocrates who gave rhetoric a high cultural and civic responsibility and deliberately placed it in opposition to philosophy as an educational ideal. This conflict between the two views persisted throughout antiquity, and in its extreme manifestations resulted in a situation in which the rhetors purposely disregarded content and the philosophers form, and in which a shift from one to the other amounted, as in the cases of Lucian or Marcus Aurelius, to a conversion, in which the one was formally renounced and the other embraced.

Aristotle first makes rhetoric philosophical and then defends it against Plato's strictures. Like dialectic it is a branch of the art of reasoning; its function is not persuasion but "the observing of all the available means of persuasion" (*Rhetoric* 1.1.14). The first two books of Aristotle's *Rhetoric* deal with techniques of argument and kinds of proof; the third is a systematic treatment of prose style. In so far as it deals with the purpose or end of its own subject matter, the *Rhetoric* is much closer to pure literary study than the impugned passages in Plato where only the moral or political effects are regarded. The transition to literary criticism proper is made in the *Poetics,* which deals with poetry mainly from the point of view of form and for itself.

Plato's rejection of poetry on political and ethical grounds (in the *Republic*) shows not that he was indifferent to art but so susceptible as to be frightened of it. In our own day Shaw has made the same point. The "imitations" which the artist achieves are not apprehended by the sure method of dialectic but by a kind of ecstasy, which the poet passes on, like a kind of electric current, through the rhapsode to his audience. The philosopher must be suspicious of an origin in ecstasy and the political teacher of anything which will heighten rather than curb emotions. Aristotle's *Poetics* is virtually an answer to Plato's objections. Poetry, he maintains, presents not badly apprehended particulars but valid universals, which are the legitimate creation of the artist and possess a truth higher than the actuality of particular experience. It is not the facts in a poem which produce its effects, but the poet's own art in representing them.

To the objection that poetry excites the emotions Aristotle answers with his doctrine of catharsis. Emotions cannot be legislated out of existence, and the sensible thing is to regulate their operation by periodic purges—it must be remembered that tragedy was presented only twice a year; more fequent opportunities, as Mr. Hamilton Fyfe has written, might produce emotional dysentery. In technical matters—language, plot, construction—Aristotle's analyses are impeccable. As in all his scientific work his method is biological, and just as the completest dissection can tell us little of the spirit of a man, so the *Poetics* show little sensitivity to what makes a tragedy great. But excursions into enthusiastic appreciation would have vitiated the usefulness of the book; its aim was to clarify the province and demonstrate the techniques of literary criticism. His intellectualism prevented Aristotle from exhibiting the kind of enthusiasm that gives the critic we call "Longinus" his special value. His penchant for classification made him insist on a hierarchy of forms, in which epic and tragedy hold the first place, and prevented him from devoting detailed analysis to a single author, such as Aristophanes had supplied in the *Frogs.*

IV. THE PROFESSIONAL CRITICS

Aristotle's shortcomings, with but few of his merits, are characteristic of his successors in literary criticism. Most of them, and particularly those influenced by the Alexandrian school, belong to the history rather of literary scholarship than of criticism; they will be mentioned in the chapter on Scholarship. But a few—Dionysius, Demetrius, "Longinus," in Greek, Horace and Quintilian in Latin —may fairly be designated critics. Even the Greeks who again essayed literary criticism did so in the Roman period and for Roman readers, and it was natural that this should be so.

With a large body of alien literature, representing centuries of production, forming a virtually exclusive canon for both form and matter, it was necessary to establish criteria of worth and principles of selection and imitation. Without exception the writers of Rome were diligent students of relevant Greek work; not only are Greek models easily detectable in Roman works, but Greek masters are often directly mentioned and sometimes evaluated. Horace thus becomes an important witness for the history of Greek literature, and Quintilian's reading list for the education of an orator (Book 10) amounts to a concise and judicious history of literature. But for instruction in Greek literature and literary theory the Romans employed Greeks, and most of the professional critical writing even in the Roman period was produced by Greek teachers and in Greek.

Dionysius of Halicarnassus was the chief of these in the Rome of Augustus. His writings, aside from the historical *Roman Antiquities* in 20 books, dealt with criticism, mainly of prose style. The most significant is *On the Order of Words*: there are also an incomplete *On the Ancient Orators*, a *First* and *Second Letter to Ammaeus*, a *Letter to Cn. Pompeius*, and lesser pieces. In a professional manner reminiscent of Aristotle's, Dionysius presents competent and useful treatments of such questions as word order, euphony, and the proper use of tropes; but he also offers perceptive aesthetic appreciations of Lysias, Thucydides, and Demosthenes.

A more successful effort to make aesthetic criticism technical is apparent in the treatise on style ascribed to Demetrius. This Demetrius is probably the acquaintance of Plutarch who eventually taught Greek and died at York, though we cannot be sure of the identity. He is almost certainly not Demetrius of Phalerum, though the obvious Peripatetic affinities of his treatise make such an identification plausible. Demetrius' main sources appear to have been the third book of Aristotle's *Rhetoric* and Theophrastus' lost work on style. The framework of the treatise shows its scientific approach: all literary expression is divided into four types—elevated, elegant, plain, and forcible—and each type is characterized and illustrated. Demetrius insists that prose style has its laws no less than poetry. To explain the different effects of the periodic and loose sentence structure he uses analogies from sculpture. The significant implication is not only that prose style is an art but that the principles of all fine arts are the same.

Because Latin literature actually started with borrowing from the Greek, awareness of technical literary problems is evident from the start. Terence's prologues are largely concerned with questions of dramatic technique, and Lucilius has remarks on poetic diction. Cicero's rhetorical treatises, his historical survey of oratory and orators, and his own practice show not only a very high technical competence but the conviction that prose style is a fine and subtle art which demands long and expert training. Cicero offers judicious appreciation of the poets also: he reveres Ennius, the symbol of pristine Roman virtue, and dislikes the neoterics who aped the Alexandrians. The cleavage between the archaizing and Alexandrian schools was sharpened in the Augustan age, and evoked a kind of compromise program from Horace, who is, at least for posterity, Rome's leading literary critic.

The most satisfactory work of ancient, perhaps of all, criticism is the treatise *On the Sublime*, ascribed to "Longinus." He alone clearly apprehends the imaginative and emotional qualities which are essential to literature. Aristotle and his Peripatetic successors may or may not have been aware of the demonic potentialities of the structures whose brick and mortar they were analyzing: "Longinus" is not only aware of what makes great art great, but he succeeds in communicating to his readers his criteria as well as his

enthusiasms. "Longinus'" aim is to define true grandeur in literature as opposed to mere turgidity and preciosity. For true grandeur
five factors are necessary, two which come from native endowment,
and three from skill. Those which must be innate are full-blooded
ideas and vehement emotion. Those which depend on skill are figures, noble diction, and elevated composition. With this grasp of
principle "Longinus" combines far-ranging taste (including an example from Genesis). His own sensitivity to great literature is as
contagious as it is obvious. *On the Sublime* is curiously not mentioned by any ancient author and it remained unknown until it
was published in 1554. Its translation by Boileau in 1674 brought
it into the center of literary discussion, and it has probably been
the most influential single work of citicism in modern times.

Like all Roman writers Horace accepts borrowing from Greek
as axiomatic, but he recommends imitation of the ancient Greek
classics—Archilochus or Alcaeus—rather than copying of the Alexandrians. This is a foreshadowing of the distinction between *imi-
tatio* and *aemulatio* which occupied the attention of Renaissance
humanists. Horace also discusses the factors of genius and of art,
and is so far an Alexandrian as to insist on meticulous care. Besides
these matters Horace's *Ars Poetica* deals with questions of artistic
unity and consistency, style and vocabulary, and meter. The dis-
proportionate space given to drama suggests that Horace was concerned with a revival of drama in his day. The tone of all Horace's
advice is sensible and practical, and its authority is enhanced by the
circumstance that Horace was himself a successful poet. The *Ars
Poetica* is indeed the only work of Latin criticism we possess from
the hand of a poet, and its authority in the 17th and 18th centuries
was enormous, and on the whole beneficial. For the modern the
interesting thing about Horace's position is that a poet so thoroughly Augustan and so hostile to any manifestation of the divine
should be so assured of his own election as a dedicated bard and
of his own immortality. Not only the use of the first person but the
sentiment itself of *non omnis moriar* and *exegi monumentum aere
perennius* rings strange in modern ears.

Subsequent writers attacked various aberrations from the norms of reasonableness. Petronius assails Lucan for deviating too sharply from the patterns established for epic, and Persius and Juvenal condemn the poetasters who do nothing but adhere to those patterns. Throughout, however, the need for maintaining artistic standards is acknowledged. In his *Dialogue on Orators* Tacitus suggests that the high formalism of Cicero might now be made more lively, but no one hints at any sort of surrender to realism or naturalism. The tide moved ever stronger in the direction of elaborate artifice, and to other conscious deviations from the model of ordinary discourse was added an increasing fondness for archaism in diction, until in the 2nd century A.D. the height of artificiality was reached in Fronto or Apuleius' *Florida*.

Perhaps a valid distinction between the ancient Greek and the Alexandrian poets is that the former were impelled to communicate while the latter sought to display. As against either, a sober purposefulness characterizes all Latin poetry—to the degree that such poetry as is not directed towards imparting some conviction is apt to be wholly frivolous, and frivolity was a charge to which the Roman was most sensitive. When Cicero speaks for the poet in *Pro Archia* he can find only utilitarian justifications: poetry affords relaxation to the statesman; it provides an armory of examples for use in his speeches; it offers the incentive of attaining immortality if his achievements are celebrated by its agency. So our best ancient critical résumé of Greek and Latin writers is found in a handbook for the training of an orator, in a section which prescribes a reading list for his education. The list occurs in the tenth of Quintilian's 12 books *On the Training of an Orator*, and though each author is evaluated in only a brief sentence or two, the estimates are in every case so just as to have met with the agreement of posterity. Of the writers in Quintilian's list discussion has been more or less continuous since his day; none not included in his list is treated by subsequent Latin writers as a classic, and of the classics no judgments significantly new are expressed. The two exegetical works of the later Empire which exerted the greatest influence on the

Middle Ages are Servius' on Vergil and Macrobius' on Cicero. These commentators obviously accept Vergil and Cicero as the established classics in verse and prose, and they have continued as such to this day. Servius' and Macrobius' explications of their authors belong not to criticism but to scholarship, which we now turn to consider.

6: *Scholarship*

I. THE ETHICAL APPROACH

IF POEMS ARE ACCEPTED AS GUIDES TO CONDUCT, then, like laws, they require exegesis almost as soon as they are written down, and it is to be expected that the conscientious teacher, like the jurist, would devote particular care to discovering the true form and meaning of the texts upon which his profession rested. The educational process (as we have gathered from *Protagoras* 325d) involved the study of the poets from which the student was expected to derive ethical precepts and patterns of conduct. This suggests that the approach to Homer and Hesiod and the gnomic poets was like that of lay study groups to the Bible. But, as the *Protagoras* passage continues, boys were also made to study the lyric poets, this time not to acquire patterns of ethical conduct but to "learn to be more gentle, and harmonious and rhythmical, and so more fitted for speech and action." The objective is still mainly ethical, but here a technical approach is essential; in the *Frogs* we find technical matters measured by an ethical gauge. Without ethical utility, the conservative Aristophanes holds, the technical approach becomes absurd: in the *Clouds* the Sophists' study of grammatical genders, obviously ancillary to their explication of texts, is ridiculed as futile display of useless cleverness.

It was Protagoras who began grammatical classification by distinguishing the three genders, and Plato who designated nouns and predications (*onomata* and *rhemata*) in a sentence. Aristotle defined other parts of speech and cases of the noun, and the Stoic grammarians, chiefly Chrysippus, carried grammatical classification further. Where study of grammar was sound, as far as it went, speculations in etymology, which were taken more seriously, were fantastic and misleading. Words were regarded not as conventional labels but as natural properties of the things they designated; to trace words to their ultimate origin, therefore, was not to recapitulate a segment of human history but to discover the "true rationale" (*etymos logos*) of nature. When Aeschylus connects "Helen" with the verb "destroy," Sophocles "Aias" with "to wail," Euripides "Pentheus" with "to grieve"—or when David connects "Nabal" with "folly"—something more than a pun is involved, though as puns the equations are effective; but the height of the absurd is reached when we are told that a grove is called *lucus* because there is no light in it (a *non lucendo*), a school a *ludus* because playing (*ludere*) is not tolerated there; or a soldier *miles* because he is not soft (*mollis*). On the other hand the study of *glossai*, which Aristotle (*Poetics* 1458b) defines as words not current in the spoken language, was on a sounder footing. Even Hesiod had misunderstood some of the strange words in Homer, and in divining the meaning of such words scholars of later antiquity employed proper philological techniques.

II. PERIPATETICS AND ALEXANDRIANS

For all matters dealing with literary as with other branches of scholarship we find the first systematic and objective approach in Aristotle and the Peripatetic school. The *Poetics* and the *Rhetoric* deal not only with criticism but also with literary history and with philology in its narrower sense; in all these fields Theophrastus and Aristotle's later successors carried his work forward. It was the Peripatetic Demetrius of Phalerum, the moving spirit in the establishment of the Alexandrian Library, who suggested the directions Alexandrian and all subsequent literary scholarship was to take. The industrious Alexandrians collected manuscripts, established critical texts, carried on researches in language, metrics, mythology, and in the lives of the poets; they embodied their results in monographs and in exegetical commentaries as well as in their own learned poetry. Callimachus, who is the most characteristic of the Alexandrian poets, was at the same time a literary historian. His *Pinakes* ("Tables") in 120 books was an enlarged catalogue. For each writer he gave a short biography and a list of works, including those lost; of each work the opening words and the number of lines were recorded, and any doubts of authenticity were noted. The whole was classified by categories such as epic, lyric, tragedy, comedy, philosophy, history, oratory. What could not be classified went into "Miscellaneous"; chance has thus preserved a list of authors on cake-baking. The impulse towards systematization is illustrated also by the "canons" of authors. The canon of the poets was probably drawn up by Aristophanes of Byzantium and included five epic poets, three iambic, five tragic, seven Old Comedy, two Middle Comedy, five New Comedy, four elegiac, nine lyric. Later scholars formulated canons of ten orators and ten historians.

In the great age of Alexandria the heads of the library were also the outstanding scholars; the roster includes Zenodotus of Ephesus, Apollonius "the Rhodian," Eratosthenes of Cyrene, Aristophanes of Byzantium, Apollonius "the Eidograph," and Aristarchus of Samothrace; Callimachus himself did not hold the office. Zenodotus (b. ca. 325 B.C.) was the first to produce an edition of Homer on the basis of collating several MSS and his edition first divided the poems into 24 books each. Dubious lines he marked with an obelus ("spit"), but he also transposed or telescoped lines and even inserted new lines. Zenodotus also edited Hesiod, Anacreon, and Pindar, and produced a Homeric glossary which opened the way to the scientific study of language. Apollonius the Rhodian, the author of the Argonautica, who figured in the famous literary quarrel with Callimachus, wrote a tract against Zenodotus. He also wrote on Archilochus, Antimachus, and Hesiod.

The most versatile of the Alexandrians was Apollonius' pupil and successor Eratosthenes. Specialists called him Pentathlos, "all-rounder," or Beta, "next-best in all lines"; he himself was the first to assume the title philologos. Besides his works on chronology, mathematics, astronomy, geography, and philosophy, and besides his original poetry, he wrote also on literary scholarship and criticism. In scholarship his main contribution was his insistence that the poet's function is to delight, not teach; hence he opposed the allegorical interpretation of Homer. The quality of Eratosthenes' mind is illustrated by a remark of his cited by Polybius (quoted in Strabo 1.2.15): "We may find out where Odysseus traveled when we find the cobbler who sewed the bag of winds." It was Eratosthenes who calculated the date of the Trojan War as 1184 B.C., which modern scholars consider reasonable. In scholarship his principal work was a treatise, in at least 12 books, *On Ancient Comedy*, in which literary, lexical, historical, and antiquarian aspects of the subject were discussed.

Eratosthenes' pupil and successor as librarian (ca. 194 B.C.) was Aristophanes of Byzantium, who was distinguished in many fields of linguistic and literary scholarship. He made the first collected edition of Pindar, but also edited Hesiod, Anacreon, Alcaeus, and he made a complete and standard edition of Euripides. His edition of Homer was an advance over that of Zenodotus; his critical acumen is suggested by the fact that he placed the end of the Odyssey at Book 23, line 296. He was interested in literary history and criticism, and some of the extant short introductions to ancient plays are abbreviations of his work. He also made contributions to lexicography and grammar.

The most influential of the Alexandrian group was doubtless Aristarchus of Samothrace (217–145 B.C.) whose name became a by-word for "critic." He made critical recensions and wrote monographs on special subjects, and he founded a school which lasted into the Roman imperial period. One of Aristarchus' pupils was Dionysius Thrax, who wrote the earliest Greek grammar, still extant (in some 15 printed pages), which remained standard for nearly a millennium and a half. The most industrious of the Alexandrians was Didymus (65 B.C.–A.D. 10), who was surnamed Chalcenterus or Brazen Gut. He wrote between 3,500 and 4,000 books, on various aspects of literary scholarship; Macrobius (5.18) refers to him as "easily the most learned of scholars and the best informed of all who exist or have existed."

The Alexandrian scholars constitute what might be called an academic succession; their publications were technical, and they addressed themselves to professional students. But aside from their productions there were others, of a sort modern publishing jargon would call "trade" books. There were popular compendia of literary or philosophical gossip, like the books of Athenaeus or Diogenes Laertius, which will be glanced at in the chapter on Literary Gossips; there were essayists like Plutarch or Dio Chrysostom who were deeply concerned with literature and made acute comments on books and authors; and there were men who stood outside the tradition and were critical of its professions and judgments. Thus the Skeptic Timon (ca. 320–230 B.C.) ridiculed literary as well as philosophic dogma. The "kept" scholars of Alexandria he sneered at as "chatterers in a bird coop." Earlier in the 4th century the Cynic Zoilus of Amphipolis protested against what he considered adulation of the traditional classics. Zoilus made Homer the special object of attack and earned the name "scourge of Homer," but he assailed Isocrates and Plato with almost equal bitterness. This is how Aelian (11.10) describes him:

Zoilus was called the Rhetorical Dog. His appearance was as follows: long beard, shaven head, short cloak not reaching the knees. He loved to bawl, and he had plenty of time to win many hatreds. The wretch was a calumniator. When a cultured man asked him why he spoke ill of everyone, he replied, "Because, though I wish to, I cannot do ill."

Zoilus' name has become proverbial for a captious and malignant critic. Thomas Browne writes (*Christian Morals* 2.2):

Bring candid eyes unto the perusal of men's works, and let not Zoilism or detraction blast well-intended labours.

III. BYZANTINES

In the early Alexandrians we sense the exhilaration of a new and exciting enterprise and a zeal for extending knowledge. But when the freshness was gone scholarship fell into pedestrian routine, and the epigoni of the Alexandrians did little more than preserve the results of Alexandrian research in specialized handbooks. Thus, in the second century A.D., Apollonius Dyscolus and his son Herodian wrote on grammar, Hephaestion on metrics, Harpocration and Hesychius (of unknown date) on lexicography. As specialization

widens the gap between scholar and reader, interest in the authors
themselves diminishes and chrestomathies and anthologies tend to
supplant complete books. The (lost) *Chrestomathy* of Proclus
(2nd century A.D.), for example, was itself used by Byzantine compilers of excerpts.

In Egypt intellectual life was quickened by a spiritual leaven.
Whereas in Rome the Christians of the first centuries were an alien
and despised sect, in Egypt men of high position and intellect devoted themselves to the service of Christianity, and those who opposed it espoused Neoplatonism with equal ardor. When men were
wrestling with momentous issues the grammarians' business reverted to its properly ancillary position. Clement of Alexandria
stands in the full stream of Greek cultural tradition, which is not
negated but rather vitalized by his Christianity. His *Stromateis* is
as richly packed a collection of literary information as Athenaeus'
Doctors at Dinner. Origen is as acute, versatile, encyclopedic, and
prolific as Eratosthenes; what distinguishes him, again, is his Christian ardor. In a later century Eusebius of Caesarea applies to the
history of Christian antiquities the same kind of research and exposition as had been found appropriate for secular history. The
schools of Athens were little concerned with technical scholarship
but maintained their interest in philosophy and rhetoric and continued in this course until they were suppressed by Justinian.
Antioch tended to combine the religious zeal of Alexandria with
the rhetorical interests of Athens. The hearth of scholarship was
Constantinople, which Christian Constantine founded at Byzantium in A.D. 330 as an Eastern replica of Rome.

Until its capture by the Turks in 1453 the literature of antiquity
was a continuous living tradition in Constantinople. Language ("to
hellenize one's tongue") and literature were the mainstays of education, and Homer, in particular, had to be learned by heart. The
nephew of Synesius (5th century), who learned 50 lines a day, knew
Homer by heart as a child, and so did Psellus in the 11th century.
Homeric tags are extremely common in Byzantine writers, who
feel no need to add "as Homer says." When Julian the Apostate
forbade Christian teachers to use Homer, Apollinaris made a

Homer out of Genesis. The scholarly work of the earlier Byzantines was directed towards making the classics intelligible to readers rather than to less practical researches in the name of science. With the utilitarian end in view they produced exegetical commentaries, dictionaries, and anthologies such as students in "survey" courses use today. Thus many excerpts from ancient authors are preserved for us in the anthology of John of Stobi, called Stobaeus (6th century), which was used in turn and praised by Photius. Photius, who was twice Patriarch of Constantinople (858–867 and 878–886) was the best of the Byzantine scholars. In his *Bibliotheca* ("Library") or *Myrobiblion* he has left us 280 paragraphs of summary and criticism of 280 prose works, many not otherwise known. Photius has also left us a Lexicon, based naturally on earlier compilations. From the 10th century we have the lexicon of Suidas (really the name of a book, not its author), which also preserves many fragments. In the 12th century John Tzetzes (a phonetic spelling of Caecius) wrote commentaries on Homer and other poets, *Allegories on Iliad and Odyssey* in 10,000 verses, and *A Historical Book*, usually called *Chiliads*, whose 12,674 verses give a highly personal review of all Greek scholarship, with quotations, frequently inaccurate, from over 400 authors. In the same century Eustathius, who became Archbishop of Thessalonica, wrote a series of commentaries on ancient authors, of which the most important are those on *Iliad* and *Odyssey*. Language, mythology, history, geography, and indeed any points that a teacher of an ancient text might bring up are treated. Eustathius is valuable as preserving the fullest precipitate of earlier scholarly work. It was shortly after the death of Eustathius that Greek literature suffered what was probably its greatest single loss, in the fires and rapine that attended the sack of Constantinople by the Crusaders of the Fourth Crusade in 1204. "The literature of the Greeks," as Gibbon observes at the close of his 60th chapter, "had almost centered in the metropolis: and without computing the extent of our loss, we may drop a tear over the libraries that have perished in the triple fire of Constantinople."

In the troubled period between the recovery of Constantinople from the Franks in 1261 and its capture by the Turks in 1453, under the dynasty of the Palaeologi, scholarship took a romantic and philological turn very like that in 19th century Germany. On the one hand the Byzantines of the 14th and 15th centuries looked back wistfully on the glories of the past and, on the other, they subjected ancient texts to their own caprices. Whereas MSS deriving from the 9th to the 12th centuries maintain the tradition of the Alexandrian and Roman ages, those of the 13th and following centuries show an eagerness to emend and to assimilate texts to metrical and other theories, again very like that which characterized 19th century scholarship. These late Byzantine scholars were the direct precursors of the Renaissance. Maximus Planudes (1260–1310), whose abridgment of the *Anthology* of Cephalas was the only *Anthology* known until the recovery of Cephalas' original in 1607, knew Latin well, and in addition to compiling historical and geographical excerpts from Greek authors he translated parts of Cicero, Caesar, and Ovid into Greek. Nicephorus Chumnus (1261–1328) foreshadowed Renaissance disputes on Platonism and Aristotelianism. Manuel Moschopulus (fl. 1300) made a catechism of Greek grammar which was much used in the Renaissance; his contemporary Thomas Magister wrote scholia on the dramatic poets. Among textual critics the foremost was Demetrius Triclinius (early 14th century), whose emendations were, however, frequently capricious. Manuel Chrysoloras, whose life extended into the 15th century, played a leading part in the revival of Greek learning in Italy, where his learning was considered prodigious; he was in fact an unworthy representative of contemporary Byzantine scholarship.

IV. ROME AND THE WEST

In pagan Rome educated men knew Greek and many, like the Emperors Hadrian or Marcus Aurelius, naturally turned to Greek to express their profoundest thoughts. But knowledge of Greek was part of pagan culture, and Roman Christianity, unlike Greek, was suspicious of pagan literature; the Latin Fathers made little use of even their brethren who had written in Greek. In parts of southern Italy Greek continued as a vernacular until modern times, and there were always a few individuals in Rome whose diplomatic or other interests in the East made them familiar with the progress of Greek studies in Byzantium. But the community of intellectual interests which had prevailed in the centuries before and after the birth of Christ was broken, and when interest in antiquity was quickened during the Renaissance the achievements of Byzantine scholarship, insofar as they reached the West at all, were welcomed as new gifts.

In scholarship as in other cultural interests Rome received light and leading from the Greeks. Suetonius (*On Grammarians* 2) is able to fix the exact date for the introduction of philological studies into Rome:

In my opinion the first to introduce the study of grammar into our city was Crates of Mallos, a contemporary of Aristarchus. He was sent to the senate by king Attalus between the second and third Punic wars, at about the time when Ennius died [169 B.C.]; and having fallen into the opening of a sewer in the Palatine quarter and broken his leg, he held numerous and frequent conferences during the whole time both of his embassy and of his convalescence, at which he constantly gave instruction, and thus set an example for our countrymen to imitate.

As was natural for men who consciously set about copying alien models, the pioneer Latin poets themselves, and especially Ennius and Lucilius, show a marked interest in linguistic usage and literary history. The first professional scholar we know is L. Aelius Stilo Praeconinus (154–74 B.C.), who studied linguistic and antiquarian subjects and inspired to similar researches the encyclopedist M. Terentius Varro (116–27 B.C.), who was the foremost scholar of Rome. Cicero (*Academics* 1.3.9) has a fine apostrophe to Varro:

'Tis you, Varro, who have revealed the life-span of our fatherland, the descriptions of the ages, the laws of our sanctities and of our priesthoods, our discipline at home and in war, the situation of our territories and demesnes, the titles, species, functions, and causes of our usages sacred and profane; you have thrown most light upon *our poets and upon Latin language and literature generally, and yourself have fashioned a composition varied and elegant in a wide choice of meters, and in many places have laid the basis for philosophy, if too slight for complete instruction, at least sufficient for instigation to further study.*

Varro was extremely prolific. St. Jerome gives a list of Varro's works along with one of Origen's to show that Origen (surely the most copious writer of antiquity) had written even more than Varro. St. Augustine (*City of God* 6.2) said of Varro that "he read so much it was a wonder he had time to write, and wrote so much it was a wonder he had time to read."

Varro's most considerable rival was P. Nigidius Figulus (98–45 B.C.) who, with Varro, invented the terminology of Latin grammar and himself wrote *Commentarii grammatici.* The foundation of the Palatine library in 28 B.C. gave a stimulus to scholarship; its first librarian, C. Julius Hyginus, wrote a commentary on Vergil. Verrius Flaccus, teacher of Augustus' grandsons, was the most learned scholar of his day; his *De verborum significatu* was the first Latin lexicon, and the abridgment of it by Festus, at the end of the 2nd century, has been drawn upon by all subsequent lexicographers. Q. Asconius Pedianus (9 B.C.–A.D. 76) wrote, besides original works, a commentary on Cicero's orations.

But some teachers found the refinements of scholarship futile and absurd; so Seneca (*Letters* 88.6 f.) writes:

It is no more to the point for me to investigate whether Homer or Hesiod was the older poet than to know why Hecuba, although younger than Helen, showed her years so lamentably. What would be the point in trying to determine the respective ages of Achilles and Patroclus? Do you raise the question, "Through what regions did Ulysses stray?" instead of trying to prevent ourselves from going astray at all times? We have no leisure to hear lectures on the question whether he was sea-tost between Italy and Sicily or outside our known world.

General interest in the problems which Seneca ridicules is indicated in an anecdote about Tiberius (Suetonius, *Tiberius* 70.3):

Tiberius used to test even the grammarians, a class of men in whom he was especially interested, by questions something like this: "Who was Hecuba's mother?" "What was the name of Achilles among the maidens?" "What were the Sirens in the habit of singing?"

But it was only the excesses that Seneca ridiculed. "Leisure without study," he wrote (*Letters* 77.3), "is death; it is a tomb for the living man." Elsewhere (*Letters* 64.7 ff.) he has a magnificent protreptic to study:

I worship the discoveries of wisdom and their discoverers; to enter, as it were, into the inheritance of many predecessors is a delight. It was for me they laid up this treasure; it was for me that they toiled. But we should play the part of a careful householder; we should increase what we have inherited. The inheritance shall pass from me to my descendants larger than before. Much still remains to do, and much will always remain, and he who shall be born a thousand ages hence will not be barred from his opportunity of adding something further.

Research and teaching received state recognition when, as Suetonius (*Vespasian* 18) tells us,

Vespasian was the first to establish a regular salary of 100,000 sesterces for Latin and Greek teachers, paid from the privy purse.

Quintilian (who held an appointment from Vespasian) provides our best summary of established views on grammar as well as on poets and orators; Aulus Gellius supplies lexicographical and grammatical as well as biographical and other information of literary interest. At the end of the 2nd century Terentianus Maurus wrote a manual on prosody, and Acro commentaries on Terence and

Horace. Similar works were produced in the following centuries, the best known being Donatus' grammar and perceptive commentaries on Terence and Vergil and Servius' commentary on Vergil, all in the 4th century. The commentary of Macrobius (5th century) on Scipio's Dream was much read in the Middle Ages; Chaucer makes it the point of departure for his *Parlement of Foules*. In Macrobius' *Saturnalia* a band of scholars is represented as discussing, with erudition and insight, antiquarian questions of various kinds, including some in language and literature. Macrobius is one of the most important channels for transmitting ancient culture to the Middle Ages. Most important for shaping European education is Martianus Capella's (6th century) *Nine Books on the Marriage of Philology and Mercury and on the Seven Liberal Arts*, which was among the half dozen most widely circulated books in the Middle Ages. The seven arts are the familiar curriculum of the schools— the *trivia* of grammar, logic, and rhetoric, and the *quadrivia* of arithmetic, music, geometry, and astronomy; Capella did not include the disciplines of medicine and architecture, which Varro had added to the seven. The fullest Latin grammar and the standard work on the subject during the Middle Ages, when commentaries were written upon it, was that of Priscian (early 6th century); Priscian is figured as representing grammar in the West Portal at Chartres. The close of the Roman age of scholarship and the beginning of the Middle Ages may be marked by the year 529, when the monastery of Monte Cassino was founded and the school of Athens closed.

V. THE "DARK AGES"

The centuries from the beginning of the 6th to the end of the 11th have been known as the Dark Ages. Gregory (540–604), who deserved his appellation "the Great" both as administrator and churchman, shows his attitude to scholarship by such sayings as "The praises of Christ cannot be pronounced by the same lips as the praises of Jove," and "It is altogether inappropriate to keep the language of the Divine Oracles in subjection to the rules of Donatus." The *History of the Franks* of Gregory of Tours (538–594) shows marked departures from classical usage in grammar; the refinements of syntactical subordination are blurred and prepositions sometimes replace case endings. Greek had almost disappeared; at the beginning of his *Opus Majus* Roger Bacon urges people to go to southern Italy to learn that language. But while accurate knowledge of Latin was declining on the continent knowledge even of Greek survived in Ireland, so that anyone who knew Greek was assumed to come from that country. The Irish monk Columban (543–615) taught in Gaul and eventually founded the monastery of Bobbio, near Pavia. Many valuable MSS now dispersed through the libraries of Rome, Milan, Turin, Naples, and Vienna originated in Bobbio. A rival of Bobbio as a treasure house of Latin literature is the monastery of St. Gallen, on the Lake of Constance, which was founded by an Irish companion of Columban named Gallus. The learning of the ancient world was gathered up for the Middle Ages in the encyclopedic *Origines* of Isidore of Seville (570–636), which covers a wide variety of subjects and contains numerous citations from earlier authorities.

Classical learning was established in England by Theodore, who was born in Tarsus and educated in Athens, and was Archbishop of Canterbury from 668 to 690. The effects of the new learning are evident in the works of Aldhelm (650–709), who was abbot at Malmesbury; of Bede (673–735), whose *Historia ecclesiastica gentis Anglorum* shows ample knowledge of Greek and Latin writers; and of Boniface or Wilfred (675–754), who converted the Saxons and Hessians and became Archbishop of Maintz. Under Boniface's sanction his follower Sturmi of Noricum founded the monastery of Fulda, which became an important seat of learning and produced such scholars as Einhard [Eginhard] and Rabanus Maurus. A pupil of Bede was Egbert, Archbishop of York, and Egbert's pupil and successor Alcuin (735–804) was the most learned and influential scholar of his age. As head of the school at York, Alcuin made its library the best of any in England or France. From 782 to 790 he was head of the school attached to the court of Charlemagne, and thus was responsible for the systematization of learning and of book production in the Carolingian age. Alcuin's own scholarly interest was chiefly in grammar, but he wrote on other subjects also. His hexameter *On the Kings, Bishops, and Saints of York* is filled with classical reminiscences; his 300 letters are in good Latin style. Greek was taught at Charlemagne's court by Paul the Deacon (725–797) who wrote the famous *History of the Lombards* after he retired to Monte Cassino. Among monasteries founded by Charlemagne that of Lorsch, near Worms, had the greatest reputation for learning. The admirable *Life of Charlemagne* by Einhard (770–840) marks the highest point attained by classical study in the Carolingian age. A lively interest in books is illustrated in the letters of Servatus Lupus, abbot at Ferrières in the middle of the 9th century which tell much of borrowing and lending of books and of literary queries and answers. The mechanical tradition handed down by Bede and Alcuin is enlivened by a fresh spirit of inquiry, in which reason asserts its claims against authority, by Joannes Scotus (810–875). Alfred the Great (849–900) made versions or free adaptations of Boethius, Orosius, Bede, and Gregory's *Cura Pastoralis*, and so merits the title of the first English translator.

The tenth is held to be the darkest of the dark centuries, and here we need only mention the nun Hrostwitha of Gandersheim (fl. 984) who wrote edifying plays in imitation of Terence—without realizing that Terence's are in verse; Pope Silvester II (950–1003), who was accounted a prodigy of learning in an age of ignorance; and Luitprand of Cremona (920–972), who had contacts with Constantinople and knew Greek. Early in the 11th century the school of Chartres under Bishop Fulbert sent forth a number of competent and influential scholars. From the 12th century to the end of the Middle Ages intellectual interests were subsumed in scholasticism, which may be defined as the reproduction of ancient philosophy under the control of ecclesiastical doctrine. This involved fuller knowledge of ancient philosophy, but also, on the part of such distinguished teachers as Abelard (d. 1142) and John of Salisbury (1110–1180), insistence on the importance of secular studies as an indispensable aid to sacred studies. The latter, educated at Chartres, was the most learned and apparently the sanest man of his time. Two of his younger contemporaries whose secular writings show expert knowledge of secular literature are the Welshman Giraldus Cambrensis (1147–1222) who wrote, among many other things, a history of the conquest of Ireland, and Walter Map, Archdeacon of Oxford in 1196, who wrote the Latin versions of the legends of Lancelot of the Lake, the Quest of the Holy Grail, the Death of Arthur, and also satirical poems in the Goliardic style. Fuller knowledge of Aristotle, derived in part from translations from Arabic, made exposition of Aristotle and defense or attack of positions taken with reference to him dominate 13th century study. Figures like Albertus Magnus, Thomas Aquinas, William of Moerbeke (who translated the Aristotle Aquinas used), Roger Bacon, Duns Scotus, belong rather to the history of philosophy than of scholarship, and indeed subservience to Aristotle prevented the university of Paris (even though he was refuted there by 1300) and northern Europe as a whole from taking the lead in the revival of classical interests. A combination of social and political conditions and the circumstance that the tradition of Latin and contact with Greek speaking regions had been continuous in Italy made that country the natural hearth of the movement we call the Renaissance. Not even in the northerly countries had the preceding centuries been as uniformly dark as has been supposed, and in Italy in particular the revival was not a sudden awakening from a comatose state. Nevertheless, in the span between the close of antiquity and our own day no other period can be as justly designated the beginning of modern times, and so we begin our brief survey of modern scholarship with the Renaissance.

VI. THE RENAISSANCE

"Episcopal" is a learned form of the same ancient word which by the natural processes of linguistic change produced "bishop," and unless bishops were a familiar phenomenon there would be no need to coin "episcopal"; the newness of the English word does not imply that the thing it represents is novel. Similarly, the fresh interest in the classics which we associate with the Renaissance does not

imply absolute novelty. The men of the Renaissance conceived a
new interest in the classics because the classics they already knew
confirmed and gave direction to new ideas already burgeoning and
they wished for further light and leading. That is why men like
Petrarch (1304–1374), Boccaccio (1313–1375), and especially Poggio (1380–1459) searched out unfamiliar texts, and why Greek
teachers like Chrysoloras (1350–1415), Gemistos Plethon (1356–
1450), Bessarion (1403–1472), and others found eager pupils in
Italy. Petrarch learned his Greek from a Calabrian monk called
Barlaam. More Greek professors came after the fall of Constantinople (1454), but it is clearly wrong to attribute Italian interest
in Greek solely to that event. Among the Italians whose scholarly
works are still of interest are Lorenzo Valla (1407–1457), who
proved the Donation of Constantine spurious on philological
grounds and translated Thucydides and Herodotus into elegant
Latin; Politian (1454–1494), poet and textual critic in both Greek
and Latin, who stimulated interest in the Silver Latin authors; and
Marsilio Ficino (1433–1499), the center of the Florentine Academy,
who sought to reconcile Platonism and Christianity. An author still
widely read whose works plainly show the effects of the new learning is Machiavelli (1469–1527), whose *Prince* and *Discourses on
the First Decade of Livy* reveal intimacy with Livy, Tacitus, Polybius, Plutarch, and other classic authors, and whose witty and polished *Mandragola* depends on the Latin comic poets. Hieronymus
Vida (1490–1566) was not only a good Latin poet but in his *Art
of Poetry* laid down laws of poetic composition which writers of
romantic epic in particular regarded as binding. Pope's *Essay on
Criticism* (705 ff.) hails him:

> *Immortal Vida: on whose honour'd brow
> The Poet's bays and Critic's ivy grow;
> Cremona now shall ever boast thy name,
> As next in place to Mantua, next in fame.*

The extreme of classicism is illustrated in Pietro Bembo (1470–
1547), who refuses to use any Latin expression not found in the
pages of Cicero, and hence, though he was papal secretary to Leo X,

cannot mention the Holy Ghost and speaks of the Virgin Mary as *dea ipsa*. In questions of style Bembo was opposed by the brilliant Gianfrancesco Pico della Mirandola (1470–1533), whose renewed emphasis on the dignity of man is a more meaningful echo of ancient humanism than any merely philological preoccupation could be. It is Bembo who delivers the Platonic discourse in the last part of Castiglione's *Cortegiano*—a book which, in Hoby's translation, did much to shape the British ideal of the gentleman. To pursue the effects of the classical revival further in Italy would be to write the history of Italian literature. In technical scholarship the Italians were soon equaled and surpassed by the transalpine peoples who took up the torch. Among subsequent Italian contributions of continuing importance we must mention the *Lexicon totius Latinitatis* of Aegidio Forcellini (1688–1768) upon which all subsequent Latin dictionaries are based, and also the impulse to study and exploit ancient topography and monuments. Among the archaeologists we might name Gianbattista Piranesi (1707–1778), copies of whose etchings of Roman ruins hang in the corridors of many universities.

It was the art of printing which so greatly facilitated the spread of humanism. Of this art the most influential practitioners were the learned and enterprising Aldus Manutius (1449–1515) and his son Paulus (1512–1574) in Venice, and Johannes Froben (1491) and his son and son-in-law who succeeded him in Basel. (It may be apposite to note that the motto on the Aldine device, *festina lente*, was rendered by Thomas Browne as "Celerity contempered with cunctation.") Erasmus (1466–1536) edited texts for both houses, but was especially attached to Froben. For his contemporaries Erasmus owed his reputation to his numerous well-printed editions of ancient books. Though his knowledge was broad and exact Erasmus was not in fact a good editor, for he was capable of preferring an inferior manuscript which was handsomely written to a superior but ill-written one. Of greater importance, in retrospect, was his effort to make Latin viable by accommodating it to contemporary needs, as against the cult of the Ciceronians, which was exemplified by Bembo. Erasmus laid down his principles in the *Ciceronianus*, and illustrated the adequacy of Latin to the needs of daily life in his *Colloquies*. His final rejection of Luther was doubtless similarly motivated by a desire to prevent Europe from becoming fragmented into disparate languages and creeds.

Whereas the Italians had studied the ancients as models for imitation, the French appear to have been interested in erudition for its own sake. It was the famous Greek scholar Budé (Budaeus; 1467–1540) who was responsible for the foundation of the Collège de France. That scholarship was not the exclusive preserve of the specialists, however, is proven by the works of Rabelais (1490–1553), who not only quotes the ancients profusely but whose humanism reflects the teachings of Politian, Valla, Budé, Erasmus, and others, and by Montaigne (1533–1592), whose abundant quotations from the ancients show that he learned from them a point of view as well as anecdotes. And they were mined by a crowd of subsequent writers. Montaigne has the highest admiration for the superb versions of Plutarch by Amyot (1513–1593), who also made masterly translations of Heliodorus and of *Daphnis and Chloe*. Influential French scholars who followed Budé are Robert Estienne (Stephanus; 1503–1559) and his son Henri (d. 1598) who were also printers, and whose pagination of such authors as Plato and Plutarch constitute our present method of reference; Julius Caesar Scaliger (1484–1558) and his more amiable son Joseph Justus Scaliger (1540–1609) who taught at Leyden; Marc-Antoine Muret (Muretus; 1525–1585); Isaac Casaubon (1559–1614) and his son Meric (1599–1671) who taught in England; Saumaise (Salmasius; 1588–1653) the opponent of John Milton; and DuCange (1610–1688), the author of a Latin dictionary which is still useful.

Of this group the most famous is Julius Caesar Scaliger, whose greatest work is an enormous *Poetics* in seven books and 944 pages (1561). None of the humanists was afflicted with self-depreciation, but the arrogance of the elder Scaliger outdoes them all. He brushes his predecessors, Horace, Aristotle, and Vida away, and says, "The Greeks are mistaken if they think we have taken anything from them except to improve it." And of a *fabula* he had written he says that it has "such novelty of invention as might suffice for seven Erasmuses, to say nothing of one." Muretus was the most eloquent rhetorician of the group. A quotation from him shows arrogance of a different complexion:

On that night [St. Bartholomew's Eve] methought the very stars shone more brilliantly forth and the river Seine rolled with more majestic flood, the quicker to sweep away and disburden into the sea the cadavers of those filthy men.

The Benedictine Jean Mabillon (1632–1707) who was reputed to be the most learned man of his day, was one of the original members of the French Academy of Inscriptions, which was founded in 1701. The original object of the Academy was not the study of epigraphy but the composition of appropriate mottoes for medals struck in honor of Louis XIV, but it soon became the focus for intensive study of history and languages. Mention must be made here of André Dacier (1651–1722) and his wife Anne (1654–1720). Both edited texts, but Mme. Dacier is the better known for her translations of *Iliad* and *Odyssey;* she also made versions of Terence, and of some of Plautus, Aristophanes, Anacreon, and Sappho. The most learned Frenchman after Mabillon was Bernard de Montfaucon (1655–1741) who not only edited such authors as Athanasius, Origen, and Chrysostom in numerous folio volumes but was also a most effective popularizer. His *Antiquité Expliquée* in 15 folio volumes was widely read and translated. A more effective and better known popularization was the *Voyage du Jeune Anacharsis en Grèce* of Jean Jacques Barthélemy (1716–1795). This presents a picture of Greek daily life as seen through the eyes of an imagined visitor, and was the model for such widely used later books as Becker's *Charicles* and *Gallus*. For the broader effectiveness of classical learning in 17th century France we need only invoke the names of Racine (1639–1699) and Molière (1622–1673). In whole scenes Racine virtually transcribes Seneca or Euripides and Molière Terence or Plautus; but they remain masters rather than slaves of their models, and their new treatment reflects and shapes contemporary viewpoints. La Bruyère (1645–1696) or Fontenelle (1657–1757) provide more immediate illustration of French exploitation of scholarly work. La Bruyère, who said that the ancients had left only gleanings for the moderns, wrote *Characters* modeled upon those of Theophrastus, which had been magnificently edited by Casaubon, and Fontenelle wrote *Dialogues of the Dead* like those of Lucian, upon which a number of scholars had recently worked.

Joseph Justus Scaliger was called to Leyden, where he was succeeded by Salmasius in 1609. Other eminent Dutch scholars whose names are still invoked are the great "polyhistor" G. J. Vossius (1577–1649) and his sons, of whom Isaac was the most distinguished; Daniel Heinsius (1580–1655) and his son Niklaas (1620–1681); Gronovius (1611–1671) and his son Jacob (1645–1716). But the greatest in the Dutch succession and the scholar who has the greatest claim on our attention in fields other than classical learning is Hugo Grotius (1583–1645) who, besides his studies in philological scholarship, produced important works in theology, history, and international law; in the latter his work remains something of a classic. Some of Grotius' important work was done in prison, to which he was committed for espousing the wrong side in a theological dispute. He escaped to Paris, and subsequently entered the service of Queen Christina of Sweden. Subsequent Dutch scholars, known chiefly as editors of texts, are Pieter Burman (1668–1741) and his like-named nephew (1714–1778); Tiberus Hemsterhuys (1685–1766); L. K. Valckenaer (1715–1785); David Ruhnken (1723–1798); and Daniel Wyttenbach (1746–1820).

Chaucer (1328–1400), who read Boccaccio and several times names Petrarch and who knew the Latin poets well, is the main channel of the Italian Renaissance to England. Poggio was in England from 1418 to 1423, and during the 15th century a number of Englishmen studied in Italy. Professional scholarship in England begins with Thomas Linacre (1460–1524), who studied in Italy under Politian, Chalcondyles, and others, edited texts and improved classical education in England. Other noted English humanists are William Grocyn (1446–1519), William Latimer (1460–1545), John Colet (1467–1519), and Thomas More (1478–1535). More's *Utopia* is a fine illustration of humanism at its best; not only is it an elegantly written Latin book, enriched from Plato and Herodotus, but its message gives contemporary relevance to ancient experience and insight on important social questions. Another humanist who gave contemporary relevance to ancient learning is the Scot George Buchanan (1506–1582), who appreciated the Psalms as literature and turned them into Latin meters, wrote a long hexameter poem on astronomy (*Sphaera*), satiric poems on education and other subjects, Latin versions of Euripides' *Alcestis* and *Medea*, and original plays on *Jephthah* and on *John the Baptist*. His selection of plays for translation shows that he understood and sympathized with Euripides' attack on masculine smugness and contempt for women, and his own *John the Baptist* is an outspoken criticism of the pretensions of absolute monarchs. It is not unlikely that the fine anonymous English version of the play is the work of John Milton, and that Milton's republicanism was reinforced by Buchanan.

Greek and Latin had become staples of English education, and Roger Ascham (1515–1568), who was tutor to Elizabeth, provided a rationale and method for the study in his *Scholemaster*. It was during his time that the Erasmian pronunciation of Greek, which attempts to reproduce ancient pronunciation, replaced the "modern" pronunciation which the teachers from Greece had used and in which, by the process called iotacism, a number of vowels and diphthongs (e, i, u, ei, oi, ui) are given the same sound. Latin pronunciation took an opposite direction. From following the usage of the Italians, which retained the ancient vowel values, Latin came to be pronounced like English. After the Reformation it was no longer necessary for the clergy to use the language of the Church, and teachers found it less troublesome to pronounce Latin as English. When an English scholar visited Scaliger at Leyden in 1608 and addressed him for a quarter hour in Latin, Scaliger apologized in good faith for his inadequate knowledge of English. It was only at the end of the 19th century that an attempt was made to restore the ancient pronunciation of Latin in English (and American) secular schools. The Church uses the Italian pronunciation; here vowels retain their ancient value, diphthongs are shortened (ae = ě), and the consonants c and g are pronounced soft before e or i.

In the pronunciation of Greek also certain national differences remain: a British or German student, for example, will pronounce the diphthong *ei* like *ai* in "aisle"—which cannot have been the original pronunciation. Until recent times the Latin equivalents of Greek names were used; today we are careful to write "Zeus," "Hermes," "Odysseus," and the like instead of "Jupiter," "Mercury," "Ulysses" when a Greek work is spoken of. Because European knowledge of Greek came through the Latin, Greek names have become current in Latin spellings, and long usage makes reform difficult. "Thoukydides," "Aiskhylos," "Alkaios," even "Hekabe," would puzzle a reader who would immediately recognize "Thucydides," "Aeschylus," "Alcaeus," or "Hecuba." When no confusion would result some writers permit themselves the use of *k* instead of the Latin *c*, and write "Sophokles" or "Sokrates." Names of authors are frequently naturalized: we say "Vergil," "Livy," "Horace," "Ovid," not "Vergilius," "Livius," "Horatius," "Ovidius," and we say "Cicero," not "Tullius" or "Tully"; the French say "Tacite," "Tite-Live," and I have once seen "Plate" for "Plato."

Ascham had said that "even the best translation . . . is but an evill imped wing to flie withall, or a hevie stompe leg of wood to go withall," but imped wings and hevie stompes found their uses. Among notable Tudor translations are the *Tenne Tragedies* of Seneca by various hands (1581), Arthur Golding's *Metamorphoses* of Ovid (1565–1567), Marlowe's *Hero and Leander* of Musaeus (completed by George Chapman), *Amores* of Ovid, and the first book of Lucan, Chapman's Homer, Thomas North's Plutarch (from Amyot's French), and Philemon Holland's Livy, Pliny, Suetonius, Ammianus Marcellinus, *Cyropedia* of Xenophon, *Moralia* of Plutarch. Other 16th and 17th century efforts, like the work of the translators, show how classical learning was integrated into the main stream of culture. The learned edition of Chrysostom in eight folio volumes by Henry Savile (1549–1622), who helped Bodley found his famous library, is a magnificent example of printing. The best example of making scholarship servant rather than master is Francis Bacon (1561–1629) who "had taken all knowledge to be his province." From so accomplished a scholar as Bacon this advice (from the *Essay on Studies*) is salutary:

To spend too much time in Studies is Sloth; To use them too much for Ornament is Affectation; To make Iudgement wholly by their Rules is the Humour of a Scholler.

How a treasure of learning could be put to pleasing and advantageous use is illustrated in the *Anatomy of Melancholy* by Robert Burton (1576–1640), which is enormous in range, filled with information, and witty. Burton's lavish quotations have been mined by subsequent writers. The learning of John Selden (1584–1654), who was a distinguished lawyer and statesman, was not only broad but sufficiently exact to edit and expound the chronicle of the Parian Marble. But the most familiar example of mastery of classical learning instead of servitude to it is John Milton (1608–1674), whose profound understanding of Greek texts is proven not only by the shrewd marginalia in his books (preserved in a number of libraries) but by his *Samson Agonistes*, which is a truer "Greek tragedy" than any adaptation of the Greeks from Seneca to Anouilh. Others besides Milton who wrote good Latin poetry are Thomas May (1595–1650), Abraham Cowley (1618–1667), and James Duport (1606–1679). Platonism was a force in 17th century England; the foremost of the "Cambridge Platonists" was Henry More (1614–1687). Richard Bentley (1662–1742) marks an epoch in European as well as English scholarship, and we may take the occasion to glance for a moment at the German scholars.

German ties with Renaissance Italy were not as strong as English, though Petrarch did encourage Charles IV to become a patron of scholarship. The best known of the German humanists are Roelof Huysman (Rudolphus Agricola, 1444–1485) who taught at Heidelberg; Johann Reuchlin (1455–1522), who studied Hebrew as well as Greek and Latin; Wilibald Pirkheimer (1470–1530), who edited texts, studied archaeology, and was a patron of humanism; and Philip Melanchthon (1497–1560), who merited the title *praeceptor Germaniae.* The Hellenized names of the German humanists indicate the extent of their preoccupation. Melanchthon ("Black Earth") was really Schwartzerd, Xylander was Holtzmann, and Opsopoieus was Koch; the Church historian Neander took that name because conversion (from Judaism) made a "New Man" of him. Reuchlin, Melanchthon and the others indicate the enormous role of humanism in promoting the Reformation and providing a scholarly armory for it. It is important to realize, for the century following, that even narrowly scholarly labors had a wider significance until, in the 18th century, classical scholarship acquired something of the same general relevance in Germany as it had had in Elizabethan England.

At the end of the 18th century the battle of the books was raging in England, and it is in that connection that the name of Bentley is familiar to the general student. Defending the ancients in his *Essay upon Ancient and Modern Learning*, Sir William Temple had written:

It may perhaps be further affirmed, in favour of the Ancients, that the oldest books we have are still in their kind the best. The two most ancient that I know of in prose, among those we call profane authors, are Aesop's Fables and Phalaris's Epistles, both living near the same time, which was that of Cyrus and Pythagoras.

William Wotton's *Reflections upon Ancient and Modern Learning* had taken the opposite view. To supply the demand for the letters of Phalaris created by Temple's advertisement, an edition of them was hastily prepared by Charles Boyle in 1695; and Wotton issued a new edition of his *Reflections* which contained Bentley's dissertation on Aesop and Phalaris. Bentley was immediately attacked by the friends of Boyle and of Sir William Temple, including Temple's pensioner Swift, who animadverts on Bentley in his *Tale of a Tub* and *Battle of the Books*. Swift denied that modern resembled ancient literature more than a spider resembles a bee. Bentley's enlarged edition of his *Dissertation on the Epistles of Phalaris* (1699) marks the inception of the critical method of scholarship which has held the field to our own day. "For me," he writes (in Latin) in his edition of Horace, "common sense and the material itself has greater validity than a hundred MSS"—and proceeds to make 700 alterations in the text of Horace and 1,000 in Terence. Some of these are brilliant, and his emendations of inscriptions have been proven correct by actual stones, but the absurdities of which the method is capable may be seen in Bentley's own emendations of *Paradise Lost*. It was reason, after all, which prompted a Dutch follower of Bentley to insist that Shakespeare had written "Sermons in books, stones in running brooks." On Homer he anticipates both Wolff and Samuel Butler's "authoress" theory:

Take my word for it, poor Homer . . . had never such aspiring thoughts. He wrote a sequel of songs and rhapsodies, to be sung by himself for small earnings and good cheer, at festivals and other days of merriment; the Ilias he made for men, and the Odysseis for the other sex. These loose songs were not collected together in the form of an epic poem till Pisistratus's time, about 500 years after.

But in Homer he also conceived the brilliant digamma hypothesis— that is, that the aspirated vowel which begins certain Homeric words stands for the consonant *waw* (digamma) which has been lost. To this digamma and to Bentley's criticism generally the famous lines in Pope's *Dunciad* (1742) refer:

> 'Mistress! dismiss that rabble from your throne:
> Avaunt—Is Aristarchus yet unknown?
> Thy mighty scholiast whose unwearied pains
> Made Horace dull and humbled Milton's strains.
> Turn what they will to verse, their toil is vain:
> Critics like me shall make it prose again.
> Roman and Greek grammarians! know your better,
> Author of something yet more great than letter;
> While tow'ring o'er your alphabet, like Saul,
> Stands our digamma, and o'ertops them all.'

Pope himself (1688–1744), Dryden (1631–1700), and Addison (1672–1719) all deserve mention as classical scholars. Pope imitated

Horace's *Satires* and made spirited translations of *Iliad* and *Odyssey* which, though quaint today, were an appropriate Homer for Pope's generation. Sandys notes that the best known line in these translations is preceded by one that owes its existence to the necessities of rhyme alone (*Odyssey* 15.74):

> True friendship's laws are by this rule exprest,
> Welcome the coming, speed the parting guest.

Dryden's *Virgil* is certainly among the best English versions, though it was criticized by both Swift and Bentley; Dryden's *Persius* and *Juvenal* are excellent, and his name is attached to many other translations (e.g., Plutarch) which are not actually his. Addison wrote *Dialogues on Medals*, *Remarks on Italy*, and some Latin poems; he also has judicious critical remarks comparing Homer and Vergil. For the place of classical learning in the education of an ordinary gentleman we turn to a letter of Lord Chesterfield to his son (1750):

> Let Greek, without fail, share some part of every day: I do not mean the Greek poets, the catches of Anacreon, or the tender complaints of Theocritus, or even the porterlike language of Homer's heroes; of whom all smatterers in Greek know a little, quote often, and talk of always; but I mean Plato, Aristotle, Demosthenes, and Thucydides, whom none but adepts know. It is Greek that must distinguish you in the learned world, Latin alone will not.

The greatest name in English scholarship after Bentley is Richard Porson (1759–1808), who combined critical genius with a somewhat rowdy way of life, and was the first to decipher the Greek text of the Rosetta Stone. Between Bentley and Porson, Thomas Tyrwhitt (1730–1786) and Thomas Twining (1734–1804) are worthy of mention. Newly awakened interest in the physical remains of classical antiquity resulted in the establishment, in 1733, of the Society of Dilettanti, which fostered such sumptuous publications as J. Stuart and R. Wood's *The Antiquities of Athens*

Measured and Delineated (1762–1816) and the epigraphical collection of Richard Chandler (1738–1810). Charles Townley (1737–1805) and Richard Payne Knight (1750–1824) gave their names to famous collections. Sir William Hamilton (1730–1803) reported early discoveries at Pompeii. The program of the Dilettanti was supported by the traveler and statesman Robert Wood (1717–1771), whose *Essay on the Genius and Writings of Homer, with a Comparative View of the Ancient and Present State of the Troade* influenced both Wolff and Goethe; Wood thought that writing was not introduced into Greece until 554 B.C.

The one work of English scholarship which enjoys indisputable rank as a literary classic in its own right is Edward Gibbon's (1737–1794) *The Decline and Fall of the Roman Empire*. The *History of Greece* was written by William Mitford (1744–1827), but Mitford had an ingrained distrust of democracy, and Greece had to await a more sympathetic treatment at the hands of George Grote. The true father of comparative philology is Sir William Jones (1746–1794), who was expert in English and Attic law (he translated Isaeus) and became judge at Calcutta and conceived a great admiration for Sanskrit. "No philologer can examine the Sanscrit, Greek, and Latin," he wrote, "without believing them to have been sprung from some common source, which, perhaps, no longer exists."

It was in Germany that critical scholarship of Bentley's type was increasingly professionalized into a science and so ultimately dehumanized that it lost all relevance to life. The first of the German academies, that of Berlin, was founded in 1700 through the efforts of the polymath G. W. Leibnitz (1646–1716). The fullest collection of bibliographical material and the most meticulous which had ever been made was the *Bibliotheca Graeca* of J. A. Fabricius (1668–1736) in many large volumes, upon which all subsequent histories of Greek literature ultimately rest. But a series of nonscientific writers emphasized the humanistic values of the classics. J. J. Winckelmann (1717–1768) was a great innovator in the aesthetic appreciation of ancient art and in bringing the ancient Greek world (which he sharply differentiated from the Roman on the basis of artistic taste) into connection with modern life. The perceptive criticism of G. E. Lessing (1729–1781) in his *Laocoön* and his *Hamburgische Dramaturgie* (which is quite possibly the best dramatic criticism ever written) introduced a new era of appreciation of Homer and Sophocles, and of Plautus, Horace, and others. In Dryden's age none questioned Vergil's superiority to Homer; it is a sign of the times that Lessing preferred Homer. So did J. G. Herder (1744–1803), who communicated his enthusiasm for primitive strength, but deplored artificial antiquarianism and regarded Greece as "the school of humanity." So, for all his wide knowledge, did the educational reformer Wilhelm von Humboldt (1767–1835) believe "that the Greek language and the old Greek culture still remain the finest product of the human intellect." The classical interests of Goethe (1749–1832) need not be dilated upon; it is worth noticing that his adaptations of Aeschylus in the Second Part of *Faust* and of Euripides in his *Iphigenia* are far more alien to the Greek spirit than Milton's *Samson Agonistes*. Where Goethe knew Greek Schiller (1759–1805) had to rely on Latin translations, but even aside from his *Iphigenia at Aulis* his works are steeped in Greek antiquity, and his *Cranes of Ibycus* and *Hero and Leander* have made these stories widely familiar. The *Lectures on Dramatic Art and Literature* of A. W. von Schlegel (1767–1845), the brilliant translator of Shakespeare, brought new appreciation to Greek tragedy. His brother F. von Schlegel (1772–1829) was less successful in his criticism of epic. The translations of Homer by J. H. Voss (1751–1826) come near to being the German "authorized version." Voss also translated Aristophanes, Vergil, Ovid's *Metamorphoses*, Tibullus, and Propertius.

VII. THE "SCIENTIFIC" AGE

Erudition, accuracy, and critical acumen had always been ideals of scholarship, but scholarship itself, to the humanists and their successors, was a means to a fuller life. In the 19th century, scholarship was virtually dehumanized. It adopted the methods of the exact sciences; its goal was the establishment of truth for its own sake, and any implications its findings might have for the fuller understanding of man were really incidental. Those who sought to make the new knowledge relevant were suspect to the esoteric, and anyone who could write readable prose forfeited his standing as a scholar. A clairvoyant intellect like Burckhardt was scorned by the professionals, and it took courage for Mommsen to acknowledge that Renan was a scholar, "even though he could write." It remains only to note that despite the prodigious industry of the 19th century German scholars and their imitators and despite their truly amazing genuine achievements, much of the structure they erected with such great assurance has been found unsound, and in many instances a return to the humanistic approach has yielded truer as well as more useful results.

The methods of the critical school had really been anticipated by such Englishmen as Richard Bentley and Humphrey Hody, but the great arena for the new scholarship was Germany, and in the modern German study of philology primacy in several senses belongs to F. A. Wolff (1759–1824). Wolff's *Prolegomena* to Homer (1795) initiated and supplied much material for the hotly fought Homeric question, and Wolff personally inspired a distinguished succession of pupils. Of Wolff's contemporaries and successors our list must be highly selective. Joseph Eckhel is the pioneer in numismatics and still the greatest name in that subject. G. F. Creuzer (1771–1858) promoted the study of mythology and of Neoplatonism. B. G. Niebuhr (1776–1831), the first critical historian of Rome, believed that all traditions of the period anterior to the Gallic invasion of 390 B.C. were based on poetic lays—such as Macaulay then attempted to reproduce in his *Lays of Ancient Rome*. Niebuhr also organized the publication of the *Corpus Scriptorum Historiae Byzantinae* and founded the periodical *Rheinisches Museum*, one of several such inaugurated in Germany at this period. Schleiermacher (1768–1834) expounded Plato and made a complete translation of him.

In German scholarship of the 19th century two clearly divergent schools must be reckoned with, a "pure" grammatical and critical school, of which the leader was Gottfried Hermann (1768–1848), and an "applied" historical and antiquarian school, of which the coryphaeus was August Boeckh (1785–1867); between the two literary understanding came near perishing. Boeckh produced acute studies of the *Public Economy of Athens* and established the *Corpus Inscriptionum Graecarum*. His principal disciple was K. O. Müller (1797–1840). Of his numerous epigoni mention may be made of G. F. Schömann (1793–1879), who wrote on Greek public antiquities; Gustav Droysen (1808–1884), who aroused interest in the Hellenistic age; and Theodor Mommsen (1817–1903), whose expertness in Roman law and public administration and own political interests gave vitality to his extremely influential *History of Rome*. It was Mommsen who initiated the great *Corpus Inscriptionum Latinarum*. The Hermann succession is even more numerous and includes the scholars whose names appear in the apparatus of most of our current classical texts and on the title-pages of standard handbooks and reference works, and who were the teachers of the Americans who introduced the "scientific" study of philology in American universities. It is significant either of their approach or of their age that, however high their reputation among fellow-specialists, their names are *not* known, as the names of true humanists were known, to wider circles. Men like Karl Lachmann (1793–1851) or Jacob Bernays (1824–1881) whose eyes wandered even slightly beyond the classical preserve were something of prodigies. Lachmann, who made a good edition of Lucretius, applied the method of Wolff's *Prolegomena* to the *Nibelungenlied* and then to Homer. Bernay's expertness in Jewish lore enabled him to illuminate certain Greek and Hellenistic-Jewish writers by each other's light. What strikes the humbler modern observer of late 19th century scholarship is its unconscious arrogance. What they studied, and by the methods they deemed correct, they studied with great success; but they could not conceive that there were other things to study in the classics or other methods of studying them. The business of the ethical dative was despatched in a lifetime of work and a fat volume; when the business of all other datives and all other similar questions should be done, knowledge would be complete and could be entered, as a possession of unalterable validity as well as accuracy, in a huge encyclopedia. It is hardly conceivable that contemporary scholars could have such assurance of the finality of their work.

So technical had German scholarship become that none but professionals could engage in it, and classical study hence tended to become insulated from the general stream of cultural life. The danger of such insulation is always present whenever studies are prosecuted with professional zeal, and early in the humanist period Montaigne (in his essay *On Pedantry*) had spoken scornfully of men who were "grammarians, not gentlemen." In England the tradition of the amateur persisted, and in that country a series of distinguished translations and interpretations of the classics has been produced by bankers and barristers. In France even works of high professional competence were leavened by an unpedantic humanism. For exhaustive treatment of any topic in classical philology, for example, the student must turn to the prodigious and still incomplete *Real-Enzyklopaedie der klassischen Altertumswissenschaft*, edited by Pauly, Wissowa, Kroll, and others; but reading Pauly-Wissowa is a serious business which no one could undertake for pleasure. The analogous French *Dictionnaire des antiquités grecques et romaines* edited by Daremberg and Saglio, though less exhaustive, is not only sound but can be read for pleasure. For the history of Greek literature, to take another example, the reference work indispensable to the scholar is that by Christ, Schmid, and Staehlin in some half dozen stout volumes in the series called "Iwan Mullers Handbuch der Altertumswissenschaft": but Christ-Schmid is to be consulted, not read. The *Histoire de la littérature grecque* of Alfred and Maurice Croiset in five volumes, though it is not nearly so exhaustive or fully documented, can be read with delight as well as confidence by any lover of literature.

In America graduate study of the classics was organized and prosecuted in the German pattern, and until the first world war study in Germany was virtually mandatory for any scholar who aspired to higher teaching in America. As in Germany the consequent professionalization almost destroyed the subject as part of general culture. But in America the humanist tradition survived, and today, through the medium of courses called Humanities or

General Education, probably a larger proportion of the population than ever before has an acquaintance, through adequate translations and interpretations, with the outstanding authors of classical antiquity.

VIII. THE DISCIPLINES OF PHILOLOGY

With so much that students must learn, to understand themselves and their world, it cannot be expected that any large proportion will devote the time necessary for mastery of classical antiquity. And in classical antiquity itself so multifarious are the specialties that have been developed that even a scholar who makes classical study his profession can center his attention upon only a few. The individual student is naturally most likely to be concerned with the ideas of the ancients, and hence with the language and literature in which those ideas have been transmitted; his main responsibility to society is as curator and disseminator of those ideas. But in order to collect the legacy of ideas, to read them intelligently, and to understand their meaning in their own historical and sociological background he must familiarize himself with a number of ancillary disciplines, some of which seem remote from a humanist's interests. The chapter headings in such works as *The Companion to Greek Studies* and *The Companion to Latin Studies* (Cambridge, 1910), which are sometimes used by students in preparation for comprehensive examinations, are an indication of the various disciplines within the field. Besides knowing the languages, literatures, and history of Greece and Rome, the student must have some knowledge of their philosophy, their art and architecture, their religion and mythology, their governmental institutions, their domestic usages and habits, and he must have some acquaintance with palaeography, epigraphy, and numismatics. Classical philology in its broader sense, then, is not a subject but a complete curriculum.

Nor can the student of antiquity blind himself to other knowledge. The political significance of a Caesar, for example, was first appreciated by a scholar who had studied Napoleon, and of Demosthenes by one who had direct experience of the diplomatic problems of the 19th century. The student of ancient religion must today be grounded in the findings of modern psychology, and the student of literature in the new techniques of criticism. But for fruitful application of new knowledge and techniques to ancient problems, a full knowledge of antiquity itself is essential. Political theorists, psychologists, students of literature who make superficial use of the ancient evidence can only mislead.

7: *Lives of the Poets*

I. THE PROPER STUDY OF MANKIND

NOTHING IS SO INTERESTING TO MEN AS THE lives of their fellow-men. People who care for no other form of literature will read biography; and novels and plays are acceptable only as their characters are credible human beings. For bookish people, at least, greatest interest naturally attaches to lives which have shaped or given direction to cultural tradition; even in a metropolis where rank is conferred by Mammon intellectual achievement comes into its own in the obituary columns, where a writer or composer at last takes precedence over a banker or a politician.

Here classical Greek literature offers a paradox. It is in its concern for men, as we have observed, that Greek literature differs most markedly from its predecessors, and yet the men with whose problems the literature of the 5th century deals are rather types than individuals. Sculpture makes this fact clear. There are no true portraits before the Hellenistic age, not because of the sculptor's inadequacy—the sculptures of the Parthenon are ample proof to the contrary—but because the sculptors of the classical age were not interested in portraying individual idiosyncrasies. The best known portrait bust of the classical period is that marked "Pericles, son of Xanthippus, Athenian," but all that we see is an idealized statesman and general, with all marks of individuality effaced. Thucydides gives us details concerning the character of Pericles and his fellow-statesmen, but only so much as we need to know in order to understand the course of history; for details concerning Pericles' relations with Aspasia or Alcibiades' lisp or Nicias' wealth we must go to Plutarch. It was only with Aristotle and the researchers of the Peripatetic school—from whom Plutarch's tradition ultimately derives—that biography in our sense became a legitimate subject for investigation. The Peripatetics not only classified characters— Aristotle's successor Theophrastus composed a book of them—but also studied the lineaments of individual physiognomies. Presumably the honest researchers of the Lyceum made no attempt to supply lives of older figures for which data were wanting, but in course of time men invented what they could not find and every classical author was supplied with a more or less plausible life. It is to the credit of ancient readers, indeed, that they were more interested in the lives of men of letters than in any other class.

II. FICTION IN BIOGRAPHY

It may be accepted as a principle, then, that no trust is to be placed in biographical details not specifically given by an author himself or a trustworthy near contemporary or by a clearly traceable tradition. What Thucydides says of himself we may believe; but how could Marcellinus, who lived many centuries later, have learned what no intervening writers seem to know, especially when we hear that Thucydides was so little known to the succeeding generation that Xenophon might have claimed his work for his own? We know Euripides' convictions from his plays, but can we trust the malicious aspersions on his private life made even by his contemporary Aristophanes? The aspersions have become traditional literary gossip, but we now know from the sober biography of Satyrus, published from papyri in 1912, that the aspersions cannot be true. On Agathon, whose work is lost, we might trust Aristophanes because Plato's *Symposium* seems to bear him out, but then we must remember that Plato probably had a bias like that of Aristophanes. In the case of the early Latin authors the situation was the same. Of the careers of Plautus and Terence we have very full details— how Plautus lost his fortune in a business venture, worked in a mill, liberated himself by writing plays as he worked; how Terence came from Africa and engaged the interest of Scipio—but this very fullness is suspicious, especially when we consider the long interval between the lives of these poets and the earliest record of their biographical details.

How then did the stories arise? They can be dismissed, after all, only if we can explain how they gained currency in the first place.

Close study has shown that in very many cases biographical details are deductions from the work of the author in question or, especially when the stories are hostile, they owe their existence to interested protagonists of views which the authors attacked or, as in the case of Euripides or Lucretius, a combination of both causes. Homer, to take a simple example, and all primitive bards may actually have been blind; but it is altogether probable that the tradition of Homer's blindness comes from the fact that his own bard Demodocus in the *Odyssey* is represented as blind. Sophocles' religiosity is a deduction from the pious utterances of his choruses; Euripides' unhappy family life and misogyny, from the naughty women who appear in some of his plays.

Data so deduced are naturally apocryphal, but it is worth observing that they need not always be. On the basis of Homer's rustic figures of farm animals and milkpails, for example, some scholars argue that Homer himself was a peasant who handled remote heroic material. After all, from the critics' point of view the main use of biographical detail is as an aid in explaining a writer's work. The fact is that too often the work is used to corroborate and illuminate biographical data, not the other way around. Only after independent documentary proof showed that Wordsworth had become a father on the continent did critics discover appropriate passages illustrating the hitherto unknown facet of Wordsworth's personality.

Even for birth dates, where we habitually accept the entries in reference books without question, there is frequently no sure basis. Most are demonstrably based on a rule-of-thumb calculation. The great event in a man's life is assumed to have taken place at his acme, which was considered to fall at the age of 40, and his birth is then dated to 40 years before the great event. Thus Thucydides' birth-year is given as 471 B.C.—just 40 years before the outbreak of the Peloponnesian War of which he wrote, and Aristophanes' as 445—just 40 years before his masterpiece, *The Frogs*, was presented. *Sub specie aeternitatis* a dozen years may be less than a watch in the night, but it would be interesting to know whether Aristophanes was actually under 20 when he wrote his masterly

Acharnians, or whether Aeschylus was past 40 before he received a prize.

III. THE TRUTH OF BIOGRAPHICAL FICTION

We are no longer shocked to find that a great artist may at the same time be a great rogue, and we are amused rather than dismayed when we find a writer with high pretensions revealing the weakness of his own flesh. Boswell was astonished that Milton, "an acrimonious and surly republican, in his domestic relations so severe and arbitrary, his head so filled with the dismal tenets of Calvinism . . . should have written . . . with beauty and even gaiety, . . . imaged delicate raptures of connubial love; nay, seemed to be animated with the spirit of revelry." Students of psychology have provided explanations for such phenomena as astonished Boswell, but Boswell's comment is squarely in the tradition of the fundamental doctrine of the ancients that an author's work must reflect his life: only a stark man could write epic, only a lover elegy, only a good man, in a word, could write good literature, for the writer can represent only such actions and viewpoints as he is himself capable of. Satyrus' biography of Euripides quotes an otherwise unknown line of Aristophanes, "As are his characters so is the man." In keeping with this principle Aristophanes has Agathon say (*Thesmophoriazusae* 149 ff.):

> *A poet, sir, must needs adapt his ways*
> *To the high thoughts which animate his soul.*
> *And when he sings of women, he assumes*
> *A woman's garb and dons a woman's habits.*
> *. . . Witness to my words*
> *Anacreon, Alcaeus, Ibycus,*
> *Who when they filtered and diluted song,*
> *Wore soft Ionian manners and attire.*

In the *Laws* (829c) Plato, following the same principle, ordains that brave soldiers must be rewarded:

And let poets celebrate them—not however every poet, but only one who in the first place is not less than fifty years of age . . . one who is good and honorable in the state, a poet of noble action.

The principle is invoked not only by an authoritarian moralizer like Plato, but even by Aristotle, who does not apply the moral gauge (*Poetics* 1448b):

Poetry soon broke up into two kinds according to the differences of character in the individual poets; for the graver among them would represent noble actions, and those of noble personages; and the meaner sort the actions of the ignoble.

Throughout antiquity the doctrine that a poet's work must reflect his own character was accepted as axiomatic. Here is perhaps the most explicit statement of the subject, from the geographer Strabo (1.2.5) who lived in the time of Augustus:

Who can assume that the poet who is capable of introducing other men in the role of orators, or of generals, or in other roles that exhibit the accomplishments of the art of rhetoric, is himself but one of the buffoons or jugglers, capable only of bewitching and flattering his hearer but not of helping him? Nor can we assume that any excellence of a poet whatever is superior to that which enables him to imitate life through the means of speech. How then can a man imitate life if he has no experience of life and is a dolt? Of course we do not speak of the excellence of a poet in the same sense as we speak of that of a carpenter or a blacksmith; for their excellence depends on no inherent nobility and dignity, whereas the excellence of a poet is inseparably associated with the excellence of the man himself, and it is impossible for one to become a good poet unless he has previously become a good man.

Similarly the perceptive "Longinus" says (9.2) that "sublimity is the true ring of a noble mind."

When, therefore, the Roman elegiac poets say, as they frequently do (e.g., Ovid, Amores 1.1), that only a lover can write love poetry, something more than a pretty conceit is involved; and when Horace maintains (Epistles 1.19.6) that Homer's praise of wine proves that Homer himself was vinosus he is not being merely whimsical. If only a lover can celebrate love and only a toper wine, then if we find praise of love or wine in a literary work, or praise of war, or any similar trait, we may legitimately deduce that the author himself possessed such traits. Grammarians who constructed an author's life out of his works were not then, in their own view, creating apocrypha but using a proper biographical source—from the point of view of the utility for criticism, a more meaningful source than vital statistics from an official register. If a book involves the essence of the poet's character then his character, or at least so much of it as concerns us, may be disengaged out of his book. The flaw in such a procedure is that in ambiguous cases the judgment of the grammarian must be subjective and may be faulty; but it is interesting to observe that the method had its rationale. And even where the judgments are most subjective they may, like any good plasma, promote understanding: it is poetically just that Lucretius should have been maddened by a love philter and have written On the Nature of Things in intervals of sanity.

IV. THE LITERARY GOSSIPERS

Deductions from an author's work, then, as well as whatever documentary data might be available were the bases of ancient literary biographies. Except for Plutarch's Lives of Demosthenes and Cicero, whose careers as statesmen admit them to his series, no complete ancient biography of a literary figure has survived. We do have shorter accounts of certain authors, of varying degrees of credibility. At one end we might put Satyrus' Life of Euripides. This is good Alexandrian work of the 3rd century B.C., but only fragments have been discovered. At the other we might put Marcellinus' Life of Thucydides, but suspicion must attach to a late author who knows details which his predecessors are ignorant of. What we have to rely on are (a) a number of rather brief lives, mostly abbreviated from longer treatments; (b) many excerpts from biographies; and (c) very many anecdotes which may or may not have been drawn from a formal biography.

In the first category the best are lives of certain Roman poets drawn, with various degrees of abridgment, from Suetonius' *De grammaticis*; the best of these are on Terence, Horace, Lucan, and Vergil, though there is doubt of the Suetonian authorship of the last. Short *Lives* of certain Greek authors, probably by Didymus, are prefixed to their texts. For the philosophers we have the biographies of Diogenes Laertius, who usually names his sources. And finally, brief biographical notes are to be found in Suidas or Photius or in scholia. For the second and third categories the source may be any bookish writer—copious and literate essayists or letter writers like Cicero or Pliny, Plutarch or Seneca; collectors of miscellanies like Athenaeus or Aelian or Aulus Gellius; factual writers like the Elder Pliny, Suetonius, Strabo, and Pausanias; and of course professed scholars such as Quintilian or Fronto.

Since these names will recur frequently in the pages to follow, brief descriptions of the works of the less familiar of them may be in place. Those most useful are connected with the classicizing movement in the reign of Hadrian which naturally directed interest to the externals of ancient books and authors. At best these epigoni made useful doxographies, like Diogenes Laertius'; at their most frivolous they made encyclopedias of anecdotes, like those of Aelian. To the historian of literature the most entertaining and also the most indispensable of these books is the *Deipnosophists* or *Doctors at Dinner*, written by Athenaeus of Naucratis in the 3rd century.

The *Deipnosophists* is a 15-book account of a dinner party, which apparently lasts three days and at which the guests, not characterized in any detail, are grammarians, philosophers, musicians, and physicians. The conversation, suggested by the food and entertainment, covers details of food and drink, cooking and serving, amusements and furnishings, parasites and hetaerae, and above all literary gossip and quotations, apt or funny or just too good to pass over. About 700 writers who would otherwise remain unknown are quoted. There can be no doubt that Athenaeus found most of his material already collected in earlier compilations, but the modern reader can only be grateful for the abundance. Originally the work seems to have been much larger: of the 15 books we have, 1, 2, and the beginning of 3 are only epitomes, made in antiquity, and there are gaps in 11 and at the end of 15. Today Athenaeus' natural habitat is the footnote; when the redoubtable Wilamowitz-Moellendorff doubted Nietzsche's theory of the birth of tragedy, Nietzsche said, "What does he want, an oracle of Delphi or a footnote to Athenaeus?"

Probably next in usefulness is the more systematic *Lives of Eminent Philosophers* of Diogenes Laertius. Diogenes' date is unknown, but can hardly have been later than the 3rd century, for he does not mention Neoplatonism though he is particularly interested in the Platonic succession. Diogenes too used earlier compilations, but since his work is the only survivor in its kind it is indispensable for the information it preserves. An introductory book glorifies Greek as compared with "barbarian" philosophies, and then enumerates the Seven Sages and their teachings. Books 2–7 deal with the Ionian succession, beginning with Anaximander; Book 8 deals with the Italian succession, beginning with Pythagoras; and Books 9–10 treat a scattered group outside these successions. The long tenth book on Epicurus is extremely valuable for the original documents it alone preserves.

Nearer in spirit to the *Doctors at Dinner* is the Latin *Attic Nights* of Aulus Gellius (ca. 123–ca. 165) which is mainly a compilation of extracts, in 20 books, from a large number of Greek and Latin writers. The collection was made, Gellius tells us in his preface, as a kind of commonplace book, and the arrangement is haphazard. His chief concern is with literature—criticism, textual matters, grammar, biographical notes—but his range also includes law, religion, history, and antiquarian interests generally. He mentions as many as 275 authors by name. Though Gellius is no scholar, in the technical sense, his eye is caught by the right things, and without him our picture of the background to our ancient books would have many gaps now filled.

Other books similar to the three mentioned yield a smaller harvest
for our present purpose. The *Stromateis* or *Miscellanies* of the
Christian Clement of Alexandria (ca. 150–212) may be compared to
the *Deipnosophists*. The eight books of the *Stromateis* quote from or
mention some 300 authors, with a view to showing the use which
devout Christians might make of the wisdom of the Greeks. Somewhat similar to Diogenes Laertius' *Lives of the Eminent Philosophers* but far less useful are the *Lives of the Sophists* of Philostratus
(ca. 170–248) and the *Lives of the Philosophers and Sophists* of
Eunapius (346–414). Both the works are chiefly concerned to heap
adulation upon third-rate oratorical virtuosi. Most like Aulus Gellius in range (but like the *Deipnosophists* in that it represents a
conversation at a fictive gathering) is the Latin *Saturnalia* of Macrobius (4th century). But whereas Aulus Gellius emptied his bushels
as they had piled up, Macrobius had digested and organized his
medley, and he distributes appropriate utterances to the well-defined
persons of his masque.

Besides these writers whose books might themselves be said to
constitute a kind of gossip column, there are a number of serious
essayists, orators, and writers on special subjects, who—like their
successors in all bookish ages—willingly employ classical tags or
anecdotes concerning classical authors "to point a moral or adorn
a tale." Plutarch (ca. 45–125) is at once the most literate and
prolific of the essayists. Plutarch's reading was very wide and his
taste excellent. He is one of the most generous and skillful quoters
in literature; his nearest analogue is Montaigne, who learned the
art from him but whose range is far less wide. At the same time
Plutarch is a connoisseur of anecdotes; he is capable of saying (*Pericles* 24), "this [really irrelevant] story coming to my recollection
as I write, it would be unnatural for me to reject it and pass it by."
It was after all Plutarch's main purpose in his *Lives* as in his *Moralia*,
to imbue his readers with Greek culture, which is embodied in
Greek books; and if today a curious reader should ask for a single
author who might communicate the fullest sense of the totality of
classical culture, the answer would have to be Plutarch.

For our purposes too, compared to Plutarch other writers are of minor significance. For authoritative opinions, as concise as they are judicious, on the merits of various classical authors we turn to the tenth book of the *Institutio Oratoria* of Quintilian (b. ca. A.D. 35). The Elder Pliny (23–79) provides information on very many things and is indispensable for sculptors and painters but has less to say on men of letters. The Greek geographer Strabo (63 B.C.–A.D. 21) has strong literary interests and expresses decided opinions on his reading. The Greek traveler Pausanias (2nd century A.D.) will include traditions of literary men connected with a monument he is describing. The "orators" of the Second Sophistic, beginning with Dio Chrysostom, will occasionally use a literary anecdote; Dio himself has a good essay comparing the tragedies on the Philoctetes theme by Aeschylus, Sophocles, and Euripides. Lucian (ca. 120–190) makes frequent allusions to literary figures in his satirical pieces; he is particularly interested in historians and has acute criticisms of inept and pretentious writing in this field. Aelian (3rd century) is frankly a collector of anecdotes, and his 14 books of *Various Histories* merely reproduce unconnected anecdotes, curious, paradoxical, or simply diverting. A number naturally refer to literary personages. The Christian writers, and St. Augustine in particular, supply an occasional piece of literary information. To list additional names is futile. It may be said in a word that except for writers of imaginative works (and even they naturally reveal their use and opinion of the classics) all writers of later antiquity show their allegiance to the traditions of their craft and hence are apt to give their work a literary flavor by literary allusions or gossip. Most of the well-known stories recur in a number of writers, but it sometimes happens that an apt story is found in only a single obscure source.

Part II

LITERARY GOSSIP

ABOUT EACH FIGURE IN CLASSICAL LITERA-
ture there has collected a precipitate of conventional information, which is regularly repeated in reference works, histories
of literature, or introductions to texts. Presumably the decisions of
successive generations of compilers and editors on what is fit to print
have been judicious; but as in the case of a newspaper which declares
it will publish only what is fit to print, one wonders what the rejected
residue may be like. Any system of labeling such a complex organism
as a creative artist must be inadequate, for correct as the label may
be, aspects and nuances for which there is no room on it may prove
to be more significant than the legend on the label. Plutarch has put
the case well, in the opening paragraph of his *Life of Alexander:*

*It must be borne in mind that my design is not to write histories,
but lives. And the most glorious exploits do not always furnish us
with the clearest discoveries of virtue or vice in men; sometimes
a matter of less moment, an expression or a jest, informs us better
of their characters and inclinations, than the most famous sieges,
the greatest armaments, or the bloodiest battles whatsoever. Therefore as portrait-painters are more exact in the lines and features of
the face, in which the character is seen, than in the other parts of
the body, so I must be allowed to give my more particular attention to the marks and indications of the souls of men, and while
I endeavor by these to portray their lives, may be free to leave more
weighty matters and great battles to be treated of by others.*

In the pages following the object is first to glean whatever "marks
and indications of the souls of men" who have produced classical
literature are available in the writings of other men, and next to
present other less familiar comment on their lives and works. Comments or opinions here offered are in no sense authoritative, and

by no means justly apportioned. In respect to both quantity and quality, here the decisive factor has been the availability of material. Frequently modern scholarship and taste occupies a position diametrically opposite to what some second-rate ancients report. For modern and more systematic opinion on ancient writers the reader will naturally turn to formal histories of literature; here nothing more than marginalia to such histories can be expected.

8: *Between Scripture and Classics*

THEIR OLDEST LITERATURE THE GREEKS RE-garded with reverence. For them Homer and Hesiod held a position somewhere between classics and Scripture, and they were quoted as freely, for substance or ornament, as we quote Bible or Shakespeare. Concerning the poets themselves (except where Hesiod provides autobiographical details) they had little more than inference to go on, but legends about them soon grew into a kind of hagiographa, and only a rationalist like Xenophanes or a rebel like Zoilus protested at what they thought was mistaken adulation.

I. LEGENDARY POETS

It is certain that there were poets before Homer, but it is almost equally certain that Orpheus and Musaeus, Philammon, Olen, Linus, and similar shadowy figures are fictions. Orpheus, whatever the origins of his legend may have been, was made to incarnate a complex of other-worldly religious beliefs, and his personality was given definite form in opposition to the worldliness of Homer. The reaction from the Homeric view is almost certainly post-Hesiodic, and likely not earlier than the 6th century. As the central figure of a sect Orpheus retained a kind of subliterary existence throughout antiquity and eventually emerged as a pagan antitype to Christ, but for the classic writers he was a definite enough entity for Socrates to look forward to encountering him, along with Homer, in another existence (*Apology* 41) and for Admetus (in Euripides' *Alcestis* 357 f.) to desire "the tongue and melody of Orpheus to charm Demeter's Maid or her husband by song."

Later systematizers made Musaeus either the pupil or teacher of Orpheus. Musaeus was associated with the cult of Demeter at Eleusis, which was concerned to emphasize the independence of the Eleusinian Mysteries from Orphism. Herodotus (7.6) says that it was Onomacritus, the oracle-expert at the court of the Pisistratids, who "set forth the prophecies of Musaeus in their order." Elsewhere (2.53) Herodotus gives it as his judgment that the named poets thought to be earlier than Homer and Hesiod are in fact "decidedly later writers," and other ancient writers who touch on the subject agree. In Alexandria, Jewish and then Christian writers interested in proving the priority of Jewish doctrine to pagan declared that "Musaeus" was only a corrupt spelling of "Moses," who was thus responsible for pagan as well as Jewish wisdom. Renaissance scholars, including the great Julius Caesar Scaliger himself, thought that the Musaeus who wrote *Hero and Leander* in the 5th century A.D. was identical with the legendary Musaeus and that his poem was better than Homer's.

Equally transparent fictions are Philammon, a creation of the cult of the Delphian Apollo, and Olen, who is associated with the cult of the Delian Apollo. "Linus" was made into a proper name from the noun *linus*, which designated a kind of dirge.

II. HOMER

Of Homer's personality we can know nothing because our ancient informants knew nothing. Legends concerning his life began to take literary shape doubtless in the 5th century, but like the familiar busts they are idealized portraits of a blind wandering poet, richly endowed and well received but poor in worldly goods. The most persistent traditions are (a) that he was born in Smyrna of the river-god Meles and the nymph Cretheis; (b) that he lived in Chios; and (c) that he was buried on the little island of Ios near Thera. The uncertainty of these data (and a refreshing indifference to them) is reflected in a number of epigrams, notably that of Antipater of Sidon (2nd century B.C.; A.P. 16.296):

Some say, Homer, that thy nurse was Colophon; some lovely Smyrna, some Chios, some Ios; while some proclaim fortunate Salamis, and some Thessaly, mother of the Lapiths, some this place, some that,

to be the land that brought thee to birth. But if I may utter openly
the wise prophecies of Phoebus, great Heaven is thy country, and
thy mother was no mortal woman, but Calliope.

The Gymnosophist Calasiris in Heliodorus' *Ethiopica* (Bk. 3),
insists that Homer was an Egyptian and that his father was Hermes:

Homer by divers reports may be ascribed to divers countries, and
indeed to the wise man no country comes amiss. But to tell the truth,
he was our countryman, an Egyptian born in Thebes of the hundred gates, and his father was putatively a prophet but in reality
the god Hermes, in whose temple the father served. For when his
mother was doing certain sacrifices after the manner of the country
she fell asleep in the temple and the god lay with her and engendered
Homer. Who indeed had about him token of unlawful generation,
for on both his thighs from birth there grew a great deal of hair.
Wherefrom, as he traveled in Greece and other countries reciting
his poems, he got his name.

Nor was there greater certainty on Homer's date. Our earliest
statement on the subject is Herodotus', who says (2.53) that both
Homer and Hesiod lived about 400 years before his own time. The
sober opinion of later antiquity, with which most moderns concur,
is that reflected in a Josephus passage (*Against Apion* 1.12):

Throughout the whole range of Greek literature no undisputed
work is found more ancient than the poetry of Homer. His date,
however, is clearly later than the Trojan War; and even he, they
say, did not leave his poems in writing. At first transmitted by
memory, the scattered songs were not united until later; to this
circumstance the numerous inconsistencies of the work are attributa-
ble.

Specimens of the arguments on the subject are given by Aulus Gellius (3.11). First Gellius quotes, with approval, arguments for the
priority of Homer; then he proceeds:

Accius, on the contrary, in the first book of his Didascalica, makes use of very weak arguments in his attempt to show that Hesiod was the elder: "Because Homer," he writes, "when he says at the beginning of his poem that Achilles was the son of Peleus, does not inform us who Peleus was; and this he unquestionably would have done, if he did not know that the information had already been given by Hesiod. Again, in the case of the Cyclops," says Accius, "he would not have failed to note such a striking characteristic and to make particular mention of the fact that he was one-eyed, were it not that this was equally well known from the poems of his predecessor Hesiod."

Accius to the contrary notwithstanding, Hesiod is the later poet, and it is with him that allusions to Homer begin. When the Muses say to Hesiod (*Theogony* 26 ff.), "We know how to speak many false things as though they were true, but we know, when we wish, to utter true things," it is surely Homer who represents the falsehood. And in the 7th century *Homeric Hymn to Apollo* (quoted also in Thucydides 3.104), the girls are bidden to answer, when they are asked who is the most delightful poet, "He is a blind man, and dwells in rocky Chios; his lays are evermore supreme." The first to name Homer is Xenophanes of Colophon (ca. 550 B.C.), and in a phrase which shows that he was already an antique and misty figure: "From the beginnings, according to Homer, for all have learned from him."

All continued to learn from him, as we saw in ch. 3, "The License to Teach," and as we can see from Xenophon (*Symposium* 4.6) where Niceratus, who had all his Homer by heart, says:

You know, doubtless, that the sage Homer has written about practically everything pertaining to man. Any one of you, therefore, who wishes to acquire the art of the householder, the political leader, or the general, or to become like Achilles or Ajax or Nestor or Odysseus, should seek my favor, for I understand all these things.

Since Homer's authority was so great, historians and moralists with more sophisticated standards found it necessary to "correct" his primitive views. So Herodotus (2.120) cannot believe that the Trojan war could have been fought for Helen's sake:

If Helen had been at Troy the inhabitants would, I think, have given her up to the Greeks, whether Paris consented to it or no. For surely neither Priam nor his family could have been so infatuated as to endanger their own persons, their children, and their city merely that Paris might possess Helen. . . . I do not believe that even if Priam himself had been married to her he would have declined to deliver her up, with the view of bringing the series of calamities to a close.

And so Thucydides (2.9), with greater sophistication:

I am inclined to think that Agamemnon succeeded in collecting the expedition, not because the suitors of Helen bound themselves by oath to Tyndareus, but because he was the most powerful king of his time. . . . It was because he inherited his power and was the greatest naval potentate of his time that he was able to assemble the expedition; and the other princes followed him, not from good will, but from fear.

Criticism on moral grounds took a similar course, with the apologists for Homer finally taking refuge, as we have seen, in allegorical interpretation. The moral objection voiced by Hesiod was echoed by the philosophers. In the 6th century Xenophanes complained that "Homer and Hesiod assigned to the gods all that is disgraceful and blameworthy among men—stealing and adultery and mutual deceit" (11b, Diels). When Pythagoras visited Hades he saw Homer and Hesiod enduring the punishments of the damned for what they had said about the gods (Diogenes Laertius 8.21), and Heraclitus used to say that "Homer deserved to be chased out of the lists and beaten with rods, and Archilochus likewise" (id. 9.1). The natural

issue of such criticism is Plato's exclusion of Homer from his ideal
state (Republic 2.377 f.; 10.598d ff.; 10.605e ff.) on the ground that
his unruly gods and unrestrained heroes set a bad educational example; of Homer's excellence as a poet Plato makes no question,
as we see in the following (Republic 10.606e):

When you meet with admirers of Homer who tell you that he has
been the educator of Hellas and that on questions of human conduct and culture he deserves to be constantly studied as a guide by
whom to regulate your whole life, it is well to give a friendly hearing
to such people, as entirely well-meaning according to their lights,
and you may acknowledge him to be the first and greatest of tragic
poets; but you must be quite sure that we can admit into our com-
monwealth only the poetry which celebrates the praises of the gods
and of good men. If you go further and admit the honeyed muse in
epic or in lyric verse, then pleasure and pain will usurp the sovereignty of law and of the principles always recognized by common
consent as the best.

It was when Aristotle asserted the legitimacy of poetic as against
historical truth (Poetics 24, 1460a) that such political and historical
strictures received their proper answer.

To Aristotle as to his world Homer is "the Poet" par excellence
(e.g., Poetics 22), and it was perhaps from Aristotle that Alexander
the Great acquired his great enthusiasm for Homer. Alexander
carried the Iliad about with him in a precious jeweled casket (Plutarch, Alexander 26), consciously modeled himself on Achilles, and
showed his impatience with pedants who claimed they could "correct" Homer's text. Alexander in turn communicated his enthusiasm to the generals who succeeded him; of Ptolemy IV Philopator
(221–204 B.C.) we know that he established a cult of Homer in
Alexandria (Aelian 13.22). It was at Alexandria that scholarly work
on Homer in the modern sense began; exegesis in the broader sense
began with the rhapsodes who recited the text. Zenodotus, who was
first head of the library at Alexandria under Ptolemy Philadelphus,
produced the first scientific edition of Homer. His text was based

on comparison of numerous manuscripts, and he marked lines he regarded spurious with a marginal *obelus*. His gauge of genuineness, however, took no consideration of the claims of historical propriety and of poetry; he rejected *Iliad* 3.423–26 because it is unbecoming for the goddess Aphrodite to carry a seat for the mortal Helen, and altered 4.88 because it is out of character for a goddess to endeavor to find the object of search. It was Zenodotus probably who first divided the poems into 24 books each. His edition was followed by those of Rhianus, Aristophanes of Byzantium, and Aristarchus. The precipitate of the great mass of Alexandrian work is to be found in the scholia and in the large commentaries of Eustathius, bishop of Salonica (1175–1192), which remained the principal subsidia for Homeric study until modern times.

Meanwhile Homer continued to be the prime ingredient in liberal education. The essay *On the Poetry of Homer* wrongly included in the corpus of Plutarch, shows admirably how a skillful teacher might interweave analysis of Homer's technical devices, narrative art, character delineation and the like to make his teaching ethically effective. Perhaps the best brief appreciation of Homer from the educational and aesthetic point of view is that of Quintilian (10.1.46–51), who gives him first and fullest place in his curriculum of readings:

Homer is like his own conception of Ocean, which he describes as the source of every stream and river; for he has given us a model and an inspiration for every department of eloquence. It will be generally admitted that no one has ever surpassed him in the sublimity with which he invests great themes or the propriety with which he handles small. He is at once luxuriant and concise, sprightly and serious, remarkable at once for his fullness and his brevity, and supreme not merely for poetic, but for oratorical power as well. For, to say nothing of his eloquence, which he shows in praise, exhortation and consolation, do not the ninth book containing the embassy to Achilles, the first describing the quarrel between the chiefs, or the speeches delivered by the counselors in the second, display all the rules of art to be followed in forensic or deliberative oratory? As regards the emotions, there can be no one so ill-educated as to deny that the poet was the master of all, tender and vehement alike. Again, in the few lines with which he introduces both of his epics, has he not, I will not say observed, but actually established the law which should govern the composition of the exordium? For, by his invocation of the goddesses believed to preside over poetry he wins the goodwill of his audience, by his statement of the greatness of his themes he excites their attention and renders them receptive by the briefness of his summary. Who can narrate more briefly than the hero who brings the news of Patroclus' death, or more vividly than he who describes the battle between the Curetes and the Aetolians? Then consider his similes, his amplifications, his illustrations, digressions, indications of fact, inferences, and all the other methods of proof and refutation which he employs. They are so numerous that the majority of writers on the principles of rhetoric have gone to his works for examples of all these things. And as for perorations, what can ever be equal to the prayers which Priam addresses to Achilles when he comes to beg for the body of his son? Again, does he not transcend the limits of human genius in his choice of words, his reflexions, figures, and the arrangement of his whole work, with the result that it requires a powerful mind, I will not say to imitate, for that is impossible, but even to appreciate his excellences? But he has in truth outdistanced all that have come after him in every department of eloquence, above all, he has outstripped all other writers of epic, the contrast in their case being especially striking owing to the similarity of the material with which they deal.

Like Dante and Shakespeare, Homer belongs to the ages, and in his pages various epochs have realized their own aspirations. Alexander the Great declared Homer to be the best and most reliable source of military science (Plutarch, Alexander 8); Horace found in him a moralist plainer and better than Chrysippus and Crantor (Epistles 1.2); in the 3rd century A.D. Porphyry saw in the Odyssean cave of the nymphs a Neoplatonic allegory (On the Cave of the Nymphs in the Odyssey); Montaigne finds all knowledge in him (2.36):

Having lived before ever the Sciences were redacted into strict rules and certaine observations, Homer had so perfect knowledge of them, that all those which since his time have labored to establish policies or Common-wealths, to manage warres, and to write either of Religion or Philosophy, in what Sect soever or of all Artes, have made use of him, as of an absolutely-perfect Master in the knowledge of all things; and of his Bookes, as of a Seminary, a Springgarden, or Storehouse of all kinds of sufficiency and learning.

Pope felt that the fire which is discerned in Vergil, flashes in Lucan and Statius, glows in Milton, and surprises us in Shakespeare, is found at its best only in Homer, "in him only it burns everywhere clearly and everywhere irresistibly" (Preface to *Iliad*).

Since the publication of F. A. Wolff's *Prolegomena to Homer* (1795) no student of ancient literature has been able to evade the Homeric question, and a word must be said of its history. Classical antiquity betrays no doubt that Homer was the author of *Iliad* and *Odyssey* and of no other poems. Reference to Homer as the author of other epics, specifically of poems in the Epic Cycle, are late and untrustworthy. Aristotle (*Poetics* 23) definitely dissociates such works from Homer, though he does speak of the burlesque *Margites* as Homer's. The separatist position (i.e., assigning *Iliad* and *Odyssey* to different authors) was first suggested in the Hellenistic age, and in the first instance in the form of a rhetorical paradox for the display of argumentative skill. That the separatists gained some credit is shown by the suggestions of "Longinus" (9) that *Iliad* was the work of Homer's youth and *Odyssey* of his old age.

Wolff went far beyond the separatist position. On the basis of Josephus, *Against Apion* 1.12 (cited above) and of ancient references to Pisistratus as having regularized the recitations of Homer, he maintained that the poems as we have them were stitched together (rhap- in "rhapsode" means "to sew") under Pisistratus. If

we descend to Byzantine times we do get an account of a Pisistra-
tian recension, somewhat as follows. When the original text of
Homer was lost, whether by fire or earthquake or flood, Pisistratus
offered rewards to any who would bring in verses of Homer they
might possess. Many batches were brought in, a few lines or a few
hundred at a time, and Pisistratus duly paid the rewards. He then
assembled a panel of 72 scholars, who were told off to select the
authentic verses and arrange them in order. The number 72 is a
clear enough indication that the story is but an echo of the Greek
recension of the Pentateuch, described in *Aristeas to Philocrates*
as having been carried out under Ptolemy Philadelphus. Whatever
its origin the story persisted and received embellishment. At any
rate Tzetzes (12th century) violently attacks a rival grammarian
named Heliodorus for propagating a similar story, and insists that
Pisistratus employed only four editors. But it is highly improbable
that Byzantines should be in possession of facts concerning Pisistratus about which all their predecessors are silent.

Wolff's successors produced a library of treatises, each of which
proved that certain portions of Homer were early and others late—
and none of which was in agreement with any other. Today not only
the Wolffians but even the separatists are largely discredited. As
an English scholar has remarked, six motor-bikes do not make a
Rolls-Royce. The reaction to conservatism has been led not so
much by scholars as by poets, who have maintained that the larger
concepts of the poems as well as their uniform excellence in detail
could derive only from a single poet.

One mark of Homer's towering position is that he could be
imitated in jest as well as in earnest. From the *Batrachomyomachia*,
or *Battle of the Frogs and the Mice*, which may be as early as the
6th century B.C., to Molly Seagrim's fierce encounters in the
churchyard, ridiculous characters have been made more ridiculous
by intentional misapplication of Homer's exalted manner. We do
not have centos of Homer like those of Vergil, but we know of
things more freakish. From Eustathius we learn that Tryphiodorus
wrote a "lipogrammatic" Odyssey; that is, the poem was rewritten
so that in each book the use of the letter by which the book was

numbered was avoided: there was no alpha in Book 1, no beta in Book 2, and so on. We hear too that one Timolaos wrote a Troica by inserting a line of his own after each line of the *Iliad*. Suidas says that Idaios doubled Homer by adding alternate lines of his own. Pigres, the brother of the famous Artemisia of Halicarnassus, inserted an elegiac line after each hexameter of Homer. Joshua Barnes published a Greek *Susias* on the story of Esther (London, 1629) in close imitation of the *Iliad*. In the first line "Haman son of Amalek" takes the place of "Achilles son of Peleus"; in the second "Hebrews" supplants "Achaeans"; in the third "mighty heads of Persians" stands for "many mighty souls," and so on. Bentley remarked that "Barnes had as much Greek, and understood it about as well, as an Athenian blacksmith." From what we can surmise of Athenian blacksmiths the remark is not so cavalier as it was evidently intended to be.

III. THE EPIC CYCLE

Homer cannot have been at once the originator of the techniques of heroic poetry and their sovereign master; but of Homer's predecessors in the field we know nothing, and of his followers very little more. A great mass of heroic poetry, almost all presupposing the existence of *Iliad* and *Odyssey*, was grouped together under the designation of Epic Cycle. It is from the material of the Cycle that such supplements to the Homeric story as are found in the second and third books of the *Aeneid* and in the *Post-Homerica* of Quintus of Smyrna derive. Notices of these poems in Photius and other Byzantine writers depend on the (lost) *Chrestomathy* of Proclus (a 2nd century grammarian, not the 5th century Neoplatonist) which in turn doubtless depended on an earlier anthology. The Alexandrians worked on these poems and probably gave them the name Cycle. The titles, authors, and lengths of the poems of the Cycle are curiously, if imperfectly, preserved for us on a stone called the *Tabula Borgiaca* (or *Iliaca*), which has reliefs illustrating the stories.

IV. HOMERIC HYMNS

The Homeric hymns are surely among the finest literary productions of Greece, and their virtual neglect by the Alexandrian antiquarians is something of a puzzle. In the MS tradition they are often associated with the hymns of Callimachus, which may account for the belated recognition given them in modern times. The finest of the hymns, indeed, that to Demeter, is extant only in a Moscow MS which was discovered at the end of the 18th century. But there can be no doubt of the genuineness or antiquity of any of the longer hymns and, indeed, a section of the hymn to Apollo is quoted by no less a writer than Thucydides. To demonstrate the antiquity of the Delian festival Thucydides (3.104) cites lines 146–50 and 165–72 of the *Hymn to Apollo:*

The character of the festival is attested by Homer in the following verses, which are taken from the hymn to Apollo:

> At other times, Phoebus, Delos is dearest to thy heart,
> Where are gathered together the Ionians in flowing robes,
> With their wives and children in the street:
> There do they delight thee with boxing and dancing and song,
> Making mention of thy name at the meeting of the assembly.

And that there were musical contests which attracted competitors is implied in the following words of the same hymn. After commemorating the Delian dance of women, Homer ends their praises with these lines, in which he alludes to himself:

> And now may Apollo and Artemis be gracious,
> And to all of you, maidens, I say farewell.
> Yet remember me when I am gone;
> And if some other toiling pilgrim among the sons of men
> Comes and asks: O maidens,
> Who is the sweetest minstrel of all who wander hither,
> And in whom do you delight most?
> Make answer with one voice, in gentle words,
> The blind old man of Chios' rocky isle.

Thus far Homer, who clearly indicates that even in days of old there was a gathering and festival at Delos.

Thucydides apparently makes no question of the Homeric authorship of the hymns, and later allusions similarly ascribe them to Homer. The first citation in which Homer is not positively given as the author is Athenaeus (226), who quotes two lines from the hymn to Apollo as "by Homer or one of the Homeridae."

V. HESIOD

The relative ages of Homer and Hesiod were a continuing subject for dispute. Herodotus calmly (2.53.2) said that both lived about 400 years before his own time. As the centuries went on the question generated more heat; there is a revealing note in Pausanias (9.30.3):

As to the age of Hesiod and Homer, I have conducted very careful researches into this matter, but I do not like to write on the subject, as I know the quarrelsome nature of those especially who constitute the modern school of epic criticism.

It is Pausanias who summarizes for us what ancient tradition knew of Hesiod. The principal passage is 9.31.3 ff.:

On Helicon tripods have been dedicated, of which the oldest is the one which it is said Hesiod received for winning the prize for song at Chalcis on the Euripus. Men too live round about the grove, and here the Thespians celebrate a festival, and also games called the Museia. . . . The Boeotians dwelling around Helicon hold the tradition that Hesiod wrote nothing but the Works, and even of this they reject the prelude to the Muses, saying that the poem begins with the account of the Strifes. They showed me also tablets of lead where the spring is, mostly defaced by time, on which is engraved the Works.

The story of the leaden tablets cannot be dismissed. It is entirely probable that such a relic should be preserved at Helicon, and

though they can scarcely have been as old as Hesiod, they do point
to a firm local tradition. The story of his death, as of the contest at
Chalcis, is constantly repeated. Thucydides tells (3.96) us that
Hesiod "is said to have been killed by the inhabitants at the temple
of Nemean Zeus in fulfilment of an oracle which foretold that he
should die at Nemea." There was no occasion for Thucydides to
refer to Hesiod's supposed crime against hospitality which caused
death, and his silence is no proof that he was ignorant of it. The
story is told most fully in a speech attributed to Solon in Plutarch's
Dinner of the Seven Sages, 162c ff.:

*Well, it is really worth hearing, and so here it is. A man from Miletus,
it seems, with whom Hesiod shared lodging and entertainment in
Locris, had secret relations with the daughter of the man who entertained them; and when he was detected, Hesiod fell under suspicion
of having known about the misconduct from the outset, and of
having helped to conceal it, although he was in nowise guilty, but
only the innocent victim of a fit of anger and prejudice. For the
girl's brothers killed him, lying in wait for him in the vicinity of the
temple of Nemean Zeus in Locris, and with him they killed his
servant whose name was Troilus. The dead bodies were shoved out
into the sea, and the body of Troilus, borne out into the current of
the river Daphnus, was caught on a wave-washed rock projecting a
little above the sea-level; and even to this day the rock is called
Troilus. The body of Hesiod, as soon as it left the land, was taken
up by a company of dolphins, who conveyed it to Rhium hard by
Molycreia. It happened that the Locrians' periodic Rhian sacrifice
and festal gathering was being held then, which even nowadays
they celebrate in a noteworthy manner at that place. When the body
was seen being carried towards them, they were naturally filled with
astonishment, and ran down to the shore; recognizing the corpse,
which was still fresh, they held all else to be of secondary importance
in comparison with investigating the murder, on account of the
repute of Hesiod. This they quickly accomplished, discovered the
murderers, sank them alive in the sea, and razed their house to the
ground. Hesiod was buried near the temple of Nemean Zeus; most*

foreigners do not know about his grave, but it has been kept concealed, because, as they say, it was sought for by the people of Orchomenos, who wished, in accordance with an oracle, to recover the remains and bury them in their own land.

The circumstances of the double burial are elaborated in Pausanias 9.38.3 ff.:

There are graves of Minyas and Hesiod at Orchomenus. They say that they thus recovered the bones of Hesiod. A pestilence fell on men and beasts, so that they sent envoys to the god. To these, it is said, the Pythian priestess made answer that to bring the bones of Hesiod from the land of Naupactus to the land of Orchomenus was their one and only remedy. Whereupon the envoys asked a further question, where in the land of Naupactus they would find the bones; to which the Pythian priestess answered again that a crow would indicate to them the place. So when the envoys landed, they saw, it is said, a rock not far from the road, with the bird upon the rock; the bones of Hesiod they found in a cleft of the rock.

For the burial at Orchomenus we have very ancient evidence. Chersios of Orchomenus (ca. 7th century B.C.) has the following sepulchral epigram (A.P. 7.54):

Ascra, the land of broad corn-fields, was my country, but the land of the charioteer Minyae (Orchomenus) holds my bones now I am dead. I am Hesiod, the most glorious in the eyes of the world of men who are judged by the test of wisdom.

And a couplet almost certainly Pindar's (frg. 238, Bergk) says:

Hail, Hesiod, twice blooming with youth and twice obtaining burial: thou didst hold the measure of wisdom for mankind.

The Contest of Homer and Hesiod (323) tells substantially the same tale of Hesiod's death, but quotes Eratosthenes' Hesiod to the effect that the seduction was committed not by Hesiod but by one Demades who was traveling with him, and that the girl hanged herself. Tzetzes' full account of Hesiod's death, finally, makes Hesiod responsible for the seduction and says that the son of the union was the poet Stesichorus.

VI. OTHER EARLY DIDACTIC POETS

For the 6th century gnomic poet Phocylides, our best testimony comes from Dio Chrysostom (36.11 ff.):

As for Phocylides, while you people do not know him, as you state, for all that he is certainly rated among the famous poets. Therefore, just as, when a merchant sails into your port who has never been there before, you do not immediately scorn him, but, on the contrary, having first tasted his wine and sampled any other merchandise in his cargo, you buy it if it suits your taste, otherwise you pass it by; just so with the poetry of Phocylides you may take a sample of small compass. For he is not one of those who string together a long and continuous poem, as your Homer does, who uses more than five thousand verses of continuous narration in describing a single battle; on the contrary, the poems of Phocylides have both beginning and end in two or three verses. And so he adds his name to each sentiment, in the belief that it is a matter of interest and great importance, in so doing behaving quite differently from Homer, who nowhere in his poetry names himself. Or don't you think Phocylides had good reason for attaching his name to a maxim and declaration such as this?

> This too the saying of Phocylides:
> The law-abiding town, though small and set
> On a lofty rock, outranks mad Nineveh.

Why, in comparison with the entire Iliad and Odyssey are not these verses noble to those who pay heed as they listen? Or was it more to your advantage to hear of the impetuous leaping and charging of

Achilles, and about his voice, how by his shouts alone he routed the Trojans? Are those things more useful for you to learn by heart than what you just have heard, that a small city on a rugged headland is better and more fortunate, if orderly, than a great city in a smooth and level plain, that is to say, if that city is conducted in disorderly and lawless fashion by men of folly?

Not much more than the quotation in this passage is preserved from Phocylides. There is a 230-line piece, in bad hexameters, with virtual quotations from the Pentateuch, which is doubtless the work of a Jewish writer of the Hellenistic age seeking to obtain currency for his doctrine by clothing it in a classical dress.

The 6th century saw a number of literary expressions of religious mysticism. We know most (from Herodotus 4.13–16) about Aristeas of Proconnesus who wrote a poem on the Arimaspeans. According to Herodotus Aristeas was able to separate himself from his body, leaving the latter in a semblance of death while he himself went elsewhere, perhaps in other than human shape, to spread his gospel. Most active were the Orphics, whose leading spirit seems to have been Onomacritus. Of him Herodotus (7.6) tells us that he "set forth the prophecies of Musaeus in their order" and that he was banished from the court of the Pisistratids when Lasus of Hermione (said to have been a teacher of Pindar) caught him foisting spurious lines into the writings of Musaeus.

Theology of a philosophical character was initiated by Xenophanes of Colophon (570–478 B.C.) who was a critic of conventional thought and conduct, and especially of Homer's and Hesiod's views of the gods. His life and doctrines are summarized in Diogenes Laertius 9.18–20 and his longer fragments are all from Athenaeus (11.462c, 10.4.13 f., 12.526a). A more systematic thinker, and a physician and statesman as well, is Empedocles of Agrigentum (484–424 B.C.). The long account in Diogenes Laertius (9.51–77) contains the various traditions of his spectacular life, and also of his theatrical death (69). A sacrifice was being performed to celebrate Empedocles' cure of a woman who had been given up by the physicians, and Empedocles rose up and walked towards Etna.

Then when he had reached it he plunged into the fiery craters and disappeared, his intention being to confirm the report that he had become a god. Afterwards the truth was known, because one of his slippers was thrown up in the flames; it had been his custom to wear slippers of bronze.

Parmenides of Elea (fl. 500) is often associated with Xenophanes and Empedocles as a philosopher in verse. Though his poem opened with a kind of apocalyptic vision which might invite legendary embellishment none seems to be recorded. What similitude we have of the man comes from Plato's *Parmenides*.

9: *Greek Lyric: Chanted, Sung, or Danced*

I. THE ELEGIAC POETS

THE EPIC POET STANDS DETACHED FROM HIS matter, and other writers of hexameter verse (except for Hesiod, who speaks in the first person and tells us much about himself) followed the convention of heroic poetry. The main distinction of lyric, aside from meter, is its subjectivity, and the remains of lyric, where they are of any extent, tell us a good deal about the poets—and have provided a basis for much ancient embroidery. Least revealing, among work broadly classified as lyric, are the elegiac poets, whose object was general admonition; the iambic poets, who indulged in personal invective, reveal more of their own personalities; and most revealing of all are the writers of solo or true lyric, whose main theme is their private perceptions of their world.

Dimmest of all are the authors of the war songs which every Spartan soldier learned in his youth. Callinus of Ephesus (7th century B.C.) is mentioned, with reference to the Cimmerian invasions of Asia Minor, by Strabo (13.604, 627; 14.647); his one extant poem, frequently translated, is in Photius. Tyrtaeus (7th century), the Spartan poet, is the subject of a familiar legend. Plato, Laws 628, mentions that Tyrtaeus was an Athenian who was given Spartan citizenship, and the scholiast explains:

This Tyrtaeus was an obscure Athenian, being a lame schoolmaster, thought little of at Athens. When the Spartans had come to their wits' end in fighting the Messenians, they were told by Apollo's oracle to fetch this man; he would be able to make them see what was to their advantage. Indeed the oracle bade them make him their adviser. When he arrived in Lacedaemon he became inspired, and urged them to renew the war by all and every means in his power, including the well-known line "Messene is good to plough and good to plant." This then is the man mentioned by the Athenian Stranger as an example of one who counseled war.

Essentially the same account appears in Pausanias 4.15.6, and Polyaenus 1.17 adds an instance of Tyrtaeus' military leadership:

When the Spartans were about to engage the Messenians, and, having resolved to conquer or die, had inscribed each man's name on a letter-stick attached to the left hand so that his friends could recognize him when the dead were taken up for burial, Tyrtaeus, desiring to strike terror into the Messenians by letting them know what the Spartans had done, gave orders that no great heed should be taken of deserting Helots, and the watch being relaxed these deserted as they chose, and told the Messenians of the desperate valor of their enemies. Terror weakened their resistance, and it was not long before they had given the Spartans the victory.

One suspects that the lame schoolmaster story is an Athenian invention, and the suspicion grows when we notice that a passage on Tyrtaeus in Athenaeus (14.630e) gives the Athenian Philochorus as a source:

The warlike character of the pyrrhic dance proves it a Spartan invention. The Lacedaemonians are a warlike people, and not only do their sons learn by rote the Embateria or Songs of the Battle-Charge which are also called Enoplia or Songs-under-Arms, but in war they themselves recite the poems of Tyrtaeus from memory and move in time to them. We are told by Philochorus that after the Spartans had defeated the Messenians by the generalship of Tyrtaeus, they made it the custom of their military expeditions that when the Paean had been sung after supper the songs of Tyrtaeus should be given one by each man, the polemarch to decide who sang the best and give the winner a prize of meat.

Mimnermus of Colophon (7th century) became the type of the soft singer of love, as we can see from a line in Horace (*Epistles* 1.6.65) which alludes to Mimnermus' most frequently quoted line: "If, as Mimnermus believes, nothing is agreeable without love and frolic, then you should live in love and frolic." Propertius, deprecating epic poetry, says (1.9.11) that "in love Mimnermus' lines count for more than Homer's." Athenaeus (13.597 f.) quotes an epigram by Hermesianax:

Mimnermus after much suffering found sweet sound and breath in the soft pentameter; he loved Nanno and often filled the gray lotus-wood (of the flute) to make revel. . . .

A couplet of Mimnermus, according to a story told in Diogenes Laertius (1.60–61), provoked a retort from Solon. Mimnermus had written

> *Would that by no disease, no cares opprest,*
> *I in my sixtieth year were laid to rest.*

Solon protested, as follows:

> *O take a friend's suggestion, blot the line,*
> *Grudge not if my invention better thine;*
> *Surely a wiser wish were thus expressed*
> *At eighty years let me be laid to rest.*

As in a sense the founder of Athenian democracy, Solon (ca. 640–560) was a revered object of legend and in particular served as hero for anecdotes which illustrated the peculiar virtues of Athenian democracy. Thus Herodotus 1.29 ff. uses the doubtless apocryphal encounter with Croesus to point the contrast between Greek and oriental views of life, and Aristotle, in the *Constitution of Athens* (6 ff.) analyzes his democratic legislation. As founder of the Athenian democracy many legends gathered about Solon. Of chief interest here are those which tell of how he presented his political poems, either himself or through a herald, with dramatic circumstances. For instance, when the question of the recovery of Salamis arose (Diogenes Laertius 1.2.46),

Solon, feigning madness, rushed into the agora with a garland on his head; there he had his poem on Salamis read to the Athenians by a herald and roused them to fury.

Plutarch's *Life* of Solon is the best presentation of what the ancients knew and believed of Solon. From Solon's own poems which Plutarch uses, it is possible to reconstruct the main outlines of his career.

Theognis (6th century B.C.) gives plain enough indication of his aristocratic bias and his belief in blood and breed. He is mentioned as a salutary teacher of morals by a number of writers, beginning with Isocrates and Plato. Stobaeus (88.14) quotes from a treatise on him by Xenophon, and Diogenes Laertius (6.15) lists a book on Theognis by Antisthenes. Aristotle quotes him several times (*Nicomachean Ethics* 1129b, 1179b; *Eudemian Ethics* 1214a), and Plutarch (*On Listening to Poetry* 23b) mentioned him among didactic writers who "borrow meter and dignity from poetry as it were a carriage, to avoid going on foot."

II. THE IAMBIC POETS

In later writers the term "iambic" signifies scurrilous invective. That connotation was given to the word by Archilochus (7th century B.C.), the first and greatest of the iambic poets. Archilochus is mentioned frequently by writers from Pindar onwards. At *Pythian* 2.99 Pindar has

Standing afar, I saw Archilochus the scold, laboring helpless and fattening on his own cantankerous hate, naught else.

Archilochus' character is fixed for most readers by lines of Horace—*Epode* 1.19.23 ff., *Ars Poetica* 79, *Epodes* 6.13. The latter passage reads

Beware, beware! I'm a tough fellow with horns ready for the wicked, like him to whom the false Lycambes would not give his daughter, or him that was so fierce a foe to Bupalus.

The scholiast explains:

He means Archilochus, who attacked Lycambes so bitterly with abusive verses that he committed suicide. Archilochus attacked him because he denied him his daughter's hand after promising it.

Aristotle (Rhetoric 1398b) says that "the Parians honored Archilochus despite his slanderous tongue," but Valerius Maximus (6.3. Ext. 1) tells us

The Spartans ordered that the books of Archilochus should be removed from their state because they considered them indecent, and would not have their children indoctrinated with writings which might do more harm to their morals than good to their wits.

Plutarch, On Music 28, and sundry grammarians naturally speak of Archilochus' metrical innovations. Archilochus' violent death is mentioned by Plutarch, On Delayed Retribution 17, and in Dio Chrysostom's oration on Archilochus (33.397):

The man who killed him was driven from his temple by Apollo, who gave answer that he had slain a servitor of the Muses, and when he protested that it was in war, said again "Archilochus a servitor of the Muses"; moreover when the poet's father had enquired of the God before his birth, Apollo had foretold that he would beget a son who should be immortal.

Appreciations of Archilochus' poetry are given by Quintilian 10.1.59—

Thus out of the three iambic writers of Aristarchus' canon, the writer that attains the highest degree of facility is Archilochus, in whom we find the greatest force of expression, a phrasing not only telling but terse and vigorous, and abundance of blood and muscle; indeed some critics hold that where he falls short it is a defect rather of his theme than of his genius.

and by "Longinus" 33.4—

Eratosthenes in the Erigone, in every respect a flawless little poem—
is he a greater poet than Archilochus, who carries along with his
flood so much which is lacking in arrangement and yet comes from
the almost uncontrollable inflow of the divine spirit?

In matching his poets to flowers Meleager (A.P. 4.1) likens Archilochus to the thistle. The Anthology also contains a number of
epigrams on Archilochus. Here is one by Leonidas (7.664):

Stand and look on Archilochus, the iambic poet of old times, whose
vast renown reached to the night and to the dawn. Verily did the
Muses and Delian Apollo love him; so full of melody was he, so
skilled to write verse and to sing it to the lyre.

And here is another by Gaetulicus (7.71):

This tomb by the sea is that of Archilochus, who first made the
Muse bitter dipping her in vipers' gall, staining mild Helicon with
blood. Lycambes knows it, mourning for his three daughters
hanged. Pass quietly by, O wayfarer, lest haply thou arouse the wasps
that are settled on his tomb.

With Archilochus it is natural to group Semonides, and in the most
interesting of the allusions to the latter he is grouped with the
former (Lucian, Liar 2):

I know too well that your life has been marked by innumerable
deeds worthy of satire, deeds such that I believe Archilochus himself
could not cope with even one of them, though he should call in the
aid of Semonides and Hipponax. Why, their satires—Orodoecides,
Lycambes, Bupalus—you have made mere child's play of every sort
of beastliness.

III. SOLO LYRIC

Elegy and iamb were intoned, to the accompaniment of flute and
lyre respectively. True lyric, whether solo or choral, was sung or

sung and danced. The true lyric poet, as the genre implies, speaks
not only in his own person but mainly of his own feelings. The line
between solo and choral is not sharp; Sappho, Alcaeus and Anacreon
wrote only solo lyric; Terpander, Alcman, Stesichorus, and Simonides wrote choral lyric as well.

Our first name in lyric is Terpander, whose technical innovations
are mentioned by many writers and discussed most fully in Plutarch, On Music. Terpander was from Lesbos, but like Tyrtaeus he
was summoned to Sparta, as Aelian 12.50 records:

*The Spartans, whose bent was for bodily exercises and feats of arms,
had no skill in music. Yet if ever they required the aid of the Muses
on occasion of general sickness of body or mind or any like public
affliction, their custom was to send for foreigners, at the bidding of
the Delphic oracle, to act as healers or purifiers. For instance they
summoned Terpander, Thales, Tyrtaeus, Nymphaeus of Cydonia,
and Alcman.*

And like Tyrtaeus', Terpander's songs became a kind of scripture
which helots were forbidden to sing (Plutarch, Lycurgus 28):

*When the Thebans made their expedition into Laconia [369 B.C.]
they ordered the helots whom they captured to sing the songs of
Terpander, Alcman, and Spendon the Spartan; but the helots declined to do so, on the plea that their masters did not allow it, thus
proving the correctness of the saying: "In Sparta the freeman is more
a freeman than anywhere else in the world, and the slave more a
slave."*

Alcman too is said to have been a newcomer in Sparta, as the
epigram of Antipater (A.P. 7.18) shows:

*Do not judge the man by the stone. Simple is the tomb to look on,
but holds the bones of a great man. Thou shalt know Alcman the
supreme striker of the Laconian lyre, possessed by the nine Muses.
Here resteth he, a cause of dispute to two continents, if he be a
Lydian or a Spartan. Minstrels have many mothers.*

The only personal idiosyncrasy of Alcman's recorded besides those which he himself mentions, is that he (and Pherecydes the Syrian) were subject to *morbus pedicularis* (Aristotle, *History of Animals* 557a).

Sappho (b. ca. 612) retained her primacy throughout antiquity. Only because Charaxus was Sappho's brother does Herodotus (2.135) find it worth mentioning that he was enamored of Rhodopis. Plato called her a tenth muse (A.P. 9.506):

Some say there are nine Muses; but they should stop to think. Look at Sappho of Lesbos; she makes a tenth.

An intelligent analogy to Socrates is given by Maximus of Tyre (24 [18]):

The love of the fair Lesbian, if it is right to argue from one age to another, was surely the same as the art of love pursued by Socrates. They both appear to me to have practised the same sort of friendship, he of males, she of females, both declaring that their beloved were many in number and that they were captivated by all beautiful persons. What Alcibiades, Charmides, and Phaedrus were to him, Gyrinna, Atthis, and Anactoria were to her, and what his rival craftsmen, Prodicus, Gorgias, Thrasymachus and Protagoras were to Socrates, that Gorgo and Andromeda were to Sappho, who sometimes takes them to task and at others refutes them and dissembles with them exactly like Socrates.

Socrates called Sappho beautiful, Maximus says, "only because her verse was beautiful; she herself was small and dark." Lucian's *Portraits* (18) suggest Sappho as a model for refinement of character, and the scholiast remarks:

Physically Sappho was very ill-favored, being small and dark, like a nightingale with ill-shapen wings enfolding a tiny body.

The traditional connection of Sappho with the Leucadian Leap is explained in Strabo 10.2.9:

The Leucadian Cliff contains the temple of Apollo Leucatas, and also the "Leap," which was believed to put an end to the longings of love. "Where Sappho is said to have been the first," as Menander says, "when through frantic longing she was chasing the haughty Phaon, to fling herself with a leap from the far-seen rock, calling upon thee in prayer, O lord and master." Now although Menander says that Sappho was the first to take the leap, yet those who are better versed than he in antiquities say that it was Cephalus, who was in love with Pterelas the son of Deioneus. It was an ancestral custom among the Leucadians, every year at the sacrifice performed in honor of Apollo, for some criminal to be flung from this rocky look-out for the sake of averting evil, wings and birds of all kinds being fastened to him, since by their fluttering they could lighten the leap, and also for a number of men, stationed all round below the rock in small fishing-boats, to take the victim in, and, when he had been taken on board, to do all in their power to get him safely outside their borders.

On Sappho's high merits all ancient critics are unanimous. In Meleager's list (A.P. 4.1) Sappho's poems are entered as "few, but roses." Plutarch, *Amatorius* 18 has:

Sappho utters words really mingled with fire, and gives vent through her song to the heat that consumes her heart, thus "healing" in the words of Philoxenus "the pain of love with the melodies of the Muse."

The two complete poems we have we owe to their being cited as illustration by critics. *To Aphrodite* is cited by Dionysius of Halicarnassus (*Composition* 23) as an example of the finished and brilliant style. Dionysius comments:

The verbal beauty and the charm of this passage lie in the cohesion
and smoothness of the joinery. Word follows word inwoven according to certain natural affinities and groupings of the letters.

Peer of the Gods He Seems to Me is cited by "Longinus" (10) to
show that the source of the sublime is "the invariable choice of the
most suitable ideas and the power to make these a whole by com-
bining them together." After giving the text "Longinus" adds:

*Is it not marvelous how she has recourse at once to spirit, body,
hearing, tongue, sight, flesh, all as quite separate things, and by contraries both freezes and burns, raves and is sane, and indeed is afraid
she is nearly dead, so that she expresses not one emotion but a con-
course of emotions? Now all such things are characteristic of the
lover, but it is the choice, as I said, of the best and the combination
of them into a single whole, that has produced the excellence of the
piece.*

Medieval knowledge of Sappho derived chiefly from Ovid's imaginary *Epistle of Sappho to Phaon*, one of the most attractive of the
Heroides (No. 15). Another passage which would make her name
and fame known to Greekless readers is Cicero's excoriation of
Verres (*Verrine* 2.4.57) for having stolen from the Syracusans a
highly prized statue of the poetess.

Sappho's fellow Lesbian Alcaeus was concerned in politics and
revolution. Herodotus 5.95 mentions his escape from battle with
the loss of his shield, and Diogenes Laertius 1.74 supplies details of
the war. Horace, *Odes* 1.32, summarizes Alcaeus' subjects as "Bacchus and the Muses, Venus and her inseparable boy, the beautiful
Lycus, dark of eye and hair." More characteristically Roman are the
judgments of Cicero and Quintilian. In *Tusculan Disputations* 4.71
Cicero says:

*Alcaeus was a brave man and eminent in the state to which he be-
longed, and yet what extravagant things he says of the love of
youths!*

And Quintilian 10.1 has:

Alcaeus is rightly awarded the "golden quill" in that part of his works where he assails the tyrants; his ethical value too is great, and his style is concise, lofty, exact, and very like Homer's; but he stoops to jesting and love-making though better fitted for higher themes.

The legend that Stesichorus was a grandson of Hesiod (q.v.) is refuted on chronological grounds by Cicero, *De republica* 2.20 and Tzetzes, *Life of Hesiod* 18. A more accurate dating and something of the nature of the man is suggested by a story in Aristotle's *Rhetoric* (2.1393b):

When the people of Himera had made Phalaris military dictator, and were going to give him a bodyguard, Stesichorus wound up a long talk by telling them the fable of the horse who had a field all to himself. Presently there came a stag and began to spoil his pasturage. The horse, wishing to revenge himself on the stag, asked a man if he could help him to do so. The man said, "Yes, if you will let me bridle you and get on to your back with javelins in my hand." The horse agreed, and the man mounted; but instead of getting his revenge on the stag, the horse found himself the slave of the man. "You too," said Stesichorus, "take care lest, in your desire for revenge on your enemies, you meet the same fate as the horse. By making Phalaris military dictator, you have already let yourselves be bridled. If you let him get on to your backs by giving him a bodyguard, from that moment you will be his slaves."

The Palinode story, alluded to in earlier writers, is given succinctly in Suidas:

It is said that for writing abuse of Helen he was struck blind, but received his sight again on writing an encomium of her in obedience to a dream. This encomium is known as the Palinode. He was called Stesichorus because he first set up choruses of singers to the lyre, his original name being Teisias.

The story of Socrates' appreciation is suspicious because it is so like a story of Solon and Croesus and because it occurs only in so late a writer as Ammianus (38.4):

The story goes that Socrates, when awaiting in prison the execution of his sentence, heard a man perform with some skill a song of the lyric poet Stesichorus, and begged him to teach it him that he might sing it before it was too late, and when the musician asked him what could be the use of it replied "I want to die knowing something more."

Ancient criticism is summarized for us by Quintilian (10.1.62):

The strength of Stesichorus' genius is shown among other things by his subject-matter. He sings of great wars and famous chieftains, sustaining all the weight of epic poetry with a lyre. Indeed he gives his characters the dignity that belongs to them both in speech and action, and if he had only kept within proper bounds might well have been counted a good second to Homer; but he is redundant and extravagant, though indeed these are the faults of a well-stored mind.

Ibycus' fame rests largely on the story of the cranes, which Schiller, for one, made famous. The story is alluded to in several ancient writers and is the subject of a neat epigram by Antipater of Sidon (A.P. 7.745). Plutarch has it in his essay On Garrulity 14:

Were not the murderers of Ibycus taken as they sat in the theater whispering with smiles together, at the sight of some cranes, that yonder were the avengers of Ibycus? For the spectators near by heard what they said, and though Ibycus had long disappeared and been mourned for dead, took up the matter of this speech and reported it to the ruling authority. Whereupon they were convicted and forthwith executed, not indeed that they were punished by the cranes, but rather compelled by their own garrulity as by some Fury or Doom-Goddess to confess to the murder they had committed.

Anacreon, we learn from Herodotus (3.121) and others who draw from him, was a familiar of Polycrates of Samos. In [Plato], *Hipparchus* 228b we read how he was invited to Athens:

Hipparchus, the eldest and wisest of the sons of Pisistratus, among other fine ways showed his wisdom not only in being the first to bring the words of Homer to this country and compelling the minstrels, as my friends here still do, to recite them in relays from beginning to end at the Panathenaic Festival, but in sending a fifty-oared galley to fetch Anacreon of Teos to Athens, and in inducing Simonides of Ceos by high pay and valuable presents to be in continual attendance upon him. This he did in order to educate his fellow-citizens and make them loyal subjects, because he believed, like a true man of culture, that wit and wisdom should never be despised.

Pausanias 1.25.1 speaks of his statue there:

On the Athenian Acropolis there are statues of Pericles son of Xanthippus and his father also who fought the Persians at Mycale. Near Xanthippus stands Anacreon of Teos, the first poet excepting Sappho of Lesbos to make his chief theme love. The statue represents him as one singing in his cups.

In Copenhagen there is a handsome statue of Anacreon, represented as singing and playing the lyre, with a large fibula pinned through his male member. There was an ancient belief that sexual indulgence spoiled a singer's voice, and infibulation (as we learn from Juvenal 6.73, 379) was a device to prevent sexual activity. Maximus of Tyre (21.7) has a revealing anecdote:

Anacreon, the poet of Teos, is said to have been punished by Love in the following way. One day at the Pan-Ionian Festival a nurse was carrying a baby in the Ionian Meeting-Place, when Anacreon came along tipsy and shouting, with a wreath on his head, and stumbling against the woman and her charge let fall some words of abuse. *The indignant nurse contented herself with expressing a pious wish that the very scoundrel who now cursed the child should live to praise him in still stronger terms—which indeed was the fact; for the God heard her prayer and, the child growing to be lovely Cleobulus, Anacreon expiated a little curse with manifold praise.*

The most highly respected sage among the lyric poets was Simonides, whose lines on the heroes of Thermopylae, quoted in Herodotus 7.228, are among the most widely known from antiquity. Plato several times (e.g., *Protagoras, Republic* 1.331e) uses lines of Simonides as texts. According to the *Life* of Aeschylus, Simonides defeated him in obtaining the commission for the elegy to commemorate the heroes of Marathon. He knew Themistocles, as appears from a story in Plutarch (*Themistocles* 5):

When Simonides made an improper request of Themistocles during the time of his command, he retorted that he would not be a good statesman if he put favor before law, any more than Simonides would be a good poet if sang out of tune.

Aristotle (*Rhetoric* 3.2, 1405b) has a fine story to illustrate Simonides' practical wit:

Simonides, when the winner of the mule race offered him a small fee, declined to write, on the ground that he did not like to write about half-asses. But when the pay was made enough, he wrote: "Hail, daughters of wind-swift steeds!"

Much of the gossip concerning Simonides is directed at his cupidity, and apparently comes from rivals who were no less mercenary. At *Peace* 697 Aristophanes has Trygaeus remark that Sophocles was changing to Simonides because "now being old and decayed he'd go sailing on a raft for profit." The scholiast explains:

Simonides seems to have been the first to connect poetry with meanness of disposition and to write it for pay; which is what Pindar hints at in his Isthmians [2.10], where he says, "For the Muse was no seeker of gain then, nor worked for hire."

On the Pindar passage the scholiast notes:

He means that nowadays they compose victory-songs for pay, a custom begun by Simonides.

Simonides' penury is dealt with in a papyrus (*Hibeh Pap.* 17) of the 3rd century B.C.:

The following sayings of Simonides are also esteemed for their truth to nature. When asked by the wife of Hiero if all things grew old, he replied "Yes, all, except love of gain; and acts of kindness sooner than anything else." Again, when he was asked why he was so penurious, he answered that it was because he got more vexation from debit than from credit; either was really negligible, though both derived importance from the passions and unreasonableness of men; and so neither of them did him any harm, or, strictly speaking, any good; but it was irksome to use another man's staff instead of one's own; moreover, borrowed money might cost little at the moment, but in the end it cost twice as much; and so we ought to count every penny. Lastly he declared that when he consumed only the necessary and natural food of man, simple food like that of the animals, he was borrowing from himself.

Theocritus (16.34.41 ff.) protests that his great predecessor gave his employers more than full value:

> They had lain forgotten of all men
> Ever and evermore with the rest of the pitiful dead folk,
> Had not a Cean bard, that wondrous and changeful singer,
> Wed to the varying tones of his harp their names as a glory
> Told to a later race.

Here are two anecdotes illustrating Simonides' frugality:

When Hiero's wife asked Simonides, "Which is best, to be rich or wise?" "Rich," he said, "for I see that the wise spend their time at the doorstep of the rich" (Aristotle, Rhetoric 2.1391a).

As a matter of fact, Chamaeleon declares, Simonides was a skinflint and greedy for gain. In Syracuse, for example, Hiero would send him general supplies for his daily needs, but Simonides would sell the greater part of what the king sent him, keeping only a small portion for himself. When somebody asked him the reason he replied, "I want to show at once Hiero's munificence and my own abstemiousness" (Athenaeus 14.656d).

Here are other specimens of his wit:

Simonides said that he had often repented speaking but had never repented holding his tongue (Plutarch, Garrulity 507a).

When Simonides saw a guest sitting silent he exclaimed: "If you're a fool, your behavior is wise; if you're wise you're a fool" (Plutarch, Dinner Talk 3 proem).

Simonides calls painting silent poetry and poetry speaking painting (Plutarch, Glory of the Athenians 3).

Simonides ascribes wine and music to the same origin (Athenaeus 2.40a).

If you seek from me a statement of my views on the existence and essential nature of God, I shall adopt the procedure of Simonides, who, when the tyrant Hiero had put the same question to him, begged for a day's indulgence, that he might ponder his answer. On the following day, Hiero demanded a reply and Simonides requested two days for deliberation; after he had several times doubled thus the number of days, Hiero in great amazement called for an explanation, and Simonides said: "Well, the longer I reflect upon *the matter, the more obscure it becomes"* (Cicero, On the Nature of the Gods 1.22).

Other allusions to Simonides refer to his longevity and to his innovations in language. For a summary of ancient criticism we turn again to Quintilian (10.1.64):

Simonides wrote in a simple style, but may be recommended for the propriety and charm of his language. His chief merit, however, lies in his power to excite pity, so much so, in fact, that some rank him in this respect above all writers of this class of poetry.

IV. CHORAL LYRIC

Simonides and other of the lyric poets mentioned above wrote choral compositions as well; Stesichorus' very name proves that his fame rested on his choral work. But for us choral lyric is associated primarily with the names of Pindar and his rival, Simonides' nephew Bacchylides. Pindar's epinician odes (but only fragments of his other works) have come down in the ordinary MS tradition; Bacchylides' were recovered from papyri in modern times. Most of our allusions to Bacchylides in other writings have to do with his rivalry with Pindar. At *Olympian* 2.154 Pindar himself contrasts the naturally gifted eagle with wordy crows; at *Nemean* 3.143 the eagle is contrasted with jackdaws; at *Pythian* 2.97 Pindar speaks of shunning slander; at 131 in the same poem apes are said to be pretty in the eyes of children; and at 166 disappointed greed is referred to. In all these cases the scholiast explains that the allusion is to Bacchylides. But Bacchylides' inferiority to Pindar is obvious to "Longinus" (33):

In lyrics, again, would you choose to be Bacchylides rather than Pindar, or in tragedy Ion of Chios rather than (save the mark!) Sophocles? In both cases the former is impeccable and a master of elegance in the smooth style. On the other hand Pindar and Sopho-

cles sometimes seem to fire the whole landscape as they sweep across it, while often their fire is unaccountably quenched and they fall miserably flat.

Other stories in which Pindar figures have to do with his rivalry with Corinna. Plutarch (*On the Glory of the Athenians* 348) says that Corinna advised Pindar "to sow with the hand, not the full sack" —in allusion to his profuse use of myth. And Pindar, according to Aelian (13.25) did not take his defeat by Corinna gracefully:

When the poet Pindar was competing in Thebes an uncultivated audience fell to his lot and he was five times defeated by Corinna. Pindar reproached their lack of cultivation and called Corinna a sow.

There are five lives of Pindar, all apparently of Byzantine date, and his own poetry enables us to follow his commissions by various princely courts and to apprehend his old-fashioned religious and social beliefs. Aside from details of family connections (which are of little interest except in showing that Pindar was so highly esteemed that such details were cherished) the tradition is preserved for us in Pausanias:

Crossing over the right side of the course (at Thebes) you come to a race-course for horses, in which is the tomb of Pindar. When Pindar was a young man he was once on his way to Thespiae in the hot season. At about noon he was seized with fatigue and the drowsiness that follows it, so just as he was, he lay down a little way above the road. As he slept bees alighted on him and plastered his lips with their wax. Such was the beginning of Pindar's career as a lyric poet. When his reputation had already spread throughout Greece he was raised to a greater height of fame by an order of the Pythian priestess, who bade the Delphians give to Pindar one half of all the first-fruits they offered to Apollo. It is also said that on reaching old age a vision came to him in a dream. As he slept, Persephone stood by him and declared that she alone of the deities had not been honored by Pindar with a hymn, but that Pindar would compose an ode to her also when he had come to her. Pindar died at once, before ten days had passed since the dream (9.23.2–4).

Crossing the river you reach the ruins of the house of Pindar, and a sanctuary of the Mother Dindymene. Pindar dedicated the image, and Aristomedes and Socrates, sculptors of Thebes, made it (9.25.3).

Not far from the hearth has been dedicated a chair of Pindar. The chair is of iron, and on it they say that Pindar sat whenever he came to Delphi, and there composed his Songs to Apollo (10.24.5).

The poet's house was revered as a relic throughout antiquity. When Alexander sacked Thebes in 335 B.C., Dio Chrysostom (2.33) tells us,

he left only that poet's house standing, directing that this notice be posted upon it: "Set not on fire the roof of Pindar, maker of song."

Arrian, Pliny, and Plutarch, who also tell the story, add that Alexander protected the poet's descendants also; and in Sonnet 8 Milton writes

> The great Emathian conqueror bid spare
> The house of Pindarus when temple and tower
> Went to the ground.

It was probably in conscious reminiscence of his model Alexander that Napoleon placed a guard at the door of Haydn's house when he occupied Vienna. Just as it was natural for Napoleon to emulate Alexander, so it was for Alexander to value the poet whose mission was the celebration of princely houses. It was in allusion to such poets as Pindar that Plato wrote (Republic 568b), "For these services poets are paid and honored, chiefly by tyrants." But Pindar was honored by Athens also. Isocrates (Antidosis 166) says:

Pindar the poet was so highly honored by our forefathers because of a single line of his in which he praises Athens as "the bulwark of Hellas" that he was made proxenus and given a present of 10,000 drachmae.

But the taint of the Medizer adhered to Pindar, and even Polybius, himself no ardent democrat, writes (4.31.5):

We do not praise the Thebans because at the time of the Persian invasion they deserted Greece in the hour of peril and took the side of the Persians from fear, nor do we praise Pindar for confirming them by his verses in their resolution to remain inactive.

Scholarly work on Pindar continued throughout antiquity, and criticism was unanimous in rating him first in the lyric canon. Critical opinion is summed up in Quintilian (10.1.61):

Of the nine lyric poets Pindar is by far the greatest, in virtue of his inspired magnificence, the beauty of his thoughts and figures, the rich exuberance of his language and matter, and his rolling flood of eloquence—characteristics which, as Horace rightly held, make him inimitable.

The reference to Horace is in Odes 4.2.1–4:

Whoever strives, Iulus, to rival Pindar, relies on wings fastened with wax by Daedalean craft, and is doomed to give his name to some crystal sea.

But in Odes 1.12 Horace himself attempts to imitate Pindar's second Olympian ode. Of an attempt by Vergil to imitate Pindar, Aulus Gellius (17.10.8) quotes the criticism of Favorinus:

Now among the passages (of the Aeneid) which particularly seem to have needed revision and correction is the one which was composed about Mount Aetna. For wishing to rival the poem which

the earlier poet Pindar composed about the nature and eruption of
that mountain, he has heaped up such words and expressions that
in this passage at least he is more extravagant and bombastic even
than Pindar himself, who was thought to have too rich and luxuriant a style. And in order that you yourselves may be judges of what
I say, I will repeat Pindar's poem about Mount Aetna, so far as I
can remember it.—Here Favorinus quotes [Pythian 1.21 ff. and
Aeneid 3.570 ff.], and continues:

Now in the first place, Pindar has more closely followed the truth
and has given a realistic description of what actually happened there,
and what he saw with his own eyes; namely, that Aetna in the daytime sends forth smoke and at night fire; but Vergil, laboring to find
grand and sonorous words, confuses the two periods of time and
makes no distinction between them. Then the Greek has vividly
pictured the streams of fire belched from the depths and the flowing rivers of smoke, and the rushing of lurid and spiral volumes of
flame into the waters of the sea, like so many fiery serpents; but
our poet, attempting to render "a lurid stream of smoke," has clum-
sily and diffusely piled up the words atram nubem turbine piceo
et favilla fumantem, "a dusky cloud smoking with eddies black and
glowing ash," and what Pindar called "founts," he has harshly and
inaccurately rendered "balls of flame." . . . and so on, in detail, to
the end of the quotation.

The precise and elaborate architectural and metrical principles
upon which Pindar constructed his odes were not fully understood
until modern times; what impressed Renaissance students was the
ancient critics' admiration of his overwhelming torrential force. In
consequence Pindar became an inspiration for an entire school
of poets, of which Pierre de Ronsard was the coryphaeus but which
spread to all the countries of Europe, who had a very imperfect
understanding of the model they professed to follow.

THERE WERE, OF COURSE, OTHER 5TH CENTURY tragic poets besides Aeschylus, Sophocles, and Euripides— we know a fair amount about Agathon, Ion, and certain others— but the unanimous judgment of their contemporaries accorded supremacy to the Three; this judgment was never questioned, but passed into a permanent tradition. General opinion separated them from the mass of writers and regarded them with peculiar veneration as models of dramatic excellence and inspired teachers of virtue and knowledge. In later Greek literature they are always described as towering above their rivals and constituting a special select group. Critics like Dionysius of Halicarnassus and Quintilian cite them as the sole representatives of tragic poetry, and philosophers and orators continually quote them as sources of wisdom and instruction. A book such as that by Heraclides Ponticus on "The Three Tragic Poets" (cited by Diogenes Laertius 5.87) did not require that the names of the Three be specified. In the 5th century it was the rule that only new work could be entered in the Dionysiac competitions; in the 4th century any choregus who wished to do so might offer a revival of a play of the Three. Actors were now known for their special interpretations of these classic works.

The best evidence for the esteem in which the Three were held are the official measures which were taken to insure the purity of their text. When in the 4th century, which was the great age of acting, certain actors took the liberty of adapting and manipulating old plays for the purpose of stage representation, the Athenians determined to prohibit the practice by law. A decree was passed (Plutarch, *Ten Orators* 841 f.) enacting that official copies of works of the Three should be deposited in the archives, and that for the future, when one of the tragedies was being exhibited, the public secretary should attend with the authorized text in his hands and follow the performance word by word so as to prevent any deviation from the original. It was the official texts of Athens which

Ptolemy III borrowed, against a deposit of the enormous sum of 15 talents, so that transcripts of them might be made for his library. Galen (*Comm. 2 on Hippocrat. Epidem 3*) tells us that Ptolemy deliberately forfeited his deposit, kept the official texts, and sent the Athenians handsome transcripts as a gift.

In 330 B.C. the orator Lycurgus enacted that bronze portrait statues of the Three should be set up in the theater of Dionysus at Athens; the fine marble figure of Sophocles in the Lateran, and the good busts of Aeschylus and Euripides in other museums are doubtless copies of these official statues.

I. AESCHYLUS

Ancient knowledge and opinion concerning Aeschylus is summarized in the extant *Life*, prefixed to many editions, which, like the *Lives* of Sophocles and Euripides, is probably the work of Didymus (ca. 65 B.C.–A.D. 10) who was surnamed Chalcenterus ("Brazen Guts") for his prodigious industry. The *Life* provides more or less reliable information on Aeschylus' dates, family connections, military career, travels, and reputation.

His service at the battles of Artemisium, Salamis, and Plataea is corroborated by a passage in Pausanias (1.14.5). The messenger's description of the battle of Salamis in *Persians* (354 ff.) is therefore an eyewitness account. The Cynegeirus of whom Herodotus tells (6.114) that he had his hand cut off when he held on to a Persian ship which was trying to escape was almost certainly Aeschylus' brother. The story that his brother displayed his empty sleeve to the court when Aeschylus was tried for revealing the mysteries is doubtless apocryphal. And the story of this trial, elaborated in Clement of Alexandria (*Stromateis* 2.387) and Aelian (5.9) might seem to be a similar invention, made plausible by Aeschylus' Eleusinian origin, but we have apparent confirmation in a passage in Aristotle's *Ethics* (3.111a): "But of what he is doing a man might be ignorant, as for instance people say . . . 'I did not know it was a secret,' as Aeschylus said of the mysteries."

The trial is one of the reasons gossip assigned for Aeschylus' re-

moval to Sicily, others being jealousy of the Athenians and Aeschylus' discomfiture at the success of his younger rivals. Jealousy
is given as the cause in an epigram by Diodorus (A.P. 7.40):

*This tombstone says that Aeschylus the great lies here, far from his
own Attica, by the white waters of Sicilian Gela. What spiteful
grudge against the good is this, alas, that ever besets the sons of
Theseus (i.e., the Athenians)?*

Failure in a competition with Sophocles is alleged as the cause in
the passage in which Plutarch (*Cimon* 8) tells how, at a tense contest, the ten generals, instead of jurors chosen by lot, were made to
serve as judges:

*The eagerness for victory grew all the warmer from the ambition to
get the suffrages of such honorable judges. And the victory was at
last adjudged to Sophocles, which Aeschylus is said to have taken
so ill, that he left Athens shortly after, and went in anger to Sicily,
where he died, and was buried near the city of Gela.*

But elsewhere (*On Exile* 13) Plutarch himself offers Aeschylus as
an example of a man who might remove to or from Athens under
no constraint. That the death took place in Sicily is indicated by the
epigram just cited, by another by Antipater of Thessalonica (A.P.
7.39)—

*Here, far from the Attic land, making Sicily glorious by his tomb,
lies Aeschylus son of Euphorion, who first built high with massive
eloquence the diction of tragedy and its beetling song.*

and by that cited in the *Life*, not improbably from Aeschylus' own
hand,

> *This tomb the dust of Aeschylus doth hide,*
> *Euphorion's son, and fruitful Gelas' pride,*
> *How tried his valor Marathon may tell*
> *And long-haired Medes who knew it all too well.*

He died, according to the familiar legend, when an eagle mistaking his bald head for a stone, dropped a tortoise upon it in order to break its shell, and so killed him. The earliest authority for the story is Sotades (3d century B.C.), who is quoted by Stobaeus (98. 9.13). The whole may rest upon a misinterpretation of a symbolic sculpture, the tortoise representing a lyre, and the flying eagle apotheosis.

Personal sayings attributed to Aeschylus are very few; probably most familiar is his declaration that his tragedies were "slices taken from Homer's mighty dinners" (Athenaeus 8.347e). Another, which probably comes from Ion of Chios and is therefore old, tells that when a boxer received a blow and the spectators cried out, Aeschylus nudged Ion and said, "Do you see what a thing training is? The man struck is silent; it is the spectators who cry out" (Plutarch, *On Progress in Virtue* 8). A story in Porphyry (*On Abstinence* 2.133) is less likely true: When the Delphians asked Aeschylus to write a paean in honor of Apollo he refused, on the grounds that everyone would prefer the antique poem of Tynnichus to his own, just as they considered the old-fashioned images of the gods far more venerable than the best of modern statues. Pausanias (9.22.7) tells how Aeschylus got material for a play: "Pindar and Aeschylus got a story about Glaucus from the people of Antheon. Pindar has not thought fit to say much about him in his odes, but the story actually supplied Aeschylus with material for a play."

Nor are there such scandalous tales about Aeschylus as there are about Sophocles and Euripides. Indeed Euripides is represented as saying to him (Aristophanes, *Frogs* 1045), "There is little of Aphrodite in your composition." Several authors speak of Aeschylus writing in a state of drunkenness (Plutarch, *Symposiacs* 7.10; Lucian, *Praise of Demosthenes* 15; Athenaeus 1.22a). The latter passage shows one way the story may have originated:

Aeschylus wrote his tragedies drunk, according to Chamaeleon. Sophocles, anyway, reproached Aeschylus with the remark that even if he wrote as he should he did it unconsciously.

The Plutarch passage suggests another possible origin:

They say that Aeschylus wrote his tragedies drunk and that they were
full of Dionysus, not, as Gorgias said [cf. Aristophanes, Frogs 1021]
full of Ares.

Aeschylus' bold loftiness of language—including its occasional
proximity to the grotesque—and the dignity of his themes and treatment were noted in antiquity. The fullest appreciation of these
qualities, at least on the part of conservative elements, is of course
in Aristophanes' *Frogs*. Sophocles, according to that play (786 ff.)
showed Aeschylus the greatest consideration:

> *When Sophocles came down, he kissed*
> *With reverence Aeschylus, and clasped his hand,*
> *And yielded willingly the chair to him.*

Euripides' ridicule of Aeschylus in *Frogs* finds actual illustration
not only in his practice but in at least two overt allusions. The recognition scene in Euripides' *Electra* is a patent criticism of the im-
probabilities in Aeschylus' handling of the same theme in *Choephoroe*, and Euripides' *Phoenician Women* 749–52—*To tell each
o'er were costly waste of time*—criticizes the improbability of the
long descriptions placed in critical juncture of action in *Seven
against Thebes*. In his *Oration* 52, which is an essay on the Philoctetes plays of the three tragic poets, Dio Chrysostom contrasts
Aeschylus' simplicity and indifference to probabilities with the
more elaborate artifice of Sophocles and Euripides. The turgidity of Aeschylus' language, to which Euripides takes exception in
Frogs, is noticed also in later critics (e.g., Dionysius of Halicarnassus, *On Ancient Writers* 10, *On Composition of Words* 22). Macrobius (5.19.17) goes so far as to ascribe Aeschylus' anomalous
coinages to his being a "thorough Sicilian." The judicious and authoritative Quintilian (10.1.66) pronounces Aeschylus "frequently
rough and inelegant; the art of Sophocles and Euripides was far
clearer."

On Aeschylus' contributions to the technique of tragedy the
classic statement is Aristotle's (*Poetics* 1449b): "Aeschylus first
introduced a second actor; he diminished the importance of the

chorus, and assigned the leading part to the dialogue." A fuller
statement, derived from Chamaeleon, an early Peripatetic scholar,
occurs in Athenaeus (1.21e):

*Aeschylus, too, besides inventing that comeliness and dignity of
dress which Hierophants and Torchbearers emulate when they put
on their vestments, also originated many dance-figures and assigned
them to the members of his choruses. For Chamaeleon says that
Aeschylus was the first to give poses to his choruses, employing no
dancing-masters, but devising for himself the figures of the dance,
and in general taking upon himself the entire management of the
piece. At any rate it seems that he acted in his own plays.*

One of his gifted dancers is mentioned by name (Athenaeus 1.22a):

*Telestes, Aeschylus' dancer, was so artistic that when he danced the
Seven against Thebes he made the action clear simply by dancing.*

Aeschylus' vivid costuming is mentioned by Pausanias (1.28.6): "It
was Aeschylus who first represented the Furies with snakes in their
hair." At the spectacle, the *Life* tells us, boys fainted and women
miscarried.

Curiously little is said of the moral dignity and the edification
which Aeschylus' innovations were intended to convey. The point
is enlarged upon in a passage of Philostratus' *Life of Apollonius of
Tyana* (6.11):

*Finding the art to be rude and inchoate and as yet not in the least
elaborated, he went to work, and curtailed the sprawling chorus,
and invented dialogues for the actors, discarding the long monodies
of the earlier time; and he hit upon a plan of killing people behind
the stage instead of their being slain before the eyes of the audience.
Well, if we cannot deny his talent in making all these improve-
ments, we must nevertheless admit that they might have suggested
themselves equally well to an inferior dramatist. But his talent was
twofold. On the one hand as a poet he set himself to make his dic-*

tion worthy of tragedy, on the other hand as a manager, to adapt
his stage to sublime, rather than to humble and groveling, themes.
Accordingly he devised masks which represented the forms of the
heroes, and he mounted his actors on buskins so that their gait
might correspond to the characters they played; and he was the first
to devise stage dresses, which might convey an adequate impression
to the audience of the heroes and heroines they saw. For all these
reasons the Athenians accounted him to be the father of tragedy;
and even after his death they continued to invite him to represent
his plays at the Dionysiac festival, for in accordance with public
decree the plays of Aeschylus continued to be put upon the stage
and win the prize anew.

It was left for Christians to remark on Aeschylus' purer theology.
Tertullian (Against Marcion 1.1) says that he shows a dim presenti-
ment of Christianity.

If Aeschylus was less frequently played and studied than his junior
rivals (even Aristotle is occupied mainly with Sophocles and Euripides and virtually ignores Aeschylus) a special sanctity continued
to be attached to his name. The story that Dionysius of Syracuse
purchased his writing tablets in order to be touched by their inspiration (Lucian, To an Illiterate Book-Fancier, 15) suggests something
of this attitude. The Athenians enacted that a statue of Aeschylus
be erected and that his works be preserved ([Plutarch] Ten Orators
841 f.).

II. SOPHOCLES

In the Life of Sophocles, which is of the same general character as
that of Aeschylus, the dominant note is of charming amiability sur-
viving through a singularly long and successful career. Good family
connections as well as marked physical endowments are proven
by his having been chosen, as an adolescent, to perform in the ritual
celebration for the victory of Salamis. The best passage on this is
in Athenaeus (1.20ef):

Sophocles, besides being handsome in his youth, became proficient in dancing and music, while still a lad, under the instruction of Lampus. After the battle of Salamis, at any rate, he danced to the accompaniment of his lyre round the trophy, naked and anointed with oil. Others say he danced with his cloak on. And when he brought out the Thamyris he played the lyre himself. He also played ball with great skill when he produced the Nausicaa.

The universal esteem in which Sophocles was held is reflected in Aristophanes' Frogs and confirmed in a fragment of the comic poet Phrynichus (2.592 Meinecke):

Blessed Sophocles who died after a long life, a man fortunate and successful who made many fine tragedies. And finely did he die, having had no evil to endure.

Two qualities for which Sophocles is frequently cited as an example by later writers are his piety and his longevity. The Life and a scholium on Electra 831 say that he was notably pious, and several stories indicating divine approval are told of him. Plutarch (Numa 4.6) cites "a story, still well attested, that Sophocles during his life was blessed with the friendship of Aesculapius and that when he died another deity procured him fitting burial." The latter may be an allusion to the story reported by Pausanias (1.21.1):

After the death of Sophocles the Lacedaemonians invaded Attica, and their commander saw in a vision Dionysus, who bade him honor the new siren with all the customary honors of the dead. He interpreted the dream as referring to Sophocles and his poetry

—and allowed him burial in occupied territory. Cicero (On Divination 25) knows that when a golden vessel was stolen from the temple of Hercules, the place of its concealment was revealed to Sophocles in a vision; and Philostratus (Life of Apollonius 8.7.8) that when winds were blowing unseasonably they were charmed by Sophocles.

Among the many references to Sophocles' longevity the most attractive are those which concern the charge of mental incompetence brought by members of his family to relieve him of business cares. Here is Cicero's account (*On Old Age* 7):

Sophocles wrote tragedies up to extreme old age, and when this preoccupation was thought to impair his attention to business matters, his sons brought him to court to prove imbecility, on a law similar to ours which deprives a householder of the management of his property if he has proved incompetent. The old poet is then said to have read to the jury the Oedipus at Colonus which he had lately written and was revising, and to have asked whether it seemed the work of an imbecile. After the reading he was acquitted.

And here is Plutarch's (*Whether an Old Man Should Engage in Politics* 785ab):

When Sophocles was a defendant on a charge of imbecility brought by his sons he is said to have read out the ode in Oedipus at Colonus which begins, "Stranger, you have come to white Colonus." The song was marvellously admired, and Sophocles was escorted from the lawcourt as from a theater, amid the applause and shouts of all present.

The *Life* tells us that he added: "If I am Sophocles I am not mad; if I am mad I am not Sophocles." An interesting echo (if the Sophocles mentioned is indeed our poet) occurs in Aristotle's *Rhetoric* (3.1416a):

Sophocles said he was not trembling, as his traducer maintained, in order to make people think him an old man, but because he could not help it; he would rather not be 80 years old.

The poet must in fact have been over ninety. Probably the best known allusion to Sophocles' old age is that near the opening of Plato's *Republic* (1.329c). Cephalus is speaking:

Sophocles the poet was once asked in my presence, "How do you feel about love, Sophocles? are you still capable of it?" to which he replied, "Hush! if you please; to my great delight I have escaped from it, and feel as if I had escaped from a frantic and savage master."

That the last was not mere hyperbole is suggested by a passage in Athenaeus (13.529a):

Even Sophocles, the tragic poet, when he was already an old man, fell in love with Theoris, the courtesan. . . . Being in his declining years, as Hegesander says, he fell in love with the courtesan Archippe, and made her in his will heiress to his property, and that Sophocles was old when Archippe lived with him is proved by what her former lover Smicrines wittily said when asked what Archippe was doing: "As the owls sit upon the tombs so sits she."

Allusions to Sophocles' fondness for boys are more numerous. Athenaeus' rather charming bit of gossip, drawn from good sources, deserves quotation at length (13.603e–604d):

Sophocles was fond of young lads, as Euripides was fond of women. The poet Ion, at any rate, in the work entitled Sojournings, writes as follows: "I met Sophocles the poet at Chios when he was sailing as general to Lesbos [440 B.C.]; he was playful in his cups, and clever. A Chian friend of his, Hermesilaus, who was consul for Athens, entertained him, when there appeared, standing beside the fire, the wine-pourer, a handsome, blushing boy; Sophocles was plainly stirred and said: 'Do you want me to drink with pleasure?' And when the boy said 'Yes' he said, 'Then don't be too rapid in handing me the cup and taking it away.' When the boy blushed still more violently he said to the man who shared his couch: 'That was a good thing Phrynichus wrote when he said: "There shines upon his crimson cheeks the light of love." ' " [There follows a discussion of such epithets as "crimson-cheeked," "golden-haired," "rosy-fingered."] Sophocles returned to the conversation with the boy. He asked him, as he was trying to pick off a straw from the cup with his little finger, whether he could see the straw clearly. When the boy declared he could see it Sophocles said, "Then blow it away, for I shouldn't want you to get your finger wet." As the boy brought his face up to the cup, Sophocles drew the cup nearer to his own lips, that the two heads might come closer together. When he was very near the lad, he drew him close with his arm and kissed him. They all applauded, amid laughter and shouting, because he had put it over the boy so neatly; and Sophocles said, 'I am practising strategy, gentlemen, since Pericles told me that whereas I could write poetry, I didn't know how to be a general. Don't you think my stratagem has turned out happily for me?' Many things of this sort he was wont to say and do cleverly when he drank or when he did anything. In civic matters, however, he was neither wise nor efficient, but like any other individual among the better class of Athenians.

Hieronymus of Rhodes says in his Historical Notes that Sophocles lured a handsome boy outside the city wall to consort with him. Now the boy spread his own cloak on the grass, while they wrapped themselves in Sophocles' cape. When the meeting was over the boy seized Sophocles' cape and made off with it, leaving behind for Sophocles his boyish cloak. Naturally the incident was much talked of; when Euripides learned of the occurrence he jeered, saying that he himself had once consorted with this boy without paying any bonus, whereas Sophocles had been treated with contempt for his licentiousness.

Sophocles, the story concludes, retorted with an epigram which charged Euripides with the actionable offense of being taken in adultery. Another passage from Hieronymus makes the same point (Athenaeus 13.557e):

When somebody remarked to Sophocles that Euripides was a woman-hater, Sophocles answered: "Yes, in his tragedies; for certainly when he is in bed he is a woman-lover."

Plutarch has another story of Sophocles' generalship which illustrates his proclivity (Pericles 8):

Once when Sophocles, who was general with him on a certain naval expedition [against Samos, 440 B.C.], praised a lovely boy, Pericles said, "It is not his hands only, Sophocles, that a general must keep clean, but his eyes as well."

The First Argument of the *Antigone* says that Sophocles was elected to this generalship because of the success of that play. But Sophocles had no illusions about his military competence, as another story in Plutarch (*Nicias* 15) shows:

Once when his fellow commanders were deliberating on some matter of general moment, Nicias bade Sophocles the poet state his opinion first, as being the senior general on the board. Thereupon Sophocles said: "I am the oldest man, but you are the senior general."

Acerbity between Sophocles and Euripides is alleged to have involved their works as well as their private lives. The scholium on *Phoenician Women* 1 speaks of mutual accusations of plagiarism, and a treatise *On Sophocles' Plagiarism* by Philostratus of Alexandria is mentioned by Eusebius. Citations in Clement of Alexandria's *Stromateis* (6.2) as well as verses in the extant plays prove that the two poets occasionally borrowed from one another, but this may be rather an indication of friendship than the reverse. Sophocles' alleged friendship with Herodotus rests upon a statement in Plutarch (*Whether an Old Man Should Engage in Politics* 785b) that Sophocles addressed a poem to Herodotus and on three Sophoclean passages which echo Herodotus: *Antigone* 905–911, an irreplaceable brother deserves greater sacrifice than a husband (cf. Herodotus 3.119); *Electra* 62, no evil omen attaches to a false report of death (cf. Herodotus 4.95); and *Oedipus at Colonus* 337, the reversal of masculine and feminine roles in Egypt (cf. Herodotus 2.35).

The most famous of Sophocles' sayings about his own work is that quoted in Aristotle (*Poetics* 1460b): "Sophocles said that he drew men as they ought to be; Euripides, as they are." Elsewhere Aristotle says (1449a) that Sophocles raised the number of actors

to three and added scene-painting. Another remark is preserved in
Plutarch (*Progress in Virtue* 79b):

*Sophocles said that only after handling with a light touch the tur-
gidity of Aeschylus and next his harshness and artificiality in composition did he, as a third step, change the character of the language,
which has most to do with moral character and goodness.*

Of Sophocles' style generally the ancients held a very high opinion. Dionysius of Halicarnassus, for example, declares (*Composition of Words* 22–24) that he combined smoothness with power,
grace with dignity, and that he was the most distinguished representative of the "middle style." But elsewhere (*Ancient Writers*
2.11) Dionysius complains of Sophocles' sudden lapses into the
commonplace. Plutarch too says (*On Listening* 45a) that "one
might find fault with Euripides for his loquacity and Sophocles for
his unevenness." The fault, and its exculpation, are best put by the
author of *On the Sublime* (33):

*Pindar and Sophocles sometimes fire the whole landscape as they
sweep across it, while often their fire is unaccountably quenched
and they fall miserably flat. Yet would anyone in his senses give
the single tragedy of Oedipus for all the works of Ion in a row?*

Similar enthusiasm was expressed by Polemo (head of the Academy,
314–276 B.C.), as quoted in Diogenes Laertius (4.20):

*Polemo loved Sophocles, particularly in those passages where it
seemed as if, in the phrase of the comic poet, "a stout Molossian
mastiff lent him aid," and where the poet was, in the words of
Phrynichus, "nor must, nor blended vintage, but true Pramnian."
Thus he would call Homer the Sophocles of epic, and Sophocles
the Homer of tragedy.*

The comparison with Homer was natural, for as Athenaeus remarks
(7.277e), "Sophocles liked the epic cycle, and even composed entire

plays in close conformity to the stories told in it." Aristotle too (*Poetics* 1462) cites Sophocles and Homer as representing tragic and epic poetry, and *Oedipus Tyrannus* and *Iliad* as types of tragic and epic poetry. Xenophon (*Memorabilia* 1.4.3) places Sophocles in the same rank with Homer, Zeuxis, and Polycleitus as the most distinguished representatives of their respective arts. And so in virtually all the Roman writers Sophocles is the tragedian par excellence. He was also the favorite of virtuoso actors. Aulus Gellius (6.4) recounts this story of the famous Polus (end of 4th century B.C.) who had recently lost a beloved son:

At that time Polus was to act the Electra of Sophocles at Athens, and it was his part to carry an urn which was supposed to contain the ashes of Orestes. The plot of the play requires that Electra, who is represented as carrying her brother's remains, should lament and bewail the fate that she believed had overtaken him. Accordingly Polus, clad in the mourning garb of Electra, took from the tomb the ashes and urn of his son, embraced them as if they were those of Orestes, and filled the whole place, not with the appearance and imitation of sorrow, but with genuine grief and unfeigned lamentation.

All sources agree that Sophocles lived beyond the age of ninety. His death is ascribed by the *Life*, variously and with equal improbability, to choking on fresh grapes, reading a long sentence of *Antigone* without stopping for breath, or excessive joy at the victory of his *Antigone*. Two bits of verse commemorating Sophocles may be cited in conclusion. One from the *Leontion* of Hermesianax of Colophon (3d century B.C., cited in Athenaeus 13.598c) has to do with his private life:

How too the Attic bee [a common designation for Sophocles] left Colonus of the many hillocks, and sang with choruses marshaled in tragedy—sang of Bacchus and of his passion for Theoris and for Erigone, whom Zeus once gave to Sophocles in his old age.

The other, by Statylius Flaccus (A.P. 9.98), celebrates his work:

Thy two Oedipuses and the relentless hate of Electra and the sun driven from heaven by the feast of Atreus and thy other writings that picture the many woes of princes in a manner worthy of the chorus of Dionysus approved thee, Sophocles, as the chief of the company of tragic poets, for thou didst speak with the very lips of the heroes.

III. EURIPIDES

Caricatures of Euripides, for which the comic poets were doubtless primarily responsible, soon crystallized into a stereotype. The entry in Aulus Gellius (15.20) is typical:

Theopompus says that the mother of the poet Euripides made a living by selling country produce. Furthermore, when Euripides was born, his father was assured by the astrologers that the boy, when he grew up, would be victor in the games; for that was his destiny. His father, understanding this to mean that he ought to be an athlete, exercised and strengthened his son's body and took him to Olympia to contend among the wrestlers. And at first he was not admitted to the contest because of his tender age, but afterwards he engaged in the Eleusinian and Thesean contests and won crowns. Later, turning from attention to bodily exercise to the desire of training his mind, he was a pupil of the natural philosopher Anaxagoras and the rhetorician Prodicus, and, in moral philosophy, of Socrates. [According to Diogenes Laertius 2.18, Socrates helped write his plays.] At the age of 18 he attempted to write a tragedy. Philochorus relates that there is on the island of Salamis a grim and gloomy cavern, which I myself have seen, in which Euripides wrote tragedies.

He is said to have had an exceeding antipathy towards almost all women, either because he had a natural disinclination to their society, or because he had had two wives at the same time (since that was permitted by a decree passed by the Athenians) and they had made wedlock hateful to him. Aristophanes also notices his

antipathy to women in the first edition of the Thesmophoriazusae
in these verses:

> Now then I urge and call on all our sex
> This man to punish for his many crimes.
> For on us, women, he brings bitter woes,
> Himself brought up 'mid bitter garden plants.

But Alexander the Aetolian composed the following lines about
Euripides:

> The pupil of stout Anaxagoras,
> Of churlish speech and gloomy, ne'er has learned
> To jest amid the wine; but what he wrote
> Might honey and the Sirens well have known.

When Euripides was in Macedonia at the court of Archelaus,
and had become an intimate friend of the king, returning home one
night from a dinner with the monarch he was torn by dogs, which
were set upon him by a rival of his, and death resulted from his
wounds. The Macedonians treated his tomb and his memory with
such honor that they used to proclaim: "Never, Euripides, shall thy
monument perish," also by way of self-glorification, because the
distinguished poet had met his death and been buried in their land.
Therefore when envoys, sent to them by the Athenians, begged that
they should allow his bones to be moved to Athens, his native land,
the Macedonians unanimously persisted in refusing.

Any reader of Euripides' plays must see that the charge of misogyny
is not only baseless but actually the reverse of the truth; and the
other personal details are equally distorted. Even without the new
evidence of Satyrus' Life (of which four papyrus pages were published in 1912) we should know that Euripides could not have been
of poor and obscure family, for he would not then have participated
in the dance to the Delian Apollo (Athenaeus 424), would not
have been celebrated as a collector of books (id. 3), would not
have been sent to negotiate peace with the Syracusans. It was doubtless our Euripides who is referred to in Aristotle's Rhetoric 2.6,

1384*b*; the scholiast says that when he found the Syracusans un-willing he said, "You ought, men of Syracuse, to respect our ex-pressions of esteem, if only because we are new petitioners."

The stories of Euripides' domestic unhappiness are clearly a fabrication based on lines from his plays. Even the second wife is probably a figment, for Choerile ("Sow") may well have been merely a nickname of his wife Melito. Similarly the influence of Anaxagoras, Prodicus, Socrates, probably rests on inference from his plays. Euripides was surely touched by the intellectual currents of his day, but he was only five years younger than Anaxagoras and about 17 years older than Socrates. The lurid details of his sex life reported by Athenaeus (557, 598, 604) and others are disproven by the silence of Aristophanes, who would surely have exploited that avenue of attack. Adaeus, who lived in the fourth century B.C. and was a Macedonian, refutes the story of Euripides' death as the result of a love adventure in Macedonia (A.P. 7.51):

Neither dogs slew thee, Euripides, nor the rage of women, thou enemy of the secrets of Cypris, but Death and old age, and under Macedonian Arethusa thou liest, honored by the friendship of Archelaus. Yet it is not this that I account thy tomb, but the altar of Bacchus and the buskin-trodden stage.

Why Euripides retired to Macedonia we cannot know; the rea-sons cannot have been the jeers of the comic poets and the infidelity of his wife, as was inevitably alleged. Archelaus gave him some of-ficial preferment and showed him great consideration. Aelian (13.4) has a rather discreditable anecdote of Euripides' stay at the Mace-donian court:

Archelaus prepared a lavish feast for his friends. As the drinking advanced, Euripides, who drank neat, gradually grew drunk. Then he embraced the tragic poet Agathon, who was sharing his couch, and kissed him, though he was about 40 years old. When Archelaus inquired whether he still seemed lovable to him, Euripides replied,

"Yes, by Zeus: not only is the spring the fairest of the fair but the autumn also."

Plutarch (*Apophthegms of Kings* 93) has a better story: When a courtier asked the king for a gold cap Archelaus gave it to Euripides, saying, "You are the sort of man to ask and not receive, Euripides the sort to receive even without asking." All the sources agree that Euripides was of a studious and retiring temperament. His portraits show the gray hair and full beard, but not the moles, of which the *Life* speaks. From Aristotle's *Politics* (5.10) we get the additional touch that his breath was foul.

The principal criticism leveled against Euripides' works is his realism. Aristotle (*Poetics* 25) quotes Sophocles to the effect that whereas he depicted men as they ought to be Euripides depicted them as they are, and Aristophanes (e.g. *Acharnians* 432 ff.) repeatedly speaks of his "ragged heroes." At several points in the *Poetics* Aristotle (whose ideal is Sophocles) speaks disparagingly of Euripides' work, but he praises highly such a recognition scene as that in *Iphigenia among the Taurians* and calls Euripides the most tragic of the poets (4). And Aristotle is ready to acknowledge Euripides' effective use of ordinary language. In the *Rhetoric* (3.2.5, 1404b) he writes: "A successful illusion is wrought when the composer picks his words from the language of daily life; this is what Euripides does and first hinted the way to do." The Platonist Crantor admired Euripides greatly on the ground that "it is hard at once to write tragedy and to stir the emotions in the language of everyday life" (Diogenes Laertius 4.26). So "Longinus" (40.2) credits Euripides with regularly achieving distinction and an effect of grandeur by the artful use of commonplace language. The rhetorical virtuosity and sophistic subtlety which Aristophanes criticized so vehemently, especially in the *Frogs*, later critics found praiseworthy. Quintilian (10.1.68) placed Euripides on a level with the greatest of orators, and Dio Chrysostom (Oration 18) says that Euripides' eloquence and sententious wisdom are exceedingly useful to a man preparing for public life. In a telling phrase Clement of Alexandria refers to Euripides (*Stromateis* 6.88) as "the philosopher on the stage."

It was doubtless the novelty of Euripides' realism and "new thought" that offended such conservatives as Aristophanes and reduced the number of his victories, but there is evidence of his great popularity before the end of the 5th century. Speaking of the miserable Athenian survivors of the Syracusan debacle Plutarch (*Nicias* 29) has a remarkable story:

Several were saved for the sake of Euripides, whose poetry, it appears, was in request among the Sicilians more than among any of the settlers out of Greece. And when any travelers arrived that could tell them some passage, or give them any specimen of his verses, they were delighted to be able to communicate them to one another. Many of the captives who got safe back to Athens are said, after they reached home, to have gone and made their acknowledgments to Euripides, relating how some of them had been released from their slavery by teaching what they could remember of his poems, and others, when straggling after the fight, been relieved with meat and drink for repeating some of his lyrics. Nor need this be any wonder, for it is told that a ship of Caunus fleeing into one of their harbors for protection, pursued by pirates, was not received, but forced back, till one asked if they knew any of Euripides' verses, and on their saying they did, they were admitted, and their ship brought into harbor.

We have epigraphic evidence to show that Euripides' plays were presented very frequently in the 4th century. Plato and Aristotle quote him more frequently than any other tragic poet. "It is not without reason," says Socrates (*Republic* 568a), "that people regard tragedy on the whole as wise, and Euripides as a master therein." Orators such as Aeschines (*Timarchus* 153) and Lycurgus (*Leocrates* 100) extol his sagacity and his patriotism. New Comedy made amends for the harshness of Old; Philemon declared that if he were sure of the existence of a future state he would hang himself in order to see Euripides. Alexander the Great quoted him constantly (e.g., Plutarch, *Alexander* 53) and at the banquet which preceded his death recited a scene of the *Andromeda* from memory (Athenaeus 537). Axionicus, a writer of Middle Comedy, made merry with the popular rage for Euripides in his *The Euripides Lover*. The rage persisted, as we can see from an amusing anecdote in Lucian (*How to Write History* 1):

There is a story of a curious epidemic at Abdera, just after the acces-sion of King Lysimachus. It began with the whole population's ex-hibiting feverish symptoms, strongly marked and unintermittent from the very first attack. About the seventh day, the fever was relieved, in some cases by a violent flow of blood from the nose, in others by perspiration not less violent. The mental effects, however, were most ridiculous; they were all stage-struck, mouthing blank verse and ranting at the top of their voices. Their favorite recitation was the Andromeda of Euripides; one after another would go through the great speech of Perseus; the whole place was full of pale ghosts, who were our seventh-day tragedians vociferating, "O Love, who lord'st it over Gods and men," and the rest of it. This continued for some time, till the coming of winter put an end to their madness with a sharp frost. I find the explanation of the form it took in this fact: Archelaus was then the great tragic actor, and in the middle of the summer, during some very hot weather, he had played the Andromeda there; most of them took the fever in the theater, and convalescence was followed by a relapse—into tragedy, the Andromeda haunting their memories, and Perseus hovering, Gorgon's head in hand, before the mind's eye.

IV. ARISTOPHANES

There are a number of Byzantine lives of Aristophanes, but except for family names their data is all patently deduced from the plays. The comedies are indeed far more revealing than Greek tragedy normally is. In the first place the choral interludes called parabases were a recognized device whereby the author could speak directly to the audience in his own person, as Terence does in his prologues.

Furthermore, where the tragic poet was constrained by his traditional material, which he could only manipulate, the comic poet
was master of his plot and characters, and freely introduced personal notes even in dialogue. The larger convictions of Aeschylus,
Sophocles, and Euripides on religious and social questions may
be deduced, but Aristophanes tells us freely what he thinks about
his contemporaries and their doings. Nor are we badly off in grasp-
ing his allusions, for in mass and quality our ancient scholia on
Aristophanes are second only to those on Homer.

Aristophanes' personal rivalries with his competitors are reflected
in a number of passages in his plays; the parabasis of the *Knights*
is in fact our best catalogue of Aristophanes' predecessors and contemporaries. The only extant contemporary who mentions Aristophanes is Plato. In the *Apology* Socrates protests that the unfair
caricature of himself by a comic poet (the reference is to the *Clouds*,
which had been presented 25 years before) had prejudiced public
opinion against him. But Plato seems to have borne Aristophanes
no ill will. In the *Symposium* Aristophanes is one of the principal
interlocutors, and is represented as discussing the nature of comedy
and tragedy with Socrates long after their fellow-topers had suc·
cumbed. The interlude of hiccoughs and the delightful explanation of the origin of love by fission of humans who were originally
spherical with four arms and legs is as thoroughly Aristophanic as
anything in Aristophanes himself.

If details of the life of Aristophanes rest only on deduction, his
reputation among critics is easy to trace. Even at the end of his
own career the impoverished and subdued city found his earlier
robust buoyancy irresponsible. Aristotle dominated the criticism
of his own and succeeding generations, and Aristotle is not the type
to appreciate Aristophanic comedy. His distaste is plain in the
Poetics (5):

*Comedy is an imitation of persons inferior—not, however, in the
full sense of the word bad, the ludicrous being merely a subdivision
of the ugly. It consists in some defect or ugliness which is not pain-*

ful or distinctive. To take an obvious example, the comic mask is
ugly and distorted, but does not imply pain.

Or again, in the Ethics (1128a):

Those who pursue the ridiculous to excess are judged to be buffoons
and vulgar, striving after humor in any and every way and at any
cost, and aiming rather at raising laughter than at saying what is
seemly and avoiding giving pain to the object of their wit. . . .
The buffoon cannot resist the ridiculous, sparing neither himself
nor anyone else so that he can but raise his laugh, saying things of
such kind as no man of refinement would say and some which he
would not even tolerate if said by others in his hearing.

Aristophanes' failure to observe the polite restraint which Aristotle
desiderated was the basis of much later criticism. In the Comparison of Aristophanes and Menander found in Plutarch's Moralia
(853–54) the criticism is explicit:

There is a vulgar, theatrical and common quality in Aristophanes'
language, and not at all in Menander's. The man in the street is
caught by his writing, but the man of culture offended. I mean especially the antitheses and rhymes and similarities of sound. Then in
his choice of words we have the tragic and the comic, the grand
and common, obscurity and ordinariness, pomp and elevation mixed
with babbling and nonsense to make one sick. Yet, with all those
differences and incongruities, his diction does not give the appropriate and natural language to each character—dignity to the king,
cleverness to the rhetor, simplicity to the woman, ordinary words
to the ordinary citizen and vulgarity to the vulgar; but tosses out
by lot, as it were, the first words that come to any speaker, so that
you cannot tell if he is a son, a father, a rustic, a god, an old woman
or a hero.
    Now Menander's language is so tempered, so polished, and so
pervaded by one atmosphere, that while passing through many pas-

sions and feelings and fitted to all kinds of characters, it yet seems one and preserves its character. . . . But Aristophanes is neither pleasing to the many nor tolerable to the thinking few. His poetry is like an old harlot who has passed her prime and imitates a very respectable married woman; the many cannot endure her airs, and the cultured are disgusted by her immorality and spitefulness.

Menander's comedies are full of salt, abundant and without bitterness, as if they were born from that sea from which Aphrodite sprang. But the salt of Aristophanes is bitter and harsh, with an astringency that bites and wounds. And I cannot see wherein that cleverness that he boasts of lies, in the words or the characters. Even what he does represent he distorts for the worse. His rascals are not like fellow-creatures, but malignant beings; his rustics not simple but idiotic; his laughter not playful but full of scorn, his treatment of love not gay but lascivious. The man seems never to have written for decent readers.

Horace recognizes the corrective function of Old Comedy in one passage (Satires 1.4.1):

The poets Eupolis, Cratinus, and Aristophanes, and other authors of Old Comedy, used great freedom in branding anyone who deserved infamy for being a rascal or thief, or for being a lecher or assassin or otherwise infamous.

But in another passage (Ars Poetica 281) he speaks of Comedy's excessive license:

To these there succeeded Old Comedy, and won considerable approval; but freedom proceeded to excess, to extremes which required regulation by law. The law was adopted, and the chorus fell into ignoble silence, deprived of its right to injure.

Quintilian (10.1.65) seems alone in just praise of Aristophanes' combination of strength and grace, though others must have said the same:

The Old Comedy is almost alone in preserving the true charm of Attic speech; at the same time it has the most expressive freedom of speech, especially in denouncing vice, though it is full of strength all through. It is grand, elegant, and charming, and—Homer always excepted, like Achilles—I doubt if any other literature is more akin to oratory or more suitable for making orators.

The fullest attack on Aristophanes in later antiquity is the 29th oration of Aelius Aristides (2nd century), entitled "One Should Not Compose Comedy" and addressed to the people of Smyrna. Apparently they had intended to inaugurate the presentation of comedy in their theater, and Aristides dissuades them from the project by calling attention to the vulgarity of comedy and emphasizing the impropriety and danger of its scurrilous attacks upon respectable personalities.

Despite the disfavor in which official criticism (but not scholarship) held him, it is strange that no epigram on him is given in the Anthology, but one from the tomb of the Alexandrian comic poet Machon (A.P. 7.708) praises Aristophanes by indirection:

Light earth, give birth to ivy that loves the stage to flourish on the tomb of Macho the writer of comedies. For thou holdest no re-dyed drone, but he whom thou clothest is a worthy remnant of ancient art. This shall the old man say: "O city of Cecrops, sometimes on the banks of the Nile, too, the strong-scented thyme of poesy grows."

V. MENANDER

Plutarch regarded Menander not only as superior to Aristophanes, but as equal, in his own way, to Homer himself. Menander was in fact the most popular author of the most popular form of literature in the Hellenistic age, and allusions to him in other writers are especially numerous; the outlines of his life given in Suidas are supplemented by remarks in many other writers. He was tall and had a handsome and sensitive face, as the portrait bust in the Boston

Museum shows. The only flaw was strabismus; Suidas says, "Though his vision was crooked his perception was keen." He had a number of literary connections. Alexis, the principal author of Middle Comedy, who is said to have written 200 plays, was his uncle. Theophrastus, the successor of Aristotle, was his teacher, and was said to have written his *Characters* for Menander to use in the composition of his comedies: all that Menander had to do, if he wished to depict a flatterer or newsmonger or the like, was to consult the proper rubric in Theophrastus. He served his ephebate, according to Strabo 14.18, with the philosopher Epicurus. A Herculaneum papyrus makes Menander a friend of the cynic Diogenes, but this is chronologically impossible. Because of his connections and early training, he was permitted, contrary to ordinary practice, to compete in the Dionysiac festival when he was only 18 and still in his ephebate. Despite his enormous reputation in later years he won only eight victories, as we learn from epigraphical data, though he competed at every festival and wrote over a hundred plays. Martial (5.10) cites him as an example of a genius unrecognized by his contemporaries:

How shall I explain why fame is refused living men and why few readers admire their own times? It is the manner of Envy, Regulus, to prefer the ancient to the modern. . . . You, O Rome, read Ennius while Vergil lived. . . . Menander, honor of the theater, was seldom applauded; only Corinna knew her Ovid. Then be not too eager, my books: if glory comes only after death, there is no hurry.

Even Dio Chrysostom (18.7) feels that he is on the defensive when recommending Menander, whom he significantly couples with Euripides.

Menander was on good terms with his rival playwrights Diphilus and Philemon, who long survived him. Aulus Gellius (17.4) tells of an interesting encounter:

In contests in comedy Menander was often defeated by Philemon, a writer by no means his equal, owing to intrigue, favor, and partisan-

ship. When Menander once happened to meet his rival he said: "Pray pardon me, Philemon, but really, don't you blush when you defeat me?"

Menander did not belong to the Epicurean school, but lived well and had the reputation of being a dandy, as we learn from a fable of Phaedrus (5.1):

Demetrius called the Phalerean, held Athens under his wicked sway. As is the vulgar manner, men vied in rushing up to him and shouting Bravo! The very nobles kissed the hand which oppressed them, groaning inwardly at the sad turn of fortune. Last of all came the laggards, who took their ease, lest not to have come be reckoned a crime. Among these was Menander, famous for his comedies, which Demetrius himself had read, not knowing the author but admiring the man's genius. Menander soaked in perfume and with garments flowing, came in with a languid and mincing gait. When the tyrant saw him at the end of the line, he said: "Who is that homosexual who has dared come into my sight?" Those nearby said, "It is the writer Menander." Demetrius fell silent. . . .

It was Demetrius, probably, who procured Menander the invitation to the court of the Ptolemies, which he rejected. Of this and of much else about Menander we learn from two letters of Alciphron (4.18,19) which are fictitious, to be sure, but based on fact. Menander's correspondent is Glycera, formerly the mistress of Harpalus, the friend of Alexander the Great. Menander lived with Glycera in his comfortable villa in the Piraeus. Here is part of the letter in which Menander informs Glycera of the invitation:

The urgent purpose of my present letter, which I write in illness at the Piraeus—you know about those periods of weakness I am subject to, which those who do not like me are wont to call self-indulgence and giving myself airs—is to convey to you, while you are staying in town for the Threshing Festival of the Goddess, the following message: I have received from Ptolemy, king of Egypt, a letter, in which he makes the most earnest entreaties, promising, in royal fashion, "all the goods of the earth," as the saying goes, and extending an invitation not only to me but to Philemon; for he says that Philemon too has received a letter. And Philemon himself has written me, disclosing his own invitation, which is in lighter vein and, since not addressed to Menander, in less elegant style; but he will look to the matter and take his own counsel.

As for me, I shall not wait for counsel; no, Glycera, you have always been and now shall be my judgment and my Council of the Areopagus and my Heliastic Court—aye everything, I swear by Athena. Well then, I am sending you the King's letter, that I may indeed bore you twice—by making you read both my letter and the King's; and I want you to know what answer I have decided to make to him. To take a sea voyage and depart for Egypt, a kingdom so distant and remote, no, by the Twelve Gods, I cannot so much as think of it. No, even if Egypt were in Aegina yonder, close at hand, even so I would not have entertained the notion of giving up my own kingdom, your love, and alone in that great throng of Egyptians, without Glycera, of looking upon a populous wilderness. With greater pleasure and less danger I woo the favor of your embraces than the courts of all the satraps and kings in the world; too great frankness is dangerous, flattery despicable, success precarious.

And here is part of Glycera's reply:

I immediately read the King's letter which you sent me. . . . When my mother and sister and friend saw that both my face and my eyes betrayed unusual happiness, they said, "Dear Glycera, what great good fortune has come to you that you now appear to us so changed in soul and in body and in every way? You are radiant all over, and your glowing beauty bespeaks happiness and answered prayer." "Ptolemy, king of Egypt," I replied, "is sending for my Menander, promising him half of his kingdom, so to speak," raising my voice and speaking with greater emphasis in order that all the women there might hear; and as I spoke I flaunted and flourished in my hands the letter with its royal seal. "Are you glad, then, to be left

behind?" said they. But it wasn't that, Menander. No, by the Goddesses, I could never be made to believe this—not even if the proverbial ox were to speak and tell me so—that my Menander would
ever be willing or able to leave me, his Glycera, behind in Athens,
and, without me, to be monarch of Egypt in the midst of all its
wealth. On the contrary, this at any rate was plain from the King's
letter, which I read: he had apparently heard about my relations
with you and wanted, by sly innuendo, with an Egyptian version of
Attic wit, to tease you good-naturedly. I am glad of this, that the
story of our love has crossed the sea even to Egypt and has reached
the King; and he certainly is convinced, by what he has heard, that
he strives for the impossible when he wants Athens to cross the sea
to him. What indeed is Athens without Menander? And what is
Menander without Glycera? For it is I who sort out the masks and
dress the actors, and I stand in the wings, gripping my fingers,
until the theater breaks into applause—meanwhile trembling with
excitement; then, by Artemis, I recover my breath, and, embracing
you, the sacred author of those famous plays, I take you into my
arms.

Pliny (N.H. 7.30.111) ascribes Menander's refusal to loftier motives, and incidentally mentions an invitation to Macedonia also:

High testimony was born to Menander's eminence in comedy by
the kings of Egypt and Macedon when they sent a fleet and an
embassy to fetch him, but higher testimony was derived from himself by his preferment of the consciousness of literary merit to royal
fortune.

Menander's connection with Demetrius was sufficiently close to
endanger him when Demetrius fell into disfavor, as we learn from
Diogenes Laertius 5.79:

Menander the comic poet, as I have learnt, was very nearly brought
to trial for no other cause than that he was a friend of Demetrius.
However, Telesphorus, the nephew of Demetrius, begged him off.

Menander died at the age of 52 by drowning while bathing in the bay of Phalerum.

Scarcely any later writer who mentions Menander does so without some laudatory epithet. Propertius calls him *doctus* and *mundus*, Athenaeus "handsome," and Themistios "golden." Aristophanes of Byzantium said, "O Menander, and O life! Which of you imitated the other?" "He showed life like itself," said Manilius (5.477), and Cicero (*De republica* 4.13) spoke of his comedies as "the imitation of life, the mirror of life, the image of manners." Caesar praised Terence by calling him "a halved Menander."

As usual, we turn for a summary of appreciation to Quintilian, who also significantly couples Menander with Euripides (10.1.69):

Menander, as he often testifies in his works, had a profound admiration for Euripides, and imitated him, although in a different type of work. Now, the careful study of Menander alone would, in my opinion, be sufficient to develop all those qualities with the production of which my present work is concerned; so perfect is his representation of actual life, so rich is his power of invention and his gift of style, so perfectly does he adapt himself to every kind of circumstance, character and emotion. Indeed, those critics are no fools who think the speeches attributed to Charisius were in reality written by Menander. . . . Indeed, such is his supremacy that he has scarce left a name to other writers of the new comedy, and has cast them into darkness by the splendor of his own renown.

Of several epigrams on Menander in the *Anthology* that of Diodorus (7.370) may be cited:

Menander of Athens, the son of Diopeithes, the friend of Bacchus and the Muses, rests beneath me, or at least the little dust he shed in the funeral fire. But if thou seekest Menander himself thou shalt find him in the abode of Zeus or in the Islands of the Blest.

LOSSES IN HISTORY HAVE BEEN AS GREAT AS IN any other form. For the ordinary reader Greek history means Herodotus and Thucydides. If he is concerned with the record of events rather than a philosophical approach or artistic presentation, he adds Xenophon as a third name. And if he is a professional student of history or historiography he will know of other historians of the 4th century and the Hellenistic period—Theopompus and Ephorus, Duris and Timaeus, and others. But even Herodotus had predecessors and rivals, for whom our *locus classicus* is the fifth chapter of Dionysius of Halicarnassus' essay on Thucydides:

Before I begin to discuss the work of Thucydides, I want to say a few words about the other historians, his predecessors and contemporaries, which will throw light on the method of the man, thanks to which he was able to excel those who went before him, and his genius. Now of earlier historians before the Peloponnesian War there were a great number in a great many different places; among them may be mentioned Eugeon of Samos, Deiochus of Proconnesus, Eudemus of Paros, Democles of Phigalia, Hecataeus of Miletus, the Argive Acusilaus, Charon from Lampsacus, and Amelesagoras from Chalcedon; and among those who go back a little way before the Peloponnesian War and extend down to the age of Thucydides, Hellanicus of Lesbos, Damastes of Sigeum, Xenomedes of Ceos, Xanthus the Lydian, and numerous others. These men all adopted a similar method as regards the choice of themes and in talents did not differ very widely from one another, some of them writing Hellenic histories (as they called them), others barbarian histories; but instead of coordinating their accounts with each other, they treated of individual peoples and cities separately and brought out separate accounts of them; they all had the one same object, to bring to the general knowledge of the pub-

lic the written records that they found preserved in temples or in
secular buildings in the form in which they found them, neither
adding nor taking away anything; among these records were to be
found legends hallowed by the passage of time and melodramatic
adventure stories, which to the modern reader seem very naïve indeed; the language which they used was for the most part similar
(as many of them as adopted the same dialect of Greek), clear,
simple, unaffected, and concise, appropriate to the subject-matter,
and not revealing any elaborate art in composition; there is nevertheless a certain charm and grace which runs through their writings,
to a greater degree in some than in others, thanks to which their
works still survive.

The 5th century Ionian writers whom Dionysius here lists are not
mentioned in the Athenian tradition; knowledge of them seems to
date only from the Alexandrian age. This circumstance illustrates
an interesting aspect of the fate of ancient books, and reminds us
that good literature was produced in places other than Athens,
whose tradition alone we have inherited. The Ionian historians
never made their way to Athens because they could not compete
with Athenian dramatists, philosophers, and poets, and with the
histories of Thucydides and Herodotus, who made Athens his
home. The Ionian historians reached Alexandria directly, not
through the medium of Athens; we cannot know how many other
non-Athenian writers failed to reach even Alexandria.

The paragraph from Dionysius (who deals with historiography
more fully than any other ancient critic) also illustrates criticism's
peculiar approach to historians. The critic dealt with history as he
did with oratory, and studied mainly the historian's language and
style and secondarily his arrangement and scope: of the historian's
perceptions, philosophic insights, or program they have little to
say. The historian's ideals of political understanding, absolute veracity, and pragmatic utility are set forth by a number of historians,
perhaps most explicitly by Polybius. But for a general and valid program for the historian we go not to a professional critic but to
Lucian's satire on the pretentiousness, bombast, and general in-

eptitude of a series of works he had just read. Here are some selected sentences from Lucian's *How to Write History*:

Here is a serious fault to begin with. It is a fashion to neglect the examination of facts, and give the space gained to eulogies of generals and commanders; those of their own side they exalt to the skies, the other side they disparage intemperately. . . . History has only one concern and aim, and that is the useful; which again has only one single source, and that is truth.

One writer started with invoking the Muses to lend a hand. What a tasteful exordium! How suited to the historic spirit! How appropriate to the style! When he had got a little way on, he compared our ruler to Achilles, and the Parthian king to Thersites; he forgot that Achilles would have done better if he had had Hector instead of Thersites to beat.

Another is a keen emulator of Thucydides, and by way of close approximation to his model starts with his own name—most graceful of beginnings, redolent of Attic thyme! Look at it: "Crepereius Calpurnianus of Pompeiopolis wrote the history of the war between Parthia and Rome, how they warred one upon the other, beginning with the commencement of the war." After that exordium what need to describe the rest—harangues, plague, and so forth.

Another puts down a bald list of events, as prosy and commonplace as a private's or a carpenter's or a sutler's diary. However, there is more sense in this poor man's performance; he flies his true colors from the first; he has cleared the ground for some educated person who knows how to deal with history.

Perhaps I should balance him with a philosophic historian . . . who subjects his readers to a dialectic catechism.

Again, it would be a sinful neglect to omit the man who begins like this: "I devise to tell of Romans and Persians"; then a little later,

"For 'twas Heaven's decree that the Persians should suffer evils"; and again, "One Osroes there was, whom Hellenes named Oxyroes"—and much more in that style.

There is another distinguished artist in words—rather more Thucydidean than Thucydides—who gives, according to his own idea, the clearest, most convincing descriptions of every town, mountain, plain, or river. I wish my bitterest foe no worse fate than the reading of them. . . . It is helplessness about the real essentials, or ignorance of what should be given, that makes them take refuge in word painting—landscapes, caves, and the like; and when they do come upon a series of important matters, they are just like a slave whose master has left him his money and made him a rich man; he does not know how to put on his clothes or take his food properly; partridges or sweetbreads or hare are served; but he rushes in, and fills himself up with peasoup or salt fish, till he is fit to burst. Well, the man I spoke of gives the most unconvincing wounds and singular deaths: some one has his big toe injured, and dies on the spot; the general Priscus calls out, and seven-and-twenty of the enemy fall dead on the spot. As to the numbers killed, he actually falsifies dispatches; at Europus he slaughters 70,236 of the enemy, while the Romans lose two, and have seven wounded!

This writer has a passion for unadulterated Attic . . . poetical phraseology . . . like an actor with one foot raised on a high buskin, and the other in a slipper . . . brilliant high-sounding prefaces of outrageous length . . . fancy geography . . . the battle of Europus in less than seven whole lines, and twenty immortal hours on a dull and perfectly irrelevant tale about a Moorish trooper.

Another entertaining person, who has never set foot outside Corinth, nor traveled as far as its harbor—not to mention seeing Syria or Armenia—starts with words which impressed themselves on my memory: "Seeing is believing: I therefore write what I have seen, not what I have been told." . . . He had never so much as seen a battle-picture.

Then there is the splendid fellow who has boiled down into the compass of 500 lines (or less, to be accurate) the whole business from beginning to end. . . . His title very narrowly misses being longer than his book. These people's uneducated antics are infinite; they have no eye for the noteworthy, nor, if they had eyes, any adequate faculty of expression; invention and fiction provide their matter, and belief in the first word that comes their style; they pride themselves on the number of books they run to.

My perfect historian must start with two indispensable qualifications; the one is political insight, the other the faculty of expression. . . . Let him be a man of independent spirit, with nothing to fear or hope from anybody. . . . The historian's task is to tell the thing as it happened . . . he must sacrifice to no god but Truth; he must neglect all else. . . . The historian's position should be precisely that of Zeus in Homer, surveying now the Mysians', now the Thracian horsemen's land.

The historian Polybius makes criticisms similar to Lucian's in the course of his remarks on some of his predecessors. In connection with his strictures on Timaeus he says (12.28.2 ff.):

It appears to me that the dignity of history also demands such a man. Plato, as we know, tells us that human affairs will then go well when either philosophers become kings or kings study philosophy, and I would say that it will be well with history either when men of action undertake to write history, not as now happens in a perfunctory manner, but when in the belief that this is a most necessary and most noble thing they apply themselves all through their life to it with undivided attention, or again when would-be authors regard a training in actual affairs as necessary for writing history. Before this be so the errors of historians will never cease.

And in criticizing Phylarchus for his pathos Polybius draws a valid contrast between history and imaginative writing (2.56.7 ff.):

In his eagerness to arouse the pity and attention of his readers he treats us to a picture of clinging women with their hair disheveled and their breasts bare, or again of crowds of both sexes together with their children and aged parents weeping and lamenting as they are led away to slavery. This sort of thing he keeps up throughout his history, always trying to bring horrors vividly before our eyes. Leaving aside the ignoble and womanish character of such a treatment of his subject, let us consider how far it is proper or serviceable to history. A historical author should not try to thrill his readers by such exaggerated pictures, nor should he, like a tragic poet, try to imagine the probable utterances of his characters or reckon up all the consequences probably incidental to the occurrences with which he deals, but simply record what really happened and what really was said, however commonplace. For the object of tragedy is not the same as that of history but quite the opposite. The tragic poet should thrill and charm his audience for the moment by the verisimilitude of the words he puts into his characters' mouths, but it is the task of the historian to instruct and convince for all time serious students by the truth of the facts and the speeches he narrates, since in the one case it is the probable that takes precedence, even if it be untrue, the purpose being to create illusion in spectators, in the other it is the truth, the purpose being to confer benefit on learners.

I. HERODOTUS

From his own book we should know that Herodotus lived until 430 B.C., for he knows events of that year, and that he died probably before 424, for he fails to mention, at the appropriate point (6.91) the destruction of the Aeginetans at Thyria (Thucydides 4.57). Thucydides does not name him, though his aspersions on his uncritical predecessors at 1.20 patently refer to Herodotus, and a parody of Herodotus is equally patent in Aristophanes' *Acharnians*, which was presented in 425. The account of the origin of the war put into the mouth of Dicaeopolis in that play (513 ff.) echoes the opening chapters of Herodotus:

Some young drunkards go to Megara and carry off the courtesan
Simaetha; the Megarians, hurt to the quick, run off in turn with
two harlots of the house of Aspasia; and so, for three gay women
Greece is set ablaze. Then Pericles, aflame with ire on his Olympian
height, let loose the lightning, caused the thunder to roll, upset
Greece. . . .

Other data—his birth, of good family, in Halicarnassus, a little before the Persian War, his relationship to the epic poet Panyasis, his
sojourn in Samos, his participation in the Athenian colonization
of Thurii in 443—come from notices in Dionysius of Halicarnassus,
Gellius, and Eusebius. Of his wide travels he himself speaks. Concerning Panyasis Suidas tells us that he was of Halicarnassus, a seer
of signs and an epic poet, and uncle to Herodotus. For the historian himself Suidas' entry, not of course reliable in every point, is
as follows:

Herodotus; son of Lyxes and Dryo, a Halicarnassian, of the better
class, and had a brother Theodorus. He removed to Samos because
of Lygdamis, the tyrant of Halicarnassus third after Artemisia. For
Pisindelis was son of Artemisia and Lygdamis of Pisindelis. In Samos
then he was practised in the Ionic dialect and wrote a history in
nine books, starting from Cyrus the Persian and Candaules king of
the Lydians. After coming back to Halicarnassus and driving out
the tyrant, when later he saw himself disliked by the citizens, he
went as a volunteer to Thurion, then being colonized by the Athe-
nians, and there he died and is buried in the agora. But some say he
died at Pella. His books are inscribed [by later hands] Muses.

The epigram which Stephen of Byzantium says was inscribed on his
tomb at Thurii may be spurious, but the connection with Thurii is
certain. Aristotle (*Rhetoric* 1409a) cites the opening sentence as
"This is the setting forth of the inquiry of Herodotus of Thurii,"
which is thus an ancient variant of our reading "of Halicarnassus."

Though Suidas says nothing of an Athenian sojourn we know
that he recited portions of his work there, and is said to have been

paid ten talents by the Athenians. The amount seems incredibly large for a literary fee; and to explain it and the source of funds for Herodotus' expensive travels some scholars have hit upon the utterly fanciful idea that he was employed in collecting intelligence for the Athenian government. Certainly Herodotus was on terms of friendship with Sophocles, who addressed a poem to him on his 55th birthday (the opening lines are quoted in Plutarch, *Whether an Old Man Should Engage in Politics* 785b) and borrowed certain motifs from him. Of these the most familiar in the extant plays are: Egyptian women do the work of men (*Oedipus at Colonus* 337; cf. Herodotus 2.35); an irreplaceable brother deserves greater sacrifice than a husband (*Antigone* 905 ff.; cf. Herodotus 3.119); and no evil omen attaches to a false report of death (*Electra* 62; cf. Herodotus 4.95).

Adverse estimates of Herodotus' reliability start with a famous chapter of Thucydides (1.20):

The way that most men deal with traditions, even traditions of their own country, is to receive them all alike as they are delivered, without applying any critical test whatever. [*Thucydides then instances the story of Harmodius and Aristogiton as told in Herodotus, but without naming him.*] *So little pains do the vulgar take in the investigation of truth. . . . I have written my work not as an essay to win the applause of the moment, but as a possession for all time.*

From being disparaged merely as an uncritical historian, Herodotus comes to be called, for example by Aristotle (*On the Generation of Animals* 756b), a teller of fables (*mythologos*), and then, "by everybody," a simple liar; so Josephus (*Against Apion* 1.16) says:

It would be superfluous for me to point out to readers better informed than myself . . . how the mendacity of Hellanicus is exposed by Ephorus, that of Ephorus by Timaeus, that of Timaeus by later writers, and that of Herodotus by everybody.

At 1.73 Josephus reports that Manetho "convicts Herodotus of being misled through ignorance on many points of Egyptian history." Herodotus' reputation as a liar is illustrated in several passages of Lucian. Describing the punishment of the wicked in his *True History* (2.31) Lucian writes:

Our guides described the life and guilt of each culprit; the severest torments were reserved for those who in life had been liars and written false history; the class was numerous, and included Ctesias of Cnidus, and Herodotus. The fact was an encouragement to me, knowing that I had never told a lie.

And in *Liar* 2 he has:

What satisfaction can there be to men of good qualities in deceiving themselves and their neighbors? . . . Look at Herodotus, or Ctesias of Cnidus. . . . Here are men of world-wide celebrity perpetuating their mendacity in black and white.

But at the same time Lucian is very appreciative of Herodotus' style (*Herodotus* 1):

I devoutly wish that Herodotus' other characteristics were imitable; not all of them, of course—that is past praying for—but any one of them: the agreeable style, the constructive skill, the native charm of his Ionic, the sententious wealth, or any of a thousand beauties which he combined into one whole, to the despair of imitators.

Roman writers of the 1st century B.C. favored the style and approach of Thucydides, and even Cicero, who gave Herodotus the title of "father of history" (*De legibus* 1.5), also said he had *innumerabiles fabulae*. It is probably in conscious reaction to this attitude that Dionysius of Halicarnassus at several points in his critical writings rises to the defense of his great fellow-townsman; his own historical writing is full of palpable imitations of Herodotus. Local patriotism is also the motive of the otherwise amiable Plutarch's treatise *On the Malignity of Herodotus*. Other critics had merely said that Herodotus was careless with the truth; Plutarch says he purposely deceived. Here are the opening sentences of the treatise:

Many readers have been deceived by Herodotus' style, which is simple, demands no effort, and runs easily along with the subject matter; but more have been deceived by his character. Not only is it, as Plato says, the extreme of injustice for a man to appear just when he is not; but it is the very height of malignity to simulate easy temper and straightforwardness and make oneself hard to unmask. Forasmuch as Herodotus has given vent to his malignity especially against the Boeotians and Corinthians, and has not spared others, I deem it incumbent upon me, in this portion of my work, to rise to the defense at once of my ancestors and of truth.

Like that Hippoclides in his own story (6.129) who danced his bride away and said "Hippoclides doesn't care," Herodotus, says Plutarch (33, 874b), danced the truth away and said "Herodotus doesn't care." "His calumnies," Plutarch closes, "must be watched out for, like insects among roses." It is his very charm that makes Herodotus dangerous, and for that charm the best testimonial remains "Longinus," who at 13.13 calls him "most Homeric" and at 26.2 exclaims:

You see, friend, how he takes you along with him through the country [Egypt] and turns hearing into sight?

The Renaissance recognized Herodotus' charm; Lorenzo Valla's translation, made in 1452–1456, was printed in 1474 and frequently thereafter. But ancient opinions on Herodotus' mendacity were so widely accepted that for his edition of Valla Henri Estienne thought it worth while to preface a defense of Herodotus' veracity. In 1566 (and eleven times during Estienne's life) this defense, decked out with numerous examples of more serious contemporary clerical deception, was printed at Geneva under the title *Introduction au traité de la conformité des merveilles anciennes avec les modernes ou traité préparatif à l'apologie pour Hérodote*. This is in effect an armory of charges against popes and priests. Another admirer was Philip Melanchthon, who thought Herodotus superior to Thucydides for teaching purposes, and illustrated his excellence in structure by contrasting his history with the amorphous Talmud. Melanchthon's selection of school authors included, besides Herodotus, Homer, Demosthenes, and Lucian. Gibbon initiated the more perceptive modern criticism when he said, "Herodotus sometimes writes for children and sometimes for philosophers." With the years specialists in social history and anthropology have come to appreciate the adult worth of even those sections of Herodotus which Gibbon thought appropriate only for children.

II. THUCYDIDES

Older editions of Thucydides are regularly prefaced by the *Life of Thucydides* by Marcellinus (probably 6th century A.D.), which gives a full account of the historian's family and career and embodies, in two of its three sections, the work of other writers who were chiefly interested in style. But the *Life* is valuable only as it is based on intelligent inferences from the pages of Thucydides: nothing beyond this is trustworthy. The fact is that we can know nothing more of Thucydides than he himself tells us; there is no mention of him in the orators or Plato or Aristotle. Three writers— Xenophon, Theopompus and Cratippus—undertook to complete his unfinished history, and of Xenophon, whose *Hellenica* is the only continuation extant, Diogenes Laertius (2.57) tells us that he could easily have suppressed the Thucydidean authorship and have claimed the work as his own. All of this suggests that Thucydides' history was little known in his own or the following generations except to professed historians. The story that Demosthenes copied the text of Thucydides with his own hand eight times is found in Lucian (*Illiterate Book Fancier* 4), but the story sounds like an invention based on an affinity in the characters of the two men and on similar stories of Demosthenes' self-discipline. Theophrastus is cited in Cicero (*Orator* 12.39) as naming Thucydides along with Herodotus as pioneers in artistic historiography, but it appears that the Alexandrians, who worked in the Peripatetic tradition, did not bestow upon Thucydides the care which they devoted to other authors. The quite logical division into eight books is probably Alexandrian (Marcellinus mentions another into 13 books, which shows that neither division was Thucydides' own), and the not infrequent citation of Thucydides in scholia follows the eight-book division.

It is in the Roman period that the name of Thucydides is most frequently invoked; indeed he becomes an issue in a war of rhetoricians, whose course can best be illustrated from Cicero. In *On the Orator* (2.13.56), written in 55 B.C., Cicero says:

After Herodotus' day, Thucydides, in my judgment, easily surpassed all others in dexterity of composition: so abounding is he in fullness of material that in the number of his ideas he well nigh equals the number of his words, and furthermore he is so exact and clear in expression that you cannot tell whether it be the narrative that gains illumination from the style, or the diction from the thought.

So in several of his letters and other early writings allusions to Thucydides are regularly complimentary. Thucydides seems to have enjoyed a special vogue in the middle of the first century B.C., of which Lucretius' close adaptation of the account of the plague may be an evidence, and adherents of the simple and concise Attic style made him a model even for oratory. To this tendency Cicero, who favored more opulent expression, objected, and in several passages (*Brutus* 287; *Orator* 9.30; *On the Best Kind of Orators* 5.15) he declares that Thucydides is an unsuitable model. "What perversity can make men feed on acorns," he says (*Orator* 31), "after grain has been discovered?"

It is to be expected then, that such an opponent of strict Atticism as Dionysius of Halicarnassus, should find fault with Thucydides. Dionysius devoted three treatises to the historian: *On the Character of Thucydides and the Other Peculiarities of the Historian; On the Peculiarities of Thucydides*, an expansion of a portion of the first; and the *Epistle to Cn. Pompey*. Dionysius criticizes Thucydides for his method of dating, for his bad arrangements (e.g. the Funeral Oration should have been better placed), and for his inequitable distribution of space. Of Dionysius' capacity as a historical critic the following (*To Cn. Pompey* 34) will afford an illustration:

Thucydides wrote only of a single war, and that neither a glorious or successful one. Better far it were for the war never to have taken place; having taken place it should have been consigned to silence and oblivion by posterity and ignored. That he had chosen an evil subject he himself makes evident in his proem, so that those who read the proem are repelled from the subject, learning that they are about to hear of Greek woes.

Quintilian, as may be expected, invokes the judgment of Cicero (10.1.33):

We must remember that Cicero thinks that not even Thucydides or Xenophon will be of much service to an orator, although he regards the style of the former as a veritable call to arms and considers that the latter was the mouthpiece of the Muses.

This dictum comes as a conclusion to general remarks on the orator's use of history (10.1.31):

History, also, may provide the orator with a nutriment which we may compare to some rich and pleasant juice. But when we read it, we must remember that many of the excellences of the historian require to be shunned by the orator. For history has a certain affinity to poetry and may be regarded as a kind of prose poem, while it is written for the purpose of narrative, not of proof, and designed from beginning to end not for immediate effect or the instant necessities of forensic strife, but to record events for the benefit of posterity and to win glory for its author. Consequently, to avoid monotony of narrative, it employs unusual words and indulges in a freer use of figures. Therefore, as I have already said, the famous brevity of Sallust, than which nothing can be more pleasing to the leisured

ear of the scholar, is a style to be avoided by the orator in view of
the fact that his words are addressed to a judge who has his mind
occupied by a number of thoughts and is also frequently uneducated, while, on the other hand, the milky fullness of Livy is hardly
of a kind to instruct a listener who looks not for beauty of exposition, but for truth and credibility.

Only Livy, among the great Roman historians, seems designedly
un-Thucydidean. Sallust, Tacitus, and especially Ammianus Marcellinus show clear signs of Thucydidean influence. One of Josephus'
Greek assistants quite clearly apes Thucydides. With the archaizing
bent of the Second Sophistic it is to be expected that there would
be high appreciation of Thucydides—and oblivion to his true greatness. So Dio Chrysostom (18.10) values Thucydides, but only as a
stylist:

Among the foremost historians I place Thucydides, and among those
of second rank Theopompus; for not only is there a rhetorical quality
in the narrative portion of his speeches, but he is not without eloquence nor negligent in expression, and the slovenliness of his diction is not so bad as to offend you. As for Ephorus, while he hands
down to us a great deal of information about events, yet the tedious-
ness and carelessness of his narrative style would not suit your purpose.

Even Plutarch (On the Glory of the Athenians 367b) praises Thucydides mainly for vividness:

In his discourse Thucydides always strives to make the auditor as
it were a spectator of events, endeavoring to induce in readers the
stirring and vehement passion of spectators.

Elsewhere he praises the sententiae of Thucydides and his noble
dignity, and he contrasts his good-will with Herodotus' ill-will. In
the Lives of heroes of the Thucydidean period Thucydides is naturally Plutarch's prime source, yet even when Plutarch acknowl-

edges his indebtedness he speaks rather of form than of matter
(*Nicias* 1):

*It will be well for me to entreat the reader, in all courtesy, not to
think that I contend with Thucydides in matters so pathetically,
vividly and eloquently, beyond all imitations, and even beyond himself, expressed by him.*

The Renaissance accepted Roman judgment in regard to Thucydides' superiority to Herodotus, to the degree, as we have seen, that
Herodotus required special defenders. And as history grew more
critical and men became more interested in the philosophy of history, respect for Thucydides increased until certain enthusiasts
reached the point of acclaiming Thucydides the greatest historian
of all time. "In the case of Thucydides," writes Grote, "the qualities necessary to the historiographer, in their application to recent
events, have been developed with a degree of perfection never since
surpassed." Not only is Thucydides supreme for his intellectual
grasp, balance, and essential truth, but his narrative and its arrangement (Dionysius to the contrary notwithstanding) is praised by so
demanding a historical critic as Macaulay, who writes:

*It must be allowed that Thucydides has surpassed all his rivals in
the art of historical narration, in the art of producing an effect on
the imagination, by skilful selection and disposition, without in-
dulging in the licence of invention.*

III. XENOPHON

Xenophon not only continued the history of Thucydides but, like
Plato, commemorated his teacher Socrates in dialogues. Hence,
fortunately, Diogenes Laertius can rate him a philosopher and sum-
marize what the ancients knew and thought of him (2.6.48 ff.):

*Xenophon, the son of Gryllus, was a citizen of Athens and belonged
to the deme Erchia; he was a man of rare modesty and extremely
handsome. The story goes that Socrates met him in a narrow pas-*

sage, and that he stretched out his stick to bar the way, while he inquired where every kind of food was sold. Upon receiving a reply, he put another question, "And where do men become good and honorable?" Xenophon was fairly puzzled; "Then follow me," said Socrates, "and learn." From that time onward he was a pupil of Socrates. He was the first to take notes of, and to give to the world, the conversation of Socrates, under the title of Memorabilia. Moreover, he was the first to write a history of philosophers.

Diogenes next tells how he was enamored of Clinias and how he became attached to Cyrus. Xenophon's friend Proxenus wrote urging him to accept service with Cyrus—

Xenophon showed this letter to Socrates and asked his advice, which was that he should go to Delphi and consult the oracle. Xenophon complied and came into the presence of the god. He inquired, not whether he should go and seek service with Cyrus, but in what way he should do so. For this Socrates blamed him, yet at the same time he advised him to go. On his arrival at the court of Cyrus he became as warmly attached to him as Proxenus himself. We have his own sufficient narrative of all that happened on the expedition and on the return home.

After the expedition of the Ten Thousand, Xenophon took service with the Spartan Agesilaus, whom he greatly admired, and in consequence lost his Athenian citizenship. At Scillus in Elis, possibly with money provided by Sparta, Xenophon acquired an estate which he endeavored to make into a miniature Ephesus, and there, "from that time forward he hunted, entertained his friends, and worked at his histories, without interruption." When Athens decided to help Sparta, Xenophon's two sons—called the Dioscuri for their handsomeness—served with the Athenians, and Gryllus, the elder, fell.

On this occasion Xenophon is said to have been sacrificing, with a chaplet on his head, which he removed when his son's death was

announced. But afterwards, upon learning that he had fallen glori-
ously, he replaced the chaplet on his head. Some say that he did not
even shed tears, but exclaimed, "I knew my son was mortal."

This is how Diogenes summarizes Xenophon's career:

He was a worthy man in general, particularly fond of horses and
hunting, an able tactician as is clear from his writings, pious, fond
of sacrificing, and an expert in augury from the victims; and he
made Socrates his exact model.

Pausanias describes Xenophon's life at Scillus, as told him by native guides, and then says (5.6.4):

At a little distance from the sanctuary he had built was shown a
tomb, and upon the grave is a statue of Pentelic marble. The neighbors say that it is the tomb of Xenophon.

Xenophon's political conservatism and military resourcefulness and
his simplicity in style and matter made him a particular favorite
with the Romans. Cicero translated the Oeconomicus and Quintilian says (10.1.82):

Why should I speak of the unaffected charm of Xenophon, so far
beyond the powers of affectation to attain? The Graces themselves
seem to have moulded his style, and we may with the utmost justice
say of him, what the writer of the old comedy said of Pericles, that
the goddess of persuasion sat enthroned upon his lips.

The one treatise in the Xenophontic corpus which is certainly
not Xenophon's is On the Constitution of Athens, of which the
author has been dubbed, in modern times, "the Old Oligarch." The
author of the Ephesiaca is naturally a much later Xenophon. Xenophon's very easy and exciting Anabasis has traditionally been the
school-boy's first Greek book, his Hellenica is our indispensable
guide to the fascinating history of the turn of the 4th and 5th cen-

turies, and his Socratic writings provide a useful pendant to Plato's, but the most influential of Xenophon's books has been his *Cyropedia*, which is a fictional account of the education of the elder Cyrus. Directly and through adaptations in various Mirrors of Princes this work has had an appreciable effect in shaping European ideas of what a gentleman should be.

IV. POLYBIUS

The names and fragments of a number of historians of the Hellenistic period are known to us, but the next Greek historian whose work is extant in complete books, and the only ancient historian worthy of being mentioned in the same breath with Thucydides is Polybius (203–120 B.C.), who was the first foreigner to understand the greatness and destiny of Rome and the weakness of his own people. In his *General Observations on the Fall of the Roman Empire in the West*, at the close of his Chapter 38, Gibbon writes:

A wiser Greek, who has composed, with a philosophic spirit, the memorable history of his own times, deprived his countrymen of this vain and delusive comfort [that their decline was due only to chance] by opening to their view the deep foundations of the greatness of Rome.

Polybius' father was Lycortas, a distinguished general of the Achaean League, and we first meet Polybius (in 183 B.C.) carrying the ashes of Philopoemen, "the last of the Greeks," in the funeral procession which his father arranged (Plutarch, *Philopoemen* 20):

They burned his body, and put the ashes into an urn, and then marched homeward, not as in an ordinary march, but with a kind of solemn pomp, half triumph, half funeral, crowns of victory on their heads, and tears in their eyes, and their captive enemies in fetters by them. Polybius, the general's son, carried the urn, so covered with garlands and ribbons as scarcely to be visible; and the noblest of the Achaeans accompanied him.

When he was only 20 Polybius went on an embassy to Egypt, and in 169 he was, as he himself tells us (28.6) Hipparch of the Achaeans. After the Roman victory at Pydna in 167 Polybius was taken to Rome as one of the thousand noble Achaean hostages the Romans demanded, and there he became attached to the philhellene circle of Scipio, of which the satirist Lucilius, the comic poet Terence, and the Stoic Panaetius were also members, and more particularly to Scipio himself, whom he accompanied on his expeditions. He was with him at the fall of Carthage, in 146. Appian (*Punica* 132) tells how Scipio was depressed by the thought of the transitoriness of human greatness, and how Polybius shared his feeling:

After meditating by himself a long time and reflecting on the inevitable fall of cities, nations, and empires, as well as of individuals, upon the fate of Troy, that once proud city, upon the fate of the Assyrian, the Median, and afterwards of the great Persian empire, and, most recently of all, of the splendid empire of Macedon, either voluntarily or otherwise the words of the poet escaped his lips:

> *The day shall come in which our sacred Troy*
> *And Priam, and the people over whom*
> *Spear-bearing Priam rules, shall perish all* (Iliad 6.448 f.).

Being asked by Polybius in familiar conversation (for Polybius had been his tutor) what he meant by using these words, Polybius says that he did not hesitate frankly to name his own country, for whose fate he feared when he considered the mutability of human affairs.

Polybius did see the fall of Corinth the same year, and was with Scipio at the fall of Numantia in 133. Velleius Paterculus 1.13 has: "Scipio was a fastidious patron and connoisseur of all liberal studies and doctrine, and kept with him, at home and in the field, Polybius and Panaetius, men of surpassing talents." Polybius' relations with Scipio are referred to by Diodorus Siculus and several times by Plutarch. When the question of releasing the Achaean hostages (of whom Polybius was one) was brought up, the Elder Cato, Plutarch tells us, remarked that it little suited the Senate's dignity to debate whether Greek or Roman undertakers should bury the derelicts. The treatise on *Long Lives* ascribed to Lucian (22) notes that

Polybius, son of Lycortas, the Megalopolitan, fell from his horse as he was returning from the country; he sickened of the fall, and died, being 82 years of age.

Among his fellow Greeks Polybius' reputation as a wise statesman, if not as a writer, was very high. Pausanias mentions several statues erected to him in Greek cities; here is his account of the one in Polybius' native Megalopolis (8.30.8):

In the market-place of that city, behind the enclosure sacred to Lycaean Zeus, is the figure of a man carved in relief on a slab, Polybius, the son of Lycortas. Elegiac verses are inscribed upon it saying that he roamed over every land and every sea, and that he became the ally of the Romans and stayed their wrath against the Greek nation. This Polybius wrote also a history of the Romans, including how they went to war with Carthage, what the cause of the war was, and how at last, not before great dangers had been run, Scipio [lacuna] whom they name Carthaginian, because he put an end to the war and razed Carthage to the ground. Whenever the Romans obeyed the advice of Polybius, things went well with them, but they say that whenever they would not listen to his instructions they made mistakes. All the Greek cities that were members of the Achaean League got permission from the Romans that Polybius should draw up constitutions for them and frame laws. On the left of the portrait-statue of Polybius is the Council Chamber.

One base of a statue bearing an honorific decree to Polybius has been preserved (Dittenberger, *Sylloge*, 317). In his treatise on *Whether an Old Man Should Engage in Politics* (790 f.) Plutarch numbers Polybius as a shining example of one who as a young man learned from active statesmen, and as a statesman taught other young men.

Virtually all subsequent historians who deal with his period have used Polybius. Livy's fine third decad is based on Polybius directly or through such intermediaries as Coelius Antipater; but Livy's mention of him as a *haudquaquam spernendus auctor*, "an author by no means contemptible" (30.45), has a faintly contemptuous ring. Strabo speaks of Polybius with respect, but at 2.4.2 ff. carries on a long polemic against what he considers Polybius' errors in geography. Cicero, on the other hand, thinks him a first-class author (*Offices* 3.32), and so do such later ecclesiastical writers as Zosimus and Xiphilinus. Even Athenaeus quotes him often and with respect.

What militated most against Polybius' reputation was his undistinguished style. Dionysius of Halicarnassus, *On the Composition of Words* 4, speaks of style as being the chief distinction of the "classic" historians, and mentions Polybius along with Phylarchus, Duris, and Psaon as being writers whom "no one can endure to read to the end." Nineteenth century educators similarly rejected Polybius as unfit, on stylistic grounds, to be put into the hands of schoolboys. But if they, like Dionysius, were blind to Polybius' real value (and his style is perfectly suitable to his matter) the Renaissance was not. Machiavelli, who could not read Greek but knew Polybius from Perotti's Latin version, would seem to have learned the essence of Machiavellism from him. Both in the *Prince* and in the *Discourses on the First Decad of Livy* a number of examples and much of the "pragmatic" outlook echoes Polybius. Critical historians of the 19th and 20th centuries put Polybius far above any other ancient writer who dealt with Rome. The great Theodor Mommsen wrote:

His books are like the sun; at the point where they begin the veil of mist which envelops the Samnite and Pyrrhic wars is raised, and at the point where they end a new and, if possible, still more vexatious twilight begins.

12: *Philosophy*

I. THE SAGES

WHEN HELLENIZED DESCENDANTS OF other ancient peoples of the Near East put forward claims to the high antiquity and excellence of their several civilizations, the Greeks insisted upon their own preeminence, basing their claim (as doubtless we should also) on their high achievement in philosophy. Here is Josephus, for example, calling the Greeks upstarts (*Against Apion* 1.6–7):

My first thought is one of intense astonishment at the current opinion that in ancient matters the Greeks alone deserve serious attention, that the truth should be sought from them, and that neither we nor any others in the world are to be trusted. In my view the very reverse of this is the case, if, that is to say, we are not to take idle prejudices as our guide, but to extract the truth from the facts themselves. For in the Greek world everything will be found to be modern, and dating so to speak, from yesterday or the day before.

Diogenes Laertius starts his account of the doctrines of the philosophers by refuting the claims of the "barbarians" and asserting the primacy of the Greeks:

There are some who say that the study of philosophy had its beginning among the barbarians. They urge that the Persians have had their Magi, the Babylonians or Assyrians their Chaldaeans, and the Indians their Gymnosophists; and among the Celts and Gauls there are the people called Druids or Holy Ones. . . . If we may believe the Egyptians, Hephaestus was the Son of the Nile, and with him philosophy began, priests and prophets being its chief exponents. Hephaestus lived 48,863 years before Alexander of Macedon, and in the interval there occurred 373 solar and 832 lunar eclipses. . . .
   These authors forget that the achievements which they attribute

to the barbarians belong to the Greeks, with whom not merely philosophy but the human race itself began. . . . The first to use the
term, and to call himself a philosopher or lover of wisdom, was
Pythagoras. . . . All too quickly the study was called wisdom and
its professor a sage, to denote his attainment of mental perfection;
while the student who took it up was a philosopher or lover of wisdom. Sophists was another name for the wise men, and not only for
philosophers but for the poets also. And so Cratinus when praising
Homer and Hesiod in his Archilochi gives them the title of sophist.
The men who were commonly regarded as sages were the following:
Thales, Solon, Periander, Cleobulus, Chilon, Bias, Pittacus. To
these are added Anacharsis the Scythian, Myson of Chen, Pherecydes of Syros, Epimenides the Cretan; and by some even Pisistratus
the tyrant. So much for the sages or wise men.

About the names of the sages there naturally gathered a mass of
anecdotes, mostly illustrating their practical sagacity rather than
their philosophical insights, to refute such mockery as this cited by
Socrates (Theaetetus 174a):

I will illustrate my meaning, Theodorus, by the jest which the clever,
witty Thracian handmaid made about Thales, when he fell into a
well as he was looking up at the stars. She said, that he was so eager
to know what was going on in heaven, that he could not see what
was before his feet. This is a jest which is equally applicable to all
philosophers. For the philosopher is wholly unacquainted with his
next door neighbor; he is ignorant, not only of what he is doing,
but whether he is or is not a human creature; he is searching into
the essence of man, and is unwearied in discovering what belongs
to such a nature to do or suffer different from any other; I think
that you understand me, Theodorus?

The proper retort to such Philistinism is the anecdote cited by Aristotle (Politics 1.11, 1259a):

There is the anecdote of Thales the Milesian and his financial device,
which involves a principle of universal application, but is attributed

to him on account of his reputation for wisdom. He was reproached for his poverty, which was supposed to show that philosophy was of no use. According to the story, he knew by his skill in the stars while it was yet winter that there would be a great harvest of olives in the coming year; so, having a little money, he gave deposits for the use of all the olive-presses in Chios and Miletus, which he hired at a low price because no one bid against him. When the harvest-time came, and many were wanted all at once and of a sudden, he let them out at any rate which he pleased, and made a quantity of money. Thus he showed the world that philosophers can easily be rich if they like, but that their ambition is of another sort.

Thales' gift for neat utterance is illustrated from the following, in Diogenes Laertius 1.26:

When he was asked why he had no children of his own he replied "because he loved children." The story is told that, when his mother tried to force him to marry, he replied it was too soon, and when she pressed him again later in life, he replied that it was too late.

But Thales could give sound political and military advice also. When the Ionians were endangered by the Persian advance, Thales advised that they federate under a single central government (Herodotus 1.170). He made a useful prophecy of the solar eclipse of 28 May 585 B.C. (id. 1.74), and enabled Croesus' army to cross the Halys by dividing its current (id. 1.75).

For the remaining sages and Ionian "physicists" we can regrettably find no room here, but of Pythagoras, though he himself left no writings, something must be said. Even for Herodotus, who alludes to his doctrine several times (2.81, 123, 4.95) Pythagoras is a dim figure. How little was actually known of him is reflected by a note in Clement of Alexandria (Stromateis 1.62):

Pythagoras son of Mnesarchus was a Samian, as Hippobotus says, but according to Aristoxenus in his Life of Pythagoras, and according to Aristarchus and Theopompus he was a Tuscan; according to

Neanthes he was a Syrian or Tyrian. According to most authorities, then, Pythagoras was barbarian by race.

The vagueness of the tradition, and at the same time the respect in which it was held, is shown by a passage in Isocrates' *Busiris* (28), written as early as 390 B.C.:

On a visit to Egypt Pythagoras became a student of the religion of the people, and was first to bring to the Greeks all philosophy, and more conspicuously than others he seriously interested himself in sacrifices and in ceremonial purity, since he believed that even if he should gain thereby no greater reward from the gods, among men, at any rate, his reputation would be greatly enhanced. And this indeed happened to him. For so greatly did he surpass all others in reputation that all the younger men desired to be his pupils, and their elders were more pleased to see their sons staying in his company than attending to their private affairs. And these reports we cannot disbelieve: for even now persons who profess to be followers of his teaching are more admired when silent than are those who have the greatest renown for eloquence.

Plato (*Republic* 10.600a) speaks in similar terms of the respect in which Pythagoras and Pythagoreans were held:

Had Homer in his life-time friends and associates who loved him and handed down to posterity an Homeric way of life, such as that which Pythagoras invented and his followers continue, who are still called after his name, and seem to have a certain distinction above other men?

It is unfair as well as unpracticable to cite the odd Pythagorean doctrines on diet and numbers without commentary. Our fullest statements concerning these matters are to be found in the writings of the Neoplatonists, by whom Pythagoras was held in special reverence and his life treated as a sacred text. Porphyry (A.D. 232–305) wrote his *Life*, as he did that of his master Plotinus, and

Iamblichus (A.D. 250–325) wrote a treatise On the Pythagorean Life. Philostratus' Life of Apollonius of Tyana follows the treatment and some of the detail of the Neoplatonist lives of Pythagoras, and Philostratus' Life of Apollonius influenced Athanasius' of St. Anthony, and so the whole succession of the lives of the saints. Jewish and Christian apologists spread the idea abroad that Pythagoras himself adopted Jewish ideas; here is the passage in Josephus (Against Apion 1.162 ff.):

Pythagoras, that ancient sage of Samos, who for wisdom and piety is ranked above all the philosophers, evidently not only knew of our institutions, but was even in those distant ages an ardent admirer of them. Of the master himself we possess no authentic work, but his history has been told by many writers. The most distinguished of these is Hermippus, always a careful historian . . . who says: "In practising and repeating these precepts he was imitating and appropriating the doctrines of Jews and Thracians."

Eusebius (Evangelical Preparation 13.12, 664a) quotes Aristobulus as saying:

Pythagoras too [as well as Plato] appropriated many things from us and introduced them into his doctrine.

It is remarkable that even without a Plato to advertise him Pythagoras' name is almost as familiar as Socrates'. He has even penetrated the forest of Arden, where Rosalind says, "I was never so berimed since Pythagoras' time, that I was an Irish rat."

II. SOCRATES

Socrates himself, like the Neoplatonist master Ammonius, the Stoic Epictetus, and other famous teachers, wrote nothing, but he is nevertheless probably the best known and best beloved of pagan teachers. For Plato the life of Socrates is itself a major text, and not the least of the aims of his Socratic dialogues is to illuminate and defend that life. The *Apology* does this directly; the others only in less degree. Perhaps the clearest case is the *Symposium*, where Plato takes pains to show that Socrates *could* get himself dressed for a party and *was* received in polite society; and any dubiety about Socrates' courage and the sincerity of his discourse on love are dispelled by the speech of Alcibiades, drunken and therefore truthful, telling of Socrates' extraordinary courage in war, his genuine "trances," and his resolute rejection of Alcibiades' own temptation to carnal love. Xenophon's Socratic writings are more outspokenly adulatory than Plato's, though, perhaps because of his own intellectual limitations, Xenophon makes Socrates something of a cracker-barrel sage rather than a profound thinker, skillful dialectician, and deeply spiritual teacher.

If the Socratics exalt the master unduly, it is certain that Aristophanes (in the *Clouds*) goes much beyond the truth in the opposite direction. Socrates did *not* potter with physical science, did *not* exploit disciples for his own profit, was *not* a sophist who taught how the worse might appear the better. If it be asked how Aristophanes could be so unfair, even in a comedy, it may be said first, as Grote has pointed out, that if any visitor to Athens should ask to see a sophist, his host even if he knew better would surely point to Socrates, whose features, figure, and gait made him a living caricature. Furthermore, in 424 B.C., 25 years before his trial, Socrates had not yet acquired the halo with which later ages endowed him. Visible evidence of the transfiguration may be seen in a chronological series of portrait busts, presented in such a collection as Anton Hekler's. The earliest show the grotesque satyr-face described by Alcibiades; in the latest the features are recognizably the same, but are regularized and softened: the eyes look upward, and the lips are partly opened.

In the case of Socrates and the Socratics, especial care must be exercised in accepting gossip. The biographies which are the source of most anecdotes on these men were influenced by the Peripatetic Aristoxenus of Tarentum, who gave vent in his writings to a pronounced bias against anyone connected with Plato. The full account of Socrates' life in Diogenes Laertius (2.5) is at several points infected by this bias. One page in Diogenes (2.35–37) contains a number of well-known bon-mots of Socrates, including those referring to Xanthippe:

When he was about to drink the hemlock Apollodorus offered him a beautiful garment to die in: "What," said he, "is my own good enough to live in but not to die in?" When he was told that so-and-so spoke ill of him, he replied, "True, for he has never learnt to speak well." When Antisthenes turned his cloak so that the tear in it came into view, "I see," said he, "your vanity through your cloak." To one who said, "Don't you find so-and-so very offensive?" his reply was, "No, for it takes two to make a quarrel." We ought not to object, he used to say, to be subjects for the comic poets, for if they satirize our faults they will do us good, and if not they do not touch us. When Xanthippe first scolded him and then drenched him with water, his rejoinder was, "Did I not say that Xanthippe's thunder would end in rain?" When Alcibiades declared that the scolding of Xanthippe was intolerable, "Nay, I have got used to it," said he, "as to the continued rattle of a windlass. And you do not mind the cackle of geese." "No," replied Alcibiades, "but they furnish me with eggs and goslings." "And Xanthippe," said Socrates, "is the mother of my children." When she tore his coat off his back in the market-place and his acquaintances advised him to hit back, "Yes, by Zeus," said he, "in order that while we are sparring each of you may join in with 'Go it, Socrates!' 'Well done, Xanthippe!' " [Abraham Lincoln said, "Go it, b'ar, go it, wife!"] He said he lived with a shrew, as horsemen are fond of spirited horses, "but just as, when they have mastered these, they can easily cope with the rest, so I in the society of Xanthippe shall learn to adapt myself to the rest of the world."

III. PLATO

The most satisfactory autobiographical writing of any classical author is Plato's *Seventh Epistle*, which modern scholarship now accepts as genuine. There are, moreover, extant lives by Apuleius, by Olympiodorus, and (far the best) by Diogenes Laertius (3.1). From these we learn that Plato's true name was Aristocles, but that he was called Plato ("broad") either from the breadth of his figure, of his forehead, or of his mind, that he was descended on his mother's side from Solon, and hence from the deities Neleus and Posidon, and on his father's side from Codrus, the last king of Athens. In his youth it is said that he wrestled, painted, wrote poems, and that when he was about to compete with a tragedy, he heard Socrates speak, and consigned his tragedy to the flames. Socrates, on his part, was warned of Plato's coming to him as a pupil by a dream of a singing cygnet. After the death of Socrates he is said to have gone to Megara, then to Cyrene, Italy, and Egypt. On the latter journey he is said to have been accompanied by Euripides; the chronological impossibility (Euripides died seven or eight years before Socrates) shows how little reliable this material is. Equally improbable is the story (*Diogenes Laertius* 3.18–21) that Dionysius I of Syracuse had Plato kidnaped and handed over to a Spartan admiral who exposed him for sale at Aegina, where he was ransomed by an acquaintance from Cyrene.

But that the tyrants of Syracuse did affect his life there can be no doubt, for Plato himself gives us the details in his *Seventh Epistle*. On his visit to Syracuse in 387 Plato met Dionysius I and won the devotion of his son-in-law Dion. When Dionysius I died 20 years later, Dion summoned Plato to Syracuse to educate Dionysius II so that he might realize Plato's ideal of the philosopher-king. But Dionysius was suspicious of Dion and banished him, and did not take kindly to Plato's instruction in geometry. A half-dozen years later Plato again went to Syracuse, on Dionysius' promise that his presence there would improve Dion's situation. But Dionysius only treated Dion more harshly, and Plato himself obtained leave to return to Athens only by the intervention of Archytas of Tarentum. Subsequently Dion expelled Dionysius from Syracuse, but was himself assassinated by persons who seem to have had something to do with Plato. The real object of the *Seventh Epistle*, addressed to Dion's party after his death, is to explain and justify Plato's part in the affair, but it also throws incidental light on Plato's conception of teaching and on his political outlook. On the former, Plato's statement (341c) will come as a shock to those who believe that his philosophy can be learned from his *Dialogues*, and indeed to any who think philosophy can be learned from a book:

One statement at any rate I can make in regard to all who have written or who may write with a claim to knowledge of the subjects to which I devote myself—no matter how they pretend to have acquired it, whether from my instruction or from others or by their own discovery. Such writers can in my opinion have no real acquaintance with the subject. I certainly have composed no work in regard to it, nor shall I ever do so in future; for there is no way of putting it in words like other studies. Acquaintance with it must come rather after a long period of attendance on instruction in the subject itself and of close companionship, when, suddenly, like a blaze kindled by a leaping spark, it is generated in the soul and at once becomes self-sustaining.

Equally important for understanding Plato's doctrine of the state is his account of his own political development (324b ff.):

When I was young, I had the same experience that comes to so many: I thought that, as soon as I should be my own master, I should enter public life. This intention was favored by certain circumstances in the political situation at Athens. The existing constitution was generally condemned, and a revolution took place. . . . Some of the leaders were relatives and friends of mine, and they at once invited me to cooperate, as if this were the natural course for me to take. No wonder that, young as I was, I imagined they would bring the state under their management from an iniquitous to a right way of life. Accordingly I watched closely to see what they would do. It was not long before I saw these men make the former constitution seem like a paradise. In particular they tried to send Socrates, my friend, then advanced in years—a man whom I should not hesitate to call the most righteous man then living— with other persons, to arrest one of the citizens by violence for execution. Their purpose, no doubt, was to implicate Socrates, with or without his will, in their proceedings. He refused, preferring to face any danger rather than be a party to their infamous deeds. Seeing all this and other things as bad, I was disgusted and drew back from the evils of the time.

Not long afterwards the Thirty fell and the whole constitution was changed. Once more I was attracted, though less eagerly, towards taking an active part in politics. In these unquiet times much was still going on that might move one to disgust, and it was no wonder that, during the revolutionary changes, some took savage vengeance upon their enemies; but on the whole the returning exiles showed great moderation. Unfortunately, however, some of the men in power brought my friend Socrates to trial on an abominable charge, the very last that could be made against Socrates—the charge of impiety. He was condemned and put to death—he who had refused to share the infamy of arresting one of the accusers' own friends when they themselves were in exile and misfortune.

When I considered these things and the men who were directing public affairs, and made a closer study, as I grew older, of law and custom, the harder it seemed to me to govern a state rightly. Without friends and trustworthy associates it was impossible to act; and these could not readily be found among my acquaintance, now that Athens was no longer ruled by the manners and institutions of our forefathers; and to make new associates was by no means easy. At the same time the whole fabric of law and custom was going from bad to worse at an alarming rate. The result was that I, who had at first been full of eagerness for a public career, when I saw all this happening and everything going to pieces, fell at last into bewilderment. I did not cease to think in what way this situation might be amended and in particular the whole organization of the state; but I was all the while waiting for the right opportunity for action.

At last I perceived that the constitution of all existing states is bad and their institutions all but past remedy without a combination of radical measures and fortunate circumstances; and I was driven to affirm, in praise of true philosophy, that only from the

standpoint of such philosophy was it possible to take a correct view
of public and private right, and that accordingly the human race
would never see the end of trouble until true lovers of wisdom should
come to hold political power, or the holders of political power
should, by some divine appointment, become true lovers of wisdom.

It was in this mind that I first went to Sicily and Italy.

Personal anecdotes about Plato are surprisingly few. One in Aelian
(4.9) shows that he could get along with ordinary people:

At Olympia Plato the son of Ariston shared a tent with some uneducated persons, to whom he himself was unknown. He so won
them over and attached them to himself by his company, joining
unaffectedly in their meals and pastimes that the strangers were
overjoyed at his sharing their society. He made no mention either
of the Academy or of Socrates; only so much did he reveal to them,
that he was called Plato. When they visited Athens he received
them very attentively. The visitors said: "Come, now, Plato, show
us your namesake, the companion of Socrates, and take us to his
Academy, and introduce us to the man, so that we may have some
profit of him." But he, smiling gently, as it was his custom to do,
said, "But I am that same man." They were astonished at having
had so important a man with them without knowing it; he had
associated with them without arrogance or bother, and had proven
that he was able to win chance companions over even without his
customary manner of speaking.

IV. ARISTOTLE

Through Plato and his other disciples the influence of Socrates on
the spiritual life of posterity may be reckoned more pervasive and
more permanent than that of any other pagan. But the Socratic
influence has been indirect, and is operative in quarters where the
name of Socrates has scarcely been heard. But with the most illus-

trious of his intellectual grandchildren the case is different. As Theodor Gomperz (4.18) has written:

Fifteen hundred years after his death he is spoken of by the great poet of the Middle Ages as the "Master of those who know." Ecclesiastical assemblies of Christian Europe penalize all deviation from the metaphysical doctrines of the heathen thinker: many a faggot blazes to consume his opponents. And the man whom Christendom delights to honour is no less the idol of Islam. In Bagdad and Cairo, in Cordova and Samarcand, the minds of men acknowledge his sway. The crusader and the Moslem forget their strife while they vie in praises of the Grecian sage.

The fullest of the ancient lives of Aristotle is that in Diogenes Laertius (5.1), and its first paragraph gives substantially all that we know of his externals:

Aristotle, son of Nicomachus and Phaestis, was a native of Stagira. His father, Nicomachus, as Hermippus relates in his book On Aristotle, traced his descent from Nicomachus who was the son of Machaon and grandson of Asclepius; and he resided with Amyntas, the king of Macedon, in the capacity of physician and friend. Aristotle was Plato's most genuine disciple; he spoke with a lisp, as we learn from Timotheus the Athenian in his book On Lives; further, his calves were slender (so they say), his eyes small, and he was conspicuous by his attire, his rings, and the cut of his hair. According to Timaeus, he had a son by Herpyllis, his concubine, who was also called Nicomachus.

For twenty years, from 367, Aristotle was a disciple in Plato's Academy. Then in 347 he seceded. In Ethics 1.6, 1096a, in rejecting the Platonic doctrine of forms, he says: "Both (i.e., Plato and truth) are dear to us, but we are bound to prefer the truth." Whether the secession left personal scars we do not know, but there is a tradition that Plato was offended: Aelian 4.9, has the following:

Plato called Aristotle colt. What did the name signify? Everyone knows that a colt, when it is satiated with its mother's milk, kicks its mother. So Plato was hinting at a certain ingratitude on the part of Aristotle. For when Aristotle had received from Plato the greatest seed and sustenance for philosophy, then when he was satiated with this excellent provender and had shaken off the reins, he built a rival school and competed in attracting disciples and companions, and was ambitious to be on a par with Plato.

Another rivalry, of which the Romans at least have more to say, was that with the orator Isocrates. The fullest passage is Cicero, On the Orator 3.35.141:

When Aristotle observed that Isocrates succeeded in obtaining a distinguished set of pupils by means of abandoning legal and political subjects and devoting his discourses to empty elegance of style, he himself suddenly altered almost the whole of his own system of training, and quoted a line from Philoctetes with a slight modification: the hero in the tragedy said that it was a disgrace for him to keep silent and suffer barbarians to speak, but Aristotle put it "suffer Isocrates to speak"; and consequently he put the whole of his system of philosophy in a polished and brilliant form, and linked the scientific study of facts with practice in style. Nor indeed did this escape the notice of that extremely sagacious monarch Philip, who summoned Aristotle to be the tutor of his son Alexander, and to impart to him the principles both of conduct and of oratory.

After leaving the Academy Aristotle became attached to Hermeias, ruler of Atarneus, whose concubine he married with Hermeias' consent. Eusebius (*Evangelical Preparation* 15.2.5) reports:

They say that to this deceased woman Aristotle offered such a sacrifice as the Athenians offer to Demeter.

Diogenes Laertius (5.1.4) leaves out "deceased" and says Aristotle was "overjoyed." Posterity gloated over this manifestation of the

master's weakness. In the Louvre there is a fine drawing by Hans
Baldung (ca. 1500), showing the bearded philosopher on all fours,
looking back passionately at the wanton perched on his back and
guiding him with a rein. For Hermeias himself Aristotle composed
a hymn to Virtue, of which Diogenes gives the text.

In 343 Aristotle went to the Macedonian court as tutor to Alexander, and remained until Alexander's accession in 336. Of his appointment to this post we read in Plutarch's *Alexander*. Philip
realized Alexander's potentialities, says Plutarch, when he saw him
tame the unbroken horse called Bucephalus, and decided to give
him the best possible education:

*Looking upon the instruction and tuition of his youth to be of
greater difficulty and importance than to be wholly trusted to the
ordinary masters in music and poetry . . . he sent for Aristotle,
the most learned and most celebrated philosopher of his time, and
rewarded him with a munificence proportionable to and becoming
the care he took to instruct his son. For he repeopled his native
city Stagira, which he had caused to be demolished a little before,
and restored all the citizens, who were in exile or slavery, to their
habitations. As a place for the pursuit of their studies and exercise,
he assigned the temple of the Nymphs, near Mieza, where, to this
very day, they show you Aristotle's stone seats, and the shady walks
which he was wont to frequent. It would appear that Alexander
received from him not only his doctrines of Morals and of Politics,
but also something of those more abstruse and profound theories
which these philosophers, by the very names they gave them, professed to reserve for oral communication to the initiated, and did
not allow many to become acquainted with. For when he was in
Asia, and heard Aristotle had published some treatise of that kind,
he wrote to him, using very plain language to him in behalf of
philosophy, the following letter. "Alexander to Aristotle, greeting.
You have not done well to publish your books of oral doctrine;
for what is there now that we excel others in, if those things which
we have been particularly interested in be laid open to all? For my
part, I assure you, I had rather excel others in the knowledge of*

what is excellent, than in the extent of my power and dominion. Farewell." And Aristotle, soothing this passion for preeminence, speaks, in his excuse for himself, of these doctrines as in fact both published and not published: as indeed, to say the truth, his books on metaphysics are written in a style which makes them useless for ordinary teaching, and instructive only, in the way of memoranda, for those who have been already conversant in that sort of learning. Doubtless also it was to Aristotle that he owed the inclination he had, not to the theory only, but likewise to the practice of the art of medicine.

To the patronage of Alexander antiquity ascribed Aristotle's facilities for biological research. This is Pliny's account (N. H. 8.17.-44):

King Alexander the Great being fired with a desire to know the natures of animals and having delegated the pursuit of this study to Aristotle as a man of supreme eminence in every branch of science, orders were given to some thousands of persons throughout the whole of Asia and Greece, all those who made their living by hunting, fowling, and fishing and those who were in charge of warrens, herds, apiaries, fishponds and aviaries, to obey his instruction, so that he might not fail to be informed about any creature born anywhere. His enquiries addressed to those persons resulted in the composition of his famous works on zoology, in nearly 50 volumes.

Other authors echo the same story; Athenaeus 9.398e, for instance, has:

The story goes that the learned Stagirite received 800 talents from Alexander to further his research on animals.

Aelian (4.19) ascribes the patronage to Philip:

Philip the Macedonian was said to be not only an excellent warrior and skillful speaker, but to have honored culture most philanthropically. For Aristotle he provided wealth with open hand, and so

became responsible for great extension of knowledge and in particular of biological science. And so the son of Nicomachus produced
his History of Animals as the fruit of Philip's wealth.

On Alexander's rebuilding Stagira for Aristotle, we have a note in
Dio Chrysostom (47.9):

I used to envy Aristotle at times because, being a native of Stagira
—Stagira was a village in the territory of Olynthus—and having
become the teacher of Alexander and an acquaintance of Philip's
after the capture of Olynthus, he brought it about that Stagira was
resettled, and they used to say that he alone had had the good fortune to become founder of his fatherland. But meanwhile, quite
recently, I came upon a letter in which he exhibits a change of
heart and laments, saying that some of these settlers are trying to
corrupt, not only the king, but also the satraps who came there, so
as to thwart any good outcome and to prevent entirely the resettle-
ment of the city.

The correspondence between Aristotle and Alexander which Plutarch quotes may possibly be genuine but is very like the manifestly
apocryphal correspondence which constitutes the bulk of the so-
called Alexander Romance, which is a late snow-ball compilation
based perhaps on the history of Alexander written by Callisthenes,
Alexander's nephew and apologist who was later involved in a conspiracy against him. This material is so manifestly spurious that
it is not worth quoting.

Upon Alexander's accession to the throne Aristotle returned to
Athens and established his school in the Lyceum. From the "walk"
(peripatos) in the school in which the students strolled they came
to be called Peripatetics. Aristotle continued as head of the Lyceum
for 13 years, until the death of Alexander. Arrian (7.27) records,
and very rightly disbelieves, a story that Aristotle was actually involved in Alexander's death:

I am aware that many other particulars have been related by historians concerning Alexander's death, and especially that poison

was sent for him by Antipater, from the effects of which he died. It is also asserted that the poison was procured for Antipater by Aristotle, who was now afraid of Alexander on account of Callisthenes. . . . These statements I have recorded rather that I may not seem to be ignorant that they have been made than because I think them worthy of credence or even of narration.

Actually, Aristotle's pro-Alexander sympathies drove him from Athens. When Alexander died in 323 and seeds of insurrection began to stir in Athens, Aristotle's well-known sympathies made him a marked man. The hymn which he had composed for Hermeias was made the basis of a charge against him, as we are told by, among others, Athenaeus (15.696):

The poem addressed by the most learned Aristotle to Hermeias of Atarneus is not a paean [which it would be a sacrilege to address to a human] as alleged by Demophilus; he, suborned by Eurymedon, caused an indictment to be drawn against the philosopher for impiety, on the ground that he impiously sang a paean to Hermeias every day in the common dining-rooms.

Discretion dictated departure from Athens. His famous explanation for leaving is reported by Aelian (3.36):

When Aristotle left Athens for fear of his trial, and someone asked him, "What manner of city is Athens?" he replied, "It is a very fine place, but in it pear tree upon pear tree waxes old, and fig upon fig" [in allusion to Odyssey 7.115]—meaning the sycophants there. And when one asked him why he had left Athens, he replied that he did not wish the Athenians to sin against philosophy twice— alluding to the passion of Socrates and his own peril.

He retired to Chalcis, and there died in the year following, of illness, or, on the dubious authority of Eumelus (quoted in Diogenes Laertius), by drinking aconite.

Preponderant scholarly opinion now holds that Aristotle's will as reproduced in Diogenes Laertius (5.11 ff.) is genuine. This formal document shows us the man himself more truly than any remarks made by his friends or enemies can do, and incidentally provides an interesting glimpse of domestic arrangements among the Greeks:

All will be well; but, in case anything should happen, Aristotle has made these dispositions. Antipater is to be executor in all matters and in general; but, until Nicanor shall arrive, Aristomenes, Timarchus, Hipparchus, Dioteles and (if he consent and if circumstances permit him) Theophrastus shall take charge as well of Herpyllis and the children as of the property. And when the girl shall be grown up she shall be given in marriage to Nicanor; but if anything happen to the girl (which heaven forbid and no such thing will happen) before her marriage, or when she is married but before there are children, Nicanor shall have full powers, both with regard to the child and with regard to everything else, to administer in a manner worthy both of himself and of us. Nicanor shall take charge of the girl and of the boy Nicomachus as he shall think fit in all that concerns them as if he were father and brother. And if anything should happen to Nicanor (which heaven forbid!) either before he marries the girl or when he has married her but before there are children, any arrangements that he may make shall be valid. And if Theophrastus is willing to live with her, he shall have the same right as Nicanor. Otherwise the executors in consultation with Antipater shall administer as regards the daughter and the boy as seems to them to be best. The executors and Nicanor, in memory of me and of the steady affection which Herpyllis has borne towards me, shall take care of her in every respect and, if she desires to be married, shall see that she be given to one not unworthy; and besides what she has already received they shall give her a talent of silver out of the estate and three handmaids whomsoever she shall choose besides the maid she has at present and the man-servant Pyrrhaeus; and if she chooses to remain at Chalcis, the lodge by the garden, if in Stagira, my father's house. Whichever of these two houses she chooses, the executors shall

furnish with such furniture as they think proper and as Herpyllis
herself may approve. Nicanor shall take charge of the boy Myrmex,
that he be taken to his own friends in a manner worthy of me with
the property of his which we received. Ambracis shall be given her
freedom, and on my daughter's marriage shall receive 500 drachmas
and the maid whom she now has. And to Thale shall be given, in
addition to the maid whom she has and who was bought, a thousand drachmas and a maid. And Simon, in addition to the money
before paid to him towards another servant, shall either have a
servant purchased for him or receive a further sum of money. And
Tycho, Philo, Olympius and his child shall have their freedom
when my daughter is married. None of the servants who waited
upon me shall be sold but they shall continue to be employed;
and when they arrive at the proper age they shall have their freedom if they deserve it. My executors shall see to it, when the images
which Gryllion has been commissioned to execute are finished,
that they be set up, namely that of Nicanor, that of Proxenus, which
it was my intention to have executed, and that of Nicanor's mother;
also they shall set up the bust which has been executed of Arimnes-
tus, to be a memorial of him seeing that he died childless, and
shall dedicate my mother's statue to Demeter at Nemea or wherever they think best. And wherever they bury me, there the bones
of Pythias shall be laid, in accordance with her own instructions.
And to commemorate Nicanor's safe return, as I vowed on his behalf, they shall set up in Stagira stone statues of life size to Zeus
and Athena the Saviors.

According to a story patently apocryphal (told by Gregory of
Nazianz in his *Fourth Oration against Julian* and repeated by
Lorenzo Valla in his *Dialogue on Free Will*) Aristotle took his
life out of chagrin at not being able to understand the tides of the
Euripus. When he found himself baffled he threw himself into
the Euripus, saying, "Since Aristotle did not grasp Euripus, Euripus
grasped Aristotle."

V. ZENO

Numerous successors of the Peripatetics as of the Platonic succession figure in the history of philosophy, but scarcely in that of literature. Nor are any of the numerous writings which Zeno (333–261 B.C.) is said to have composed extant, but as the founder of the most influential philosophy in later antiquity his name is important in the tradition of books. Zeno is an excellent illustration of the expanded ramifications of Hellenism after Alexander; not only to writers like Cicero and Diogenes Laertius but to his contemporaries Timon and Crates he was "the Phoenician." Actually, he was from Citium in Cyprus, which Diogenes (7.1) says was a Greek city with Phoenician population, and Cicero (De finibus 4.20.56) says its inhabitants "came from Phoenicia." Cyprus was in fact, as the antiquities in the Cesnola collection in the Metropolitan Museum show, a meeting place of the Greek and Semitic traditions. The name of Zeno's father, sometimes given as Demeas, is more often given (as by Pausanias and Plutarch) as Mnaseas, which has a Semitic ring.

Of his origin and appearance the most succinct account is the paragraph of Diogenes Laertius' section on him (7.1):

Now the way he came across Crates was this. He was shipwrecked on a voyage from Phoenicia to Piracus with a cargo of purple. He went up into Athens and sat down in a bookseller's shop, being then a man of thirty. As he went on reading the second book of Xenophon's Memorabilia, he was so pleased that he inquired where men like Socrates were to be found. Crates passed by in the nick of time, so the bookseller pointed to him and said, "Follow yonder man." From that day he became Crates' pupil, showing in other respects a strong bent for philosophy, though with too much native modesty to assimilate Cynic shamelessness. Hence Crates, desirous of curing this defect in him, gave him a potful of lentil-soup to carry through the Ceramicus; and when he saw that he was ashamed and tried to keep it out of sight, with a blow of his staff he broke the pot. As Zeno took to flight with the lentil-soup flowing down his legs, "Why run away, my little Phoenician?" quoth Crates, "nothing terrible has befallen you."

A teacher whose main concern is with ethics rather than with First Philosophies naturally gathers about himself many stories illustrating his own personality and conduct, and his own followers are likely to exalt him to sainthood and his opponents to denigrate him as a charlatan. Most of the recurrent stories concerning Zeno are to be found in Diogenes, who seems to have drawn both on friendly and unfriendly sources. Here are some passages from Diogenes 7.12 ff.:

He made a hollow lid for a flask and used to carry about money in it, in order that there might be provision at hand for the necessities of his master Crates. It is said that he had more than a thousand talents when he came to Greece, and that he lent this money on bottomry. He used to eat little loaves and honey and to drink a little wine of good bouquet. He rarely employed men-servants; once or twice indeed he might have a young girl to wait on him in order not to seem a misogynist. . . . He disliked, they say, to be brought too near to people, so that he would take the end seat of a couch, thus saving himself at any rate from one half of such inconvenience. Nor indeed would he walk about with more than two or three. He would occasionally ask the bystanders for coppers, in order that, for fear of being asked to give, people might desist from mobbing him, as Cleanthes says in his work On Bronze. When several persons stood about him in the Colonnade [Stoa] he pointed to the wooden railing at the top round the altar and said, "This was once open to all, but because it was found to be a hindrance it was railed off. If you then will take yourselves off out of the way you will be the less annoyance to us." . . .

Zeno himself was sour and of a frowning countenance. He was very niggardly too, clinging to meanness unworthy of a Greek, on the plea of economy. If he pitched into anyone he would do it concisely, and not effusively, keeping him rather at arm's length. I mean, for example, his remark upon the fop showing himself off. When he was slowly picking his way across a water-course, "With good reason," quoth Zeno, "he looks askance at the mud, for he can't see his face in it." When a certain Cynic declared he had no oil in his flask and begged some of him, Zeno refused to give him any. However, as the man went away, Zeno bade him consider which of the two was the more impudent. Being enamored of Chremonides, as he and Cleanthes were sitting beside the youth, he got up, and upon Cleanthes expressing surprise, "Good physicians tell us," said he, "that the best cure for inflammation is repose." When of two reclining next to each other over the wine, the one who was neighbor to Zeno kicked the guest below him, Zeno himself nudged the man with his knee, and upon the man turning round, inquired, "How do you think your neighbor liked what you did to him?" To a lover of boys he remarked, "Just as schoolmasters lose their common-sense by spending all their time with boys, so it is with people like you." He used to say that the very exact expressions used by those who avoided solecisms were like the coins struck by Alexander: they were beautiful in appearance and well-rounded like the coins, but none the better on that account. Words of the opposite kind he would compare to the Attic tetradrachms, which, though struck carelessly and inartistically, nevertheless out-weighed the ornate phrases.

Athenaeus has some anecdotes, relating to his own special interests, mostly from a work on Zeno by Antigonus of Carystus, who was a worker in bronze as well as writer:

Zeno of Citium, who was very harsh and choleric toward his acquaintances, became gentle and bland after absorbing quantities of wine; and when people asked him to explain this change of manner, he answered that he underwent the same process as the lupines; for they too are very sour before they are soaked, but when steeped they become very sweet and mild (2.55 f.).

Antigonus of Carystus, in his Life of Zeno, writes as follows: "King Antigonus (Gonatas) used to have revels at the house of Zeno.

On one occasion, coming away from a drinking party at day-break, he rushed to Zeno's and persuaded him to join in a revel at the house of Aristocles the harp-singer, whom the king loved greatly" (13.603e).

Antigonus of Carystus, in his Life of Zeno, records a remark made by Zeno of Citium, the founder of Stoicism, to the gourmand with whom he lived for a long time. It happened that a large fish was served to them without any other course. Zeno took the entire fish from the platter and made as if he were going to eat it. When the other looked at him reproachfully he said, "What then, think you, must those who live with you suffer, if you can't endure my gluttony for a single day?" (8.345d).

Antigonus of Carystus writes: "Zeno of Citium, when Persaeus bought a little flute-player at a drinking-party, but hesitated to take her home because he lived in the same house with Zeno, no sooner perceived this than he pulled the lass into the house and shut her up with Persaeus" (13.607e).

Myrtilus cast a glance at those who hold the principles of the Porch, first quoting the verses from the Iambics of Hermeias of Curium: "Hear, ye Styacs, vendors of twaddle, hypocritical mouthers of words who alone by yourselves gobble up everything on the platters before the wise man can get a share, and then are caught doing the very opposite of what you solemnly chant"; oglers of boys you are, and in that alone emulating the founder of your philosophy, Zeno the Phoenician, who never resorted to a woman, but always to boy-favorites, as Antigonus of Carystus records in his biography of him (13.563d).

As for your wise Zeno, says Antigonus of Carystus, he, having a premonition, as it would seem, of the lives you were to lead, and of your hypocritical profession, asserted that they who listened casually to his precepts and failed to understand them would be filthy and mean. . . . And so most of you are like that, all wizened and foul not only in your manners but also in your morals (13.565c).

The most important fact in the external history of Zeno is doubtless his connection with the powerful Antigonus Gonatas, son and successor of Demetrius the Besieger. Antigonus' invitation is quoted from Apollonius of Tyre's book on Zeno by Diogenes Laertius (7.7):

King Antigonus to Zeno the philosopher, greeting:
While in fortune and fame I deem myself your superior, in reason and education I own myself inferior, as well as in the perfect happiness which you have attained. Wherefore I have decided to ask you to pay me a visit, being persuaded that you will not refuse the request. By all means, then, do your best to hold conference with me, understanding clearly that you will not be the instructor of myself alone but of all the Macedonians taken together. For it is obvious that whoever instructs the ruler of Macedonia and guides him in the paths of virtue will also be training his subjects to be good men. As is the ruler, such for the most part it may be expected that his subjects will become.

Zeno welcomes the proposal but cannot himself go to Antigonus. He closes his reply as follows:

But I am constrained by bodily weakness, due to old age, for I am 80 years old; and for that reason I am unable to join you. But I send you certain companions of my studies whose mental powers are not inferior to mine, while their bodily strength is far greater, and if you associate with these you will in no way fall short of the conditions necessary to perfect happiness.

Zeno's attitude toward the great man is described by Epictetus (2.14):

When Zeno was going to meet Antigonus he was not anxious, for Antigonus had no power over any of the things which Zeno admired; and Zeno did not care for those things over which Antigonus had power. But Antigonus was anxious when he was going to meet Zeno, for he wished to please Zeno, but this was a thing out of his powers. But Zeno did not want to please Antigonus; for no man who is skilled in any art wishes to please one who has no such skill.

The independence of the sage in the face of external power is reflected in the following, from Plutarch, *How to Listen to Poetry*, 33d:

Zeno amended the lines of Sophocles—

> Whoever comes to traffic with a king
> To him is slave however free he come—

and rewrote it thus—

> Is not a slave if only free he come.

An anecdote illustrating Zeno's austerity despite his intimacy with Antigonus is this from Aelian (9.26):

King Antigonus treated Zeno of Citium with great reverence and assiduity. Once when he was soaked in wine he revelled with Zeno; he kissed him and threw his arms around him, being inebriated, and bade him ask anything of him, swearing upon oath, with youthful earnestness, that he would not fail to obtain his request. Zeno said to him, "Go out and vomit,"—thus austerely and high-mindedly rebuking his inebriation and showing concern for him, lest he burst of his satiety.

Aelian also tells us (7.14) that he rendered the Athenians important political services by his influence with Antigonus. At any rate, as Diogenes 7.6 says:

The people of Athens held Zeno in high honor, as is proved by their depositing with him the keys of the city walls, and their honoring him with a golden crown and a bronze statue.

The decree, or perhaps a conflation of two decrees, is quoted *in extenso* by Diogenes (7.10–12).

Ancient critics, always more concerned for form than matter, spoke disparagingly of Zeno's faulty Greek. Chrysippus, who was much concerned with grammar, wrote a treatise on Zeno's *Proper Use of Nouns;* a quotation from this in Galen deplores Zeno's "innovations in nouns." Cicero echoes this remark when he calls Zeno (*Tusculan Disputations* 5.12.34) *advena quidam et ignobilis verborum opifex,* "an upstart and vulgar carpenter of words." His solecisms, Polemo (quoted in Diogenes Laertius 7.25) said, were a means of concealing his plagiarisms. Cicero repeats this charge also, at several places; "Zeno changed the terminology," he writes (*Laws* 1.13.38), "without altering the ideas"; or (*Tusculan Disputations* 2.12.29), "Zeno labors over the word, not the thing." In point of fact Cicero is not unsympathetic to the Stoic philosophy; it is mainly its impractical perfectionism that he ridicules. That Zeno was scrupulous if not fastidious in his choice of words we learn from a saying of his quoted in Plutarch (*Phocion* 5.2):

Zeno used to say that a philosopher should immerse his words in meaning before he utters them.

It was natural that the adherents of so spiritual a doctrine as Zeno's should be more deeply committed to the master than was the case in other schools. On this too we have a remark of Zeno himself (Plutarch, *Progress in Virtue* 78e):

Zeno, seeing that Theophrastus was admired for having many pupils, said, "It is true his chorus is larger, but mine is more harmonious."

Zeno died, at a very advanced age and by his own choice, when he received a premonition of approaching death. The treatise on *Long Lives* ascribed to Lucian (19) has:

Zeno the leader of the Stoic philosophy was 98 years old. They say that when he stumbled upon entering the ecclesia, he cried out,

"Why are you calling to me?" He turned around and went home, and by abstaining from food ended his life.

This is Zenodotus' epigram on him (A.P. 7.117):

Zeno, reverend grey-browed sage, thou didst found the self-sufficient life, abandoning the pursuit of vain-glorious wealth; for virile (and thou didst train thyself to foresight) was the school of thought thou didst institute, the mother of dauntless freedom. If thy country were Phoenicia what reproach is that? Cadmus too, from whom Greece learnt writing, was a Phoenician.

VI. EPICURUS

Because Epicurus denied divine providence, which must be a central article of faith in all religions, his name has become a byword for infidel among believers in several religions. Bitter criticism of Epicureanism is plentiful, not only in Christian writers but in pious pagans like Plutarch and in disciplined ones like Cicero. But there is surprisingly little personal vilification of the master himself, possibly because his own decency and modesty and frugality were too well known, and what there is manifestly derives from bitter resentment of his system. On the other hand, admiration for Epicurus reaches the point of adulation on the part of his devotees, and in particular in such a figure as Lucretius.

Diogenes Laertius is more valuable on Epicurus than on any other writer; his Book 10 contains the only extant specimens of Epicurus' writing, and he has the fullest account of Epicurus' life and the richest collection of stories about him, both slanderous and adulatory, though his material is utterly confused, chronologically and otherwise. From Diogenes we learn that Epicurus was born probably on Samos, whither his father Neocles had gone as a colonist, but that he retained Athenian citizen rights and in due time entered the ephebate. His parents were poor, and hostile stories alleged (Diogenes Laertius 10.4) "that he used to go round with his mother to cottages and read charms, and assist his father in his school for a pitiful fee." This sounds suspiciously like Demosthenes' denigration of Aeschines (On the Crown 258); if it is true that he assisted his mother in her work, we may have an explanation for his subsequent contempt for superstition. He was converted to philosophy at the age of 14, when his teachers could not explain the meaning of "chaos" in Hesiod. Sextus Empiricus, Against the Mathematicians 10.18 tells the story:

Some say that this was the reason why Epicurus devoted himself to philosophy. When he was still a young lad [Epicurus himself is elsewhere quoted as saying he was 14 at the time] he inquired of the teacher who was reading to him from Hesiod "First chaos came into being." Epicurus wished to know from what chaos itself had come into being if it was indeed the first. The teacher replied that it was not his business to teach such matters but that of the men called philosophers. "Well then," said Epicurus, "it is to them I must go if they know the truth of the matter."

The poverty of his boyhood is usually given as a reason for the inadequacy of Epicurus' education. Sextus Empiricus 1.1 cites him along with Pyrrho as having opposed the "Professors":

Epicurus took the ground that the subjects taught are of no help in perfecting wisdom; and he did this, as some conjecture, because he saw in it a way of covering up his own lack of culture (for in many matters Epicurus stands convicted of ignorance, and even in ordinary converse his speech was not correct). Another reason may have been his hostility towards Plato and Aristotle and their like who were men of wide learning.

Cicero (De finibus 1:7.26) says:

For my part I could have wished either that he were himself better instructed in doctrine—he is indeed insufficiently polished in those arts which bestow the title of scholar upon those who possess them —or that he would not have deterred others from such studies.

A sample of the personal vilification heaped upon Epicurus by adherents of other schools may be cited from Diogenes Laertius (10.6 f.):

In the book entitled Merriment *Timocrates, who was Epicurus' disciple and then left the school, asserts that Epicurus vomited twice a day from over-indulgence, and goes on to say that he himself had much ado to escape from those notorious midnight philosophizings and the confraternity with all its secrets; further, that Epicurus' acquaintance with philosophy was small and his acquaintance with life even smaller; that his bodily health was pitiful, so much so that for many years he was unable to rise from his chair; and that he spent a whole mina daily on his table, as he himself says in his letter to Leontion and in that to the philosophers at Mitylene. Also that among other courtesans who consorted with him and Metrodorus were Mammarion and Hedia and Erotion and Nikidion.*

The stories of Epicurus' personal excesses naturally derive from inference from his doctrine. The basis is his statement on pleasure, quoted in several authors, but most fully in Athenaeus 280ab:

Epicurus used to maintain with a shout: "The beginning and root of all good is the satisfaction of the belly, and all wise and notable things have in this their standard of reference." Again, in the work on the End he says something like this: "As for myself, I cannot conceive of the good if I exclude the pleasures derived from taste, or those derived from sexual intercourse, or those derived from entertainments to which we listen, or those derived from the motions of a figure delightful to the eye." And proceeding further (Chrysippus says), Epicurus declares: "We should prize the good and the virtues and such things as that, provided they give us pleasure; if they do not give pleasure we should renounce them."

But in the more respectable authors what we get is ridicule of Epicurus' physics rather than personal vilification. In reference to

his doctrine of phenomenal objects being formed by fortuitous con-
catenation of atoms, for example, Plutarch (*Oracles at Delphi* 399e)
has:

*If that were so, what is to hinder someone else from declaring that
Epicurus did not write his* Leading Principles, *but that by chance
and accidentally the letters fell in with one another as they now
stand, and the book was completed?*

Lucilius, the writer of comic epigrams, has this (A.P. 11.103):

*Epicurus wrote that all the world consisted of atoms, thinking,
Alcinous, that an atom was the most minute thing. But if Diophantus had existed then he would have written that it consisted of
Diophantus, who is much more minute than the atoms. Or he would
have written that other things were composed of atoms, but the
atoms themselves, Alcinous, of Diophantus.*

Vilification like that quoted from Diogenes Laertius but more lurid
may be cited from Aelian (fragment 39), if only to show that
popular attitudes to dissident groups regarded as subversive have
not materially changed:

*Epicurus reckoned the divine as nothing. He had three brothers,
who were plagued by myriad diseases and died miserably. Epicurus
himself, even when he was a young man, could not easily leave his
bed; he was blear-eyed and could not endure the rays of the sun.
Hateful to the most brilliant and radiant of deities, he could not
even tolerate the light of a fire. His blood could be discerned through
its extremest passages. So far was his body emaciated that he was
unable to bear the weight of loose garments. Metrodorus also, and
Polyaenus, both companions of Epicurus, died in most wretched
wise. And so for his atheism he suffered retribution by no means
undeserved. So far did Epicurus succumb to pleasure that in his
last will and testament he wrote to his father and mother and
brothers that they should celebrate the anniversary of the death*

of the above mentioned Metrodorus and Polyaenus once annually
and his own death twice—so excessively did that sage, forsooth,
honor luxury, even in such a connection. And he desired, like the
gourmand and glutton he was, stone tables to be fashioned and
placed as votive offerings upon his grave. These things he ordered,
though his means were far from abundant. In his appetites he was
a raging maniac—as if they too were not going to perish with him.

The Epicureans were expelled from Rome by a common decree
of the Senate, and the Messenians in Arcadia expelled those fat-
tened in that same sty, on the grounds that they corrupted the
youth and infected philosophy with a stain by reason of their ef-
feminacy and atheism, and they bade them betake themselves out
of the boundaries of the Messenian country before the setting of
the sun. Further, they ordered the priests to purify the temples
and the Timochoi (so the Messenians call their magistrates) to
purify the whole city, as if it had been purged of infectious dregs.
In Crete the Lycteans expelled certain Epicureans who had made
their way to that place, and a law was inscribed in their native dialect
to the effect that banishment from Lyctos should be proclaimed
for those who introduced an effeminate, ignoble, and disgraceful
philosophy and were moreover enemies to the gods. And if any con-
temning the law should in brazen disregard of its provisions appear, he should be made fast in a pillory by the government house
for 30 days, stripped nude and besmeared all over with honey and
milk, so that he should furnish a feast for bees and flies, who would
consume him within the stated period of time. And if, when this
shrift was passed he were still alive, he should be attired in woman's
garb and hurled down a steep cliff.

A less lurid if not more credible story told by Plutarch (Pyrrhus 20)
illustrates the Roman attitude to Epicureans. After Pyrrhus' emis-
sary Cineas had first tried in vain to corrupt Appius Claudius' emis-
sary with gold, and then to frighten him by suddenly confronting
him with a trumpeting elephant, he then sought to demoralize him
with Epicureanism:

He set forth the doctrines of that school concerning the gods, civil government, and the highest good, explaining that they made pleasure the highest good, but would have nothing to do with civil government on the ground that it was injurious and the ruin of felicity and that they removed the Deity as far as possible from the feelings of kindness or anger or concern for us, into a life that knew no care and was filled with ease and comfort. But before Cineas was done, Fabricius cried out and said: "O Hercules, may Pyrrhus and the Samnites cherish these doctrines, as long as they are at war with us."

Christian writers are scarcely more gentle. Without exception, all who mention him do so with some opprobrious epithet. Dante (*Inferno* 10.14) makes him the prototype of those who deny immortality:

In this part are entombed with Epicurus all his followers, who made the soul die with the body.

But the devotion of the Epicureans to their founder was as ardent as the devotion of the Stoics to theirs. Each year, as we know from several sources, they celebrated the founder's birthday. Cicero (*De finibus* 2.101), for example, mentions Epicurus' provision for the observance and finds it inconsistent:

What I want to know is this: if all sensation is annihilated by dissolution, that is, by death, and if nothing whatever that can affect us remains, why is it that Epicurus makes such precise and careful provision and stipulation "that his heirs, Amynochus and Timocrates, shall after consultation with Hermarchus assign a sufficient sum to celebrate his birthday every year in the month of Gamelion, and also on the 20th day of every month shall assign a sum for a banquet to his fellow-students in philosophy, in order to keep alive the memory of himself and Metrodorus"? That these are the words of as amiable and kindly a man as you like, I cannot deny; but what business has a philosopher, and especially a natural philosopher,

which Epicurus claims to be, to think that any day can be anybody's
birthday?

Cicero does not deny that Epicurus was "an amiable and kindly
man." Diogenes Laertius preserves the good as well as the bad that
was spoken of Epicurus, and prefers (as do his modern readers) to
believe the good, though that too is doubtless exaggerated (10.9 f.):

But these maligners of Epicurus are stark mad. For our philosopher
has abundance of witnesses to attest his unsurpassed goodwill to
all men—his native land, which honored him with statues in bronze;
his friends, so many in number that they could hardly be counted
by whole cities, and indeed all who knew him, held fast as they
were by the siren-charms of his doctrine, save Metrodorus of Stra-
tonicea, who went over to Carneades, being perhaps burdened by
his master's excessive goodness; the School itself which, while nearly
all the others have died out, continues for ever without interruption through numberless reigns of one scholarch after another; his
gratitude to his parents, his generosity to his brothers, his gentle-
ness to his servants, as evidenced by the terms of his will and by
the fact that they were members of the School, the most eminent
of them being the aforesaid Mys; and in general, his benevolence
to all mankind. His piety towards the gods and his affection for his
country no words can describe. He carried deference to others to
such excess that he did not even enter public life. He spent all
his life in Greece, notwithstanding the calamities which had befallen her in that age; when he did once or twice take a trip to
Ionia, it was to visit his friends there. Friends indeed came to him
from all parts and lived with him in his garden. This is stated by
Apollodorus, who also says that he purchased the garden for eighty
minae; and to the same effect Diocles in the third book of his
Epitome speaks of them as living a very simple and frugal life; at
all events they were content with half a pint of thin wine and
were, for the rest, thoroughgoing water-drinkers. He further says
that Epicurus did not think it right that their property should be
held in common, as required by the maxim of Pythagoras about

the goods of friends; such a practice in his opinion implied mistrust, and without confidence there is no friendship. In his correspondence he himself mentions that he was content with plain bread and water. And again: "Send me a little pot of cheese, that, when I like, I may fare sumptuously." Such was the man who laid down that pleasure was the end of life.

The will which he mentions, as well as certain of Epicurus' letters, Diogenes quotes, and these bear out his generous estimate of Epicurus' personality. One item may be added from Plutarch's *Demetrius* (34). The Athenians besieged by Demetrius were in such straits that a father and son fought for the possession of a dead mouse.

At this time, we are told, the philosopher Epicurus sustained the lives of his associates with beans, which he counted out and distributed among them.

For praise of Epicurus amounting to beatification we go to the author of the only considerable Epicurean work which has survived, but in a tenuous manuscript tradition, from antiquity. Lucretius, whom Christian writers like Calvin therefore call "blasphemous," makes Epicurus the savior of mankind. At the opening of his poem he pays this tribute to the master (1.62 ff.):

When the life of man lay foul to see and groveling upon the earth, crushed by the weight of religion, which showed her face from the realms of heaven, lowering upon mortals with dreadful mien, 'twas a man of Greece who dared first to raise his mortal eyes to meet her, and first to stand forth to meet her: him neither the stories of the gods nor thunderbolts checked, nor the sky with its revengeful roar, but all the more spurred the eager daring of his mind to yearn to be the first to burst through the close-set bolts upon the doors of nature.

And towards its end he hails him as a very god (5.8 ff.):

He was a god, yea a god, noble Memmius, who first found out that principle of life, which now is called wisdom, and who by his skill saved our life from high seas and thick darkness, and enclosed it in calm waters and bright light.

13: *The Attic Orators*

IN THE HIERARCHY OF LITERARY FORMS OUR OWN evaluations are generally analogous to those of the Greeks. The great exception is oratory, which among ourselves is fallen into disrepute but which the Greeks, who insisted upon the practical as well as the beautiful, placed very high in the scale of values. On this some good sentences from Macaulay may be quoted:

It may be doubted whether any compositions which have ever been produced in the world are equally perfect in their kind with the great Athenian orations. Genius is subject to the same laws which regulate the production of cotton and molasses. The supply adjusts itself to the demand. The quantity may be diminished by restrictions, and multiplied by bounties. The singular excellence to which eloquence attained at Athens is to be mainly attributed to the influence which it exerted there. In turbulent times, under a constitution purely democratic, among a people educated exactly to that point at which men are most susceptible of strong and sudden impressions, acute, but not sound reasons, warm in their feelings, unfixed in their principles, and passionate admirers of fine composition, oratory received such encouragement as it has never since obtained. And even after loss of liberty had put a period to the practical effectiveness of oratory, it retained its high position in the public esteem as a fine art, and was practised, with resounding financial success, by a galaxy of "stars."

Oratory, as has been noted, was seriously put forward as a legitimate successor to poetry. The significant common element is that the orator like the lyric poet addresses his audience directly in his own person and attempts to persuade them by the artistic presentation of his own convictions—not by an account, real or imaginary, of events that befell others. A far larger proportion of ancient criti-

cal writing is devoted to oratory than to any other genre, and even
in the criticism of other genres the gauge is frequently, as notably
in the case of Quintilian, usefulness for the study of oratory. The
archaizing revival of the 2nd century A.D., known as the Second
Sophistic, was centered mainly on imitation of the classic orators.
In the Alexandrian age a canon of ten orators, like the canon of
nine lyric poets was drawn up; included were Antiphon, Andocides,
Lysias, Isocrates, Isaeus, Aeschines, Lycurgus, Demosthenes, Hyperides, Dinarchus. A series of biographies of these ten is found in
a treatise wrongly included in the works of Plutarch under the title
Lives of the Ten Orators. All later scholars and critics respected
the Alexandrian canon. Of no orator not included in the canon
are whole speeches extant, except for such things as Pericles' Funeral
Oration quoted in Thucydides; but of seven of the ten a large body
of work has been transmitted in the usual manuscript tradition,
and of an eighth considerable fragments have been recovered in
papyri.

I. GORGIAS

The man mainly responsible for giving the new artistic prose its
character and prestige is not included in the ten. He was Gorgias
of Leontini (483–376 B.C.), whose rhetoric took Athens by storm
when he appeared there in 427 as the envoy of his native city.
Diodorus Siculus 12.53 says of him:

He was the foremost man of his age in rhetorical skill. The clever
Athenians, with their fondness for eloquence, were struck by the
foreign air of his style, by the remarkable antitheses, the symmetrical
clauses, the parallelisms of structure, the rhyming terminations,
and the other similar figures of speech, which were then welcomed
because of their novelty.

Gorgias gives his name to one of Plato's principal treatises on
rhetoric (the other is the *Phaedrus*). In the *Gorgias* Plato declares
that rhetoric so far from being an art is only a happy knack acquired
by practice (463b, 501a), and Gorgias and his pupil are taken to

task as representatives of the current rhetoric of the day. Elsewhere also, notably in the *Symposium*, Plato takes a fling at Gorgianic excesses. Aristotle (*Rhetoric* 3.1404a) speaks with disapproval of the innovation introduced by Gorgias:

As the poets seemed to have won their reputation, even when their thoughts were poor, by force of their style, the first prose style was led to become poetical, like that of Gorgias. To this day, indeed, the mass of the uneducated think that such persons are the finest talkers. It is not so, however; the diction of prose and the diction of poetry are distinct.

Elsewhere in the third book of his *Rhetoric* Aristotle criticizes certain extravagant expressions of Gorgias: "beggar-poet flatterer" (1405b); "forsworn or ultra-veracious" (*ibid.*); "events fresh with the blood in them still" (1406b). He praises Gorgias' facility in introducing one theme after another in an epideictic speech (1418a):

This is what Gorgias meant by saying that matter of discourse never failed him. In speaking of Achilles he praises Peleus, and then Aeacus, and then the god, and valor, and this or that.

Aristotle also approves of Gorgias on jokes (1419b):

Jokes seem to be of some service in debate; Gorgias said that we ought to worst our opponents' earnest with mockery, and his mockery with earnest; a good saying.

There are a number of fragments of Gorgias which celebrate the validity of rhetoric. In connection with the discussion of poetic truth we have cited his remark "the poet who deceives is more just than the poet who does not deceive, and he that is deceived is wiser than he who is not deceived." On Gorgias' view of the power of persuasion we may cite a portion of Professor Van Hook's translation of the fragmentary *Helen*, which happily presents some of the sound effects of the original:

Persuasion is a powerful potentate, who with frailest, feeblest frame works wonders. For it can put an end to fear and make vexation vanish; it can inspire exultation and increase compassion. I will show how this is so. For I must indicate this to my hearers for them to predicate. All poetry I ordain and proclaim to be composition in meter, the listeners of which are affected by passionate trepidation and compassionate perturbation and likewise tearful lamentation, since through discourse the soul suffers, as if its own, the felicity and infelicity of property and person of others. Come, let us turn to another consideration. Inspired incantations are provocative of charm and revocative of harm. For the power of song in association with the belief of the soul captures and enraptures and translates the soul with witchery. For there have been discovered arts twain of witchery and sorcery, which are consternation to the heart and perturbation to art. Now, it has been shown that, if Helen was won over by persuasion, she is deserving of commiseration, and not condemnation.

An anecdote in Aelian (2.35) refers to Gorgias' death:

When Gorgias of Leontini, grown old and near the term of life, was seized by a certain disease and fell into a gradual sleep, one of his kinsmen came to visit him and asked how he did. Gorgias replied, "Sleep has already begun to hand me over to his brother."

II. ANTIPHON

To the oratorical ability of Antiphon (480–411 B.C.) we have an extraordinary ancient testimonial. When Antiphon was on trial for his life for his part in the oligarchic conspiracy of 411, his unsuccessful plea moved Thucydides to this expression of opinion (8.68):

The real author and maturer of the whole scheme, who had been longest interested in it, was Antiphon, a man inferior in excellence to none of his contemporaries, and possessed of remarkable powers of thought and gifts of speech. He did not like to come forward in the assembly, or in any other public arena. To the multitude, who were suspicious of his great abilities, he was an object of dislike; but there was no man who could do more for any who consulted him, whether their business lay in the courts of justice or in the assembly. And when the government of the Four Hundred was overthrown and become exposed to the vengeance of the people, and he being accused of taking part in the plot had to speak in his own case, his defense was undoubtedly the best ever made by any man tried on a capital charge down to my time.

Illustrating the qualities of the great-spirited man, Aristotle (*Eudemian Ethics* 1232b) speaks of the tragic poet Agathon's praise of the same speech:

A great-spirited man would consider more what one virtuous man thinks than what many ordinary people think, as Antiphon after his condemnation said to Agathon when he praised his speech for his defense.

The section on Antiphon in the *Lives of the Ten Orators* cites a treatise on him by Caecilius of Calacte, the rival of Dionysius of Halicarnassus, and reports some good things, including an abortive venture in psychiatry (833b):

Antiphon sailed to Syracuse in an embassy when the tyranny of the Elder Dionysius was in its heyday. When at a drinking party the question arose what bronze was best and various opinions were offered, Antiphon said, "That bronze is best of which the statues of the tyrannicides Harmodius and Aristogiton are fashioned." When Dionysius heard this he took it to be an incitement to an attack upon himself and ordered Antiphon to be killed. Others say he was angry at Antiphon for hissing his tragedies. . . . Plato Comicus and Pisander represent him as avaricious in their comedies.
He is said to have composed tragedies, both alone and with Dionysius. When he was still devoted to poetry, he set up a scheme for relieving spiritual distress, like the treatment of physical dis-

eases by physicians. He built him a kind of office in Corinth near the market-place and advertised that he was able to cure persons in anguish through words alone. He would inquire the causes of his patients' distress and give them relief. But he thought that that practice was beneath his dignity, and so turned to rhetoric.

Antiphon's extant speeches say nothing of his own politics, poetry, or psychiatry, but deal only with murder cases, probably hypothetical. For each case he has a tetralogy, or set of four speeches, two for the prosecution and two for the defense.

III. ANDOCIDES

The speeches of Andocides (440–390 B.C.), on the other hand, provide very full biographical details, being largely devoted to defenses growing out of charges that he participated in the mutilation of the Hermae and in Alcibiades' parody of the Eleusinian Mysteries. The events are described in Thucydides 6, and an account of them is given in Plutarch's *Alcibiades* and in the *Lives of the Ten Orators*. The latter says "About all these things he himself tells in his compositions," and nothing that others say adds much to our picture of the man.

IV. LYSIAS

Lysias (459–380 B.C.) possesses greater interest for the student of ancient literature. For one thing he provides the acknowledged norm for correct prose style—Dionysius of Halicarnassus (*On the Judgement of Lysias*) calls him the "canon"; for another, we know his personality well from his own speeches, his reputation from Plato's *Phaedrus*, and his charming father Cephalus and elder brother Polemarchus from Plato's *Republic* 1. Phaedrus, in the dialogue of that name, had become enamored of a discourse on love by Lysias and had committed it to memory. It is quite probable that the discourse as given in the *Phaedrus* is actually by Lysias. The theme of the discourse is the paradox that it is more expedient to grant favors to a nonlover than to a lover. Socrates demolishes the theme as immoral, but Lysias himself Socrates represents as being at the height of his fame and vogue (228a) and as being the cause of more discourses, either by delivering them himself or being the occasion of their delivery by other men, than any living person with the exception of Simmias of Thebes.

From his own speeches and from references to his family in the *Republic* we can see that Lysias was a man of wit, integrity, and high patriotism, and that he moved in the highest circles; nevertheless being only a metic or resident alien he could not himself address the Athenian ecclesia on political subjects. He could, however, address the assembled Hellenes at the Olympian festival, and the speech he delivered there, probably in 384, portions of which are quoted in Dionysius of Halicarnassus, is a powerful thing. Here is a partial translation of it by George Grote (10.306):

The Greek world is burning away at both extremities. Our eastern brethren have passed into slavery under the Great King, our western under the despotism of Dionysius. The two are the great potentates, both in naval force and in money, the real instruments of dominion: if both of them combine, they will extinguish what remains of freedom in Greece. . . . Let us not lie idle, waiting until Artaxerxes and Dionysius attack us with their united force; let us check their insolence at once, while it is yet in our power.

Dionysius himself was present at the festival, in a court pavilion decorated with purple and gold, which Lysias charged he had extorted from the Greeks he had enslaved. In Diodorus Siculus 14.9 we read that the audience was so moved by Lysias' exhortation that they set about pulling the magnificent pavilion to pieces.

In the polemics between Atticists and Asianists in Rome of the first century B.C. Lysias was naturally invoked as the master of the spare Attic style. To appreciate the criticism of Cicero (*Brutus* 16 f.), therefore, we must not only allow for his Roman chauvinism in making Cato Lysias' equal, but also his own bias in favor of a modified Asianic as against a pure Attic style:

Now Cato's speeches are almost as numerous as those of Lysias of Athens—to whom, I believe, more have been ascribed than to any other man. I say 'of Athens' since he was certainly born there, discharged all the duties of citizenship there, and finally died there, although Timaeus, proceeding as though the Athenians had enacted a Licinian or a Mucian Law, demands that he be considered a Syracusan. Now Lysias and Cato are not entirely unlike: both are adroit, elegant, witty, concise. Of the two, however, our Greek has enjoyed far wider fame; he has ardent followers who strive after slenderness, rather than sturdiness, of body and who are even willing to go so far as to present an appearance of emaciation, so long as their health is not affected. Now, although Lysias often displays flashes of a lusty muscularity which is extraordinarily impressive, yet upon the whole his style tends rather toward a sparse simplicity. In spite of this fact, he has his devotees who greatly rejoice in his limitation of rhetorical embellishment. . . . And how ignorant we are! The very same men who go into raptures over the primitive era of Greek literature and who delight in that unadorned simplicity which they call Attic are utterly unaware of the fact that Cato displays precisely the same characteristic. They yearn to emulate Hyperides and Lysias. Excellent! But why do they not take Cato as their model? They aver that they are enraptured by the Attic style. I applaud, but I could wish they would seek to imitate its flesh and blood and not alone its bones. And yet, their ambition is laudable; why, therefore, do they lavish their adoration upon Lysias and Hyperides and completely ignore Cato?

V. ISOCRATES

The "old man eloquent," as Milton called Isocrates (436–338 B.C.), has become a byword for two things: he continued his active literary career until the age of 97, and he amassed a great fortune by teaching. For posterity Isocrates suffers by the stigma of the rhetorician; he is overshadowed as a moral teacher by the Socratics and as a political guide by Demosthenes. But judgment may be qualified on both counts; at all events Isocrates is the greatest educationist of antiquity. The best testimonial for Isocrates' youthful promise is

that which Plato puts into the mouth of Socrates at the end of
the *Phaedrus*:

*I think that Isocrates has a genius which soars above the orations of
Lysias, and he has a character of a finer mould. My impression of
him is that he will marvelously improve as he grows older, and that
all former rhetoricians will be as children in comparison of him. And
I believe that he will not be satisfied with this, but that some divine
impulse will lead him to things higher still. For there is an element
of philosophy in his nature.*

As a student, he himself tells us (*Antidosis* 161), "I was more
famous and better known amongst my fellow pupils than I am
now amongst my fellow citizens." Among his teachers were both
Gorgias and Socrates, and though he was never admitted to the
inner Socratic circle, when Socrates died Isocrates wore mourning.
His intellect was apparently respectable enough for him to be entertained by Plato, as we read in Diogenes Laertius (3.8):

*Plato was a friend of Isocrates. Praxiphanes represents them as con-
versing about poets at a country seat where Plato was entertaining
Isocrates.*

But Isocrates turned from speculative philosophy to rhetoric and
journalism and became a teacher of oratory and practical politics.
He himself delivered no speeches; a weak voice and nervousness, he
tells us (*Panathenaicus* 10) prevented him from pleading cases or
haranguing the assembly. When he was asked how it was that being
himself unable to speak he could teach others to do so, he replied
(*Lives of the Ten Orators* 838c), "Whetstones are themselves unable to cut, but they give a cutting edge to iron." His school was
the most celebrated in antiquity, and trained virtually all the public
men of the generation following his maturity. Of it Cicero writes
(*On the Orator* 2.94):

*Then behold! there arose Isocrates, the Master of all rhetoricians,
from whose school, as from the Horse of Troy, none but leaders*

emerged, but some of them sought glory in ceremonial, others in action. And indeed the former sort, men like Theopompus, Ephorus, Philistus, Naucrates, and many more, while differing in natural gifts, yet in spirit resemble one another and their Master too; and those who betook themselves to lawsuits, as did Demosthenes, Hyperides, Lycurgus, Aeschines, Dinarchus and several others, although of varying degrees of ability, were none the less all busy with the same type of imitation of real life, and as long as the imitation of these persisted, so long did their kind of oratory and course of training endure. Afterwards, when these men were dead and all remembrance of them gradually grew dim and then vanished away, certain other less spirited and lazier styles of speaking flourished.

So exorbitant was Isocrates' tuition fee that Demosthenes is said to have had to content himself with a less celebrated teacher (Plutarch, Demosthenes 5.4):

Demosthenes employed Isaeus as his guide to the art of speaking, although Isocrates was lecturing at the time; either, as some say, because he was an orphan and unable to pay Isocrates his stipulated fee of ten minas [about $200 but many times that in purchasing power], or because he preferred the style of Isaeus for its effectiveness and adaptability in actual use.

As we should suspect from his general attitude to things Greek, the Elder Cato ridiculed the school (Plutarch, Marcus Cato 23.2):

Cato made fun of the school of Isocrates, declaring that his pupils kept on studying with him till they were old men, as if they were to practise their arts and plead their cases before Minos in Hades.

But for Aristotle Isocrates' teaching was not theoretical enough. Not only had he turned from speculative philosophy, but his approach to rhetoric was not as scientific as Aristotle would have it, and later writers, at least, speak of sharp rivalry between the two. Both Cicero and Quintilian, as we have seen in the section on

Aristotle, speak of Aristotle's envy of Isocrates' popularity (Cicero, *On the Orator* 3.141; Quintilian 3.1.14). In politics, however, the two saw eye to eye. Isocrates' dominant idea was the union of all Greeks, under a strong leader, against Persia. At first he hoped that Dionysius of Syracuse would be that leader, and then he turned to Philip of Macedon. Such a policy was precisely what men like Demosthenes feared; Isocrates was in a sense the spiritual begetter of Alexander, as this story in Aelian (13.11) shows:

I have heard it said that the orator Isocrates was the cause of the slavery which the Macedonians inflicted upon the Persians. When the report of the Panegyric speech which Isocrates delivered to the Hellenes reached Macedonia at first it aroused Philip against Asia, and then when he died it prepared his son and heir Alexander to succeed to his father's ambition.

That Isocrates was not happy in the political atmosphere of Athens we infer from another story in Aelian (12.52):

The orator Isocrates used to say of the city of Athens that it was like a courtesan. Those who were captivated by her beauty were eager to cohabit with her, but none was so low-spirited as to wish to marry her. So Athens too was agreeable for a sojourn, and in this respect surpassed all the cities of Hellas. But to live with it was safe for no one. By this he alluded to the sycophants who lived in Athens and to the schemes of its demagogues.

Partly because Aristotle shared Isocrates' Macedonian sympathies, and partly because Isocrates' artificial style provides good illustrations for rhetorical expressions, Aristotle cites Isocrates copiously in his *Rhetoric*. As many as ten citations can be found in a single chapter (3.10).

Isocrates' principal stylistic innovation is the avoidance of hiatus, that is, never allowing one word ending in a vowel to be followed by another beginning with a vowel. There is a good deal of critical comment on his style, mainly in Dionysius of Halicarnassus. For

our purposes perhaps the best appreciation is that in Cicero's history
of oratory, the *Brutus* (32):

Then Isocrates appeared; his home, wide open to the whole of
Greece, was a sort of lecture room and laboratory of eloquence. He
was a superb orator and a supremely gifted teacher, although he
shunned the white light of publicity and pursued glory within his
own walls—and in my judgment he attained it in fuller measure
than any of his successors has done. He was a voluminous and
brilliant writer and taught his students to write. Besides, he not only
surpassed his predecessors in other elements of style, but he was
the first to see that even in prose, while verse-forms were to be
eschewed, yet a certain rhythm and cadence should be sought. Before him there was no well ordered structure, so to speak, of words,
nor were sentences brought to rhythmical conclusions; or if such
stylistic phenomena did occur, they displayed no evidence of design.
That may possibly be worthy of applause; but at any rate they owed
their occasional appearance in the works of earlier writers to chance
and natural bent and not to any plan or intention.

It was natural that Isocratean refinements should provoke jeers
in certain quarters. The most merciless perhaps is that in the essay
On the Fame of Athenians (350de) which Plutarch wrote (if write
it he did) as a youthful display piece:

Isocrates, although he had declared [Panegyricus 86] that those who
had risked their lives at Marathon had fought as though their souls
were not their own, and although he had hymned their daring and
their contempt of life, himself (so they say), when he was already
an old man, replied to some one who asked him how he was getting
on, "Even as does a man over 90 years of age who considers death
the greatest of evils." For he had not grown old sharpening his
sword nor whetting his spear-point nor polishing his helmet nor
compaigning nor pulling at the oar, but in gluing together and
arranging antitheses, balanced clauses, and inflexional similarities,
all but smoothing off and proportioning his periods with chisel and

file. How could this person do other than fear the clash of arms and the impact of phalanxes, he who feared to let vowel collide with vowel, or to utter a phrase whose balance was upset by the lack of a single syllable? . . . Isocrates consumed almost 12 years in writing his Panegyric; and during this period he took part in no campaigns, nor served on any embassy, nor founded any city, nor was dispatched as commander of a fleet, although this era brought forth countless wars.

A passage in Cicero's essay On Old Age (5) seems to be a direct refutation of this jeer:

Not everyone can have stormings of cities, battles by land and sea, general commands, and triumphs to recall. But there is also the calm and serene old age of a life passed peacefully, simply, and gracefully. Such, we have heard, was Plato's, who died at his desk in his 81st year; such was Isocrates', who was 94 when he wrote his Panathenaicus and lived five years more. His teacher Gorgias of Leontini rounded out 107 years without suspending his diligence or his pursuits.

Though the defeat at Chaeronea (338 B.C.) which put a period to Athenian liberty was the logical outcome of Isocrates' policy, and though he congratulated Philip on his victory (Epistle 3), the issue must have clouded his last days. According to Dionysius of Halicarnassus he died a few days after the battle, in the 98th year of his age, in accordance with his wish to end his own life together with the fortunes of the state, since it was not clear what use Philip was likely to make of his victory. According to the Lives of Ten Orators (837e) on receiving the news while in the palaestra of Hippocrates, he recited the first line of three Euripidean plays:

Danaus the father of fifty daughters; Pelops the Tantalid came to Pisa; and Cadmus upon a time left Sidon town.

The common denominator of Danaus, Pelops, and Cadmus was that all were alien intruders into Greece; the plain implication was

that Philip was now the fourth intruder. He then abstained from
food for four days and died, "being unwilling to see Hellas enslaved for the fourth time." Pausanias (1.18.8) mentions his statue
in Athens:

*On a pillar is a statue of Isocrates, whose memory is remarkable for
three things: his diligence in continuing to teach to the end of his
98 years, his self-restraint in keeping aloof from politics and from
interfering with public affairs, and his love of liberty in dying a vol-
untary death, distressed at the news of the battle of Chaeronea.*

It is to this that Milton's sonnet alludes:

> As that dishonest victory
> At Chaeronea, fatal to liberty,
> Killed with report that old man eloquent.

VI. ISAEUS

Perhaps because his speeches deal exclusively with testamentary
law Isaeus is not mentioned by any writer before Dionysius of
Halicarnassus, whose opening paragraph in his essay on him gives
all that we know of his life:

*Isaeus, the teacher of Demosthenes—and this is his chief title to
fame—was according to some an Athenian by birth, according to
others a Chalcidian. He flourished after the Peloponnesian War,
as I gather from his speeches, and survived into the reign of Philip.
I cannot state the exact date of his birth and death, nor can I give
any account of his manner of life or political principles, nor do I
know whether he held any particular views; in fact I am ignorant on
all such points, since I have never come across any account of him.
Even Hermippus, who wrote about the pupils of Isocrates, though
he gives details about the others, has only recorded two facts about
Isaeus, namely, that he was a pupil of Isocrates and that he taught
Demosthenes.*

No later writer has anything substantial to add. That he was not altogether unknown is indicated by the last sentence in the short paragraph on Isaeus in the *Lives of the Ten Orators*:

Mention is made of Isaeus by the comic writer Theopompus in his Theseus.

VII. AESCHINES

Aeschines indubitably had merits—an impressive presence, a sonorous voice, and skill in political manipulation—but what we know about him is all bad because it comes from Demosthenes' bitter attacks upon him. Demosthenes opposed Philip out of deep-rooted principle; Aeschines supported Philip, and Demosthenes charged that he was in Philip's pay. In 343 B.C. each accused the other of treason, in extant speeches *On the Embassy*. In 337 Ctesiphon proposed the award of a crown to Demosthenes, and Aeschines indicted Ctesiphon for illegality. His speech *Against Ctesiphon* is naturally filled with invective against Demosthenes. Demosthenes' *On the Crown* defends Ctesiphon and Demosthenes' own career, and is even fuller of invective against Aeschines. Here is a choice bit (258):

But you, the man of dignity, who spit upon others, look what sort of fortune is yours compared with mine. As a boy you were reared in abject poverty, waiting with your father on the school, grinding the ink, sponging the benches, sweeping the room, doing the duty of a menial rather than a freeman's son. After you were grown up, you attended your mother's initiations, reading her books and helping in all the ceremonies: at night wrapping the novitiates in fawnskin, swilling, purifying, and scouring them with clay and bran, raising them after the lustration, and bidding them say, "Bad I have scaped and better I have found"; priding yourself that no one ever howled so lustily—and I believe him! for don't suppose that he who speaks so loud is not a splendid howler! In the daytime you led your noble orgiasts, crowned with fennel and poplar, through the high-

ways, squeezing the big-cheeked serpents, and lifting them over your head, and shouting Evoe Saboe, and capering to the words Hyes Attes, Attes Hyes, saluted by the beldames as Leader, Conductor, Chest-bearer, Fan-bearer, and the like, getting as your reward tarts and biscuits and rolls; for which any man might well bless himself and his fortune!

When you were enrolled among your fellow-townsmen—by what means I stop not to inquire—when you were enrolled, however, you immediately selected the most honorable of employments, that of clerk and assistant to our petty magistrates. From this you were removed after a while, having done yourself all that you charge others with; and then, sure enough, you disgraced not your ante-cedents by your subsequent life, but hiring yourself to those rant-ing players, as they were called, Simylus and Socrates, you acted third parts, collecting figs and grapes and olives like a fruiterer from other men's farms, and getting more from them than from the playing, in which the lives of your whole company were at stake; for there was an implacable and incessant war between them and the audience, from whom you received so many wounds, that no wonder you taunt as cowards people inexperienced in such en-counters.

But passing over what may be imputed to poverty, I will come to the direct charges against your character. You espoused such a line of politics (when at last you thought of taking to them) that, if your country prospered, you lived the life of a hare, fearing and trembling and ever expecting to be scourged for the crimes of which your conscience accused you; though all have seen how bold you were during the misfortunes of the rest. A man who took courage at the death of a thousand citizens—what does he deserve at the hands of the living? A great deal more that I could say about him I shall omit: for it is not all I can tell of his turpitude and infamy which I ought to let slip from my tongue, but only what is not disgraceful to myself to mention.

Of the trial and what befell Aeschines thereafter Plutarch (Demos-thenes 24) tells:

During this time it was that the indictment against Ctesiphon, concerning the crown, was brought to trial. The action was commenced a little before the battle in Chaeronea, when Chaerondas was archon, but it was not proceeded with till about ten years after, Aristophon being then archon. Never was any public cause more celebrated than this, alike for the fame of the orators, and for the generous courage of the judges, who, though at that time the accusers of Demosthenes were in the height of power, and supported by all the favor of the Macedonians, yet would not give judgment against him, but acquitted him so honorably, that Aeschines did not obtain the fifth part of their suffrages on his side, so that, immediately after, he left the city, and spent the rest of his life in teaching rhetoric about the island of Rhodes, and upon the continent in Ionia.

An incident in his Rhodian sojourn is recounted in the Lives of the Ten Orators (840d):

For purposes of display Aeschines recited to the Rhodians his speech Against Ctesiphon. When they expressed astonishment that, having delivered such a speech, he was nevertheless worsted, he said: "You would not be astonished, men of Rhodes, if you had heard Demosthenes speak in opposition."

A more interesting if less credible version of the same story is given by Cicero (On the Orator 3.213):

The story goes that when Demosthenes was asked what is the first thing in speaking, he assigned the first role to delivery, and also the second, and also the third; and I constantly feel that this answer was actually outdone by the remark of Aeschines. That orator, having had a discreditable defeat in a lawsuit, had left Athens and betaken himself to Rhodes; there it is said that at the request of the citizens he read the splendid speech that he had delivered against Ctesiphon, when Demosthenes was for the defense; and when he had read it next day he was asked also to read the speech that had been made in reply by Demosthenes for Ctesiphon. *This he did, in a very attractive and loud voice; and when everybody expressed admiration he said, "How much more remarkable you would have thought it if you had heard Demosthenes himself!" thereby clearly indicating how much depends on delivery, as he thought that the same speech with a change of speaker would be a different thing.*

VIII. DEMOSTHENES

About Demosthenes we are better informed than about any other classical author. Because he was a statesman as well as a writer he is included among Plutarch's worthies, and his *Life* is among the fullest and most reliable the master of biography has left us. Besides Plutarch's, which is based on good sources, there are seven other lives of Demosthenes: those in the *Lives of the Ten Orators,* in Photius, and in Suidas; those of the distinguished 4th century orator Libanius, of Zosimus of Ascalon (5th century), and one anonymous; and, most rewarding, the *Encomium of Demosthenes* ascribed to Lucian. As a check upon these we have not only Demosthenes' account of himself in his own speeches, but the invective in those of his rival Aeschines. Demosthenes' perseverance in overcoming handicaps and his devotion to lofty principles of patriotism made him a favorite text for moralizers, who allude to him repeatedly. Moreover, antiquity universally regarded him as the most accomplished of the orators, and devoted to his writings a body of technical criticism which probably surpasses, in volume and value, that on any other classic.

From this abundance the most economical procedure is to present the anecdotes concerning Demosthenes' education and death from Plutarch, an appreciation of his political insight and integrity from Lucian, and an estimate of his technical excellence from Quintilian, which are respectively the best in their kind. Here are excerpts from the first 11 sections of Plutarch's *Demosthenes:*

At the age of seven, Demosthenes was left by his father in affluence, since the total value of his estate fell little short of 15 talents; but he was wronged by his guardians, who appropriated some of his property to their own uses and neglected the rest, so that even his teachers were deprived of their pay. It was for this reason, as it seems, that he did not pursue the studies which were suitable and proper for a well-born boy, and also because of his bodily weakness and fragility, since his mother would not permit him to work hard in the palaestra, and his tutors would not force him to do so. For from the first he was lean and sickly, and his opprobrious surname of Batalus is said to have been given him by the boys in mockery of his physique. . . . When Demosthenes heard the teachers and tutors agreeing among themselves to be present at a famous trial at which Callistratus was to speak, with great importunity he persuaded his own tutor to take him to the hearing. This tutor, having an acquaintance with the public officials who opened the courts, succeeded in procuring a place where the boy could sit unseen and listen to what was said. Callistratus won his case and was extravagantly admired, and Demosthenes conceived a desire to emulate his fame. . . . When Demosthenes came of age he began to bring suits against his guardians and to write speeches attacking them. They devised many evasions and new trials, but Demosthenes won his cause, although he was able to recover not even a small fraction of his patrimony. However, he acquired sufficient practice and confidence in speaking, and got a taste of the distinction and power that go with forensic contests, and therefore essayed to come forward and engage in public matters. And just as Laomedon the Orchomenian—so we are told —practised long-distance running by the advice of his physicians, to ward off some disease of the spleen, and then, after restoring his health in this way, entered the great games and became one of the best runners of the long course, so Demosthenes, after applying himself to oratory in the first place for the sake of recovering his private property, by this means acquired ability and power in speaking, and at last in public business, as it were in the great games, won the first place among the citizens who strove with one another on the bema.

And yet when he first addressed the people he was interrupted by their clamors and laughed at for his inexperience, since his discourse seemed to them confused by long periods and too harshly and immoderately tortured by formal arguments. He had also, as it would appear, a certain weakness of voice and indistinctness of speech and shortness of breath which disturbed the sense of what he said by disjoining his sentences.

In his dejection he was encouraged by an old man who remembered Pericles and said Demosthenes' style was like Pericles', and by the actor Satyrus, who showed him how proper delivery could heighten his effectiveness:

After this, we are told, he built a subterranean study, which, in fact, was preserved in our time, and into this he would descend every day without exception in order to form his action and cultivate his voice, and he would often remain there even for two or three months together, shaving one side of his head in order that shame might keep him from going abroad even though he greatly wished to do so. . . . For this, many of the popular leaders used to rail at him, and Pytheas, in particular, once told him scoffingly that his arguments smelt of lamp-wicks. To him, then, Demosthenes made a sharp answer. "Indeed," said he, "thy lamp and mine, O Pytheas, are not privy to the same pursuits." . . . Moreover, he used to declare that he who rehearsed his speeches was a true man of the people: for such preparation was a mark of deference to the people, whereas heedlessness of what the multitude will think of his speech marks a man of oligarchical spirit, and one who relies on force rather than on persuasion.

For his bodily deficiencies he adopted the exercises which I shall describe, as Demetrius the Phalerian tells us, who says he heard about them from Demosthenes himself, now grown old. The indistinctness and lisping in his speech he used to correct and drive away by taking pebbles in his mouth and then reciting speeches. His voice he used to exercise by discoursing while running or going up steep places, and by reciting speeches or verses at a single breath. Moreover, he had in his house a large looking-glass, and in front of this he used to stand and go through his exercises in declamation.

At ch. 12 Plutarch takes up Demosthenes' political career, but includes in his account such anecdotes and comment as the following:

The political attitude of Demosthenes was manifest even while peace still lasted, for he would let no act of the Macedonian pass uncensured, but on every occasion kept rousing and inflaming the Athenians against him. Therefore Philip also made most account of him; and when Demosthenes came to Macedonia in an embassy of ten, Philip listened indeed to them all, but took most pains to answer his speech. As regards all other marks of honor and kindly attention, however, Philip did not treat Demosthenes as well as the others, but courted rather the party of Aeschines and Philocrates. And so when these lauded Philip as most powerful in speaking, most fair to look upon, and, indeed, as a most capable fellow-drinker, Demosthenes had to say in bitter raillery that the first encomium was appropriate for a sophist, the second for a woman, and the third for a sponge, but none of them for a king (16).

When messengers brought news of Philip's death the Athenians proceeded to make thank-offerings for glad tidings and voted a crown for Pausanias. And Demosthenes came forth in public dressed in a splendid robe and wearing a garland on his head, although his daughter had died only six days before, as Aeschines says [Against Ctesiphon], who rails at him for this and denounces him as an unnatural father. And yet Aeschines himself was of a weak and ungenerous nature, if he considered mournings and lamentations as the signs of an affectionate spirit, but condemned the bearing of such losses serenely and without repining (22).

Demosthenes told the Athenians the story of how the sheep surrendered their dogs to the wolves, comparing himself and his fellow-orators to dogs fighting in defence of the people, and calling Alexander "the Macedonian arch-wolf." Moreover, he said further: "Just as grain-merchants sell their whole stock by means of a few kernels of wheat which they carry about with them in a bowl as a sample, so in surrendering us you unwittingly surrender also yourselves, all of you" (23).

Pytheas, we are told, said that just as we think that a house into which asses' milk is brought must certainly have some evil in it, so also a city must of necessity be diseased into which an Athenian embassy comes; whereupon Demosthenes turned the illustration against him by saying that asses' milk was given to restore health, and the Athenians came to bring salvation to the sick (27).

After the renewed hopes of liberation were dashed by Antipater at Crannon in 322, he sent Archias "the exile hunter" to arrest Demosthenes, who had taken refuge at the temple of Poseidon at Calauria. At first Archias tried cajolery (29):

After Archias had said many kindly things to him, Demosthenes, just as he sat, looked steadfastly at him and said: "O Archias, thou didst never convince me by thine acting, nor wilt thou now convince me by thy promises." And when Archias began to threaten him angrily, "Now," said he, "thou utterest the langauge of the Macedonian oracle; but a moment ago thou wert acting a part. Wait a little, then, that I may write a message to my family." With these words, he retired into the temple, and taking a scroll, as if about to write, he put his pen to his mouth and bit it, as he was wont to do when thinking what he should write, and kept it there some time, then covered and bent his head. The spearmen, then, who stood at the door, laughed at him for playing the coward, and called him weak and unmanly, but Archias came up and urged him to rise, and reiterating the same speeches as before, promised him a reconciliation with Antipater. But Demosthenes, now conscious that the poison was affecting and overpowering him, uncovered his head; and fixing his eyes upon Archias, "Thou canst not be too soon now," said he, "in playing the part of Creon in the tragedy and casting this body out without burial. But I, O beloved Poseidon, will depart from thy sanctury while I am still alive; whereas Antipater and the Macedonians would not have left even thy temple undefiled." So speaking, and bidding someone support him, since he was now trembling and tottering, he had no sooner gone forth and passed by the altar than he fell, and with a groan gave up the ghost.

Other versions say that Demosthenes carried the poison in a belt, in a bracelet, or in a ring.

In the course of the *Encomium of Demosthenes* Lucian (if the treatise is indeed his) has an imaginary scene between Archias and his employer. When Archias reports his failure to bring Demosthenes alive, Antipater expresses deep regret. First he speaks of Demosthenes' overpowering eloquence, and then continues (33 ff.):

Yet to that I give but a secondary place, as a tool the man used. It was the man himself I marveled at, his spirit and his wisdom, and the steadiness of soul that steered a straight course through all the tempests of fortune with never a craven impulse. And Philip was of my mind about him; when a speech of his before the Athenian assembly against Philip was reported, Parmenio was angry, and made some bitter jest upon him. But Philip said: "Ah, Parmenio, he has a right to say what he pleases; he is the only popular orator in all Greece whose name is missing in my secret service accounts, though I would far rather have put myself in his hands than in those of clerks and third-rate actors. All the tribe of them are down for gold, timber, rents, cattle, land, in Boeotia if not in Macedonia; but the walls of Byzantium are not more proof against the battering-ram than Demosthenes against gold.

"This is the way I look at it, Parmenio. An Athenian who speaking in Athens prefers me to his country shall have of my money, but not of my friendship; as for one who hates me for his country's sake, I will assault him as I would a citadel, a wall, a dock, a trench, but I have only admiration for his virtue, and congratulations for the State that possesses him. The other kind I should like to crush as soon as they have served my purpose; but him I would sooner have here with us than the Illyrian and Triballian horse and all my mercenaries; arguments that carry conviction, weight of intellect, I do not put below force of arms. . . . Are you afraid of these town-

bred generals and their men? Their fleet, their Piraeus, their docks,
I snap my fingers at them. What is to be looked for from people
whose worship is of Dionysus, whose life is in feasting and dancing?
If Demosthenes, and not a man besides, had been subtracted from
Athens, we should have had it with less trouble than Thebes or
Thessaly; deceit and force, energy and corruption, would soon have
done the thing. But he is ever awake; he misses no occasion; he makes
move for move and counters every stroke. . . .

"He rouses his reluctant countrymen out of their opiate sleep,
applies to their indolence the knife and cautery of frank statement,
and little he cares whether they like it or not. He transfers the rev--
enues from state theatre to state armament, re-creates with his navy
bill a fleet disorganized to the verge of extinction, restores patriotism to the place from which it had long been ousted by the passion
for legal fees, uplifts the eyes of a degenerate race to the deeds of
their fathers and emulation of Marathon and Salamis, and fits them
for Hellenic leagues and combinations. You cannot escape his vigi-
lance, he is not to be wheedled, you can no more buy him than the
Persian King could buy the great Aristides. . . ."

All Roman writers on oratory accept it as axiomatic that Demosthenes is the greatest of the Greek orators. Even when Cicero had
been canonized as beyond question the greatest Roman orator, such
an ardent admirer of Cicero as Quintilian still refuses to make him
equal to Demosthenes. Here is Quintilian on Demosthenes (10.-
1.76):

Of the ten remarkable orators which Athens alone produced in the
same generation Demosthenes is far the greatest: indeed he came
to be regarded as almost the sole pattern of oratory. Such is the force
and compactness of his language, so muscular his style, so free from
tameness and so self-controlled, that you will find nothing in him
that is either too much or too little.

And here Quintilian brings Cicero and Demosthenes together
(10.1.105):

*It is our orators, above all, who enable us to match our Roman elo-
quence against that of Greece. For I would set Cicero against any
one of their orators without fear of refutation. I know well enough
what a storm I shall raise by this assertion, more especially since I
do not propose for the moment to compare him with Demosthenes;
for there would be no point in such a comparison, as I consider
that Demosthenes should be the object of special study, and not
merely studied, but even committed to memory.*

Statuesque figures like Demosthenes are peculiarly liable to stories
calculated to expose their clay feet. Here are two often alluded to,
the first from Aulus Gellius, quoted from Sotion (1.8):

*Lais of Corinth used to gain a great deal of money by the grace and
charm of her beauty, and was frequently visited by wealthy men
from all over Greece; but no one was received who did not give what
she demanded, and her demands were extravagant enough. . . .
The great Demosthenes approached her secretly and asked for her
favors. But Lais demanded ten thousand drachmas—a sum equiv-
alent in our money to ten thousand denarii. Amazed and shocked at
the woman's great impudence and the vast sum of money demanded,
Demosthenes turned away, remarking as he left her: "I will not buy
regret at such a price."*

More widely cited is the story which illustrated the great man's
vanity. Here is Cicero's telling of it (*Tusculan Disputations* 5.36.-
103):

*Surely it was petty of my favorite Demosthenes to say he was de-
lighted with the whispered remark of a poor woman carrying water,
as is the custom in Greece, and whispering in her fellow's ear—
"Here is the great Demosthenes!" What could be more petty?*

IX. HYPERIDES

Of the remaining three orators of the canon, Hyperides, Dinarchus,
and Lycurgus, no speeches have come down in manuscript tradition,
though substantial fragments of Hyperides have been recovered

from papyri. Of the three the most impressive figure is Lycurgus, who reformed the political administration of Athens and did a good deal for its culture; it was he who provided that statues of the tragic poets should be set up in the theater of Dionysius.

The most intriguing figure of the three is Hyperides, of whom we have an excellent appreciation in "Longinus" (34):

If excellence were to be judged by the number of merits and not by greatness, Hyperides would then be altogether superior to Demosthenes. He has more strings to his lute and his merits are more numerous. He may almost be said to come a good second in every competition, like the winner of the Pentathlon. In each contest he loses to the professional champion, but comes first of the amateurs. Besides reproducing all the virtues of Demosthenes, except his skill in arrangement, Hyperides has, moreover, embraced all the merits and graces of Lysias. He talks plainly, where necessary, does not make all his points in a monotonous series, as Demosthenes is said to do, and has the power of characterization, seasoned moreover (Heaven knows) by simplicity and charm. Then he has an untold store of polished wit, urbane sarcasm, well-bred elegance, supple turns of irony, jests neither tasteless nor ill-bred, apposite according to the best models of Attic wit, clever satire, plenty of pointed ridicule and well-directed fun, and therewithal what I may call an inimitable fascination. Nature endowed him fully with the power of evoking pity and also of telling a tale fluently and winding his way through a description with facile inspiration, while he is also admirably versatile.

"Longinus" goes on to say that Demosthenes could never have handled the defense of Phryne, which was doubtless the best exhibition of Hyperides' wit and urbanity. That speech, unfortunately, has not been recovered, but we know the details of the case. Phryne was the mistress and model of Praxiteles (and so the pattern for all subsequent statues of Venus), and was indicted on the same charge as Socrates, that of corrupting the young. The *Lives of the Ten Orators* (849e) tells how Hyperides won his case:

When Phryne was about to be found guilty he brought her forward
and pulled off her dress, exhibiting the woman's bosom. The judges
gazed upon her beauty, and absolved her.

Other authors supply further details. Most entertaining, perhaps
is the letter of gratitude which Alciphron (4.3) imagines that
Bacchis addressed to Hyperides:

We courtesans are all grateful to you, and each one of us is just as
grateful as Phryne. The suit that was brought by that scoundrei
Euthias involved Phryne alone, but it meant danger to us all. . . .
Now we shall not find fault with our profession because Euthias
showed himself a rascally lover; but because Hyperides showed himself a gentleman we shall regard it with pride. Blessings on you,
then, for your kindness, and many of them! You have not merely
saved a good mistress for yourself but you have put the rest of us
in a mood to reward you on her account. And furthermore, if you
would write out the speech that you composed in Phryne's defense,
then we courtesans would really and truly set up your statue in gold
wherever in Greece you may wish.

Phryne and Praxiteles are both well known to literature, and a
story of their relationship from Pausanias (1.20) may well be repeated:

Phryne once asked of Praxiteles the most beautiful of his works,
and the story goes that loverlike he agreed to give it, but refused to
say which he thought the most beautiful. So a slave of Phryne
rushed in saying that a fire had broken out in the studio of Praxiteles,
and the greater number of his works were lost, though not all were
destroyed. Praxiteles at once started to rush through the door crying that his labor was all wasted if indeed the flames had caught his
Satyr and his Love. But Phryne bade him stay and be of good courage, for he had suffered no grievous loss, but had been trapped into
confessing which were the most beautiful of his works.

14: *Hellenistic and Later Greek Poets*

OMMENTS ON THE CLASSICAL AUTHORS, even when found in compilations of the Roman period, usually derive from the antiquarian studies of the Alexandrian age. Their own contemporaries the Alexandrian antiquaries naturally did not regard as classics, and so our information about them is sparse in quantity and of a different character than the stories which gathered about the names of the remote great. What scholars were interested in with regard to their contemporaries were technical matters, and the *odium philologicum* having always run a close second in intensity to the *odium theologicum*, we have such spectacles as the famous feud between Callimachus and Apollonius.

I. CALLIMACHUS

Callimachus (305–240) is the typical Alexandrian. He was a scholar and critic, wrote poetry to illustrate his scholarship and his critical theories, and waged polemics with protagonists of different theories. For his life we rely mainly on the notice in Suidas:

Callimachus, son of Battus and Mesatma, of Cyrene, grammarian, pupil of Hermocrates of Iasos, the grammarian, married the daughter of Euphrates of Syracuse. His sister's son was Callimachus the younger, who wrote an epic, On Islands. So diligent was he that he wrote poems in every metre and also wrote a great number of works in prose. The books written by him amount in all to more than eight hundred. He lived in the times of Ptolemy Philadelphus [reigned 285–247 B.C.]. Before his introduction to that king he taught grammar in Eleusis, a hamlet of Alexandria. He survived to the time of Ptolemy, surnamed Euergetes.

Battiades, the name by which Catullus and Ovid call Callimachus, refers not only to his father Battus but to Battus the founder of

Cyrene. Strabo 17.837 says: "Cyrene is a foundation of Battus; Callimachus declares that this Battus was his own ancestor."

Callimachus' own convictions that poetry must be fresh in subject matter, brief, and highly polished may be deduced from certain of his own utterances as well as from his works. In Epigram 30 he says: "I hate the cyclic poem, nor do I take pleasure in the road which carries many to and fro." Athenaeus (2.72a) tells us that "Callimachus the scholar said that a big book is a big evil." In his *Hymn to Apollo* Callimachus says (2.105 ff.):

Spake Envy privily in the ear of Apollo: "I admire not the poet who singeth not things for number as the sea." Apollo spurned Envy with his foot and spake thus: "Great is the stream of the Assyrian river, but much filth of earth and much refuse it carries on its waters."

On the word "refuse" in this passage the scholiast says:

Here he reproaches those who mocked him as being unable to write a big poem; in consequence he was forced to compose his Hecale.

In the epitaph he wrote for himself (Epigram 23) he says that "he sang songs beyond the reach of envy." The "envy" is generally attributed to Apollonius, who wrote his *Argonautica* to refute Callimachus' position that long poems could no longer be written. Apollonius' opinion of Callimachus occurs in an epigram, which he probably wrote on the margin of a copy of Callimachus' *Origins* (A.P. 11.275):

Callimachus the outcast, the butt, the wooden head! The origin is Callimachus, who wrote the Origins.

The heaviest gun in the duel was Callimachus' lost *Ibis*, which we know by description and from Ovid's imitation. What an insult it was to call a man an ibis we can gather from Strabo's description of that bird (17.823):

Tamest of all is the *Ibis*, which is like a stork in shape and size, and is of two colors, one storklike, the other all black. Every crossing in Alexandria is full of them, in some respects usefully, in others not usefully. Usefully, because they pick up all sorts of vermin and the offal in the butchers' shops and fish-shops. They are detrimental, because they are omnivorous and unclean and are with difficulty prevented from polluting in every way what is clean and what is not theirs.

Suidas describes the *Ibis* as "a poem of studied obscurity and abuse on one Ibis, an enemy of Callimachus: this was Apollonius, who wrote the *Argonautica*." Studied obscurity and abuse characterize Ovid's imitation, as we see from 53 ff.:

Finally, if you persist, the iambic volume dyed in the blood of Lycambes will provide me weapons against you. The curses which Battiades invoked upon his enemy Ibis I shall soon invoke upon you and yours. And as he did, I shall wrap my poem in dark enigmas. Myself I am not in the habit of following such a course. But I shall be spoken of as imitating his ambiguities in the *Ibis*, oblivious of my usual habit and my judgment.

Callimachus was a prime model for the Latin elegists, and especially for Propertius, who begins his third book with an invocation to him:

Shade of Callimachus and sacred rites of Philetas, suffer me, I pray, to enter your grove. I am the first with priestly service from an unsullied spring to carry Italian mysteries among the dances of Greece. . . . Let verse run smoothly, polished with fine pumice. 'Tis by such verse as this that Fame lifts me aloft from earth, and the Muse, my daughter, triumphs with garlanded steeds, and tiny Loves ride with me in my chariot, and a throng of writers follows my wheels. Why strive ye against me vainly with loosened rein? Narrow is the path that leadeth to the Muses. Many, O Rome, shall add fresh glories to thine annals, singing that Bactra shall be thine empire's bound; but this work of mine my pages have brought down from the Muses'

mount by an untrodden way, that thou mayest read it in the midst
of peace.

II. APOLLONIUS

Neither of Callimachus' antagonist do we have much beyond what
pertains to the feud. The text of Apollonius is included in the fine
10th century Laurentian MS which contains Aeschylus and Sophocles also, and is equipped with good scholia. To these are appended
two epitomes of a life of Apollonius, which are our principal source
on the subject. The first reads:

Apollonius the poet of the Argonautica was an Alexandrian by birth,
the son of Silleus, or as some have it, Illeus, of the tribe of Ptolemais,
and was a pupil of Callimachus. At first he associated with his own
teacher Callimachus, but later he turned to composing poetry. They
say that he exhibited his Argonautica while he was still quite young,
and when he could not endure being shamed by his fellow-citizens
nor the insults and slanders of other poets, he decided to forsake
his country and migrate to Rhodes. There he polished and corrected his poems and then exhibited them, and gained very high
opinions. It is for this reason that he inscribes himself a Rhodian in
his poems. He was a brilliant cultural influence in Rhodes, and
was by the Rhodians esteemed worthy of citizenship and distinction.

The second epitome is in substantial agreement with the first, but
adds:

Some say that he returned to Alexandria, and there again exhibited
his work and gained high reputation, so that he was esteemed worthy
of the leadership of the Library and Museum and of being buried
with Callimachus himself.

Older scholarship tended to doubt that Apollonius was ever Librarian, and represented him as Callimachus' inferior; the publication of a papyrus listing the Alexandrian librarians (Oxyrhynchus

1241) shows that Apollonius held the office after Zenodotus and before Eratosthenes. Callimachus, though he worked in the library and made a catalogue of it, was actually Apollonius' subordinate, and the disparity of their positions may have had something to do with their quarrel.

Of the personality of Apollonius nothing more can be said, but his poem has left its mark in Latin literature, and through Vergil, whose Dido and Aeneas episode is a palpable adaptation of Argonautica 3, on European literature. How closely Vergil studied Apollonius is shown by a passage where the text of the master can be corrected by the pupil's copy. At 3.756 ff. Apollonius has:

And as a sunbeam dances on the rooms of a house, reflected from the water newly poured into a cauldron or perchance a pail; hither and thither it darts and flashes from the swift eddy—even so did the heart of the maiden throb and quiver in her breast.

In Aeneid 8.20 ff. we read:

Now hither now thither he swiftly throws his mind, casting it in diverse ways, and turning it in all directions; as when in brazen cauldrons a flickering light from water, flung back by the sun or moon's glittering form, flits far and wide o'er all things, and now mounts high and smites the fretted beams of the high ceiling.

Rooms in the Apollonius passage renders the Greek domois; Vergil evidently read dokois ("beams") in his text, and that is probably the true reading, since it is natural for a scribe to substitute the familiar domois for the unfamiliar dokois. It is interesting to observe that Ariosto (Orlando Furioso 8.71) borrows the same figure, from Vergil, not Apollonius:

> Qual d'acqua chiara il tremolante lume,
> Dal Sol percossa, o da' notturni rai,
> Per gli ampli tetti va con lungo salto
> A destra ed a sinistra, e basso ed alto.

But Vergil was not the only channel through which Apollonius reached the Romans. Catullus, Ovid, Propertius, and Lucan show definite acquaintance with him. Varro of Atax (82–37) made a Latin version of the *Argonautica* (lost except for fragments) which was highly esteemed. Ovid, *Amores* 1.15–21 says: "What age does not know Varro and the pioneer vessel and the golden fleece sought for the Aesonian chief?" The extant *Argonautica* of Valerius Flaccus, whose recent death Quintilian (10.1.90) regrets, is a reworking rather than a translation of Apollonius, but obviously leans heavily on him. How familiar the story of the quest of the golden fleece had become in Roman literature is indicated by its prominent place in the list of mythological themes which Juvenal says, at the beginning of the first satire, have exhausted his patience.

The two best critics of the Roman period express essentially similar judgments on Apollonius. "Longinus" (33.4) says:

Apollonius in his Argonautica *is an impeccable poet. . . . Yet would you not rather be Homer than Apollonius?*

Apollonius, in other words, while no genius, is steady and shows infinite capacity for taking pains. Quintilian says (10.1.54):

Apollonius is not admitted to the lists drawn up by the professors of literature, because the critics, Aristarchus and Aristophanes, included no contemporary poets. None the less, his work is by no means to be despised, being distinguished by the consistency with which he maintains his level as a representative of the intermediate type.

III. THEOCRITUS

The pastorals of Theocritus are a very different, and to modern taste a more genuine, kind of poetry than Apollonius' learned epic, but our information concerning Theocritus is of the same character as that concerning Apollonius. The basic passage again is the anonymous life prefixed to a number of MSS:

Theocritus, the poet of the Bucolics, was a Syracusan by birth
. . . as he himself says—"Simichidas, whither draggest thy feet
at noonday?" [7.21]. Some say that Simichidas was merely a nickname. They say that he was snub-nosed in appearance, and that he
had Praxagoros for father and Phalina for mother. He was a pupil
of Philetas and Asclepiades, of whom he makes mention. He attained his prime under the Ptolemy surnamed Lagus, and having
proven himself a virtuoso in bucolic poetry, he attained a great
reputation. According to some, the man called Moschus was named
Theocritus, but we must note that Theocritus was contemporary
with Aratus and Callimachus and Nicander. He lived in the time of
Ptolemy Philadelphus.

From the Arguments prefixed to the individual poems and the
scholia upon them we get additional details:

Theocritus flourished in the 124th Olympiad (= 284–280 B.C.;
Arg. 4). When Theocritus went to Ptolemy at Alexandria, he so-
journed on Cos and became a friend to Prasidamos and Antigenes
(Arg. 7). Theocritus converses with the physician Nicias, a Milesian
by birth, who had been a fellow student of Erasistratus, who was
also a physician (Arg. 11). This idyll was written to Hiero son of
Hierocles, the last tyrant of Sicily. . . . When he received nothing
from Hiero he inscribed this idyll Charitae (Arg. 16).

In Thalysia (No. 7) where a number of poets masquerade under
borrowed names, the scholia provide identifications.

In the quarrel concerning the feasibility of writing epic in the
Alexandrian age, Theocritus was on the side of Callimachus and
opposed to Apollonius. An epigram of his (A.P. 7.45) says:

I hate all birds of the Muses that vainly toil with their cackling note
against the Minstrel of Chios (Homer).

And at 16.20 he says, "Homer is enough for all," which suggests the
futility of competing in epic.

It is probable that by any absolute criteria Theocritus is a greater poet than Callimachus or Apollonius; in the esteem of posterity he surpasses them by an even greater interval than poetic merit alone would suggest, because whereas they worked in traditional forms which grew hackneyed, Theocritus' pastoral provided a new genre which found enthusiastic imitators in all European languages. Again the great intermediary is Vergil, whose own youthful Eclogues are incidentally the best testimonial to Theocritus. Both (and all subsequent writers of pastoral) idealize reality and make it artificial, but Theocritus is free of the superfluities and conceits which are already apparent in Vergil's imitations. Here are some lines of passionate soliloquy in Theocritus (2.28–32):

As I melt this wax with the help of Heaven, so may the Myndian Delphis now melt with love; and as this brazen wheel is whirled by Aphrodite's power, so may he be whirled one day about my door! (Magic wheel, draw thou that man to my house.)

And here is Vergil's adaptation (Eclogues 8.80–84):

As this loam grows hard, and this wax soft in one and the same fire: so may Daphnis in the fire of my love! Sprinkle meal and kindle the crackling laurel-leaves with pitch. The evil-hearted Daphnis burns me and I burn this laurel-leaf in Daphnis' name. (Bring Daphnis home from the city, bring him home, my songs.)

After Theocritus had discovered Arcady and Vergil had named and publicized it, it became a favorite province of European poesy. In antiquity the romance of Daphnis and Chloe is pure pastoral, and even borrows its names from Theocritus. In the Renaissance pastoral enjoyed a great vogue, of which Spenser's *Shepherd's Calendar* may fairly be reckoned the culmination. In the Epistle which accompanies the *Calendar*, Spenser gives an apologia and a history of the form:

Colin, vnder whose person the Author selfe is shadowed . . . following the example of the best and most auncient Poetes, which deuised this kind of wryting, being both so base for the matter, and homely for the manner, at the first to trye theyr habilities: and as young birdes, that be newly crept out of the nest, by little first to proue theyr tender wyngs, before they make a greater flyght. So flew Théocritus, as you may perceiue he was all ready full fledged. So flew Virgile, as not yet well feeling his winges. So flew Mantuane, as being not full somd. So Petrarque. So Boccace; So Marot, Sanazarus, and also diuers other excellent both Italian and French Poetes, whose foting this Author euery where followeth, yet so as few, but they be wel sented can trace him out. So finally flyeth this our new Poete, as a bird, whose principals be scarce growen out, but yet as that in time shall be hable to keepe wing with the best.

IV. ARATUS

The poet of whom Paul speaks in Acts 17.28, "as certain also of your poets have said, For we are also his offspring," is Aratus, and the reference is to line 5 of his *Phaenomena*. Only the curious know Aratus today, for we like our science modern and in prose, but he was familiar to every educated Roman and was translated or paraphrased at least four times. The earliest is Cicero's, of which nearly 700 lines are preserved. Cicero himself mentions this version several times, and with satisfaction; at *On the Nature of the Gods* 2.41, for example, he has an interlocutor say:

I shall avail myself of your youthful translation of Aratus' poetical works, which so delight me in the Latin form you have given them that I remember many of the lines.

A second version was made by Varro of Atax (82–37 B.C.), who translated Apollonius' *Argonautica* also, and so justified the remark of Quintilian (10.1.87), "He achieved a reputation as the interpreter of the work of others." Of Varro's version only slight fragments are extant, but we have some 850 lines of the translation made by Germanicus Caesar (15 B.C.–A.D. 19), the nephew of the Emperor Tiberius. In the 4th century Rufus Festus Avienus, who was

proconsul of Africa in 366, made an (extant) paraphrase of the
Phaenomena in 1878 lines. The influence of the *Phaenomena* is
plainly apparent in Lucretius and Vergil and especially in the
Astronomica of Manilius, who wrote under Tiberius.

Aratus' own contemporary Leonidas of Tarentum, himself a better poet than Aratus, wrote this appreciation of him (A.P. 9.25):

*This is the book of the learned Aratus, whose subtle mind explored
the long-lived stars, both the fixed stars and the planets with which
the bright revolving heaven is set. Let us praise him for the great
task at which he toiled; let us count him second to Zeus, in that
he made the stars brighter.*

But other critics complain of Aratus' faulty astronomy, saying that
he took it from the work of Eudoxus which he understood imperfectly. So Cicero (*Republic* 1.22):

*Gallus told us that the other kind of celestial globe, which was solid
and contained no hollow space, was a very early invention, the first
one of that kind having been constructed by Thales of Miletus,
and later marked by Eudoxus of Cnidus (a disciple of Plato, it was
claimed) with the constellations and stars which are fixed in the sky.
He also said that many years later Aratus, borrowing this whole
arrangement and plan from Eudoxus, had described it in verse,
without any knowledge of astronomy, but with considerable poetic
talent.*

And in *On the Orator* 1.16 he says:

*The learned world is agreed that Aratus, though quite ignorant of
astronomy, has composed a most eloquent and artistic poem on the
heavens and the stars.*

The fullest criticism in this kind is that of Leontius, a 6th century
commentator:

It must be noted that what Aratus says about the stars is not well
said, as can be learned from the writings of Hipparchus and Ptolemy
on the subject. The reason is, in the first place, that he did not fully
comprehend the work of Eudoxus, whom he mainly follows; and
in the second place, that he did not aim at precision, as the commentator Sporos points out, but made his composition useful for
seafarers.

The respectable 2nd century rhetorician Theon defends Aratus
against such strictures, and says:

Their violence is immoderate. Mathematical expertness is necessary
even in making a paraphrase, and we find Aratus for the most part
a careful student of Eudoxus.

Quintilian (10.1.55) gives the literary man's estimate:

The subject chosen by Aratus is lifeless and monotonous, affording
no scope for pathos, description of character, or eloquent speeches.
However, he is adequate for the task to which he felt himself equal.

V. OTHER DIDACTIC AND HEROIC POETRY

Besides the four poets already dealt with in this chapter, and besides the many epigrammatists whose work will be mentioned in
the section following, many others wrote in the period between
the Alexandrian age and the end of antiquity. Most are only names,
but even of those of whom considerable complete works remain—
Herodas, Nicander, Lycophron, Oppian, Quintus, Nonnus, Colluthus, Tryphiodorus, and Musaeus—most are known only to specialists, and indeed deserve no better.

Herodas (3rd century), whose first English translator called
him the "realist of the Aegean," is in a special case. Before the discovery (in 1890) of the papyrus containing eight of his mimes he
was virtually unknown; all other papyrus discoveries were of works
known to have existed. And although Herondas' mimes bear a relationship to Theocritus', their calculated vulgarity sets them apart

from almost everything else in Greek literature and made them particularly sympathetic to an age that was discovering realism. But their subject matter and linguistic difficulty alike made them unsuitable for school use, and though philologers have reveled in them for half a century knowledge of them has not penetrated beyond seminar walls.

Nicander (3rd century) wrote many poems which could not help being more interesting than his two long didactic poems, the *Theriaca* and the *Alexipharmaca*. The first deals with the poisons of noxious creatures, chiefly snakes, and their antidotes, and the second with other poisons. There are one or two laudatory references in later writers to Nicander's other work, but the only comment that could be made on his poison-poems (and this very justly) is that a versified treatise does not make a poem.

Lycophron (3rd century) is similarly useful as a horrible example. His *Alexandra* is a single monologue, in 1475 tragic iambics, in which a slave reports the prophecies of Alexandra (Cassandra) to Priam. No person, place, or thing is called by its name, but everything is referred to by most tortuous allusions. Lycophron tried hard to be difficult, and succeeded. The first explicit reference to the poem is in Statius' piece on his father (*Silvae* 5.3.157) who, as a teacher of literature, had among other things "to unravel the riddles of cramped Lycophron."

The *Cynegetica* and *Halieutica*, on hunting and fishing respectively, were probably written by separate Oppians, in the 2nd and 3rd century A.D. The *Halieutica* in particular is a witty and informing poem, and can be read with real pleasure in the Jacobean translation of John Jones. In a list of poets who wrote on fishing Athenaeus 1.13b mentions "Oppian of Cilicia, who was born a little before us." The *Life* preserved in the MSS of the poem is interesting enough to merit reproduction:

Oppian the poet was the son of Agesilaus and Zenodote, and his birthplace was Anazarbos in Cilicia. His father, a man of wealth and considered the foremost citizen of his native city, distinguished too for culture and living the life of a philosopher, trained his son on the same lines and educated him in the whole curriculum of education—music and geometry and especially grammar. When Oppian was about 30 years of age, the Roman Emperor Severus visited Anazarbos. And whereas it was the duty of all public men to meet the Emperor, Agesilaus as a philosopher and one who despised all vainglory neglected to do so. The Emperor was angered and banished him to the island of Melite in the Adriatic. There the son accompanied his father and there he wrote these very notable poems. Coming to Rome in the time of Antoninus, son of Severus—Severus being already dead—he read his poetry and was bidden to ask anything he pleased. He asked and obtained the restoration of his father, and received further for each verse or line of his poetry a golden coin. Returning home with his father and a pestilence coming upon Anazarbos he soon after died. His fellow-citizens gave him a funeral and erected in his honour a splendid monument with the following inscription:

"I, Oppian, won everlasting fame, but Fate's envious thread carried me off and chilly Hades took me while still young—me the minstrel of sweet song. But had dread Envy allowed me to remain alive long, no man would have won such glory as I."

He wrote also certain other poems and he lived for thirty years. He possessed much polish and smoothness coupled with conciseness and nobility—a most difficult combination. He is particularly successful in sententious sayings and similes.

Oppian's fanciful zoology is notorious but he can be profitable nevertheless, as Thomas Browne notes in his Hydrotaphia:

Abating the annual mutation of sexes in the hyaena, the single sex of the rhinoceros, the antipathy between two drums, of a lamb's and a wolf's skin, the informity of cubs, the venation of Centaures, the copulation of the murena and the viper, with some few others, Oppian may be read with great delight and profit.

People nurtured on Homer will find the 14-book Posthomerica of Quintus of Smyrna (4th century A.D.) the most interesting of this group. Quintus tells, in order, the stories connected with the Trojan War from the point where the *Iliad* leaves off. The single fact known about him is what he himself tells us at 12.310, "What time I fed my goodly sheep on Smyrna's pasture-lea." This line has been taken, with no probability, to imply that Quintus was a bishop, and with great probability that he was of Smyrna, and hence he is now so named. Earlier writers, John Milton among them, call him Quintus of Calabria, from the circumstance that it was in Otranto in Calabria that Cardinal Bessarion discovered the first MS of the *Posthomerica* in the 15th century.

Of other poets who dealt with parts of the tale of Troy we have the *Rape of Helen* of Colluthus (5th century) and the *Taking of Ilium* of Tryphiodorus (4th century). Information on each is very meager, consisting mainly of a brief note in Suidas. A note in the Ambrosian MS of Colluthus says that the *Rape of Helen* was a familiar poem in Apulia; of Tryphiodorus Suidas tells us further that he wrote a lipogrammatic *Odyssey*, which is an *Odyssey* in which the letter alpha is not found in the first book, beta is not found in the second, gamma in the third, and so on.

The Egyptian Nonnus (5th century) composed, besides a paraphrase of the Gospel of St. John, the 48-book *Dionysiaca*, which describes the origin of the god and his triumphal progress to India. The huge *Dionysiaca* is remarkable for a wild kind of new energy growing out of corruption of the old. All that we have concerning the author is an anonymous epigram (A.P. 9.198):

I am Nonnus; my native city was Panoplis, but in Alexandria I mowed down by my vocal sword the children of the giants [i.e., in the battle between Dionysus and Typhoeus in the Dionysiaca].

Far the best known of this group to European readers is Musaeus (5th century). Through Marlowe's *Hero and Leander*, enormously expanded by Chapman, through Grillparzer who made a tragedy of the story and through Schiller who made a ballad of it, Musaeus' poem has become a familiar part of the European tradition, and none of his followers tells the story better than does Musaeus himself. Renaissance scholars, including even the great Julius Caesar Scaliger, thought that the author was the ancient seer who came long before Homer, and that his poem was superior to Homer's. In his folio edition of the heroic poets (1566) H. Stephanus prints Musaeus after Tryphiodorus; he notes that a friend who assured him he had seen a MS in which Musaeus was called "a grammarian" had confirmed his own feeling that there was nothing Homeric in the poem.

VI. THE ANTHOLOGY

Some of the most exquisite poems of antiquity are found in the so-called *Palatine Anthology*, which covers a span of 1,500 years and contains 9,000 pieces. Our anthology is an accretion. About the middle of the first century B.C. Meleager of Gadara chose short poems of 46 writers from Sappho's day to his own for a *Garland*. His introductory poem (A.P. 4.1) lists his "contributors," with a highly appropriate flower for each:

Dear Muse, for whom bringest thou this gardenful of song, or who is he that fashioned the garland of poets? Meleager made it, and wrought out this gift as a remembrance for noble Diocles, inweaving many lilies of Anyte, and many martagons of Moero, and of Sappho little, but all roses, and the narcissus of choral Melanippides budding into hymns, and the fresh shoot of the scented flowering iris of Nossis, on whose tablets Love melted the wax, and with her, marjoram from sweet-breathing Rhianus, and the delicious maiden-fleshed crocus of Erinna, and the hyacinth of Alcaeus, vocal among the poets, and the dark-leaved laurel-spray of Samius, and withal the rich ivy-clusters of Leonidas, and the tresses of Mnasalcas' sharp pine. . . .

Meleager's *Garland* was the nucleus for the *Anthology* of Philip of Thessalonica, of the 2nd century A.D. Other collections were made by Strato of Sardes (2nd century) and Agathias of Byzantium (5th century). These collections and many new epigrams went into the huge anthology made in the 10th century by Constantine Cephalas. In 1301 the monk Maximus Planudes edited the *Anthology* of Cephalas, ejecting many fine poems on moral grounds and adding many others in what is called the *Planudean Appendix*. Cephalas' original disappeared from view, and the only anthology known to the Renaissance was the *Planudean*, which was printed by John Lascaris at Florence in 1484. In 1606 Salmasius (Saumaise), then only 18 but already an accomplished scholar, discovered a MS of the *Anthology* of Cephalas in the library of the Counts Palatine at Heidelberg. He copied from it and circulated in manuscript the epigrams hitherto unknown but never edited the whole work. In 1623, when Heidelberg was captured by the Archduke Maximilian of Bavaria in the Thirty Years War, the MS of the *Anthology* along with many others was sent as a gift to Pope Gregory XV and placed in the Vatican Library. In 1797 it was taken to Paris by order of the French Directory, and after the Napoleonic Wars it was restored to the Palatine Library.

The little we know of the poets of the *Anthology* (except for those like Simonides or Plato) is what they say of themselves or each other, but it may be useful to list and say a word about the principal ones. Anyte of Tegea (ca. 300 B.C.) whose "lilies" head Meleager's list is represented by 24 exquisite and spirited pieces. Her reputation was deservedly high; Antipater (A.P. 9.26) calls her "the female Homer." Asclepiades of Samos, represented by 43 fine pieces, is mentioned by Theocritus (7.39) along with Philetas of Cos (not represented) as his masters in style. There are over a hundred pieces of Leonidas of Tarentum (early 3rd century) which, probably for their diffuseness, Meleager characterizes as "ivy-clusters." Euphorion (3rd century) has only two pieces, but may be mentioned for his great influence on the Romans. Cornelius Gallus, the friend of Vergil, translated him into Latin, and Cicero (*Tusculan Disputations* 3.19) has a famous sneer for the *Cantores Euphorionis*. Alcaeus of Messene (ca. 200 B.C.) has 22 pieces, many on historical events. Antipater of Sidon, who lived at the beginning of the first century B.C. and Antipater of Thessalonica, who lived at its end, have between them 178 epigrams of which the proper distribution is not always easy. Philodemus of Gadara, an Epicurean philosopher who lived at Rome, who is mentioned by Cicero and Horace, and whose treatises have been recovered from Herculaneum, has 30-odd rather scabrous pieces. Crinagoras was a prominent Greek poet in Augustan Rome, and is represented by 51 epigrams. Most like the epigrams of the Roman Martial are those of Lucilius, who was a pensioner of Nero and has some 140 epigrams in the *Anthology*. Strato lived under Hadrian and specialized in pederastic pieces. He was the editor of the third revision of Meleager's *Garland*, and it was his work to which Planudes chiefly took exception. He himself is represented by about a hundred pieces.

Peculiar interest attaches to the personalities of a group of later writers in the *Anthology*. The most astringent is Palladas (4th century), whose 150 poems show his contempt for humanity; Palladas is one of the last pagans to speak out against Christianity. Agathias (6th century) was a Christian, a historian, and himself an anthologist. He is represented by almost 100 rather diffuse but pretty poems. The best poet in the later group is Paul the Silentiary (the function of a silentiary was to procure silence for certain rituals in the Eastern Church), who was a friend of Agathias. Each speaks approvingly of the other.

15: *Greek Prose under Roman Sway*

INTELLECTUALLY ROME WAS A PROVINCE OF HEL-
lenism. Latin literature is dominated by Greek forms and motifs,
and only during some three centuries, centering in the beginning
of our era, was creative writing of the first order produced in the
Latin language. At the Republican end of the span Romans like
Fabius Pictor wrote their own history in Greek, and at the other
end emperors like Hadrian or Marcus Aurelius turned to Greek
to express their inward thoughts. In the eastern half of the empire
the primacy of Greek was never interrupted and the making of
books was continuous. Reference works list more than a thousand
Greek writers of the Roman period, and of these some 25, aside
from the writers of Christianity, are represented by extant works
considerable enough in scope and significance to merit treatment
in the most summary account of ancient literature.

I. LITERATURE OF KNOWLEDGE

Most of the extant writing of the period is utilitarian in nature.
The fullest category is history, in which, besides numerous fragments, we have substantial portions of the work of respectable
writers. Dionysius of Halicarnassus (fl. 30 B.C.) wrote, besides his
critical works, the *Archaeology of the Romans*, which sought to
interpret Rome to Greek readers and establish its place in the
new oecumene. The *Library* of Diodorus Siculus (fl. 90 B.C.) consists mainly of excerpts of earlier historians of diverse peoples, and
aims to present the world as a single brotherhood, in accordance
with Stoic principles. Josephus (fl. A.D. 80) sought to persuade
the gentile world of the antiquity and dignity of the Jews, to the
end of procuring their recognition also as members of the family
of peoples. If an English household, two centuries ago, possessed
but one book besides the Bible that book was apt to be Josephus.
Arrian's (A.D. 95–175) *Anabasis* is our best account of the career

of Alexander the Great; he also put into writing the spoken *Discourses* of Epictetus. Appian of Alexandria wrote the history of Rome in sensible geographical segments. We have the letter of recommendation of Fronto (1.263 Haines) which procured him his procuratorship:

For two years now I have been your suppliant for my friend Appian, between whom and myself there has been both a long-standing intimacy and almost daily practice of mutual studies. . . . It is to enhance his dignity in old age that he desires to attain this distinction, and not from ambition or coveting the salary of a procurator.

Dio Cassius Cocceianus (A.D. 155–235) wrote the most complete history of Rome, in 80 books. The short *History of Events after Marcus* by the Syrian Herodian (3rd century A.D.) was used as a text book of history in 18th century England. More widely read, perhaps, than the historians proper are the geographers Strabo and Pausanias. The 17-book *Geography* of Strabo (63 B.C.–A.D. 21; his larger history is lost) is an encyclopedia of information concerning the various countries of the then known world. The 10-book *Description of Greece* of Pausanias is a traveler's guide, containing legends, myths, folklore, prophecies, scraps of history, and a very little art criticism.

More clearly in the realm of the text and reference book are the critical essays of Dionysius of Halicarnassus, Demetrius, and "Longinus," which have been mentioned in Chapter 5 on the Critics, and the collections of Diogenes Laertius, Athenaeus, and Aelian, which are listed in Chapter 7 on the Gossipers. One of the older of the four related writers named Philostratus (170–248) wrote a gossipy compilation called *Lives of the Sophists*; it is not cited in the present gossipy compilation because its trivial heroes have all been forgotten. Philostratus' reverent *Life of Apollonius of Tyana* is a work of a different order; through Athanasius' *Life of St. Anthony* it influenced all subsequent biographies of saints. A later Philostratus wrote *Imagines*, a series of talks on paintings, and a Callistratus (3rd or 4th century) a similar *Descriptions of Statues*. In imitation of Philostratus' *Lives of the Sophists*, Eunapius (346–414) wrote an even more trifling *Lives of the Philosophers and Sophists*.

II. LITERATURE OF POWER

Utility of a different sort was the object of a group of earnest men, mainly Stoic at first and then (omitting the Christians) Neoplatonic, who sought to make themselves and their fellows at home in the world. Some, like Epictetus or Plotinus, addressed their disciples; others, like Dion of Prusa or Maximus of Tyre, addressed large audiences; still others, like Plutarch and the Neoplatonists, addressed a reading public. A group of orators, including Themistius and Libanius, aimed rather at entertainment than edification. Perhaps Lucian, who deserves a place in the shortest list of ancient books worth the modern reader's attention, shares the functions of teacher and entertainer. His imaginative writings make a transition to the Greek romances, which exerted a very great influence on our own fictional forms. In the paragraphs following we shall deal cursorily with such of these writers as have left their mark on posterity, and first with the philosophic teachers.

III. EPICTETUS

Epictetus (late first century A.D.) is the most spiritual of the Stoic teachers. He himself published nothing; his *Discourses* were taken down, obviously verbatim, by Arrian. We know that he was a slave, from other sources and from an epigram (*A.P.* 7.676):

> Slave, poor as Irus, halting as I trod,
> I, Epictetus, was the friend of God.

The halting, several sources tell us, was due to a brutal beating by his master; Suidas attributes it to rheumatism. He was long unmarried, which makes the point in Lucian's gibe (*Demonax* 55):

Epictetus once urged the cripple Rufinus, with a touch of reproof, to take a wife and raise a family—for it beseemed a philosopher to leave some one to represent him after the flesh. But he received the home-thrust: "Very well, Epictetus; give me one of your daughters."

When Domitian banished the philosophers from Rome, Epictetus went to Nicopolis in Epirus, where he continued to teach. Of all pagan teachers his doctrine stands closest to the teachings of Jesus, and he has had a devoted following in all ages. The finest tribute to Epictetus is perhaps that of Justus Lipsius:

He was a man who relied wholly upon himself and God, but not on Fortune. In origin low and servile, in body lame and feeble, in mind most exalted, and brilliant among the lights of every age. . . . So help me God, what a keen and lofty spirit in his Discourses! a soul aflame, and burning with love of the honorable! There is nothing in Greek their like, unless I am mistaken; I mean with such notable vigor and fire. A novice or one unacquainted with true philosophy he will hardly stir or affect, but when a man has made some progress or is already far advanced, it is amazing how Epictetus stirs him up, and though he is always touching some tender spot, yet he gives delight also. . . . There is no one who better influences and shapes a good mind. I never read that old man without a stirring of my soul within me, and, as with Homer, I think the more of him each time I re-read him, for he seems always new; and even after I have returned to him I feel that I ought to return to him yet once more.

IV. MARCUS AURELIUS

All readers of Marcus Aurelius' *To Himself* have been impressed by the author's saintliness. The impression is not marred (though not greatly strengthened) by the correspondence between him and the rhetorician Marcus Cornelius Fronto, discovered in a Vatican palimpsest in 1815. Dio (71.35.6) says of Marcus: "By nature a good man, his education and the moral training he imposed upon himself made him a better one." And Aristides (A.D. 117–189) says (*To Regulus* 106): "As was natural to one who had beatified his soul with every virtuous quality he was innocent of all wrongdoing." Before Suidas the only direct mention of Marcus' book is in the orator Themistius (A.D. 350). It is not mentioned again until the 12th century, when Tzetzes quotes and Planudes makes excerpts from it. It was first printed in 1558 by Xylander, and has since gone through innumerable editions and translations. In England alone (as J. W. Legg's *Bibliography of Marcus Aurelius*, 1908, notes) 26 editions of Marcus Aurelius have appeared in the 17th century, 58 in the 18th, 81 in the 19th, and 30 in the 20th up to 1908. The earliest English translation is that of Meric Casaubon (1634). Countless moderns have cherished Marcus' book, but it is notable that men of action—Frederick the Great, Maximilian of Bavaria, Captain John Smith of Virginia, and "Chinese" Gordon —have been particularly attached to it.

V. PLUTARCH

The master of biography, it is a cliche to say, is himself without a biography. And yet in his voluminous writings Plutarch (A.D. 50–120) talks so freely (but unobjectionably) about himself, his family and friends, and his career that his personality comes into clearer focus than does that of any other Greek writer. The significant fact in Plutarch's biography is that though he had a brilliant career in Rome and even received the consular dignity from Trajan, he nevertheless preferred to return to his native Chaeronea, there to hold a minor magistracy, to be a priest of Delphi, and to teach the local youth the subjects that distinguished Hellenes from other men. "As for me," he writes (*Demosthenes* 2.2) "I live in a small city, and I prefer to dwell there that it may not become smaller still." In effect Plutarch devoted his life to making of Hellenism a cult of civilization which could survive the loss of national sovereignty.

No author conveys a more complete sense of the political and intellectual climate of the Greco-Roman world. Neither as thinker

or poet, nor yet in his contribution to Europe's intellectual outlook, does Plutarch rank with Greece's greatest, but he has indubitably had more European readers than any other pagan Greek and
has been the greatest single channel for communicating to Europe
a general sense of the men and manners of antiquity. Plutarch's
reputation started early. Apuleius and Marcus Aurelius both honored his nephew Sextus for his sake. Porphyry and the other Neoplatonists studied him, and so did Julian the Apostate and the
orators Themistius and Libanius. The great Christian teachers of
the 4th century—John Chrysostom, Gregory of Nazianz, Gregory
of Nyssa, and Basil—use him. At the end of the 12th century Maximus Planudes systematized the text of the *Moralia* and assured
their preservation. During the Renaissance Plutarch was one of
the most eagerly read Greek authors, and many of the humanists
paid especial attention to him.

The greatest intermediary for general knowledge of Plutarch was
the masterly translation of Amyot, which made him the common
possession of all educated men and the most widely read author
in 16th and 17th century France. Montaigne repeatedly acknowledges his obligations to Plutarch, as for example in the following,
taken from Florio's translation:

*The Bookes that serve me are Plutarke, since he spoke French
[the allusion is to Amyot's translation] and Seneca. . . . Seneca
full-fraught with points and sallies, Plutarke stuft with matter
(2.10).*

*From Plutarke or Seneca (as the Danaides) I draw my water, un-
cessantly filling, and as fast emptying (1.25).*

*What profit shall he not reap reading the lives of our Plutarke? . . .
To some kind of men, it is a meere gramaticall studie, but to others
a perfect anatomie of Philosophie.*

North's English version of Amyot was published in 1579 and dedicated to Queen Elizabeth. Shakespeare owned the 1612 edition of
North and also the 1603 edition of Florio's translation of Mon-

taigne. Not only in Shakespeare's Roman tragedies but also in those of Corneille and Racine is Plutarchan influence patent; Brunetière has said that Plutarch played the same role in French tragedy as Homer did in Greek. To list further influences of Plutarch and name the great who expressed special affection for him is futile; but it may be mentioned that Jean Jacques Rousseau counted Plutarch his favorite reading, and that Plutarch's "republicanism" provided encouragement and an armory of examples for the instigators of the French Revolution.

It was partly reaction from the revolution, partly a new sense of the greatness of the creative spirits of classical Greece, partly the romantic reaction against Plutarch's conventional morality and patriotism, partly the new scientific historiography which found him a mere journalist, that caused a decline in Plutarch's fortunes in the 19th century. But the 19th century also saw, in Ralph Waldo Emerson, Plutarch's most ardent publicist. "We cannot read Plutarch," Emerson wrote, "without a tingling of blood"; and Emerson's advocacy carried even to Europe.

VI. LUCIAN

The fun of Lucian of Samosata in Syria (A.D. 120–190) is less explosive than Aristophanes', but also less dependent on time and place; in consequence there is hardly a wit or satirist in European literature after the Renaissance who cannot be shown to have been influenced by him. The only significant facts we know of his life are those he himself tells us, particularly in his *Dream*, where he tells us why he left his statuary uncle to whom he had been apprenticed to devote himself to literature. Suidas' note on him says:

He was killed, it is said, by dogs, after that he had been exceeding mad against the truth. For in his Life of Peregrinus he attacks Christianity and, all guilt-stained as he is, blasphemes the Christ himself. Wherefore at this present he has paid fitting penalty for this madness and in the time to come shall be joint heir with Satan of the fire everlasting.

The charge is baseless, being merely inferred from Lucian's mockery of all authoritarian doctrine, but it does explain early Christian hostility to him. Nevertheless, as Gibbon (ch. 15) notes:

When Tertullian or Lactantius employ their labours in exposing the falsehood and extravagance of Paganism, they are obliged to transcribe the eloquence of Cicero or the wit of Lucian.

One striking manifestation of Lucianic influence is in the arts: Botticelli, Raphael, Mantegna, Rembrandt, Albrecht Dürer, and others transferred pictures from Lucian to canvas or paper. In literature the list is naturally longer: Erasmus and More, Reuchlin and Melanchthon, Rabelais and Hans Sachs, Cervantes and Quevedo, all translated or adapted portions of Lucian. Cyrano de Bergerac's comic histories and his Voyage to the Moon are clearly Lucianic, and Fontenelle dedicates his Dialogues des Morts "à Lucien, aux champs Elysiens." Fénelon's Dialogues des Morts are as obviously inspired by Lucian. In Swift, Voltaire, and a host of others the influence of Lucian may be less direct but it is nevertheless unmistakable.

VII. THE ROMANCES

The European legacy of writers like Apollonius and Theocritus, Plutarch and Lucian, is relatively easy to assess because their imitators can be identified and the forms they pioneered are relatively uncommon. The legacy of the Greek romancers is hard to assess because their imitators are hard to identify and their influence has pervaded (but nevertheless remains present in) the form which has dominated English literature for two centuries and which, translated into film, today attracts larger audiences than any other art form. The structural characteristics of fiction are easy to recognize, but it is not easy to recognize some of its ethical conventions, which are essentially as artificial as its structure in that they do not correspond to the experiences of life. Nevertheless, these conventions have become so naturalized into our habits of thought that their artificiality is no longer apparent; like the essentially artificial conduct of a Launcelot or a Tristan they may indeed have so shaped ethical outlooks that their artificiality has become realism. Similar artificialities in structure and ethical premises characterize both Greek and modern prose fiction. Though no broad and clearly marked highway leads from ancient to modern novels, their similarities are not accidental. The trail is very clearly marked through the period of the Elizabethans; thenceforward it is indeterminate though nevertheless real.

To the shaping of the Greek romance antecedent forms have manifestly contributed; it has learned architecture from the *Odyssey*, suspense and peripety from New Comedy, lay characters and perfumed rusticity from the pastorals. Perhaps the prime impulse to the creation of the novel was the desire of subjugated peoples to bolster their self-esteem and impress their environment by "histories" of their glorious past. We can see the historical element giving way to the erotic as our extant specimens progress from the fragments of the *Ninus Romance*, to Chariton's *Chaereas and Callirhoe*, to the *Ephesian Tale* of Xenophon of Ephesus, to Heliodorus' *Ethiopica* (or *Theagenes and Chariclea*), to Achilles Tatius' *Leucippe and Clitophon*. Longus' *Daphnis and Chloe* is in a different category, because of the preponderance of the pastoral element.

Of none of these authors is anything positive known. Chariton, for example, whom Erwin Rohde's great work on the Greek novel had placed last in the series, perhaps in the 4th century, is now proven by papyrus fragments to be the earliest, not later than the 2nd century A.D. The opening sentence of *Chaereas and Callirhoe* reads "I am Chariton of Aphrodisia, secretary to the advocate Athenagoras." Chariton and Athenagoras both occur as names in inscriptions of Aphrodisia in Caria in Asia Minor, and there is no reason to doubt Chariton's identification of himself. Heliodorus identifies himself in the last sentence of his book:

Here endeth the Ethiopian history of Theagenes and Chariclea, the author whereof is Heliodorus of Emesus, a city of Phoenicia, son of Theodosius who fetched his pedigree from the sun.

The *Ecclesiastical History* of Socrates (5.22) says that both Heliodorus and Achilles Tatius, author of *Leucippe and Clitophon*, were
bishops. There is no actual disproof of this statement, but it has
been suggested that the episcopal title was attached to the names
in order to make their books respectable reading for Byzantine
monks, who were exceedingly fond of the novels and apparently
had many more to read than the few which have survived. Photius
is enthusiastic in his praise of the novels and summarizes both
Heliodorus and Achilles Tatius as well as lost novels of Iamblichus
and Antonius Diogenes. Many stories in the *Gesta Romanorum*
clearly derive from Greek novels, and through Boccaccio have made
their way into the European tradition.

The Greek novels were translated into modern languages in the
16th century and enjoyed an enormous vogue, partly as a reaction
from the romances of chivalry. Heliodorus was translated into
French by Amyot in 1547 and by Warschewiczki into Latin in 1551.
Thomas Underdowne's translation from the Latin, published in
1587, was very widely read. His understanding of even the Latin
was imperfect, and he makes comical mistakes. The verb *veniam*
("I shall come"), for example, he takes as a noun, and renders "O
sweet soul, pardon me." *Daphnis and Chloe* was beautifully rendered into French by Amyot in 1559, and Amyot's French was
freely rendered into English by Angel Day in 1587. Achilles Tatius
was translated into English by William Burton, elder brother of
the author of the *Anatomy of Melancholy*, in 1601. The English
author who made fullest use of these books and was himself most
fully used by others is Sir Philip Sidney. Samuel L. Wolff, whose
Greek Romances in Elizabethan Fiction (New York, 1912) is an
admirable treatment of the subject, concludes his study of *Arcadia*
as follows:

Once more the reader receives the impression that Sidney has
learned the very accent of Greek Romance; once more he feels that
Sidney has deliberately written Greek Romance in English. And
this is the abiding impression. The separate conclusions reached

upon analysis of the "Arcadia" into its elements are confirmed upon a retrospect of the whole. Its material in plot and character, however diffuse and various, is held firmly within the Heliodorean frame; its descriptive matter is strongly flavored with the Greek Romance ecphrasis; its structure has been deliberately recast in the mould of Heliodorus; its style speaks with the voice of the Greek Romancers. Sidney has domesticated the genre.

Sidney had learned Greek but probably used translations. Henri Estienne's dedication of an edition of Herodian (1581) to Sidney reveals the scholar's suspicion that the courtier had let his Greek slip.

The prolific Robert Greene repeatedly transcribed long sections from the Greek novels. In Thomas Lodge the influence of the Greek novels is present but less extensive. Wolff concludes his study with the following perceptive comment:

It appears not only that the Greek Romances contributed variously to Elizabethan fiction itself, but also that, mediately, by way of Elizabethan fiction, they made two distinct further contributions to English literature. The one contribution, which is quite beyond doubt, is a contribution to the drama: it can be definitely identified at its highest in "King Lear" and in "The Winter's Tale." The other contribution—the contribution to the development of the novel—will remain somewhat problematic until the exact nature of the influence of Elizabethan fiction upon the Eighteenth Century is cleared up. Meanwhile it seems not too much to suggest, tentatively, as a proposition not yet fully established but not lightly to be denied, that the Greek Romances, partly through French Romance of the Seventeenth Century, partly through a single Elizabethan Romance—the "Arcadia," helped to give to the English novel that gift which Greek literature has so often conferred,—the gift of sustained and complex form. . . . whatever of the Greek Romances may survive in the modern novel is not their illusion, but that architectonic power in them which despite themselves makes against illusion and toward law.

But form is surely not the only thing which the English pioneers of the novel learned from the Greeks. The love of the store-model hero and heroine, their temptations, separations, and eventual reunion in endless felicity, and most of all, the exaggerated importance attached to them, remained a pattern which greater spirits transcended but never wholly left behind.

16: *Romans of the Republic*

THE ATTITUDE OF THE ROMANS TO THEIR OWN pioneers in literature was ambivalent: more polished ages were ashamed of their crudity, and at the same time proud of their achievements. A Cicero or a Horace acknowledged their lack of refinement but admired their stalwart ruggedness. It was in the archaizing age of Fronto that the ancients ceased to be merely old-fashioned and became classics. Fronto incessantly urges the ancients upon his royal pupil, Marcus Aurelius, as in this letter (2.5 Haines): "Polish your style with Plautus, saturate yourself with Accius. Soothe yourself with Lucretius, fire yourself with Ennius." Cicero he deprecates because (1.5 Haines) "he seems far from disposed to *search out* words with especial care"; Horace "is dead and done with as far as I am concerned" (1.39 Haines). He praises a composition of his pupil by saying (1.13 Haines) that "it could be put in a book of Sallust's without jarring or showing any inferiority"—Sallust himself being a pioneer in archaizing.

I. FROM LIVIUS TO THE FIRST CENTURY

It is an index of the artificiality of Latin literature that we can name its first writer and his first work. Tradition made Livius Andronicus a captive Tarentine Greek, who was manumitted by Livius Salinator. For the year 187 B.C. Jerome's chronicle has this entry:

Titus Livius, the writer of tragedies, enjoyed fame. Because of his genius he was deservedly given his liberty by Livius Salinator, whose children he had educated.

As a teacher Livius found he had no Latin books to teach, and so produced a version of the *Odyssey*, which is regarded as the earliest Latin book. Its first line is quoted by Aulus Gellius (18.9.5):

In the library at Patras I found a manuscript of Livius Andronicus
of undoubted antiquity, entitled Odyssey, in which the first line
contained the word insece without the letter u: Virum mihi,
Camena, insece versutum, "Tell me, O Muse, about the crafty man."

Livy (27.37.7) tells us that in the year 207 B.C., in consequence
of a series of unfavorable prodigies,

The pontiffs decreed that thrice nine virgins should go through the
city singing a hymn . . . which was composed by the poet Livius.

In his account of the origins of drama Livy (7.2) says that Livius
was the first to abandon saturae and compose a play with a plot.
The plots were of course taken from Greek plays. Cicero (Brutus
18) agrees with a remark of Ennius that he was the first Roman
poet:

This is no idle boasting, either; it is a plain statement of fact. For
the Latin Odyssey might well be likened to a statue from the chisel
of Daedalus [i.e., is primitive], and the plays of Livius are not worth
a second reading.

Livius was still a school author in Horace's day, as Horace (Epistles
2.1.69) ruefully remembers:

I do not rail against old poets nor think the works of Livius should
be blotted out; I remember them from the dictation of my teacher
Orbilius, who was ready with his switch, when I was a boy.

Naevius was an independent spirit, and both his tragedies and
his epic (on the Punic war) bore a distinctively Roman stamp. His
political independence brought him into the conflict with the
powerful Metelli, of which several subsequent authors speak. Cicero
(Verrines 1.10.29) speaks of the quarrel, and Aulus Gellius (3.3.15)
of his incarceration:

So too we are told of Naevius that he wrote two plays in prison, the
Soothsayer and the Leon, when by reason of his constant abuse and
insults aimed at the leading men of the city, after the manner of
the Greek poets, he had been imprisoned at Rome by the triumvirs.
And afterwards he was set free by the tribunes of the commons,
when he had apologized for his offenses and the saucy language with
which he had previously assailed many men.

Cicero (*On Old Age* 14.49) speaks of the *Bellum Punicum* as the
work of Naevius' old age, and Varro wrote comments upon it.
Jerome reports his death under the year 201 B.C.:

Naevius, the comic poet, died at Utica, having been driven from
Rome by the faction of the nobles and especially Metellus.

His epitaph he composed for himself (Aulus Gellius 1.24.2):

The epitaph of Naevius, although full of Campanian arrogance,
might have been regarded as a just estimate, if he had not written
it himself:
> If that immortals might for mortals weep,
> Then would divine Camenae weep for Naevius.
> For after he to Orcus as treasure was consigned,
> The Romans straight forgot to speak the Latin tongue.

Of Plautus Jerome tells us, under the year 200 B.C.:

Plautus, from Sarsina in Umbria, died at Rome; because of difficulty
of livelihood he hired himself out to turn a hand mill, and in the
intervals of his work he used to write plays and sell them.

Aulus Gellius (3.3.14) gives the story more fully:

Now Varro and several others have recorded that the Saturio, the
Addictus, and a third comedy, the name of which I do not now
recall, were written by Plautus in a bakery, when, after losing in

trade all the money which he had earned in employments connected
with the stage, he had returned penniless to Rome, and to earn a
livelihood had hired himself out to a baker, to turn a mill, of the
kind which is called a "push-mill."

Some modern critics have doubted the whole tale as fabricated on
the basis of passages in Plautus. How little was known of Plautus
even in the first century B.C. is shown by these informing extracts
from Aulus Gellius (3.3.1 ff.):

*I am convinced of the truth of the statement which I have heard
made by men well trained in literature, who have read a great many
plays of Plautus with care and attention: namely, that with regard
to the so-called "doubtful" plays they would trust, not the lists of
Aelius or Sedigitus or Claudius or Aurelius or Accius or Manilius,
but Plautus himself and the characteristic features of his manner
and diction. Indeed, this is the criterion which we find Varro using.
For in addition to those 21 known as "Varronian," which he set
apart from the rest because they were not questioned but by common consent were attributed to Plautus, he accepted also some
others, influenced by the style and humor of their language, which
was characteristic of Plautus; and although these had already been
listed under the names of other poets, he claimed them for
Plautus. . . .*

*In that same book of Varro's we are told also that there was
another writer of comedies called Plautius. Since his plays
bore the title "Plauti," they were accepted as Plautine, although
in fact they were not Plautine by Plautus, but Plautinian by Plautius.*

*Now there are in circulation under the name of Plautus about
130 comedies; but that most learned of men Lucius Aelius thought
that only 25 of them were his. However, there is no doubt that those
which do not appear to have been written by Plautus but are attached to his name, were the work of poets of old but were revised
and touched up by him, and that is why they savor of the Plautine
style.*

Dubiety concerning Plautine authorship is also indicated in Servius
(Preface to *Aeneid*):

Some say that Plautus wrote 21 plays, others 40, others a hundred.

For later Romans Plautus was an assured classic. Cicero (*Offices*
1.29.104) pays him the compliment of coupling him with Aristophanes and the Socratics:

*The manner of joking is reducible under two denominations—one
that is ill-bred, insolent, profligate, and obscene; another that is
elegant, polite, witty, and good-humored. We have abundance of
this last, not only in our Plautus, and the authors of the old Greek
comedy, but in the writings of the Socratic philosophers.*

But there were purists who demurred; here is the judgment of
Horace (*Epistles* 2.1.170):

*'Tis thought that Comedy, drawing its themes from daily life, calls
for less labor; but in truth it carries a heavier burden, as the indulgence allowed is less. See how poorly Plautus maintains the part of
the youthful lover, how poorly that of the close father, or of the
tricky pander; what a Dossennus he is among his greedy parasites;
with what a loose sock he scours the scene. Yes, he is eager to drop
a coin into his pocket and, that done, he cares not whether his play
fall or stand square on its feet.*

Sidonius Apollinaris (23.149) stoutly maintains that "Plautus'
charm surpasses the Greek wit," but after his day Plautus seems to
have fallen into oblivion until, in the Renaissance, he gave drama
a fresh impulse which continues vital.

The greatest, most prolific, and most influential of the Roman
pioneers was Ennius (239–169 B.C.), of whom all subsequent
writers speak with reverence. Quintilian (10.1.88) sets the proper
note:

Let us venerate Ennius like the groves, sacred from their antiquity, in which the great and ancient oaks are invested not so much with beauty as with sacred associations.

Ennius was born in Calabria and was at home in three languages (Aulus Gellius 17.17.1):

Quintus Ennius used to say that he had three hearts, because he knew how to speak Greek, Oscan, and Latin.

Other details are given by Jerome (in 240 B.C.) probably from Suetonius:

Q. Ennius the poet was born at Tarentum. He was brought to Rome by the quaestor Cato and lived on the Aventine at a frugal outlay, being content with the service of a single housemaid.

The report of the lone servant is probably based on the good story in Cicero (*On the Orator* 2.68.276):

Scipio Nasica had called upon the poet Ennius and, when he inquired for him at his front-door, had been told by the housemaid that her master was not at home, which reply Nasica perceived to have been given by the master's order, he being in fact in the house. A few days later Ennius called at Nasica's, and asked for him at the entrance, whereupon Nasica called out that he was not at home. "What?" cries Ennius, "Do I not know your voice?" To which Nasica rejoined, "You are a shameless fellow; when I asked for you, I believed your maid when she said you were not at home; do you not believe me when I tell you the same thing at first hand?"

Ennius himself wrote *numquam poetor nisi si podager*, "I never poetize unless I have the gout," and Horace (*Epistles* 1.19.7) wrote: "Ennius never sallied forth to sing of arms unless he was drunk." Marcus Fulvius Nobilior, consul in 189 B.C., took Ennius with him on his expedition to Aetolia, Cicero tells us (*For Archias* 11.27), to celebrate his achievements. Cicero also tells us that Ennius left out a detail of the Punic war because Naevius had treated of it, and incidentally compares the two poets (*Brutus* 19.76):

Granted that Ennius is the more polished author, as he assuredly is; yet if he had actually regarded Naevius with the contempt he pretends to feel for him, he would not have touched so lightly on that bitterly waged First Punic War, in his comprehensive description of our military campaigns. But he himself offers this explanation: "Others have dealt with this subject in poetry"—in excellent poetry, too, Ennius, even though it is less smooth and finished than yours; moreover, you ought to be the first to agree with me, inasmuch as you have borrowed at length from Naevius, if you are prepared to acknowledge the debt; if you decline to give him proper credit, then you are a plagiarist.

From Cicero too we have (*Tusculan Disputations* 1.15.34) Ennius' own inscription for his bust:

Behold, my countrymen, the bust of the old man Ennius: he penned the record of your fathers' mighty deeds—

and also his inscription for his tomb:

Let none embellish me with tears nor weep at my funeral. And why? Living I fly from lips to lips of men.

Almost every subsequent author for whom it was appropriate to do so mentions, alludes to, or borrows from Ennius. Only a few of the testimonia can be cited here. Lucretius (1.117) calls him

Our own Ennius, who first bore down from pleasant Helicon the wreath of deathless leaves, to win bright fame among the tribes of Italian peoples.

Cicero praises Ennius repeatedly, and his lengthy quotations from him are our fullest source for fragments. In several passages of the

Aeneid Servius calls attention to Vergil's borrowing from Ennius, and according to the expanded life of Vergil by Donatus Vergil used to say that "he gathered gold from Ennius' dung heap." According to Horace (*Epistles* 2.1.50) the critics called Ennius "wise, valiant, the second Homer." Martial notes (5.10.7) that Ennius was read even when Vergil was available, and Hadrian, according to his life (*S.H.A. Hadrian* 16.5), preferred Ennius to Vergil, as he preferred Cato to Cicero and Coelius to Sallust. Macrobius in his day complains of the neglect of Ennius (6.99):

Because our age has deserted Ennius and the whole library of ancients we are ignorant of many things which would not have escaped our knowledge if the reading of the ancients were a familiar practice.

Of Ennius' nephew Pacuvius Jerome (under 154 B.C.) says:

Pacuvius of Brundisium was regarded a famous writer of tragedies. He was nephew of Ennius and lived at Rome, painting and selling plays. Then he moved to Tarentum and died at the age of nearly 90.

These details are confirmed by various other authors, and his works receive moderate praise from Cicero, Quintilian, and others. Aulus Gellius (13.2) has a story of an encounter between Pacuvius and Accius:

Pacuvius when already enfeebled by advanced age and constant bodily illness, had withdrawn from Rome to Tarentum. Then Accius, who was a much younger man, coming to Tarentum on his way to Asia, visited Pacuvius, and being hospitably received and detained by him for several days, at his request read him his tragedy entitled Atreus. Then Pacuvius remarked that what he had written seemed sonorous and full of dignity, but that nevertheless it appeared to him somewhat harsh and rugged.

Aulus Gellius (1.24.4) also records Pacuvius' own epitaph, remarking on its dignity and good taste:

> Young man, although you haste, this little stone
> Entreats thee to regard it, then to read its tale.
> Here lie the bones of Marcus, hight Pacuvius.
> Of this I would not have you unaware. Good bye.

Caecilius, who came between Plautus and Terence, was by some regarded as a better poet than either. Notices concerning him are of the same character as those concerning his predecessors, and because his fragments are so slight, hardly worth recording. The one event in his life which has meaning for us is that of his connection with Terence, and appears in the life, doubtless by Suetonius, prefixed to Donatus' commentary on Terence. That life is worth excerpting rather fully:

Publius Terentius Afer, born at Carthage, was the slave at Rome of Terentius Lucanus, a senator, who because of the young man's talent and good looks not only gave him a liberal education, but soon set him free. . . . He lived on intimate terms with many men of high rank, in particular with Scipio Africanus and Gaius Laelius. . . . He wrote six comedies, and when he offered the first of these, the Andria, to the aediles, they bade him first read it to Caecilius. Having come to the poet's house when he was dining, and being meanly clad, Terence is said to have read the beginning of his play sitting on a bench near the great man's couch. But after a few lines he was invited to take his place at table, and after dining with Caecilius, he ran through the rest to his host's great admiration. . . .
It is common gossip that Scipio and Laelius aided Terence in his writings, and he himself lent color to this by never attempting to refute it, except in a half-hearted way, as in the prologue to the Adelphi. . . . After publishing his comedies before he had passed his twenty-fifth year, either to escape from the gossip about publishing the work of others as his own, or else to become versed in Greek manners and customs, which he felt that he had not been wholly successful in depicting in his plays, he left Rome and never returned. . . . Quintus Cosconius writes that he was lost at sea as he was returning from Greece with 108 plays adapted from Menan-

der; the rest of our authorities declare that he died at Stymphalus
in Arcadia, or at Leucadia, in the consulship of Gnaeus Cornelius
Dolabella and Marcus Fulvius Nobilior, having fallen ill from grief
and annoyance at the loss of his baggage, which he had sent on to
the ship, and with it of the new plays which he had written. He
is said to have been of moderate height, slender and of dark
complexion. . . . Cicero in his Limo gives him this much
praise:

Thou, Terence, who alone dost reclothe Menander in choice
speech, and rendering him into the Latin tongue, dost present him
with thy quiet utterance on our public stage, speaking with a certain
graciousness and with sweetness in every word.

Also Gaius Caesar:

Thou too, even thou, art ranked among the highest, thou half-
Menander, and justly, thou lover of language undefiled. But would
that thy graceful verses had force as well, so that thy comic power
might have equal honor with that of the Greeks, and thou mightest
not be scorned in this regard and neglected. It hurts and pains me,
my Terence, that thou lackest this one quality.

During the Middle Ages Terence enjoyed a vogue for his easy and
pure Latin style, and in the 10th century the nun Hrostwitha of
Gandersheim wrote a series of pious plays following the Terentian
models, but without realizing that Terence's were in verse. Here is
Hrostwitha herself justifying her enterprise:

There are some who cleave to the sacred pages but who, though
they spurn other writings of the gentiles, read the fictions of Terence all too frequently, and in taking pleasure in the sweetness of
his discourse are sullied by familiarity with wicked matters. Wherefore I, the Strong Voice of Gandersheim, have not, while others
cultivate him in perusal, refused to imitate him in utterance, to
the end that by that same fashion of discourse by which the foul
bawdiness of lewd women are set forth, the admirable chastity of
holy virgins should be celebrated, according to the capacity of my
small gifts.

Modern scholars have suggested that both Hrostwitha and the plays
are fabrications of Humanist scholars.

The one form in which Rome claimed originality was Satire—
Quintilian (10.1.93) says *satura tota nostra est*—and the great
master of satire was Lucilius. Though Lucilius' own writings survive only in fragments his influence is palpable in Persius and Juvenal and especially Horace, whose two most famous satires, *The
Journey to Brundisium* and *The Bore*, are copies of Lucilian originals. Here is Horace on his great predecessor (*Satires* 1.4.1–13):

*Eupolis and Cratinus and Aristophanes, true poets, and the other
good men to whom Old Comedy belongs, if there was anyone deserving to be drawn as a rogue and thief, as a rake or cut-throat, or as
scandalous in any other way, set their mark upon him with great
freedom. It is on these that Lucilius wholly hangs; these he has
followed, changing only meter and rhythm. Witty he was, and of
keen-scented nostrils, but harsh in framing his verse. Herein lay his
fault: often in an hour, as though a great exploit, he would dictate
two hundred lines while standing, as they say, on one foot. In his
muddy stream there was much that you would like to remove. He
was wordy, and too lazy to put up with the trouble of writing—of
writing correctly, I mean; for as to quantity, I let that pass.*

But in 1.10 Horace is somewhat more generous:

*To be sure I did say that the verses of Lucilius run on with halting
foot. Who is a partisan of Lucilius so in-and-out of season as not
to confess this? And yet on the self-same page the self-same poet
is praised because he rubbed the city down with much salt. . . .
But I did say his stream runs muddy, and often carries more that you
would rather remove than leave behind. Come, pray, do you, a
scholar, criticize nothing in the great Homer? Does your genial
Lucilius find nothing to change in the tragedies of Accius? Does he
not laugh at the verses of Ennius as lacking in dignity, though he
speaks of himself as no greater than those he has blamed? And as we*

read the writings of Lucilius, what forbids us, too, to raise the question whether it was his own genius, or whether it was the harsh nature of his themes that denied him verses more finished and easier in their flow than if one were to put his thoughts into six feet and, content with this alone, were proud of having written two hundred lines before and two hundred after supping? . . . Grant, say I, that Lucilius was genial and witty: grant that he was also more polished than you would expect one to be who was creating a new style untouched by the Greeks, and more polished than the crowd of older poets: yet, had he fallen by fate upon this our day, he would smooth away much of his work, would prune off all that trailed beyond the proper limit, and as he wrought his verse he would oft scratch his head and gnaw his nails to the quick.

II. LUCRETIUS

Under the year 94 B.C. Jerome's Chronicle has:

T. Lucretius the poet is born. Later he was rendered insane by a love potion. In his intervals of sanity he wrote several books, which Cicero afterwards emended. He killed himself by his own hand in the 44th year of his life.

The date, no less than the madness, suicide, and Cicero's editorship, has been questioned, but no more reliable information is available. A biography by Girolamo Borgia, written in 1502, has been shown to be without authority. The earliest and indeed only sound reference to Lucretius and his poem is in a letter of Cicero in which he agrees with his brother's estimate of the poem (To Quintus His Brother 2.9.3):

The poems of Lucretius show, as you write, many flashes of genius and also much art.

The date of this private letter is 55 B.C.; it is curious to note that in his Tusculan Disputations (2.7), published ten years later, Cicero says that he has not read Epicurean books in Latin, as no good could come from the Epicurean school. The explanation is that in the interval Epicureanism had become politically suspect, and it was imprudent to show any special interest in the subject. That may be the explanation for the silence of other Latin writers on Lucretius, though a number show unmistakable familiarity with his poem. Vergil, for example, surely alludes to Lucretius in *Georgics* 2.490:

Felix qui potuit rerum cognoscere causas—Blessed is he who has been able to win knowledge of the causes of things, and has cast beneath his feet all fear and unyielding Fate, and the howls of hungry Acheron.

Aulus Gellius (1.21.7) remarked that "Vergil not only adopted single words of Lucretius but also closely followed very many verses and passages almost in their entirety." Of the other Latins who mention Lucretius by name only Ovid has good words for him (*Amores* 1.15.23): "Then will the verses perish of the sublime Lucretius when the same day shall give the world to destruction."

It was natural for the Christian Middle Ages to eschew the Epicurean, and when Rabanus Maurus used the poem he explained that it was "in order to interpret Ecclesiasticus and Genesis and to illuminate physical questions which touch upon Christian dogma." The Renaissance knew Lucretius from the single MS which Poggio Bracciolini found. It was Politian who suggested to Botticelli, on the basis of the opening of Lucretius' poem, the picture of Venus as the goddess of Nature in his Primavera. Editors long thought it necessary to apologize for their labors on Lucretius. Lambinus protests that in editing other authors he would not adopt their erroneous opinions, and Faber prints a sermon before the especially dangerous third book. Lemaire was forbidden by Louis XVIII to publish Lucretius in the original series of the Bibliotheca Classica Latina. Lipsius acknowledged that "Lucretius murders common sense." Even Lord Byron (*Don Juan* 1.43) prudently states that

Lucretius' irreligion is too strong
For early stomachs to prove wholesome food.

In the opinion of many modern students Lucretius is the most eminent intellect in pagan Rome.

III. CATULLUS

Catullus' poems make his life an open book. We know too a good deal about many people in his environment, from Cicero and others, and especially about his Lesbia, whose true name was Clodia. Concerning Catullus himself the single meaningful reference is in Suetonius (*Julius* 73):

Valerius Catullus, as Caesar himself did not hesitate to say, inflicted a lasting stain on his name by the verses about Mamurra [*Catullus* 29 and 57]; yet when he apologized, Caesar invited the poet to dinner that very same day, and continued his usual friendly relations with Catullus' father.

From Nepos (*Atticus* 12) we know that contemporaries regarded him, along with Lucretius, as one of the two best poets of the day:

Since the death of Lucretius and Catullus I think I may truly say that Calidus is the most graceful poet our age has produced.

His position as the lyric poet remains unchallenged, even by Horace; and all subsequent Latin lyricists, from Ovid, Statius, and Martial (who is particularly indebted to Catullus) to Ausonius and Dracontius have allusions to or imitations of Catullus. The Middle Ages lost sight of Catullus except for a single poem (No. 62) included in a florilegium. In 965 Bishop Rather of Verona confesses that he had been eagerly reading Catullus, apparently in the sole copy that survived antiquity. In the 14th century the Verona MS turns up again, and in the century following, before it disappeared from view, copies now located in Oxford, Paris, and Rome were made from it. Petrarch's enthusiasm gave Catullus a great vogue; to trace subsequent Catullan influence is to write the history of lyric poetry in Europe. English poetry in particular shows the Catullan strain, which appears, more or less pronounced, in virtually all lyricists from Chaucer to Tennyson. And Catullus himself has enjoyed a steady vogue. Here is what Macaulay, towards the close of his life, said of the poet (*Life* 2.378):

I have pretty near learned all that I like best in Catullus. He grows on me with intimacy. One thing he has—I do not know whether it belongs to him or to something in myself—but there are chords of my mind which he touches as nobody else does. The first lines of Miser Catulle; the lines to Cornificius, written evidently from a sick-bed; and part of the poem beginning Si qua recordanti, affect me more than I can explain. They always move me to tears.

IV. CAESAR

Quite apart from his military and political achievements Caesar must rank as a major literary figure. Suetonius' *Life* of Caesar has a chapter on the subject (56):

He left memoirs too of his deeds in the Gallic war and in the civil strife with Pompey. . . . With regard to Caesar's memoirs Cicero also, in the Brutus, speaks in the following terms: "He wrote memoirs which deserve the highest praise; they are naked in their simplicity, straightforward yet graceful, stripped of all rhetorical adornment, as of a garment; but while his purpose was to supply material to others, on which those who wished to write history might draw, he haply gratified silly folk, who will try to use the curling-irons on his narrative, but he has kept men of any sense from touching the subject." Of these same memoirs Hirtius uses this emphatic language: "They are so highly rated in the judgment of all men, that he seems to have deprived writers of an opportunity, rather than given them one; yet our admiration for this feat is greater than that of others; for they know how well and faultlessly he wrote, while we know besides how easily and rapidly he finished his task." Asinius

Pollio thinks that they were put together somewhat carelessly and without strict regard for truth; since in many cases Caesar was too ready to believe the accounts which others gave of their actions, and gave a perverted account of his own, either designedly or perhaps from forgetfulness; and he thinks that he intended to rewrite and revise them. He left besides a work in two volumes On Analogy, the same number of Speeches Criticising Cato, in addition to a poem, entitled The Journey. He wrote the first of these works while crossing the Alps and returning to his army from Hither Gaul, where he had held the assizes; the second about the time of the battle of Munda, and the third in the course of a 24 days' journey from Rome to Farther Spain. Some letters of his to the senate are also preserved, and he seems to have been the first to reduce such documents to pages and the form of a memorial volume, whereas previously consuls and generals sent their reports written right across the sheet. There are also letters of his to Cicero, as well as to his intimates on private affairs. . . . We also have mention of certain writings of his boyhood and early youth, such as the Praises of Hercules, a tragedy Oedipus, and a Collection of Apophthegms; but Augustus forbade the publication of all these minor works in a very brief and frank letter sent to Pompeius Macer, whom he had selected to set his libraries in order.

Caesar's writings are naturally mentioned by many other writers, usually as an example of the literary preoccupations of a great man. So Cicero (*Brutus* 72.253):

In the very midst of his strenuous activities Caesar composed that precise and accurate essay on the correct use of language.

And so Fronto writing to Marcus Aurelius (2.29 Haines):

With respect to what you say that you can scarcely read anything except by snatches and by stealth in your present anxieties, recall to your mind and ponder the fact that Gaius Caesar, while engaged in a most formidable war in Gaul, wrote besides many other military works two books of the most meticulous character On Analogy, *discussing amid flying darts the declension of nouns, and the aspiration of words and their classification mid the blare of bugles and trumpets.*

Possibly because the man so far overshadowed his writings little is said of the latter. Livy and Tacitus, Plutarch, Appian, and Dio naturally use—and displace—him. In the 13th century Planudes translated him into Greek. In the Renaissance Petrarch wrote a biography of Caesar, using his *Gallic* and *Civil War*. Moderns have devoted careful study to the man, and left his books to schoolboys.

V. SALLUST

Judging from his monographs on *Jugurtha* and on the *Catilinarian Conspiracy* the *History* of Sallust, if it had survived, might have proved him the greatest of the Roman historians. Because he was a Caesarian the senatorial party blackened his character; this may be the origin of a story Aulus Gellius (17.18) quotes from Varro:

Marcus Varro, a man of great trustworthiness and authority in his writings and in his life, in the work which he entitled Pius; or, On Peace, *says that Gaius Sallustius, the author of those austere and dignified works, whom we see in his history writing and acting like a censor, was taken in adultery by Annius Milo, soundly beaten with thongs, and allowed to escape only after paying a sum of money.*

But to counter this and other belittling remarks we have high praise from good critics. Velleius Paterculus (2.36.2) calls him "the rival of Thucydides," and Quintilian says (10.1.101) "I should not hesitate to balance Thucydides with Sallust." Tacitus (*Annals* 3.30) calls Sallust "a most admirable historian," and imitates his style. In the archaizing age of Hadrian, Sallust was a major figure, and Fronto repeatedly speaks in his praise.

After the revival of learning, when Ciceronianism became paramount, Sallust came to be regarded as crude. Here is a comment of John Cheke, quoted by Ascham:

Sallust by gathering truth out of Cato smelleth much of the rough-ness of his style; even as a man that eateth garlick for his health shall carry away with him the savour of it also, whether he will or not.

VI. CICERO

His significance as a statesman and writer and the ample materials available in his voluminous private correspondence and other writings have made Cicero a tempting subject for biographers, beginning with Plutarch, and his life is more fully known to the reading public than that of any other ancient. From his own day onward no other Roman writer has been more universally accepted as a classic; pages could be filled with laudatory comments upon him, ancient and modern. Even when Latin prose style consciously deviated from the Ciceronian model Cicero's own position as a classic was never threatened. His poetry, on the other hand, did not enjoy such immunity, though Plutarch says that at one time Cicero was considered the best poet as well as the best orator of Rome. "Caesar and Brutus wrote poems," says Tacitus (*Dialogue* 21), "not better than Cicero but more fortunately, for fewer people know that they did it." Here is Juvenal on the notorious *O fortunatam natam me consule Romam* (10.122 f.):

> O happy fate for the Roman State
> Was the date of my great Consulate!

Had Cicero always spoken thus, he might have laughed at the swords of Antony.

Upon the Latin Fathers Cicero exerted more influence than any other pagan author: Lactantius was called "the Christian Cicero," Jerome reproached himself with being a Ciceronian rather than a Christian, and Augustine was directed to philosophy by reading the (lost) *Hortensius* of Cicero. This interest may have had something to do with preserving Cicero through the Middle Ages. With the revival of learning Petrarch's fanatical devotion to Cicero gave rise to a cult of Ciceronianism which refused to tolerate any word or usage not found in the pages of Cicero. The Church objected that it was unchristian to imitate the pagans, but by the 16th century, under the leadership of Cardinal Bembo, a society of *litterati* bound its members by oath not to use any word which could not be found in Cicero. Into the Latin of the Church Bembo introduced such terms as *res publica* for the Church and *magistri* for its officials, besides using the Roman method of dating by Kalends, Nones, and Ides. In his *History of Venice* he calls the nuns *virgines vestales*, the saints *divi*, and the cardinals *senatores*. Heated polemics on the Ciceronian question passed between Poggio Bracciolini and Lorenzo Valla, Politian and Scala, Bembo and Pico. Extreme Ciceronianism would of course make of Latin a dead language and, because he ardently wished to keep Latin alive in order to preserve the homogeneity of Europe, Erasmus opposed the movement, most effectively in his witty *Ciceronianus* (1528). Erasmus was violently assailed for his position, among others by Julius Caesar Scaliger in his *An Oration in Defence of Cicero against Erasmus* (1531). Others supported Erasmus' position. Muretus, pointing out that some of Cicero's works are lost, in whole or part, goes on to say:

If a rat or a moth had eaten a bit of a page, or mold and decay had ruined it, or a spark from the lamp had fallen on some certain part of the book, today the words pigrandi *and* contraversandi *and many others would be barbarisms.*

And Sir Philip Sidney, in his *Apologie for Poetrie,* says:

Truly I could wish, if at least I might be so bold as to wish in a thing beyond the reach of my capacity, the diligent imitators to Tullie and Demosthenes (most worthy to be imitated) did not so much keep Nizolian Paperbookes of their figures and phrases, as by attentive translation (as it were) devoure them whole and make them wholly theirs.

Neither Ciceronians nor anti-Ciceronians could prevent the rise of nationalisms and their devotion to their several vernaculars, and Ciceronianism became an academic question. But Cicero himself continued a persistent force in the intellectual life of Europe.

17: *The Empire*

THE TOWERING FIGURES OF THE AUGUSTAN age—Vergil, Horace, and Livy—sought to promote the Augustan program, chiefly through the patronage of Maecenas. The independent elegiac poets—Ovid, Tibullus, Propertius—were "gentlemen" preoccupied with their private emotions. After the Golden Age freedom of expression was curtailed. Silver Latin literature is more concerned with form than with substance. The principal figures are the essayist and tragic poet Seneca, his nephew Lucan and other writers of epic, the satirical Martial and Petronius and the more formal satirists Persius and Juvenal, the encyclopedist Pliny and his nephew, the historian Tacitus and the biographer Suetonius. After the first century A.D. there are a number of influential pagan writers in Greek and many Christian in both Greek and Latin, but there are no more pagan Latin writers of the first magnitude.

I. VERGIL

As with Cicero in prose, Vergil has been universally recognized as Rome's greatest poet from his own day onwards. Vergil, indeed, was revered as well as respected, even by Christians, because of the strain of mysticism in his writings. By the time of Suetonius his life had become a kind of hagiographa, as may be seen from the excerpts given below. Because Suetonius' *Life* summarizes what the ancients knew and believed of Vergil these must be rather full. After recording Vergil's birth of humble parents at Andes, a village near Mantua, on 15 October 70 B.C. the *Life* continues:

While he was in his mother's womb, she dreamed that she gave birth to a laurel-branch, which on touching the earth took root and grew at once to the size of a full-grown tree, covered with fruits and flowers of various kinds; and on the following day, when she

was on the way to a neighboring part of the country with her husband, she turned aside and gave birth to her child in a ditch beside
the road. They say that the infant did not cry at its birth, and had
such a gentle expression as even then to give assurance of an unu-
sually happy destiny. . . . Vergil spent his early life at Cremona
until he assumed the gown of manhood . . . , moved from Cremona to Mediolanum, and shortly afterwards from there to Rome.
He was tall and of full habit, with a dark complexion and a rustic
appearance. His health was variable; for he very often suffered from
stomach and throat troubles, as well as with headache; and he also
had frequent hemorrhages. He ate and drank but little. He was
especially given to passions for boys, and his special favorites were
Cebes and Alexander, whom he calls Alexis in the second poem of
his Bucolics. . . . For the rest of his life he was so modest in speech
and thought, that at Naples he was commonly called "Parthenias,"
and that whenever he appeared in public in Rome, where he very
rarely went, he would take refuge in the nearest house, to avoid
those who followed and pointed him out. . . . He made his first
attempt at poetry when he was still a boy. . . . Then he wrote the
Catalepton, Priapea, Epigrams and the Dirae, as well as the Ciris
and the Culex when he was 16 years old. . . . He also wrote the
Aetna, though its authorship is disputed. Presently he began to
write of Roman story, but thinking himself unequal to the subject,
turned to the Bucolics, especially in order to sing the praises of
Asinius Pollio, Alfenus Varus, and Cornelius Gallus, because at the
time of the assignment of the lands beyond the Po, which were
divided among the veterans by order of the triumvirs after the victory at Philippi, these men had saved him from ruin. Then he wrote
the Georgics in honor of Maecenas, because he had rendered him
aid, when the poet was still but little known, against the violence
of one of the veterans, from whom Vergil narrowly escaped death
in a quarrel about his farm. Last of all he began the Aeneid, a varied
and complicated theme, and as it were a mirror of both the poems
of Homer; moreover it treated Greek and Latin personages and
affairs in common, and contained at the same time an account of
the origin of the city of Rome and of Augustus, which was the poet's

special aim. When he was writing the Georgics, it is said to have
been his custom to dictate each day a large number of verses which
he had composed in the morning, and then to spend the rest of
the day in reducing them to a very small number, wittily remarking
that he fashioned his poem after the manner of a she-bear, and
gradually licked it into shape. In the case of the Aeneid, after writing a first draft in prose and dividing it into 12 books, he proceeded
to turn into verse one part after another, taking them up just as he
fancied, in no particular order. And that he might not check the
flow of his thought, he left some things unfinished, and, so to speak,
bolstered others up with very slight words, which, as he jocosely used
to say, were put in like props, to support the structure until the solid
columns should arrive.

The Bucolics he finished in three years, the Georgics in seven,
the Aeneid in twelve. The success of the Bucolics on their first appearance was such, that they were even frequently rendered by
singers on the stage. . . . Hardly was the Aeneid begun, when its
repute became so great that Sextus Propertius did not hesitate to
declare [2.34.65 f.]:

> Yield, ye Roman writers; yield, ye Greeks:
> a greater than the Iliad is born.

Augustus indeed (for it chanced that he was away on his Cantabrian
campaign) demanded in entreating and even jocosely threatening
letters that Vergil send him "something from the Aeneid"; to use
his own words, "either the first draft of the poem or any section of
it that he pleased." But it was not until long afterwards, when the
material was at last in shape, that Vergil read to him three books in
all, the second, fourth, and sixth. The last of these produced a remarkable effect on Octavia, who was present at the reading; for it
is said that when he reached the verses about her son, "Thou shalt
be Marcellus" [6.884 f.], she fainted and was with difficulty revived.
He gave readings also to various others, but never before a large
company, selecting for the most part passages about which he was
in doubt, in order to get the benefit of criticism. . . . In the 52nd
year of his age, wishing to give the final touch to the Aeneid, he

determined to go away to Greece and Asia, and after devoting three
entire years to the sole work of improving his poem, to give up the
rest of his life wholly to philosophy. But having begun his journey,
and at Athens meeting Augustus, who was on his way back to Rome
from the Orient, he resolved not to part from the emperor and even
to return with him; but in the course of a visit to the neighboring
town of Megara in a very hot sun, he was taken with a fever, and
added to his disorder by continuing his journey; hence on his arrival at Brundisium he was considerably worse, and died there on
the eleventh day before the Kalends of October [Sept. 21, 19 B.C.],
in the consulship of Gnaeus Sentius and Quintus Lucretius. His
ashes were taken to Naples and laid to rest on the via Puteolana
less than two miles from the city, in a tomb for which he himself
composed this couplet:

Mantua gave me the light, Calabria slew me; now holds me
　　Parthenope. I have sung shepherds, the country, and wars.

. . . He had arranged with Varius, before leaving Italy, that if anything befell him his friend should burn the Aeneid; but Varius had
emphatically declared that he would do no such thing. Therefore
in his mortal illness Vergil constantly called for his book-boxes, in-
tending to burn the poem himself; but when no one brought them
to him, he made no specific request about the matter, but left his
writings jointly to the above mentioned Varius and to Tucca, with
the stipulation that they should publish nothing which he himself
would not have given to the world. However, Varius published the
Aeneid at Augustus' request, making only a few slight corrections,
and even leaving the incomplete lines just as they were. . . .

Vergil never lacked detractors, which is not strange; for neither
did Homer. . . . Asconius Pedianus, in a book which he wrote
Against the Detractors of Vergil, sets forth a very few of the charges
against him, and those for the most part dealing with history and
with the accusation that he borrowed a great deal from Homer; but
he says that Vergil used to meet this latter accusation with these
words: "Why don't my critics also attempt the same thefts? If they
do, they will realize that it is easier to filch his club from Hercules

than a line from Homer." Yet Asconius says that Vergil had intended to go into retirement, in order to prune down everything to
the satisfaction of carping critics.

Almost as soon as Vergil was dead his books became school texts.
Quintilian (1.8.5) recommends them as such, and Juvenal (7.227)
speaks of schoolboys thumbing a begrimed Vergil. Post-Vergilian
Latin literature is as saturated with Vergilian adaptations and allusions as post-Shakespearian English literature is with Shakespearian.
Men sought guidance for the future by the *Sortes Vergilianae*, that
is, opening a Vergil at random and interpreting the first words in the
passage. The Emperors Hadrian, Clodius Albinus, Alexander Severus, and Claudius all received prophecies of their destiny from
the *Sortes*, and belief in their efficacy lingered on into the 17th
century. Vergil's birthday, like Augustus', was registered in the
official Calendar. Poets like Statius and Silius Italicus (Younger
Pliny 3.7.8) worshiped at his tomb as at a shrine. Alexander Severus
placed his bust in the imperial chapel, where divine honors were
accorded it. Vergil retained a similar status under Christianity, for
Constantine, Eusebius, and St. Augustine accepted his *Fourth
Eclogue* as a direct prophecy of the birth of Christ. Numerous
centos, composed exclusively of lines and half-lines from Vergil
were written; many were ingeniously forced into a Christian sense,
though the most famous, the Nuptial Cento of Ausonius, is merely
obscene. Numerous legends gathered about Vergil's name. St. Paul
was said to have visited his tomb on his way from Puteoli to Rome
and to have wept because he died before the light had come into
the world. The service for St. Paul's day at Mantua includes the
following hymn:

> Ad Maronis mausoleum
> Ductus, fudit super eum
>   Piae rorem lacrymae;
> Quem te, inquit, reddidessem
> Si te vivum invenissem,
>   Poetarum maxime!

When to Maro's tomb they brought him
Tender grief and pity wrought him
To bedew the stone with tears;
What a saint I might have crowned thee,
Had I only living found thee,
Poet first and without peers!

There were popular as well as sacred legends. Vergil the prophet
became Vergil the magician, and fantastic tales, many in the *Gesta
Romanorum*, gathered about his name.

Meanwhile, through the commentaries of Servius and Donatus,
serious study of Vergil as a poet continued. It was Vergil whom
Dante acknowledged as his guide and master. To Dante Vergil is
"sage," "guide," "sweet father," "high teacher," "grand commander," "eternal treasure," "supreme virtue," "faithful escort,"
"ocean of all wisdom," or, most eloquent of all, simply *il poeta*,
"the poet." From Dante a highroad of Vergilian influence leads to
all the literature of Europe. Hieronymus Vida, the literary theorist
who carried greatest weight with the humanists, wrote, " 'Tis an
impiety for bards to hope to carry poesy further." Here is Vida's
apostrophe to Vergil (*Poemata Selecta*, 266):

Hail, light of Italy, thou brightest of the bards! Thee we worship,
thee we adore with wreaths, with frankincense, with altars; to thee,
as duty bids, for everlasting will we chaunt our holy hymns. Hail,
consecrated bard! No increase to thy glory flows from praise, nor
needs it voice of ours. Be near, and look upon thy votaries; come,
father, and infuse thy fervor into our chaste hearts, and plant thyself within our souls.

II. HORACE

Of Horace too we have a *Life* by Suetonius, of which the essentials
may here be excerpted:

Quintus Horatius Flaccus of Venusia had for a father, as he himself
writes, a freedman who was a collector of money at auctions; but

it is believed that he was a dealer in salted provisions, for a certain man in a quarrel thus taunted Horace: "How often have I seen your father wiping his nose with his arm!" Horace served as tribune of the soldiers in the war of Philippi, at the instance of Marcus Brutus, one of the leaders in that war. When his party was vanquished, he was pardoned and purchased the position of a quaestor's clerk. Then contriving to win the favor, first of Maecenas and later of Augustus, he held a prominent place among the friends of both. . . . Besides this, among other pleasantries, Augustus often calls him "a most immaculate libertine" and "his charming little man," and he made him well to do by more than one act of generosity. As to his writings, Augustus rated them so high, and was so convinced that they would be immortal, that he not only appointed him to write the Secular Hymn, but also bade him celebrate the victory of his stepsons Tiberius and Drusus over the Vindelici, and so compelled him to add a fourth to his three books of lyrics after a long silence. Furthermore, after reading several of his Talks, the Emperor thus expressed his pique that no mention was made of him: "You must know that I am not pleased with you, that in your numerous writings of this kind you do not talk with me, rather than with others. Are you afraid that your reputation with posterity will suffer because it appears that you were my friend? . . ."

In person he was short and fat, as he is described with his own pen in his satires and by Augustus in the following letter: "Onysius has brought me your little volume, and I accept it, small as it is, in good part, as an apology. But you seem to me to be afraid that your books may be bigger than you are yourself; but it is only stature that you lack, not girth. So you may write on a pint pot, that the circumference of your volume may be well rounded out, like that of your own belly." It is said that he was immoderately lustful; for it is reported that in a room lined with mirrors he had harlots so arranged that whichever way he looked, he saw a reflection of venery. He lived for the most part in the country on his Sabine or Tiburtine estate, and his house is pointed out near the little grove of Tiburnus. . . . He was born on the sixth day before the Ides of December in the consulate of Lucius Cotta and Lucius Torquatus [Dec. 8,

65 B.C.], and died on the fifth day before the Kalends of the same
month in the consulship of Gaius Marcius Censorinus and Gaius
Asinius Gallus [Nov. 27, 8 B.C.], 59 days after the death of Maecenas, in his 57th year. He named Augustus as his heir by word of
mouth, since he could not make and sign a will because of the sudden violence of his ailment. He was buried and laid to rest near
the tomb of Maecenas on the farther part of the Esquiline Hill.

Like Vergil, Horace became a school text, and knowledge of him
is evident in post-Horatian lyricists, both pagan and Christian,
though his influence is not nearly so weighty. Probus in the age of
Nero, Terentius Scaurus in the age of Hadrian, Acro and Porphyrio
in the 3rd century, made editions of Horace's works. During the
Middle Ages knowledge of Horace fades, though it does not wholly
disappear. Petrarch acquired a copy of Horace's works in 1347 and
was responsible for the revival of interest in him. His "letter" to
Horace begins

> Hail, Sovereign of the lyric measure,
> Hail, Italy's great pride and treasure;

and closes

> So great the love that bindeth me to thee
> So ruleth in my heart thy minstrelsy.

It was almost a century before Horace achieved print but, between
1470 and 1500, 44 editions of the poet appeared in Italy and more
than a dozen in France and Germany. An inventory made in 1906
lists 90 translations of the complete Odes of Horace in English, 70
in German, 100 in French, 48 in Italian. Other classics have had
far greater influence in shaping the thought and expression of
Europe, but none has been so completely naturalized in succeeding
generations.

III. TIBULLUS, PROPERTIUS, OVID

Ovid, whom ancients and moderns alike have considered the best of the group, himself presents the roster of Roman elegists (*Tristia* 4.10.51–55):

Vergil I only saw; and greedy fate vouchsafed Tibullus no time for my friendship. It was Tibullus who succeeded you, Gallus, and Propertius succeeded Tibullus: I myself was the fourth in order of time.

The four elegists are grouped together in Quintilian's criticism (10.1.93):

We also challenge the supremacy of the Greeks in elegy. Of our elegiac poets Tibullus seems to me to be the most terse and elegant. There are, however, some who prefer Propertius. Ovid is more sportive than either, while Gallus is more severe.

Gallus committed suicide because of political disgrace, and his poetry has perished. To Tibullus there are a number of allusions in his successors, and his position as a standard author is shown by the fact that his book was considered a suitable present for a guest at a dinner party (Martial 14.193), but his influence is only a thin trickle. Propertius is in similar case, though verses of his scribbled on walls in Pompeii suggest that he was more popular, and his vigorous personality has attracted more translators and interpreters in modern times.

The one poet of the group who has left an indelible mark on the literature of Europe is Ovid. In *Tristia* 4.10 Ovid himself supplies a full autobiography, of which the central fact is his exile, by order of Augustus for some undefined dereliction, to Tomis (Constanza) on the Black Sea. This misfortune entailed the banning of his books from three public libraries in Rome (*Tristia* 3.1.60 ff.), and in his discouragement he burned the first draft of his *Metamorphoses*. But his popularity was very wide; busts of him were multiplied and,

the Elder Seneca reports (*Controversiae* 3.7), "he filled the age
with his quotations." The Middle Ages show little Ovidian influence, but by the 12th century he had become a school author. His
influence is perceptible in the poetry of the Goliards and of the
Troubadors. Chrestien de Troyes translated the *Art of Love*, and the
Romance of the Rose has many reminiscences of Ovid. Through
allegorical interpretation Ovid was made a teacher of ethics and
theology. Chaucer learned much from Ovid; one of the pillars in
the House of Fame is erected to

> *Venus clerk, Ovyde,*
> *That hath y-sowen wonder wyde*
> *The grete god of Loves name.*

In the Renaissance Ovid's chief apostle was Boccaccio, and affection for him spread rapidly across the Alps. The Elizabethans knew
and loved him, and Ovidian influences are easy to detect in their
writings. Among the most successful translations of Ovid into any
language are Christopher Marlowe's versions of Ovid's love elegies.

IV. LIVY

Livy is a prose counterpart to the *Aeneid*; his object, like Vergil's
was to glorify Rome and its destiny, and he enjoyed high repute
among those who sympathized with that object. It is significant
that the two should be coupled in Caligula's hostility (Suetonius,
Caligula 34):

Caligula all but removed the writings and the busts of Vergil and
of Titus Livius from all the libraries, railing at the former as a man
of no talent and very little learning, and the latter as a verbose and
careless historian.

On the other hand, the prevalent opinion represented by Quintilian
(10.1.101) rated Livy very high:

Herodotus could not resent Livy being placed on the same level as himself. Livy has a wonderful charm and transparency in narrative, while his speeches are eloquent beyond description; so admirably adapted is all that is said both to the circumstances and the speaker; and as regards the emotions, especially the more pleasing of them, I may sum him up by saying that no historian has ever depicted them to greater perfection.

A familiar story illustrating Livy's fame is that recorded by the Younger Pliny (2.3.8):

Surely you have read the story of that man from Cadiz? He was so roused by the name and fame of Titus Livy that he came from the farthest ends of earth merely to see him, and when he had done so immediately departed again.

Livy became a standard author at once, and because of his bulk epitomes of him were made; so Martial (14.190) says:

These little skins contain great Livius, whom complete my entire library would not hold.

Virtually all subsequent historians, both Greek and Latin, who deal with Livy's period use him, and on the basis of these and with the guidance of the epitomes scholars like the 17th century Freinshemius have been able to supply substitutes for Livy's books that are lost. The fact that we possess as much of him as we do is due, as colopha to certain MSS show, to the efforts of Symmachus who, when Christianity had won the upper hand, was eager to propagate loyalty to Roman traditions. There is little evidence of knowledge of Livy during the Middle Ages. John of Salisbury (d. 1180) knew him, and Dante (*Inferno* 28.12) speaks of *Livio che non erra*. The Renaissance was particularly eager to embrace Livy, not merely as a Latinist but as a guide to restoring ancient ways of life, and the most strenuous efforts were made to recover the lost decades. Livy was Cola di Rienzo's favorite reading and Machiavelli used the first decad of Livy as a text for his *Discorsi* on political institutions. The history of modern countries came to be written quite in the Livian manner; thus large stretches of Hector Boece's *Historia Scotorum*, for example, are little more than transcripts from Livy. The 19th century turned its back on Livy because of his uncritical approach to history: in point of fact the "classic" histories of modern times are more influenced by the national and patriotic approach of Livy than by the detachment of Thucydides or Polybius.

V. SENECA

By reason of the scope and volume of his writings and of his influence on later European literature Seneca is easily the most important literary figure in the first century of the empire. His like named father, the rhetor, came from Spain, and Seneca himself was born there, though he was brought to Rome as an infant. His elder brother was Gallio, the deputy of Achaia, before whom Paul was brought to trial (Acts 18.12 f.). His younger brother was the father of the epic poet Lucan. Despite a sickly childhood Seneca had attained such distinction as an orator and writer by the time of Caligula's accession as to affront that emperor's megalomania. Dio Cassius (59.19) says:

Caligula ordered the death of Seneca but let him off because he believed a certain woman with whom he was intimate who told him that Seneca suffered from a malignant consumption and would die in a short time.

In Claudius' first year Messallina procured Seneca's banishment to Corsica on the improbable charge of adultery with Julia Livilla, Claudius' niece. His abject appeals for recall from Corsica show an egregious lack of Stoic fortitude, just as his enormous wealth, accumulated mainly through usury, is a poor example of Stoic "indifference." In A.D. 49, Tacitus (*Annals* 12.8) says:

Agrippina, that she might not be conspicuous only by her evil deeds, procured for Annaeus Seneca a remission of his exile, and with it the praetorship. She thought this would be universally welcome, from the celebrity of his attainments, and it was her wish too for the boyhood of Domitius to be trained under so excellent an instructor, and for them to have the benefit of his counsels in their designs on the throne. For Seneca, it was believed, was devoted to Agrippina from a remembrance of her kindness, and an enemy to Claudius from a bitter sense of wrong.

Together with the praetorian prefect Burrus, Seneca exercised a salutary influence on the young ruler (*Annals* 13.2):

Burrus and Seneca guided the emperor's youth with an unity of purpose seldom found where authority is shared, and though their accomplishments were wholly different, they had equal influence. Burrus, with his soldier's discipline and severe manners, Seneca, with lessons of eloquence and a dignified courtesy, strove alike to confine the frailty of the prince's youth, should he loathe virtue, within allowable indulgences.

In A.D. 62 Seneca's relations with the Emperor grew strained, and in 65 he was implicated in the Pisonian conspiracy and bidden to take his life. Tacitus records the manner of his death (15.62 f.):

Quite unmoved, Seneca asked for tablets on which to inscribe his will, and, on the centurion's refusal, turned to his friends, protesting that as he was forbidden to requite them, he bequeathed to them the only, but still the noblest possession yet remaining to him, the pattern of his life, which, if they remembered, they would win a name for moral worth and steadfast friendship. At the same time he called them back from their tears to manly resolutions, now with friendly talk, and now with the sterner language of rebuke. . . . Then by one and the same stroke he and his wife sundered with a dagger the arteries of their arms. Seneca, as his aged frame, attenuated by frugal diet, allowed the blood to escape but slowly, severed also the veins of his legs and knees. Worn out by cruel anguish, afraid too that his sufferings might break his wife's spirit, and that, as he looked on her tortures, he might himself sink into irresolution, he persuaded her to retire into another chamber. Even at the last moment his eloquence failed him not; he summoned his secretaries, and dictated much to them which, as it has been published for all readers in his own words, I forbear to paraphrase.

Roman critics show decided reservations about Seneca. The disparagement of the Emperor Caligula, uttered before Seneca had become politically important, is an example (Suetonius, *Caligula* 53.2):

Caligula used to say that Seneca, who was very popular just then, composed "mere school exercises," and that he was "sand without lime."

Aulus Gellius (12.2) reports similar judgments of later critics:

Some think of Annaeus Seneca as a writer of little value, whose works are not worth taking up, since his style seems commonplace and ordinary, while the matter and the thought are characterized, now by a foolish and empty vehemence, now by an empty and affected cleverness; and because his learning is common and plebeian, gaining neither charm nor distinction from familiarity with the earlier writers. Others, on the contrary, while not denying that his diction lacks elegance, declare that he is not without learning and a knowledge of the subjects which he treats, and that he censures the vices of the times with a seriousness and dignity which are not wanting in charm.

The fullest statement is in Quintilian (10.1.125 ff.):

I have deliberately postponed the discussion of Seneca in connection with the various departments of literature owing to the fact that there is a general, though false, impression that I condemn

and even detest him. It is true that I had occasion to pass censure
upon him when I was endeavoring to recall students from a de-
praved style, weakened by every kind of error, to a severer standard
of taste. But at that time Seneca's works were in the hands of every
young man, and my aim was not to ban his reading altogether,
but to prevent his being preferred to authors superior to himself,
but whom he was never tired of disparaging; for, being conscious
of the fact that his own style was very different from theirs, he was
afraid that he would fail to please those who admired them. . . .
Seneca had many excellent qualities, a quick and fertile intelligence
with great industry and wide knowledge, though as regards the last
quality he was often led into error by those whom he had entrusted
with the task of investigating certain subjects on his behalf. . . .
If he had only despised all unnatural expressions and had not been
so passionately fond of all that was incorrect, if he had not felt
such affection for all that was his own, and had not impaired the
solidity of his matter by striving after epigrammatic brevity, he
would have won the approval of the learned instead of the enthusiasm of boys. But even as it is, he deserves to be read by those whose
powers have been formed and firmly moulded on the standards
of a severer taste, if only because he will exercise their critical facul-
ties in distinguishing between his merits and his defects. For, as
I have said, there is much in him which we may approve, much
even that we may admire.

Dio Cassius presents the severest indictment of Seneca on moral
grounds. Though at 59.19 he says that Seneca "was superior in wisdom to all the Romans of his day and to many others as well,"
in 61.10 he excoriates him:

While denouncing tyranny, Seneca was making himself the teacher
of a tyrant; while inveighing against the associates of the powerful,
he did not hold aloof from the palace himself; and though he had
nothing good to say of flatterers, he himself had constantly fawned
upon Messalina and the freedmen of Claudius, to such an extent,
in fact, as actually to send them from the island of his exile a book

containing their praises—a book that he afterwards suppressed out
of shame. Though finding fault with the rich, he himself acquired
a fortune of 300,000,000 sesterces; and though he censured the
extravagances of others, he had five hundred tables of citrus wood
with legs of ivory, all identically alike, and he served banquets on
them. In stating thus much I have also made clear what naturally
went with it—the licentiousness in which he indulged at the very
time that he contracted a most brilliant marriage, and the delight
that he took in boys past their prime, a practice which he also taught
Nero to follow.

Perhaps these unfavorable opinions have a political basis; Seneca
had been condemned as a traitor, and Quintilian and Dio were both
functionaries of the state. Those who had no such loyalty speak
differently. The Latin Fathers of the Church were particularly attached to Seneca. Tertullian, who has a very low tolerance for pagan
writers speaks (*De anima* 20) of "our Seneca"; Lactantius (*In-
stitutes* 4.24) says, "Seneca could have been a true worshiper of God
if anyone had shown him the way." Jerome (*De viris illustribus* 12)
has:

*Lucius Annaeus Seneca of Cordova . . . lived a most continent
life. I should not be placing him in the catalogue of saints were I
not impelled to do so by those widely read letters of Paul to Seneca
and of Seneca to Paul. Though he was a minister and the most
powerful personage of his day he said that he would prefer to have
among his own people the place which Paul had among Christians.*

Augustine believed in the genuineness of the correspondence and
agrees (*Epistles* 153.14) with Jerome's judgment. Modern scholars
are agreed that Seneca's correspondence with Paul (the letters are
extant) is no more genuine than Vergil's prophecy of the birth of
Christ, but the error in the case of Seneca assured his writings a
vogue in the Middle Ages like Vergil's. He was frequently excerpted,
anthologized, and invoked. As in the case of Vergil he is not much
noticed in the Renaissance because he did not need to be discovered.

But Erasmus edited him and Calvin commented on his *On Clemency*. Montaigne couples him with Plutarch as his favorite reading, and Diderot's long essay on him (1779) kept his memory alive. F. W. Farrar's widely read *Seekers after God* made him familiar to the pious in our father's time.

But for students of literature Seneca's most significant influence by far is that on Elizabethan tragedy. Without the pattern of Seneca it is inconceivable that Elizabethan tragedy could have had its characteristic shape and texture, its gore, its rhetoric, its very structure. There can be no question that Shakespeare learned from Seneca, though estimates of his borrowing may differ. In his Introduction to the Tudor translation of *The Tenne Tragedies of Seneca* T. S. Eliot has this to say:

I am not here concerned with Shakespeare's "borrowings" (where I am inclined to agree) but with Shakespeare the voice of his time, and this voice in poetry is in the most serious matters of life and death, most often the voice of Seneca.

VI. LUCAN AND OTHER LATIN EPIC POETS

For Lucan we have the *Life* of Suetonius:

Marcus Annaeus Lucanus of Corduba made his first appearance as a poet with a Eulogy of Nero at the emperor's Quinquennial Contests, and then gave a public reading of his poem on the Civil War waged between Pompey and Caesar. . . . He was recalled from Athens by Nero and made one of his intimate friends, besides being honored with the quaestorship; but he could not keep the emperor's favor. For piqued because Nero had suddenly called a meeting of the senate and gone out when he was giving a reading, with no other motive than to throw cold water on the performance, he afterwards did not refrain from words and acts of hostility to the prince, which are still notorious. Once for example in a public privy, when he relieved his bowels with an uncommonly loud noise, he shouted out this half line of the emperor's, while those who were

*there for the same purpose took to their heels: "You might suppose
it thundered 'neath the earth."*

*He also tongue-lashed not only the emperor but also his most
powerful friends in a scurrilous poem. Finally he came out almost
as the ringleader in the conspiracy of Piso, publicly making great
talk about the glory of tyrannicides, and full of threats, even going
to the length of offering Caesar's head to all his friends. But when
the conspiracy was detected, he showed by no means equal firmness
of purpose; for he was easily forced to a confession, descended to
the most abject entreaties, and even named his own mother among
the guilty parties, although she was innocent, in hopes that this
lack of filial devotion would win him favor with a parricidal prince.
But when he was allowed free choice of the manner of his death,
he wrote a letter to his father, containing corrections for some of
his verses, and after eating heartily, offered his arms to a physician,
to cut his veins. I recall that his poems were even read in public,
while they were published and offered for sale by editors lacking
in taste, as well as by some who were painstaking and careful.*

There is a famous criticism of Lucan in the Satyrica of his contemporary Petronius, put into the mouth of the old reprobate Eumolpus
(118):

*Eumolpus broke in on this duet. "My young friends," said he, "many
a young fellow is tripped up when he takes to poetry. As soon as
he has constructed a line that scans and has wrapped up a senti-
mental idea in a cloud of words, he imagines that he has climbed
straight into Mount Helicon."*

Eumolpus then criticizes both purple patches and prosiness and
invokes as examples of excellence Homer and the Greek lyric poets,
Vergil and Horace. The term *curiosa felicitas* applied to Horace
is one of the aptest and best known in all the literature of criticism.
Then, with obvious reference to Lucan, he continues,

*Behold, a Civil War is a mighty theme, and whoso essays it, if he
be not ripe of scholarship, will faint under the burden. For not
in a poem can we describe the deeds of men—the historians do*

this far better; nay, through dark ways and the service of the gods, through the tossing maelstrom of the imagination, must the free spirit be hurled, so that it may seem rather the prophecy of a soul inspired than the prosaic record of authenticated fact.

Eumolpus then proceeds to dash off a 300-line poem on the same theme to show how it really should be done.

Lucan himself had written (9.985), "My *Pharsalia* shall live; no age shall condemn it to darkness," and he did in fact enjoy a great vogue. In the course of a fine birthday ode to him his contemporary Statius says (*Silvae* 2.7.75–80):

The untutored Muse of bold Ennius shall give way to thine, and the towering frenzy of learned Lucretius, he too who led the Argonauts through the narrow seas, and he who changes bodies from their former shapes. What greater praise can I give? the Aeneid itself, as thou singest to Roman folk, shall do thee homage.

Lucan was much read and commented upon in the Middle Ages. Dante (*Inferno* 4) gives him a place among the first six poets. Marlowe, a kindred spirit, essayed to translate him. Shelley said the poem appeared to him "of wonderful genius and transcending Vergil." Lord Byron's copy of Lucan has this note:

The Pharsalia is not sufficiently appreciated—though harsh and irregular I consider it an epic poem of great merit which read on classic ground is by no means uninteresting.

And Macaulay writes (1.462):

When I consider that Lucan died at 26 I cannot help ranking him among the most extraordinary men that ever lived.

Statius reveals much of his career and character in the occasional pieces in his *Silvae*, but these were unknown to the Middle Ages, and Statius was so exclusively identified with his *Thebais* that Chaucer called him Stace of Thebes. Antiquity too paid little attention to the *Silvae* but applauded the *Thebais* (Juvenal 7.82–87):

When Statius has gladdened the city by promising a day, people flock to hear his pleasing voice and his loved Thebais; so charmed are their souls by his sweetness, with such rapture does the multitude listen to him. But when his verses have brought down the house, poor Statius will starve if he does not sell his virgin Agave to Paris.

Paris was a performer of mimes, and Agave apparently a libretto which Statius wrote for him. For another mention of Statius we wait till Sidonius Apollinaris, Bishop of Clermont in the 5th century, who imitates him closely and alludes to him several times, as in the following (22.6):

If anyone thinks that a longish poem is blameworthy because it exceeds the minuteness of an epigram it is transparently clear that he has never had the habit of reading anything at all of our dear Statius.

The Middle Ages cherished a tradition that Statius was converted to Christianity at Puteoli by St. Paul, and he was accordingly much read. Dante accepted the story of Statius' conversion, and has him say (Purgatory 21):

Statius folk yonder still do name me; I sang of Thebes, and then of the great Achilles; but I fell by the way with the second burden.
The sparks, which warmed me, from the divine flame whence more than a thousand have been kindled, were the seeds of my poetic fire:
Of the Aeneid I speak, which was a mother to me, and was to me a nurse in poesy; without it I had not stayed the weight of a drachm.
And to have lived yonder, when Vergil was alive, I would consent to one sun more than I owe to my coming forth from exile.

Dante, and Alcuin of York, Boccaccio, and Chaucer, who also mention Statius, knew only the epics. The Silvae were discovered by Poggio in 1417, and towards the end of the 15th century Politian lectured on the poems. Here is an extract:

While I am not prepared to deny that in the great body of Latin literature work may be found which will easily surpass these slight Silvae, either in the weight of their subject-matter or in the importance of their argument, or in flow of language, yet I think I am entitled to describe them as being of such a character that for epic power, for variety of theme, for skill, for knowledge of places and legends, history and custom, for command of recondite learning and the arcana of letters, there is nothing superior to them in all Latin literature. . . . Just as in the Thebais and the Achilleis Statius made good his claim to be considered the second poet in his own line, so in these Silvae—in the composition of which he had no rival—he, to my thinking, excelled himself as much as in the epics just mentioned he had been excelled by Vergil.

In modern times, after the writers of romantic epic who learned much from him, Statius has had few ardent admirers, though some favorable judgments may be found. Pope thought him second only to Vergil among Latin poets. Goethe, who had not known the poet, read him at the suggestion of a Jena scholar, and then commented:

Statius is a very laudable poet and worthy of diligent study. I am not offended by the copious effusions of his genius, but in him I admire the art, which every good poet should have, of clear comprehension and precise description. Observe how accurately he paints Domitian's horse, how faithfully he renders Hercules' statue, how subtly he describes rural regions and the decorations of the baths. The things which he outlines in words seem present to our very eyes.

To Valerius Flaccus the only specific ancient reference is a line of Quintilian (10.1.90) which expresses regret at his recent death. Silius Italicus, the author of the inferior *Punica*, was a rich patron of literature and active in politics, and is naturally mentioned by Martial in connection with his patronage and by Tacitus in connection with his politics. A full and sympathetic account of him is given by the Younger Pliny (3.7):

*I am just now informed that Silius Italicus has starved himself to
death, at his villa near Naples. Having been afflicted with an im-
posthume, which was deemed incurable, he grew weary of life under
such uneasy circumstances, and therefore put an end to it with the
most determined courage. . . . He was highly respected and much
sought after, and though he was bedridden, his chamber was always
thronged with visitors, who came not merely out of regard to his
rank. He spent his time in philosophical discussion, when not engaged in writing verses; these he sometimes recited, in order to try
the sentiments of the public, but he discovered in them more industry than genius.*

VII. THE SATIRISTS

After Lucilius and Horace the only writers of satire in the ancient
technical sense are Persius and Juvenal; in a broader sense Martial
and Petronius may also be called satirists, and will be included in
this section. For Persius we have a good *Life* by Suetonius, which
tells of his birth, education, associates, and then continues:

*He was very gentle in manner, of virginal modesty and very hand-
some; and he showed an exemplary devotion to his mother, sister,
and aunt. He was good and pure. He left about two million sesterces
to his mother and sister, and a letter addressed only to his mother.
. . . He wrote rarely and slowly. This very volume [to which the
Life was attached] he left unfinished, and some verses were taken
from the last book, that it might have the appearance of completion. . . . As soon as his book appeared, men began to admire it
and to buy it up rapidly. He died of a stomach trouble in the thir-
tieth year of his age.*

Persius' little book won the esteem of connoisseurs. Martial (4.29.7)
says, "Persius gains more by a single book than Marsus by his whole
Amazonid"; and Quintilian (10.1.94), "Though he wrote but one
book Persius has acquired a high and well-deserved reputation."
But subsequent traces of Persius are hard to discover. He has usually

been hitched to the chariot wheels of Juvenal, as in the quaint English version of Holyday (1673), the vigorous translation of Gifford
(1802), and in the translation of all of Persius and part of Juvenal
by Dryden; the latter are quite the best of all Dryden's excellent
translations.

None of the several *Lives* of Juvenal is reliable; the best, dating
probably from the 4th century, gives the following:

*Junius Juvenalis, the son or the alumnus (it is uncertain which)
of a rich freedman, practised declamation till near middle life, more
for amusement than by way of preparing himself for school or
forum. Afterwards, having written a clever Satire of a few verses on
Paris the pantomime, and a poet of his time, who was puffed up
with his paltry six months' military rank, he took pains to perfect
himself in this kind of writing. . . . Juvenal, therefore, fell under
suspicion as one who had covertly censured the times; and forthwith, under color of military promotion, though he was 80 years
of age, he was removed from the city, and sent to take command
of a cohort which was stationed in the furthest part of Egypt. That
sort of punishment was determined upon as being suited to a light
and jocular offense. Within a very short time he died of vexation
and disgust.*

Juvenal was a solitary nature, and it is not surprising that the only
contemporary who mentions him is his admirer Martial, who protests his friendship for Juvenal (7.24), sends him a gift for the
Saturnalia (7.91), and writes him from his retirement in Spain
(12.18):

*While you may be wandering, Juvenal, through the clamorous
Subura, or mounting Diana's hill; while you may be treading the
thresholds of the great, fanned by your sweaty toga, tired with the
larger Caelian and the smaller: I, after so many Decembers, have
been received and accepted by my Bilbilis, proud of its gold and
iron.*

In the 4th century Juvenal was read by people who read little else. Ammianus Marcellinus, deploring indifference to literature, writes (28.4.14):

Some of them hate learning as they do poison, and read with attentive care only Juvenal and Marius Maximus, in their boundless idleness handling no other books than these, for what reason it is not for my humble mind to judge.

A line of Rutilius Namatianus (5th century) shows that Juvenal was the classic satirist, and one of Sidonius Apollinaris (9.269–273) that the story of Juvenal's exile at the instance of the actor Paris was current in his day. Servius cites Juvenal several times, and Ausonius and Claudianus imitate him. Juvenal was acceptable to the Middle Ages because of his ethical tone and his quotable sententiae. Dante (Purgatory 22) mentions him, and a number of Renaissance scholars edited him. Juvenal became the model for verse satire, in Italy, France, and especially England. The English tradition includes such names as Thomas Wyatt, George Gascoigne, John Donne, Joseph Hall, John Marston, John Dryden, Alexander Pope, and culminates in the closest imitations of Juvenal of all, Samuel Johnson's London, which is adapted from Juvenal 3, and his Vanity of Human Wishes, adapted from Juvenal 10.

Upon the death of Martial, the Younger Pliny, who had given him money and to whom he had written a poem, wrote of him to a friend (3.21):

I have just heard of the death of poor Martial, which much concerns me. He was a man of an acute and lively genius, and his writings abound in both wit and satire, combined with equal candor. . . . Do you not think that the poet who wrote in such terms of me, deserved some friendly marks of my bounty then, and that he merits my sorrow now? For he gave me the most he could, and it was want of power only, if his present was not more valuable. But to say truth, what higher can be conferred on man than fame, and applause, and immortality? And though it should be granted, that

his poems will not be immortal, still, no doubt, he composed them
upon the contrary supposition.

Martial himself, in the opening poem of his first book, is sure of his
vogue and durability

Here is he whom you read, whom you search for, Martial, known
the whole world over for his witty books of epigrams. He to whom,
while still alive, you have given, studious reader, a glory which poets
obtain but seldom even after they are dead.

His popularity continued after his death. Of Hadrian's adoptive son
Aelius Verus we read (*S.H.A. Aelius* 5.9):

He always kept the Recipes of Caelius Apicius and also Ovid's
Amores at his bedside, and declared that Martial, the writer of epi-
grams, was his Vergil.

Martial has always had readers and imitators. Translations into English begin with the age of Elizabeth and continue numerous. Of
these a certain notoriety attaches to the version of James Elphinston
(1721–1809) who published a specimen and solicited subscriptions
to bring out the whole work. Boswell, under date of April 9, 1778,
records that Garrick told Elphinston he was no epigrammatist, that
Johnson was not consulted, and that Elphinston's brother-in-law,
the printer Strahan, sent him 50 pounds but promised 50 more
if he would abandon the project. The book was handsomely published nevertheless, in 1782, and was derided on all hands. Here is
Robert Burns on Elphinston's version:

> *O thou whom Poesy abhors,*
> *Whom Prose has turned out of doors!*
> *Heardst thou that groan? Proceed no further;*
> *'Twas laurell'd Martial roaring Murther!"*

Most truly might it be said of Petronius, Nero's Arbiter of Elegance, that nothing became him like his death. Here is Tacitus'
account of it (*Annals* 16.18–19):

Petronius passed his days in sleep, his nights in the business and pleasures of life. Indolence had raised him to fame, as energy raises others, and he was reckoned not a debauchee and spendthrift, like most of those who squander their substance, but a man of refined luxury. . . . He was chosen by Nero to be one of his few intimate associates, as a critic in matters of taste (arbiter elegantiae) while the emperor thought nothing charming or elegant in luxury unless Petronius had expressed to him his approval of it. Hence jealousy on the part of Tigellinus, who looked on him as a rival and even his superior in the science of pleasure. . . . Yet he did not fling away life with precipitate haste, but having made an incision in his veins and then, according to his humor, bound them up, he again opened them, while he conversed with his friends, not in a serious strain or on topics that might win for him the glory of courage. And he listened to them as they repeated, not thoughts on the immortality of the soul or on the theories of philosophers, but light poetry and playful verses. To some of his slaves he gave liberal presents, a flogging to others. He dined, indulged himself in sleep, that death, though forced on him, might have a natural appearance. Even in his will he did not, as did many in their last moments, flatter Nero or Tigellinus or any other of the men in power. On the contrary, he described fully the prince's shameful excesses, with the names of his male and female companions and their novelties in debauchery, and sent the account under seal to Nero. Then he broke his signet-ring, that it might not be subsequently available for imperilling others.

Mention of Petronius' picaresque novel is extremely rare, and even in the Renaissance, where one would expect he would be eagerly embraced, he had only a slight vogue. The only portion of his work which was continuously known and admired was the story of the Widow of Ephesus. It was not until the 17th century that *Trimalchio's Dinner*, which is today the most widely known portion of the *Satyrica*, was found, and this aroused wide interest in Petronius. In Germany and France of the 18th century *Trimalchio's Dinner* was enacted in all its details for the entertainment of royalty. Alexander Pope (*Essay on Criticism* 667–68) wrote,

> *Fancy and art in gay Petronius please:*
> *The Scholar's learning, with the courtier's ease.*

But Petronius' naughtiness was always a block in England: Johnson, Warton, and Edwin criticized Pope for his reference to Petronius, and English translations of him have omitted the objectionable passages or presented them in French or Italian.

VIII. THE PLINYS AND QUINTILIAN

The fullest evidence for the lives of both Plinys is in the *Letters* of the Younger. In a letter to Tacitus (6.16) he gives circumstantial details of his uncle's death in the eruption of Vesuvius in A.D. 79, and in another he gives an account of his uncle's career, a catalogue of his literary works, and a description of his prodigious diligence:

In the country his whole time was devoted to study without intermission, excepting only while he bathed. But in this exception I include no more than the time he was actually in the bath; for all the while he was rubbed and wiped, he was employed either in hearing some book read to him, or in dictating himself. In his journeys, as though released from all other cares, he found leisure for this sole pursuit. A shorthand writer, with book and tablets, constantly attended him in his chariot, who, in the winter, wore a particular sort of warm gloves, that the sharpness of the weather might not occasion any interruption to his studies; and for the same reason my uncle always used a sedan chair in Rome. . . . By this extraordinary application he found time to write so many volumes, besides 160 which he left me, consisting of a kind of common-place, written on both sides, in a very small character; so that one might fairly reckon the number considerably more. I have heard him say that when he was comptroller of the revenue in Spain, Larcius Licinus offered him 400,000 sesterces for these manuscripts: and yet they were not then quite so numerous.

Antiquity and the Middle Ages alike used Pliny as an encyclopedia. Among those who give evidence of having done so are Martianus Capella, Isidore of Seville, and the Venerable Bede. The authority of the *Natural History* continued high until science came of age; the book is still a *vade mecum* for antiquarians in several specialties.

The *Letters* naturally tell us more about their amiable author. They became, as they were intended to become, a classic in their kind. In the 4th century Symmachus published his own *Letters* in nine books because Pliny had published nine of his; the exchanges with Trajan, which have given Pliny an undeserved reputation as a persecutor of Christians, constituted a separate book. The imperial Panegyrists of the 3rd and 4th centuries similarly followed Pliny's *Panegyric to Trajan*, and themselves became the pattern for addresses and dedications to royalty in later history.

Pliny twice (2.14.9, 6.6.3) mentions Quintilian as his teacher, and Quintilian was doubtless the teacher of Tacitus also. The apostrophe of Martial (2.90), "Quintilian, supreme moderator of impetuous youth, Quintilian, glory of the Roman toga," alludes not only to his teaching but to his eloquence, and so Juvenal (6.279) has a lady in need of persuasiveness cry, "Speak, speak, Quintilian, give me some of your colors!" Quintilian was the first salaried professor of rhetoric at Rome (Suetonius, *Vespasian* 18). His reputation continued high. Lactantius, Ausonius, Hilary of Poitiers, and St. Jerome allude to him. Cassiodorus regarded him as the best guide to thorough education. The *Ars rhetorica* of Julius Victor (6th century) is largely borrowed from Quintilian. Poggio's discovery of a complete text of Quintilian was hailed as a great event. G. A. Campani, who edited the first edition (1470) has this in his preface:

Concerning Quintilian this is the case: Next after the unique and blessed boon of Cicero, whom all must look up to and as it were adore as the very peak, Quintilian is the sole particular guide one may have in eloquence. If you follow him, then whatever you lack in attaining perfection you must seek from nature, not art.

As long as rhetoric has been of concern, Quintilian's reign was unquestioned. Milton's *Tractate on Education* strongly recommends the first books of Quintilian, and in Sonnet 11, referring to the roughness of northern nomenclature, Milton says:

> Those rugged names to our like mouths grow sleek
> That would have made Quintilian stare and gasp.

IX. TACITUS AND SUETONIUS

Pliny is so sure that the histories of his friend Tacitus will be immortal that he asks (7.33) to be mentioned in them. But in point of fact there seems to be a conspiracy of silence concerning Rome's greatest historian, and it is not until the 18th century that his true worth is recognized. Interest shifted from expository history to biographies of the ruling princes, Christians disliked his aspersions upon Christianity, and the cult of Ciceronianism objected to his purposeful deviations from Ciceronian style. Ammianus Marcellinus obviously intended his own history to be a continuation of Tacitus. The Emperor Tacitus (A.D. 275–276), who claimed the historian as an ancestor, ordered that ten copies of his works be transcribed annually and deposited in public libraries (*S.H.A. Tacitus* 10). Orosius obviously read Tacitus, and there are sporadic allusions to him in succeeding centuries. Boccaccio used Tacitus. Further Tacitean material was found (though Poggio's search was in vain) and Lipsius published his masterly edition of the historian in 1574. A series of good scholars occupied themselves with Tacitus, but interest in him grew mainly with the new concern for theories of government, and with the new appreciation of Tacitus' dramatic potentialities. Tacitus was the source of Corneille's *Otho* (1665), and of Racine's *Brittanicus* (1669); and many lesser dramatic and fictional works have been based upon Tacitus.

Suetonius has left far more abundant traces in antiquity. The imperial biographies in the *Scriptores Historiae Augustae* show how completely Suetonius' technique had established itself. Virtually all subsequent historians of the relevant period, Greek and Latin, use Suetonius; so closely had his name become attached to the history of the Caesars that Orosius' error in ascribing the *Gallic Wars* to Suetonius was quite natural. The Suetonian pattern is apparent in Einhard's *Life of Charlemagne* and in Petrarch's *De viris illustribus*. When Plutarch became available to Europe he preempted the market for biography; but Suetonius has always had a following, among readers curious either about the political personalities whom he describes or about the lurid sexual aberrations of some of them.

BIBLIOGRAPHICAL NOTES

Bibliographical Notes

GENERAL WORKS

The standard reference work for the subjects dealt with in this book is the *Real-Enzyklopädie der klassischen Altertumswissenschaft,* edited by Pauly, Wissowa, Kroll, and others (Stuttgart, 1894 ff.); a much shorter work, but usually with modern bibliography, is the *Oxford Classical Dictionary* (Oxford, 1949). Sections on Books and Writing, Palaeography, Epigraphy, History of Scholarship and various other relevant themes are to be found in *A Companion to Greek Studies,* ed. L. Whibley (Cambridge, 1905), and *A Companion to Latin Studies,* ed. J. E. Sandys, ed. 3, (Cambridge, 1921).

Documentation for the lives of ancient authors and bibliographical hints for investigating their posthumous fortunes are to be found in the standard histories of literature in the *Iwan Müller Handbuch der klassischen Altertumswissenschaft,* each in several volumes. The first volumes of each, in the most recent revision, are: W. Schmid— O. Stählin, *Geschichte der griechischen Literatur,* I,i (Munich, 1929); M. Schanz—C. Hosius, *Geschichte der römischen Literatur,* I,i (Munich, 1927). Introductions to scholarly editions of various authors usually present similar material, sometimes very fully. The posthumous fortunes of individual classical authors are dealt with in the series called Our Debt to Greece and Rome (early volumes, Marshall Jones Company, Boston; later volumes, Longmans Green Company, New York) which includes some 40 volumes of widely varying merit. Unified treatment of the influences of classical upon subsequent literature are to be found in Gilbert Highet, *The Classical Tradition* (Oxford, 1949), and Ernst R. Curtius, *European Literature and the Latin Middle Ages,* translated by W. R. Trask (New York, 1953).

Listed below are books relevant to the various chapters, followed by indications of the sources of the translations used. No separate citations are given for a number of authors frequently cited, and it is to be assumed that quotations from them are drawn (frequently with revisions) from the following:

ARISTOTLE: The "Oxford" Aristotle, reprinted in The Basic Works of Aristotle, ed. R. McKeon (Random House, 1941)

ATHENAEUS: C. B. Gulick (Loeb Classical Library, Harvard University Press)

DIO CHRYSOSTOM: J. W. Cohoon (L.C.L.)

DIOGENES LAERTIUS: R. D. Hicks (L.C.L.)

AULUS GELLIUS: J. C. Rolfe (L.C.L.)

GREEK ANTHOLOGY (A.P.): W. R. Paton (L.C.L.)

HERODOTUS: George Rawlinson (reprinted in Everyman and elsewhere)

ISOCRATES: G. Norlin and L. R. Van Hook (L.C.L.)

JOSEPHUS: H. St. J. Thackeray (L.C.L.)

LONGINUS: W. H. Fyfe (L.C.L.)

LUCIAN: H. W. and F. G. Fowler (Oxford, 1905)

PAUSANIAS: W. H. S. Jones (L.C.L.)

PLATO: B. Jowett, Dialogues of Plato, reprinted in Random House edition, 1937

PLINY, Letters: Melmoth's translation, revised by W. M. Hutchinson (L.C.L.)

PLINY THE ELDER: H. Rackham (L.C.L.)

PLUTARCH, Lives: Dryden-Clough (reprinted in Everyman and elsewhere)

PLUTARCH, Moralia: F. C. Babbitt (L.C.L.)

QUINTILIAN: H. E. Butler (L.C.L.)

SENECA, Letters: R. M. Gummere (L.C.L.)

SENECA, Moral Essays: J. W. Basore (L.C.L.)

STRABO: H. L. Jones (L.C.L.)

SUETONIUS: J. C. Rolfe (L.C.L.)

TACITUS: A. J. Church and W. J. Brodribb (reprinted in Modern Library)

THUCYDIDES: B. Jowett (reprinted in The Greek Historians, Random House, 1942)

XENOPHON, Memorabilia: E. C. Marchant (L.C.L.)

In other cases where no source is indicated the translation is the writer's own.

CHAPTER 2

BIRT, T., Das Antike Buchwesen (Berlin, 1882); Die Buchrolle in der Kunst (Leipzig, 1907)

DIRINGER, D., The Alphabet (New York, 1948)

FRIEDLAENDER, L., Sittengeschichte Roms, ed. 9–11, 4 vols. (Leipzig, 1921–23); Eng. tr. from 7th German ed. 4 vols. (London, 1908–1913)

HALL, F. W., A Companion to Classical Texts (Oxford, 1913)

JOHNSTON, H. W., The Private Life of the Romans, ed. 2 (Chicago, 1932)

KENYON, F. G., Books and Readers in Ancient Greece and Rome, ed. 2 (Oxford, 1951)

KIRCHNER, J., Lexikon der Buchwesens, 2 vols. (Stuttgart, 1952)

MITTEIS, L., and U. WILCKEN, Grundzüge und Chrestomathie der Papyruskunde, 2 vols. (Leipzig, 1912)

PACK, R. A., The Greek and Latin Literary Texts from Greco-Roman Egypt (Ann Arbor, 1952)

PARSONS, E. A., The Alexandrian Library (Houston, 1952)

RICHARDSON, E. C., The Beginning of Libraries (Princeton, 1914)

ROBERTS, E. S., An Introduction to Greek Epigraphy (Cambridge, 1887)

SANDYS, J. E., Latin Epigraphy, ed. 2 (Cambridge, 1927)

SCHUBART, W., Einführung in die Papyruskunde (Berlin, 1918); Das Buch bei den Griechen und Römern, ed. 2 (Berlin, 1921)

THOMPSON, E. M., Introduction to Greek and Latin Palaeography (Oxford, 1912)

THOMPSON, J. W., Ancient Libraries (Berkeley, 1940)

ULLMAN, B. L., Ancient Writing and Its Influence (New York, 1932)

Sources of Quotations in the Present Work

8 ff.   PLINY: adapted from Kenyon, Books and Readers

12 f.   PERSIUS: G. G. Ramsay (L.C.L.)

23   ARISTEAS: M. Hadas (Harper, 1951)

31 f.   DE BURY: Anonymous, reprinted in A. Taylor, Philobiblon (Berkeley, 1948)

CHAPTER 3

ATKINS, J. W. H., Literary Criticism in Antiquity, 2 vols. (Cambridge, 1934)

SIKES, E. E., The Greek View of Poetry (London, 1931); Roman Poetry (London, 1923)

Sources of Quotations in the Present Work
35 HESIOD: Edwin Arnold
38 PLATO: W. R. M. Lamb (L.C.L.)

CHAPTER 4

DOBSON, J. F., The Greek Orators (London, 1918)

FLICKINGER, R. C., The Greek Theater and Its Drama, ed. 4 (Chicago, 1936)

HAIGH, A. G., The Tragic Drama of the Greeks (Oxford, 1896)

PICKARD-CAMBRIDGE, A. W., Dithyramb, Tragedy, and Comedy (Oxford, 1947)

PUTNAM, G. H., Authors and Their Public in Ancient Times (New York, 1894)

See also under Chapter 2.

Sources of Quotations in the Present Work
51 f.   ST. AUGUSTINE: E. B. Pusey (Everyman and other editions)
54 f.   VITRUVIUS: F. Granger (L.C.L.)
65   DIGEST: adapted from J. W. Thompson, *Ancient Libraries*

CHAPTER 5

FYFE, W. H., Introduction to L.C.L. Aristotle, Poetics, etc.

RHYS ROBERTS, W., Greek Rhetoric and Literary Criticism (New York, 1928)

SPINGARN, J. E., A History of Literary Criticism in the Renaissance (New York, 1924)

See also under Chapter 3.

CHAPTER 6

PECK, H. T., A History of Classical Philology (New York, 1911)
REINACH, S., Manuel de Philologie Classique (Paris, 1890)
SAINTSBURY, G., A History of Criticism and Literary Taste in Europe from the Earliest Texts to the Present Day, vol. 1 (Edinburgh, 1900)
SANDYS, J. E., A History of Classical Scholarship, 3 vols.: vol. 1, ed. 3 (Cambridge, 1921), vols. 2 and 3 (1908)
STURTEVANT, E. H., The Pronunciation of Greek and Latin (Chicago, 1920)

CHAPTER 7

LEO, F., Die Griechische-Römische Biographie (Leipzig, 1901)
MISCH, G., A History of Autobiography in Antiquity, 2 vols. (Harvard, 1951; first German ed. 1907)
STUART, D. R., Epochs of Greek and Roman Biography (Berkeley, 1928)

Sources of Quotations in the Present Work
   125   ARISTOPHANES: B. B. Rogers (reprinted in L.C.L. and elsewhere)

CHAPTERS 8–17

For bibliographies for individual authors, see under General Works, above.

Sources of Quotations in the Present Work
   139   HELIODORUS: T. Underdowne (1587)
   145   MONTAIGNE: John Florio (1603)
   166   AMMIANUS: J. C. Rolfe (L.C.L.)
   169   THEOCRITUS: J. H. Hallard, The Greek Bucolic Poets (London, n.d.)
   170 f.   CICERO: H. M. Poteat (Univ. of Chicago Press, 1950)
   178   AESCHYLUS EPITAPH: E. H. Plumptre

181 f. PHILOSTRATUS: F. C. Conybeare (L.C.L.)

201 ff. ALCIPHRON: F. A. Wright (London, n.d.)

205 f. DIONYSIUS OF HALICARNASSUS: from L. Pearson, Early Ionian Historians (Oxford, 1939)

223 APPIAN: H. White (L.C.L.)

234 ff. PLATO: L. A. Post, Epistles of Plato (Oxford, 1925)

237 THEODOR GOMPERZ, Greek Thinkers (New York, 1908)

241 f. ARRIAN: E. J. Chinnock, reprinted in The Greek Historians (Random House, 1943)

249 f. EPICTETUS: W. A. Oldfather (L.C.L.)

259 f. LUCRETIUS: C. Bailey (Oxford, 1910)

262 DIODORUS SICULUS: C. H. Oldfather (L.C.L.)

264 GORGIAS: L. R. Van Hook, Greek Life and Thought (New York, 1923)

268 CICERO: H. M. Poteat (University of Chicago Press, 1950)

275 f. DEMOSTHENES: C. R. Kennedy (reprinted in Everyman)

287 ALCIPHRON: F. A. Wright (London, n.d.)

297 CICERO, Republic: C. W. Keyes (L.C.L.)

302 MELEAGER: J. W. Mackail, Select Epigrams from the Greek Anthology (London, 1906)

306 FRONTO: Haines (L.C.L.)

314 f. S. L. WOLF, Greek Romances in Elizabethan Fiction (New York, 1912)

341 f. HYMN FOR ST. PAUL'S DAY: J. A. Symonds, Renaissance in Italy (Modern Library Giant ed., 1.356)

342 VIDA: J. Symonds, ibid., 1.549

348, 351 f. DIO CASSIUS: E. Cary (L.C.L.)

354 f. PETRONIUS: J. M. Mitchell (London, 1922)

356 DANTE: Carlyle-Wicksteed (Modern Library)

INDEX

Index

DATES of ancient authors are frequently only approximate; Roman numerals refer to centuries, and unless the contrary is indicated are to be read as A.D. The principal entry is in italics.